The Legacy of Southwestern

The Legacy of Southwestern

Writings That Shaped a Tradition

James Leo Garrett, Jr.
Editor

C. W. Brister   R. Bruce Corley   Al Fasol   Harry Leon McBeth
Associate Editors

Smithfield Press
North Richland Hills, Texas

Smithfield Press
An imprint of D. & F. Scott Publishing, Inc.
P.O. Box 821653
N. Richland Hills, TX 76182
817 788-2280
info@dfscott.com
www.dfscott.com

**Smithfield
Press**

Printed in the United States of America

05 04 03 02 01   5 4 3 2 1

Library of Congress Cataloging-in-Publication Data
The legacy of Southwestern : writings that shaped a tradition /
James Leo Garrett, Jr., editor ; C.W. Brister ... [et al.], associate
editors.
p. cm.
Includes bibliographical references.
ISBN 1-930566-27-1 (hard cover : alk. paper)
1. Southwestern Baptist Theological Seminary—Faculty—Bio
-bibliography. I. Garrett, James Leo. II. Brister, C. W.
BV4070.S86L44 2002
230'.07'3617645315—dc21
2002009573

Photo credits:
Engelhart-Darwin: pages 132, 206
Olan Mills: page 170

CONTENTS

Contents

CONTRIBUTORS

Nathan Larry Baker is pastor of First Baptist Church, Sun City West, Arizona.

Paul A. Basden is co-senior pastor of Preston Trail Community Church, Frisco, Texas.

C. W. Brister is distinguished professor emeritus of pastoral ministry and holds the Warren C. Hultgren Chair of Pastoral Care at Southwestern Baptist Theological Seminary.

Karen O'Dell Bullock is associate professor of church history and associate dean for the Ph.D. degree, School of Theology, Southwestern Baptist Theological Seminary.

R. Bruce Corley is professor of New Testament and holds the Huber L. Drumwright, Jr., Professorship of New Testament at Southwestern Baptist Theological Seminary.

David E. Crutchley is professor of New Testament and former dean, School of Theology, Southwestern Baptist Theological Seminary.

Al Fasol is distinguished professor of preaching and holds the E. Hermond Westmoreland Professorship of Preaching at Southwestern Baptist Theological Seminary.

Roy J. Fish is distinguished professor of evangelism and holds the L. R. Scarborough Chair of Evangelism at Southwestern Baptist Theological Seminary.

James Leo Garrett, Jr., is distinguished professor emeritus of theology at Southwestern Baptist Theological Seminary.

Robert I. Garrett, Jr., is professor of missions and holds the George W. Bottoms Chair of Missions at Southwestern Baptist Theological Seminary.

William E. Goff is professor of Christian ethics at Southwestern Baptist Theological Seminary.

Paul L. Gritz is professor of church history at Southwestern Baptist Theological Seminary.

John L. Harris is associate professor of Old Testament and dean of the School of Christian Studies, East Texas Baptist University, Marshall, Texas.

Rick L. Johnson is professor of Old Testament at Southwestern Baptist Theological Seminary.

Contributors

Paul Griffin Jones, II is executive director of the Mississippi Religious Leadership Conference and retired executive director-treasurer of the Christian Action Commission of the Mississippi Baptist Convention, Clinton, Mississippi.

William David Kirkpatrick is professor of theology at Southwestern Baptist Theological Seminary.

John (Jack) William MacGorman is distinguished professor emeritus of New Testament at Southwestern Baptist Theological Seminary.

Frank Louis Mauldin is professor of philosophy, University of Tennessee at Martin, Martin, Tennessee.

Harry Leon McBeth is distinguished professor of church history at Southwestern Baptist Theological Seminary.

David W. Music is professor of church music at Baylor University, Waco, Texas.

Siegfried S. Schatzmann is professor of New Testament at Southwestern Baptist Theological Seminary.

William A. (Budd) Smith is professor of foundations of education and holds the J. M. Price Chair of Religious Education at Southwestern Baptist Theological Seminary.

James T. Spivey, Jr., is associate professor of church history at Southwestern Baptist Theological Seminary and associate dean of Southwestern Seminary in Houston.

Stephen M. Stookey is associate professor of church history at Southwestern Baptist Theological Seminary.

Mark E. Taylor is assistant professor of New Testament at Southwestern Baptist Theological Seminary.

William B. Tolar is distinguished professor emeritus of Biblical backgrounds and archaeology and special consultant to the president, emeritus, at Southwestern Baptist Theological Seminary.

PREFACE

Four score and fourteen years ago the Baylor Theological Seminary in Waco, Texas, under the leadership of Benajah Harvey Carroll was, with approval of the Baptist General Convention of Texas, chartered as Southwestern Baptist Theological Seminary and thus separated from Baylor University. Relocated in 1910 in the suburbs of Fort Worth, the seminary was in 1925 transferred to the Southern Baptist Convention (SBC). Despite the acute hardships of the Great Depression, the dislocations of wars, and acrimonious division fostered by denominational controversy, Southwestern became the largest SBC theological seminary during the latter 1940s, and then the world's largest free-standing theological school. Southwestern alumni came to serve in all the states of the United States both in local churches and in other ministries. During the latter twentieth century, one-half of the missionaries supported by the SBC's International Mission Board had been students at Southwestern, and today nearly 250 international students (with non-U.S. passports) are studying at Southwestern. Indeed the sun never sets on those who have been influenced by this institution.

The story of this seminary during its first thirty years was told by its second president, Lee Rutland Scarborough,[1] and its history for seventy-five years was written by one of its distinguished church historians, Robert Andrew Baker.[2] By nature institutional histories must focus on presidencies, buildings, enrollments, finances, curricula, and personnel.

Sensing that there is also a need for an examination of the writings and thought of Southwestern professors and their effects on the seminary and a wider realm and with approval of his faculty, David E. Crutchley, dean of the School of Theology, appointed on 17 May 2001 a committee of five professors, active and emeritus (C. W. Brister, R. Bruce Corley, Al Fasol, James Leo Garrett, Jr., chairman, Harry Leon McBeth), to undertake the production of such a book for the School of Theology.

The committee soon recognized the need for a basis for selecting those authors to be treated and then determined that a corpus of published writings, especially books, and some impact on Southwestern would constitute basic criteria. Subsequent research would demonstrate that the Southwestern faculty in all three schools—theology, educational ministries, and church music—have authored, coauthored, edited, or coedited at least seven hundred books.[3] All but two of the professors selected for inclusion have taught at Southwestern for twenty or more years. Twenty-two of the authors of the twenty-five chapters of this book have known personally the professors about whom they have written. Although given a fivefold format for the development of each chapter, each author has been permitted to craft his chapter to fit the personality and work of the professor-subject. To declare that Southwestern has a heritage or a legacy is a defensible statement, for continuity has coexisted with change.

Numerous indeed have been those who have labored to bring this volume to completion. Dean Crutchley has provided support and encouragement, as has Jack D. Terry, Jr., vice president for institutional advancement. The members of the *Legacy* committee for a year have faithfully made decisions and read typescripts. The living subjects of these chapters have been helpful in supplying information. Barbara Ann Isbell has provided extraordinary secretarial service with accuracy and skill for the entire project and has been virtually an assistant editor. Michael T. Pullin, archivist of Roberts Library, has been responsible for the photographs used, and he and his staff, especially Mayeli (Mrs. Jason) Jones, have provided recurrent help in the writing and the editorial processes. Fran (Mrs. John Ed) Wilson, administrative assistant for the School of Theology, has managed the budget. Foreign language consultants have transliterated book titles: Samuel Shahid (Arabic), T. Timothy Chen (Chinese), Ebbie C. Smith (Indonesian), Yao-ting Lee (Japanese), Dong Sun Cho (Korean), Justice C. Anderson (Spanish), Thurmon E. Bryant (Portuguese), and Taegug Shim (Thai). Others who have assisted include Terry Caywood, J. Edgar Ferrer, Helen (Mrs. John) Hanson, Hubert R. Martin, Jr., Richard McCormack, Robert L. Phillips, Bill Taylor, and Joy (Mrs. Jamie) Willis. We are also greatly indebted to William R. Scott of D. and F. Scott Publishing for his expertise.

Hopefully this volume will afford the readers an opportunity to reenvision Southwestern Seminary through the lives and writings of those treated within its pages. For those who have had no intimate knowledge of Southwestern it may serve as an introduction. For Southwestern's many alumni it may serve as a lane to vivid and thankful memories of yesteryear and as an invitation beckoning to tomorrow.

James Leo Garrett, Jr.
May 2002

Benajah Harvey Carroll
(1843–1914)
English Bible

James T. Spivey, Jr.

BIOGRAPHY

Benajah Harvey Carroll was born 27 December 1843 into a large family near Carrollton, Mississippi.[1] In 1850 the Carrolls moved to Arkansas, where Harvey started school. Although he felt strangely resistant to religion, at age thirteen Carroll was baptized at a revival meeting—a superficial exercise that left him unconverted and an avowed "infidel."[2] In 1858 the family migrated to Texas, and six months later he entered Baylor University at Independence. Carroll became a reputed debater and was headed for a promising legal career when, just before graduation, he volunteered for Confederate service in McCullough's Rangers. Returning home to attend his dying father, he fell in love with and married Ophelia Crunk of Caldwell in December 1861. When she refused to move to West Texas, Carroll returned to duty alone, and Ophelia soon broke her marriage vows. The fact that a jury granted him a divorce on the basis of her infidelity did not console Harvey. Deeply depressed, he abandoned all hope, severed ties with his church, rejected the Bible, and enlisted in the Seventeenth Texas Infantry Regiment that was deploying to the front lines. Carroll threw himself with abandon into the heat of every battle. Finally, when a "Minnie ball" nearly killed him at Mansfield, Louisiana (April 1864), he was sent home to convalesce. He opened a school at Yellow Prairie and then moved it to Caldwell. Even more deeply depressed, Carroll

1

began searching the Scriptures for help. Aroused at a Methodist camp-meeting by the preacher's challenge to test the claims of Christianity and listening to hymns after the meeting, he was overcome by a vision of Jesus' invitation in Matt. 11:28. That evening while reading *Pilgrim's Progress* at his mother's bedside, Carroll felt God calling him to preach. Days later, he was baptized by Baylor schoolmate W. W. "Spurgeon" Harris. In 1866 Dove Baptist Church licensed and ordained Carroll. Soon he began to court Ellen Bell, from Starkville, Mississippi, and in December 1866 they were married in Caldwell by Baylor ex-president Rufus C. Burleson.[3] After eking out a living as a teacher, farmer, evangelist and part-time pastor of Post Oaks Church in Burleson County, he was called in 1869 as pastor of New Hope Baptist Church at Goat Neck in McLennan County. Throughout 1870 he preached twice monthly at First Baptist Church, Waco, where Burleson, then president of Waco University, was interim pastor. When Burleson left, the church called Carroll, and in March 1871 he began a ministry that spanned twenty-eight years. That year Carroll defeated famed Methodist polemicist Orceneth Fisher in a highly publicized debate at Davilla. Accounts of his victory made him an instant hero among Texas Baptists and well known in the Southern Baptist Convention (SBC).

Carroll did the entire work of the pastor: he preached, indoctrinated, disciplined, raised funds, and conducted his own annual revival meetings with great success. He systematically organized and employed every resource of the Waco church. It led Texas Baptists in planting churches, at one time providing half of the support for missionaries sponsored by Waco Baptist Association and raising one-third of all mission funds in the state. During his pastorate, First Baptist added 2,325 members, grew from 424 to 1,000 members, and became one of the largest churches in Texas. He also used this position as a catalyst for civic reform in Waco and across Texas.[4]

Carroll was an even more influential denominational leader. While holding several key positions in Baptist life, he became chairman of a committee that led to the consolidation of the two Texas Baptist colleges and the formation of the Baptist General Convention of Texas (BGCT).[5] When the state mission board was in jeopardy, Carroll and George W. Truett raised enough funds to keep it solvent. He delivered the keynote sermon at the 1878 session of the SBC, preached at almost every meeting from 1891 through 1908, and hosted the 1883 session in Waco. He was a trustee of Southern Baptist Theological Seminary (1894–1911) and the Texas member of the SBC Foreign Mission Board (FMB). He convinced Texas Baptists to align with the SBC Home Mission Board (HMB) rather than with the northern American Baptist Home Mission Society (ABHMS) when the latter promised greater financial aid. He convinced SBC messengers not to dismantle the HMB but to give it their full support;[6] he persuaded them to adopt J. M. Frost's plan to form the Sunday School Board;[7] and his advocacy led to the HMB's establishing a Department of Evangelism.[8]

Carroll was a champion of Baptist unity and orthodoxy. He stopped evangelist M. T. Martin from spreading heterodox doctrine about assurance among Texas Baptists (1880s). When T. P. Crawford launched his offensive against organized missions (early 1890s), Carroll rallied Texas churches in support of the FMB. His successful defense of the state mission board (late 1890s) led to the expulsion of Samuel Hayden from the BGCT and his forming the rival Baptist Missionary Association. As a trustee of Southern Seminary, Carroll led a group that forced the resignation of its president, W. H. Whitsitt, because he challenged Landmark views popular with many Southern Baptists.[9] In each instance, Carroll insisted that his purpose was to promote unity. Against Hayden, he urged Texas Baptists to unite in the systematic support of missions. In the Whitsitt dispute his motive was to prevent the disintegration of Southern unity and the dismemberment of the SBC.

Carroll's most influential legacy was in theological education. He led a campaign to endow Waco University and later raised money to liquidate the debt of Baylor University at Waco and finance its expansion.[10] As early as 1872 in his study he was tutoring ministerial students in the English Bible and ecclesiology.[11] After Baylor University was chartered at Waco (1886), Carroll was elected chairman of its board of trustees and remained in that position twenty years. In 1894, when Carroll was elected to the faculty, he was put in the unique position of working for the very institution which he governed.[12] After his wife's death, at his brother James's urging, Carroll resigned his pastorate and took charge of the Texas Baptist Education Commission.[13] While in that office (1899–1902), he became dean of the Baylor Bible Department and married Hallie Harrison of Waco.[14]

Pursuant to a vision he had while travelling by train through the Texas Panhandle, Carroll began in 1905 to raise funds to establish a seminary for the Southwest. In August the Baylor trustees approved his plan to constitute Baylor Theological Seminary and to start classes that fall.[15] After the BGCT voted to separate the seminary from Baylor (1907), Carroll obtained a charter for the Southwestern Baptist Theological Seminary in Waco (14 March 1908) and expanded the faculty.[16] In 1909 Carroll agreed to move the seminary to Fort Worth when civic leaders promised to raise $100,000 for its support and provided a suitable site south of the city. His vision was realized when he convened classes there with seven faculty members and 126 students on Monday, 3 October 1910. Carroll died 11 November 1914.[17] His deathbed charge instructed his successor, Lee R. Scarborough, how to safeguard his most important legacy:

> Lee, keep the Seminary lashed to the cross. If heresy ever comes in the teaching, take it to the faculty. If they will not hear you and take prompt action, take it to the trustees of the Seminary. If they will not hear you, take it to the Convention that appoints the Board of Trustees, and if they will not hear you, take it to the great common people of our churches. You will not fail to get a hearing then.[18]

WRITINGS

Despite his limited formal education,[19] Carroll became one of the best informed and most articulate Baptists leaders of his day. He read relentlessly—about three hundred pages daily—in his quest for practical excellence. He read everything from classical philosophy to modern science, ever gleaning insights to inform his preaching and teaching. What Carroll learned he never forgot. Renowned for his mental powers, he could instantly cite virtually every pertinent fact he had ever read, particularly in the Bible. Its study was his passion. He navigated its passages with great familiarity and demonstrated his skill as a biblical expositor. Although his secular knowledge earned him credibility in debate with civic leaders, his touchstone was always the Bible.

Carroll, although a brilliant scholar, did not write books. His power was in persuasive oratory. His written works were sermons, addresses, lectures, and articles that were published as pamphlets or in newspapers. Twenty pamphlets have survived: three doctrinal sermons,[20] four sermons preached at annual sessions of the SBC,[21] three sermons preached at annual meetings of the BGCT,[22] two apologetic sermons,[23] a history of Baylor University;[24] four lectures,[25] and three works on social issues.[26] The most important newspaper items include: curriculum material for the Baylor Bible Department,[27] articles tracing the establishment of Southwestern Seminary,[28] arguments on social issues,[29] and accounts of his opposition to Fisher,[30] Martin,[31] Hayden,[32] and Whitsitt.[33]

Carroll made no systematic effort to publish his sermons and lectures until persuaded to do so by Gatesville editor J. B. Cranfill, who met Carroll in 1883. The following year Cranfill published Carroll's sermon *The Agnostic*.[34] In 1886 he moved to Waco and joined Carroll's congregation. After purchasing the *Texas Baptist Standard* (1892), Cranfill made his pastor's sermons a weekly feature of the paper for the next twelve years.[35] Wanting to perpetuate her husband's legacy, Ellen helped Cranfill to persuade Carroll that his works should be collected and printed as books.[36] In 1893 Cranfill compiled thirty sermons, but a fire at his press delayed printing of *Sermons and Life Sketch of B. H. Carroll* until 1895.[37] One of these sermons, *My Infidelity and What Became of It*, was already popular. J. M. Frost had published it in the HMB journal *Kind Words* and had distributed it to Sunday School teachers across the SBC.[38] Rightly anticipating the demand for *Sermons*, Cranfill boosted circulation of the *Standard* by offering Carroll's book as a premium to readers who recruited new subscribers.[39] No further effort was made to print other collected works until 1906, when Carroll's student, J. W. Crowder, suggested that it should be done, and Carroll charged him with that responsibility.[40] Crowder compiled Carroll's expository lectures and, under Carroll's supervision, arranged them for Cranfill to edit as *An Interpretation of the English Bible*. In 1913 they produced the first two commentaries, first on Revelation and then on Genesis, plus two companion volumes of sermons, *Baptists and Their Doctrines*[41] and *Evangelistic Sermons*.[42] These were followed in 1914 by two commentaries covering Exodus through Ruth.

After Carroll's death, Crowder compiled and Cranfill edited the rest of the commentaries (1915–17), which were translated into Spanish and ran into four English editions.[43] Carroll left his written material to his wife and Cranfill, with the suggestion that Crowder assist them in publishing his works.[44] During the Great Depression, Cranfill, relying chiefly on Broadman Press, published seven volumes and introduced Carroll to the next generation of Southern Baptists: *The River of Life*,[45] *Inspiration of the Bible*,[46] *Studies in Romans*, *Studies in Romans, Ephesians, and Colossians*,[47] *The Day of the Lord*,[48] *Studies in Genesis*, and *The Ten Commandments*.[49] Crowder collated Carroll's sermons into fourteen typed manuscripts for publication,[50] but as convention support waned, Cranfill had to turn to other sources for help. Advanced subscriptions and support from benefactors such as Dallas surgeon G. D. Mahon and Jewish banker Fred F. Florence[51] enabled him to publish ten of these volumes: *Jesus the Christ*,[52] *Revival Messages*,[53] *The Holy Spirit*,[54] *Ambitious Dreams of Youth*,[55] *The Faith That Saves*,[56] *Christ and His Church*,[57] *The Providence of God*,[58] *Christ's Marching Orders*,[59] *Saved to Serve*,[60] and *The Way of the Cross*.[61] In 1942 renewed interest in Carroll led Broadman Press to reprint an expanded edition of *An Interpretation*[62] and to publish Cranfill's last edited work before his death, *Messages on Prayer*.[63] This left Crowder to publish the remaining manuscripts: *The Supper and Suffering of Our Lord*;[64] *Christian Education and Some Social Problems*;[65] and *Patriotism and Prohibition*.[66]

THOUGHT

The two ideals controlling Carroll's life were "an authoritative Bible and the reality of Christian experience."[67] His theology was intensely biblical, experiential, and corporate: the Bible reveals how to be saved, and believers who faithfully receive and obey its doctrine will know God's fullness by seeing the Spirit of God at work in the churches. Carroll formulated a practical, biblical-pastoral theology that called the church to evangelism and social responsibility. His biblical theology was imbedded in *An Interpretation of the English Bible*; his pastoral theology was expressed in his eighteen volumes of sermons. For a fuller understanding of his thought, one must also consult Carroll's other published sermons, addresses, and lectures; his books *Baptists and Their Doctrines* (1913), *Inspiration of the Bible* (1930), and *Patriotism and Prohibition* (1952); and eight of his unpublished manuscripts.[68] These reveal that Carroll's main doctrinal emphases were biblical revelation, soteriology, ecclesiology, and eschatology.

"B. H. Carroll was rock-ribbed in his reverent belief in God's Word."[69] Asserting its infallibility, he said that the Bible not only contains the word of God but also *is* God's very word. He taught verbal, plenary inspiration. Giving primacy to the New Testament as the "Law of Christianity," he refused to make the Old Testament a model for Christian ethics or institutions. While affirming that individuals could interpret the Scriptures correctly, he rejected exclusively private interpretation. He was not a biblicist; he used covenants and confessions.

Carroll's theology was Trinitarian: each Person is equal in divine perfection, but the Holy Spirit proceeds from the Father and from the Son (*filioque*) and is subordinate in office to the Son, as the Son is to the Father. Accepting Archbishop Ussher's dating of creation (4004 B.C.), he taught that God made the universe not in a literal week but in six twenty-four hour bursts. Carroll rejected Darwinian evolution but accepted development within the species. He believed that God guides everything toward his purpose without impinging on human freedom. God's will in respect to human sin is preventive, permissive, directive, and determinative, as A. H. Strong had taught.[70] Carroll affirmed the virgin birth and the full deity and humanity of Christ. On the work of Christ he ascribed a fourth role to Christ, "sacrifice," in addition to prophet, priest, and king. At Pentecost the Holy Spirit "occupied" the church and "accredited" it by miraculous signs. This "baptism of the Spirit" was for the whole church, not just individuals, and was for a limited time. Only the "graces" of faith, hope, and love continued. Today believers receive the Holy Spirit as a blessing of God after they repent and believe, not as a "regenerating grace."

Carroll taught that Adam, though created mortal, could have lived indefinitely by continually eating of the tree of life. Adam conveyed "original sin" to all persons, who inherit their souls from male issuance, not female conception. This sin is corporate, but since it still brings the condemnation of death to individuals, God's grace intervenes to save dying infants. With actual sin comes the condemnation of guilt, which makes repentance and belief necessary for salvation. Although the seed of life and sin descends from the male, not the female, Jesus, being of the Holy Spirit, did not inherit Adam's sin. Christ had a human soul, but God's Spirit controlled his entire being. Carroll left unresolved the dilemma of this traducian anthro-

7

pology: how did Christ get his perfect human soul since he did not inherit it from a depraved earthly father?

For Carroll, four elements comprise salvation: redemption, atonement, justification, and adoption. The buying back of the sinner (redemption) is achieved through the atonement and applied through regeneration. Christ's atonement was sacrificial, voluntary, vicarious, penal, and satisfactory; in expiation it purges sin; in propitiation it reconciles humans to the Father. Regeneration, a unified and not a multi-stage process, begins with divine conviction. It continues with human contrition, prevenient grace that prompts prayer, repentance, confession, conversion, faith, and remittance of sin—the legal product of justification. Justification is distinct from pardon: justification is God's justice in paying the debt; pardon is God's mercy in canceling the debt. Justification is forensic and irrevocable: sinners are pronounced permanently righteous when they believe. This lays the foundation for adoption. Sanctification is not a "second blessing" but the lifelong process that perpetuates regeneration. Justification is God's heavenly declaration of an external condition instantly certified on earth; sanctification is the internal process accomplished on earth and certified in heaven.

According to Carroll, the church is a spiritual, visible, local assembly of regenerate believers who form an autonomous, non-hierarchical, democratic body. Baptist churches do not comprise the kingdom of God; they are constituent parts of the kingdom and called to a missionary purpose. The two ordinances symbolize salvation: baptism represents regeneration, the Lord's Supper portrays sanctification. Carroll admitted as members only persons baptized in Baptist churches, and he administered "close communion." The pastor and the deacon are the two ordained officers. Deacons are not a ministerial order but assist the pastor so that he can do ministry. Carroll affirmed the office of deaconess but said that it did not warrant ordination. Nor did he allow a woman to be a pastor, to pray in open assembly, or to teach in a position of authority over men. Carroll's views resembled Landmarkism: he emphasized the local church and disregarded its universal nature; he believed that John was the first "Baptist" and that true churches resembling Baptists had continued since the apostolic era. His role in the Whitsitt dispute might suggest a Landmark agenda, but this is unlikely. Carroll tried to avoid taking action against Whitsitt.

When he did so, he claimed that it was to preserve denominational unity. Conversely, he opposed Landmarkers Crawford and Hayden when they threatened Texas Baptist solidarity. Furthermore, certain of his practices opposed Landmarkism. He refused to equate local churches with the kingdom of God and encouraged associational discipline and cooperation.

Carroll emphasized eschatology as foundational to all biblical interpretation.[71] His postmillennialism complemented his soteriology and ecclesiology. Progressive sanctification fitted with the gradual consummation of the kingdom of God, and the missionary purpose of the church anticipated the transformation of society. Although respecting premillennialists such as Charles H. Spurgeon and Dwight L. Moody, he reckoned their eschatology to be dogmatic and shallow; it relegated the gospel to failure and undercut motivation for missions. Yet Carroll could not abide liberal postmillennialists who dismissed supernaturalism and the literal second coming.

Conservative Baptists influenced Carroll's theology, especially Boyce, Strong, Spurgeon, and Broadus. He disdained modernism, agreed with the conservative tenets of *The Fundamentals: A Testimony to the Truth*, and was a moderate Calvinist in line with the New Hampshire Confession. He taught supralapsarianism but also single election—that humanity never had been divided into two predetermined lots. His doctrine of atonement was not limited; though Christ's death is effective only for the elect and everyone will not be saved, he died for all persons. Those who never hear the gospel will be judged according to their light, opportunities, and attitude toward Christ. Carroll rejected antinomianism and Hyper-Calvinism.

J. B. Gambrell said, "President Carroll, Bible in hand, standardized orthodoxy in Texas. He rallied the hosts of Baptists to the vital, ruling doctrines of the Holy Scriptures."[72] As a pastor-polemicist, he employed his biblical-pastoral theology against any movement threatening doctrinal purity or Baptist unity. The same was true of Carroll the ministerial educator. A man of "leonine orthodoxy," he was determined that his students be "saturated with the conviction that the Bible was God's Book and not in any way to be trifled with." He often declared "'that orthodoxy is to make its last stand on Seminary Hill.'"[73]

INFLUENCE

B. H. Carroll's reputation never equaled the man himself. He became a truly larger-than-life personality as pastor, denominational leader, and educator. He led his congregation to become the strongest evangelistic, mission-minded church in Texas. From this platform he helped to transform every level of denominational life and profoundly affected the sociopolitical life of Texas.[74] Yet his greatest pastoral influence was as a preacher. Carroll captivated generations of Baylor students who gravitated to his pulpit. He was strikingly handsome, with his Moses-like beard, and physically impressive. Standing six feet and four inches tall and weighing 250 pounds, he had a bearing that was always erect and stately. His strong voice and persuasive oratory personified self-assurance and matched the style of master orators such as William Jennings Bryan and Woodrow Wilson.[75] George W. Truett and L. R. Scarborough ranked him among the all-time greatest preachers.[76] Carroll's logic was so convincing and his scriptural evidence so exhaustive that his pronouncements were irresistible. He electrified students with white-hot conviction and fiery logic, relentlessly pressing to triumphal declaration of eternal truths. Hundreds of them fanned out to fill pulpits across Texas and the South. The *Baptist Standard* carried Carroll's sermons into thirty thousand homes, and ten thousand Baptist ministers fed on them weekly.[77] His reputation as an expositor became legendary. According to one country minister, Carroll could "'dig deeper to find God's truth and climb higher to reveal it than any man that ever lived.'"[78]

Involved throughout his ministry in every major concern at each level of Baptist life, Carroll was a true "Kingdom builder."[79] He helped to consolidate the BGCT and Baylor University, defended the HMB and the FMB against the ABHMS and Gospel Missionists, opposed dismantling of the HMB, and supported creation of the Sunday School Board. He was a prominent trustee of the FMB and of Southern Seminary. He was at center stage in the disputes against Martin, Crawford, Hayden, and Whitsitt. Denominational leaders relied on his advice at critical junctures such as the polity negotiations with Northern Baptists and the problem of heterodoxy at the University of Chicago. Acknowledging his influence, John R. Sampey wrote to Carroll after John A. Broadus's death, "You are now—since Broadus is gone—our natural leader in the Southern Convention."[80]

Carroll played several key roles in Texas Baptist education: consolidating its colleges, strengthening the finances of Baylor, leading the Education Commission, and serving for twenty years as a Baylor trustee. Yet his greatest passion was for the students themselves. Even before his election to the Baylor faculty, he was feeding them an entire seminary course from the pulpit and mentoring them in his private study. Altogether he tutored or lectured in the classroom for forty-three years and extended this influence through his publishing curriculum material in the *Baptist Standard*.[81] In this way, "He did more to formulate the theology and shape the ideals of the young preachers of Texas than all other men combined."[82] Carroll also had a gift for identifying and cultivating future Baptist leaders.[83] Two of his greatest discoveries were Scarborough and Truett, who lived with him for three years. Projecting Carroll's influence well into the next century, they became vital parts of his most enduring legacy, which, according to Truett, was closest to his heart:

> The crowning work of his life, probably, was his leadership in the establishing of the Southwestern Baptist Theological Seminary. No other task in all his life seemed so completely to enthrall his thoughts and energies as the task of Ministerial Education . . . [T]his man, in season, out of season, pleaded forever for the better education of God's preachers.[84]

BIBLIOGRAPHY

1. Primary

BOOKS

Ambitious Dreams of Youth: A Compilation of Discussions of Life and Its Obligations. Comp. J. W. Crowder and ed. J. B. Cranfill. Dallas: Helms Printing, 1939.

Baptists and Their Doctrines. Ed. Timothy George and Denise George. Nashville: Broadman and Holman, 1995.

Baptists and Their Doctrines: Sermons on Distinctive Baptist Principles. Comp. J. B. Cranfill. New York: Fleming H. Revell, 1913; Nashville: Broadman, n.d.

Christ and His Church: Containing Great Sermons concerning the Church of Christ . . . Comp. J. W. Crowder and ed. J. B. Cranfill. Dallas: Helms Printing, 1940; Nashville; Broadman, n.d.

Christian Education and Some Social Problems: Sermons. Comp. and ed. J. W. Crowder. Fort Worth: pvt.ptg., 1948.

Christ's Marching Orders: Comprising a Compilation of Vital Messages on the Great Commission and Christian Stewardship. Comp. J. W. Crowder and ed. J. B. Cranfill. Dallas: Helms Printing, 1941.

The Day of the Lord. Comp. J. W. Crowder and ed. J. B. Cranfill. Nashville: Broadman, 1936

Evangelistic Sermons. Comp. J. B. Cranfill. New York: Fleming H. Revell, 1913.
> *Sermones Evangelisticos.* Trans. Sara A. Hale. El Paso: Casa Bautista de Publicaciones, 1936. [Spanish]

The Faith That Saves: A Compilation of Pungent Pulpit Messages on the Vitalities of ScriptureTeaching. Comp. J. W. Crowder and ed. J. B. Cranfill. Dallas: Helms Printing, 1939.

The Holy Spirit: Comprising a Discussion of the Paraclete, the Other Self of Jesus, and Other Phases of the Work of the Spirit of God. Comp. J. W. Crowder and ed. J. B. Cranfill. Grand Rapids: Zondervan, 1939.

Inspiration of the Bible: A Discussion of the Origin, the Authenticity and the Sanctity of the Oracles of God. Comp. and ed. J. B. Cranfill. New York: Fleming H. Revell, 1930; Orlando, Fla.: Christ for the World Publishers, 1980; Nashville: Thomas Nelson, 1980.

An Interpretation of the English Bible, 13 vols. Edited by J. B. Cranfill. New York: Fleming H. Revell, 1913–16; 13 vols. Nashville: Sunday School Board of the Southern Baptist Convention, 1913–16; 17 vols. Nashville: Broadman, 1942–43 and 1947–48; 6 vols. Grand Rapids: Baker Book House, 1976.
> *Una Interpretacion de la Biblia.* 12 vols. Trans. Sara A. Hale. El Paso: Casa Bautista de Publicaciones, 1932–47. [Spanish]

Jesus the Christ: A Compilation of Sermons concerning Our Lord and Savior, and Touching upon the Mountain-peaks of His Ministry, His Earthly Life and His Messiahship. Comp. J. W. Crowder and ed. J. B. Cranfill. Nashville: Baird-Ward, 1937.

Messages on Prayer: Comprising Pungent and Penetrating Sermons on a Subject Perennially Vital to Every Christian. Comp. J. W. Crowder and ed. J. B. Cranfill. Nashville: Broadman, 1942.

Patriotism and Prohibition: Addresses and Articles. Comp. and ed. J. W. Crowder. Fort Worth: pvt. ptg., 1952.

The Providence of God: Comprising Heart-searching Sermons on Vital Themes concerning God and His Overruling Providence among Men. Comp. J. W. Crowder and ed. J. B. Cranfill. Dallas: Helms Printing, 1940.

Revival Messages: A Compilation of Pungent and Winsome Appeals to Wanderers from God. Comp. J. W. Crowder and ed. J. B. Cranfill. Grand Rapids: Zondervan, 1939.

The River of Life and Other Sermons. Comp. and ed. J. B. Cranfill. Nashville: Sunday School Board of the Southern Baptist Convention, 1928; (coauth.) *River of Pearls.* Nashville: Broadman, 1936.

Saved to Serve: Comprising Appealing and Vital Messages on the Duties of Christians to Give of Their Time, Thought and Means to God. Comp. J. W. Crowder and ed. J. B. Cranfill. Dallas: Helms Printing, 1941.

Sermons and Life Sketch of B. H. Carroll, D.D. Compiled by J. B. Cranfill. Philadelphia: American Baptist Publication Society, 1893; Dallas: Evangel, 1957; Gallatin, Tenn.: Church History Research and Archives, 1986.

    Sermones y Bosquejo de la Vida de B. H. Carroll, D. D. Trans. Sara A. Hale. El Paso: Casa Bautista de Publicaciones, 1936. [Spanish]

Seven Churches of Asia. Little Rock: Challenge, 1972.

Studies in Genesis. Ed. P. E. Burroughs. Nashville: Broadman, 1937.

    Chuang Shi Ji Yan Jiu. Translated by Si-hui He. Hong Kong: Baptist Press, 1963. [Chinese]

Studies in Romans. Ed. P. E. Burroughs. Nashville: Sunday School Board of the Southern Baptist Convention, 1935.

    Comentario sobre la Epistola a los Romanos. Trans. Sara A. Hale. El Paso: Casa Bautista de Publicaciones, 1941. [Spanish]

(coauth.) *Studies in Romans, Ephesians, and Colossians.* Nashville: Broadman, 1936.

The Supper and Suffering of Our Lord: Sermons. Comp. and ed. J. W. Crowder. Fort Worth: [Seminary Hill Press], 1947.

The Ten Commandments. Nashville: Broadman, 1938.

The Way of the Cross: Comprising a Luminous Discussion of Both the Law and the Gospel. Comp. J. W. Crowder and ed. J. B. Cranfill. Dallas: Helms Printing, 1941.

PAMPHLETS

The Agnostic: A Sermon. Gatesville, Tex.: Advance Printing, 1884.

Baptism: Its Law, Its Administrator, Its Subjects, Its Form, Its Design. Waco: Baptist Standard, 1893.

The Baptist One Hundred Years Ago. Nashville: Sunday School Board of the Southern Baptist Convention, 1900.

Baylor University, at Waco, Texas: An Historical Sketch. Waco, Tex.: Kellner Printing, n.d. [c. 1890].

The Bible Doctrine of Repentance: Lectures Delivered before the Bible School of Baylor University. Louisville: Baptist Book Concern, 1897.

Christian Education: A Sermon Preached at San Antonio, Texas, Sunday, January 28, 1900. Waco: Kellner Printing, 1900.

Communion, from a Bible Standpoint: A Sermon. Dallas: Texas Baptist Printing, 1876.

Course in the English Bible. Waco: Kellner Printing, n.d. [c. 1900].

Distinctive Baptist Principles: A Sermon before the Pastors' Conference at Dallas, November 4, 1903. Dallas: n.p., 1903.

Ecclesia—The Church: Bible Class Lecture, February, 1903. Louisville: Baptist Book Concern, 1903; Ashland, Ky.: Baptist Examiner, n.d.; Little Rock: Challenge Press, n.d.; partially reprinted in Thomas Theodore Martin, *The New Testament Church,* 35–59. Kansas City, Mo.: Western Baptist, 1917.

Four Good Works for 1895: Two Sermons. Waco: Baptist Standard, n.d. [1895].

My Infidelity and What Became of It. N.p.p.: n.p., n.d. [c. 1892]; Waco: Baptist Standard, n.d. Also in his *Sermons and Life Sketch of B. H. Carroll, D. D.,* ed. J. B. Cranfill, 13–23, and in J. B. Cranfill, *From Memory: Reminiscences, Recitals, and Gleanings from a Bustling and Busy Life,* 135–48. Nashville: Broadman, 1937.

The Nature and Person of Our Lord: A Sermon Preached by Special Appointment before the Southern Baptist Convention at Hot Springs, Ark., May 15, 1908. Nashville: Sunday School Board, Southern Baptist Convention, 1908.

An Office Magnified: A Sermon to Preachers before the State Convention of Texas. Philadelphia: American Baptist Publication Society, 1898.

Opening of the Course in the English Bible: Introductory Lecture. Waco: Kellner Printing, 1902.
Papal Fields: An Address Delivered before the Southern Baptist Convention at Nashville, Tenn., May 13, 1893. Waco: Baptist Standard, 1893.
Personal Liberty: A Lecture by Rev. B. H. Carroll, DD, Delivered at Waco, Texas, January 18th, 1887. N.p.p.: n.p., 1887.
Prohibition: A Sermon. Austin: J. B. Link, 1886.
Sermon on the Modern Social Dance. Dallas: Texas Baptist, 1877.
The Statewide Prohibition Question. Houston: Statewide Prohibition Amendment Association Headquarters, n.d.
(coauth.) *Suggestions for Associational Committees.* N.p.p: n.p., n.d. [1900].
The Theology of the Bible. N.p.p.: n.p., n.d.

JOURNAL ARTICLES

"The Greatest Man in History." *The Southwestern Theological Review* 1 (November 1903): 17–30.
"Distinctive Baptist Principles." *The Southwestern Theological Review* 1 (December 1904): 67–84.
"Man's Forgiveness of Man." *Southwestern Journal of Theology* o.s. 8 (January 1924): 37–55.
"Our Articles of Faith, Article 1: The Scriptures." *Southwestern Journal of Theology* o.s. 5 (April 1921): 3–13.
"Our Articles of Faith, Article 2: The True God." *Southwestern Journal of Theology* o.s. 5 (July 1921): 10–16.
"Our Articles of Faith, Article 3: The Fall of Man." *Southwestern Journal of Theology* o.s. 5 (October 1921): 38–45.
"Our Articles of Faith, Article 4: The Way of Salvation." *Southwestern Journal of Theology* o.s. 6 (January 1922): 63–72.
"Our Articles of Faith, Article 5: Justification." *Southwestern Journal of Theology* o.s. 6 (April 1922): 3–12.
"Our Articles of Faith, Article 6: The Freeness of Salvation." *Southwestern Journal of Theology* o.s. 6 (July 1922): 29–38.
"Our Articles of Faith, Article 7: Grace in Regeneration." *Southwestern Journal of Theology* o.s. 6 (October 1922): 69–79.
"Our Articles of Faith, Article 8: Repentance and Faith." *Southwestern Journal of Theology* o.s. 7 (January 1923): 26–35.
"Our Articles of Faith, Article 9: God's Purpose of Grace." *Southwestern Journal of Theology* o.s. 7 (April 1923): 38–46.
"Our Articles of Faith, Article 14: Baptism and the Lord's Supper." *Southwestern Journal of Theology* o.s. 8 (April, 1924): 26–35.
"The Second Advent and the Millennium." *The Southwestern Theological Review* 1 (January 1904): 162–74.

MISCELLANEOUS ARTICLES

"Notice of an Editorial, 'Affirming: The Present Existence of an Universal, Invisible, Spiritual Church, Composed of All the Redeemed of All Ages.'" *Baptist Argus*, 16 April 1903, 2–3.
"Shall the Atlanta Board Be Instructed to Employ Evangelists?" *Baptist Standard*, 31 May 1906, 1–2.

2. Secondary

DISSERTATIONS AND THESES

Beck, Rosalie. "The Whitsitt Controversy: A Denomination in Crisis." Ph.D. diss., Baylor University, 1984.

Blackaby, Melvin Duane. "The Nature of the Church and Its Relationship to the Kingdom of God in Baptist Theology: John Leadley Dagg, Benajah Harvey Carroll, and Dale Moody." Ph.D. diss., Southwestern Baptist Theological Seminary, 1997.

Bugg, Charles Basil. "The Whitsitt Controversy: A Study in Denominational Conflict." Ph.D. diss., Southern Baptist Theological Seminary, 1972.

Cates, John Dee. "B. H. Carroll: The Man and His Ethics." Th.D. diss., Southwestern Baptist Theological Seminary, 1962.

Cogburn, Keith Lynn. "B. H. Carroll and Controversy: A Study of His Leadership among Texas Baptists, 1871–1899." M.A. thesis, Baylor University, 1983.

Early, Joseph E., Jr. "The Hayden Controversy: A Detailed Examination of the First Major Internal Altercation of the Baptist General Convention of Texas." Ph.D. diss., Southwestern Baptist Theological Seminary, 2002.

Lefever, Alan J. "The Life and Work of Benajah Harvey Carroll." Ph.D. diss., Southwestern Baptist Theological Seminary, 1992.

Mitchell, R. Varnell. "A History of Martinism with Particular Emphasis on the Controversy between M. T. Martin and B. H. Carroll." Th.D. diss., Mid-America Baptist Theological Seminary, 1990.

Moore, Nellie Garrett. "B. H. Carroll and His Educational Values to Texas." M. Ed. thesis, University of Texas, 1940.

Robinson, Robert Jackson. "The Homiletical Method of Benajah Harvey Carroll." Th.D. diss., Southwestern Baptist Theological Seminary, 1956.

Shirley, Timothy Wade. "J. P. Boyce and B. H. Carroll: Two Approaches to Baptist Theological Education." Th.M. thesis, Southern Baptist Theological Seminary, 1987.

Stewart, Wilson Lanning. "Ecclesia: The Motif of B. H. Carroll's Theology." Th.D. diss., Southwestern Baptist Theological Seminary, 1959.

Watson, Thomas L. "The Eschatology of B. H. Carroll." Th.M. thesis, Southwestern Baptist Theological Seminary, 1960.

BOOKS

Cranfill, J. B. *B. H. Carroll and His Books*. Nashville: Broadman, n.d. [1943].

Crowder, J. W., comp. and ed. *Dr. B. H. Carroll: The Colossus of Baptist History*. Fort Worth: pvt. ptg., 1946.

Fountain, Edwin B. *Scriptural Index to B. H. Carroll's "An Interpretation of the English Bible."* Shelbyville, Tenn.: Bible and Literature Missionary Foundation, 1978.

Hayden, Samuel Augustus. *The Complete Conspiracy Trial Book: Being an Historical, Philosophical, Ethical and Judicial Analysis of Eleven Baptist Lawsuits in Texas*. Dallas: Texas Baptist Publishing, 1907.

Lefever, Alan J. *Fighting the Good Fight: The Life and Work of Benajah Harvey Carroll*. Austin: Eakin, 1994.

McDaniel, George W. *A Memorial Wreath: A Giant of the Southwest, B. H. Carroll; Our Great Commoner, J. B. Gambrell*. N.p.p.:n.p., n.d.

Ray, Jefferson Davis. *B. H. Carroll*. Nashville: Sunday School Board of the Southern Baptist Convention, 1927.

Scarborough, L. R. *A Modern School of the Prophets*. Nashville: Broadman, 1939.

CHAPTERS IN BOOKS

Baker, Robert A. "The Founder," "Immediate Antecedents," and "Southwestern Seminary Founded." In *Tell the Generations Following: A History of Southwestern Baptist Theological Seminary, 1908–1983*, 53–187. Nashville: Broadman, 1983.

Burkhalter, Frank E. "Dr. Carroll Begins His Ministry" and "Dr. Carroll Continues His Marvelous Leadership." In *A World-Visioned Church: Story of the First Baptist Church, Waco, Texas*, 72–151. Nashville: Broadman, 1946.

Burroughs, P. E. "Benajah Harvey Carroll." In *Ten Men from Baylor*, ed. J. M. Price, 63–78. Kansas City, Kan.: Central Seminary Press, 1945.

Crowder, J. W. "B. H. Carroll: Biographical Sketch." In *Southwestern Men and Their Messages*, ed. J. M. Price, 29–31. Kansas City, Kan.: Central Seminary Press, 1948.

Spivey, James T, Jr. "Benajah Harvey Carroll." In *Baptist Theologians*, ed. Timothy George and David S. Dockery, 307–29. Nashville: Broadman, 1990. Rpt. in *Theologians of the Baptist Tradition*, ed. George and Dockery, 163–80. Nashville: Broadman and Holman, 2001.

ARTICLES

Alexander, Charles T. "Four Sonnets to B. H. Carroll." *Southwestern Journal of Theology* o.s. 7 (October 1923): 3–4; condensed as "Ode to Dr. Carroll, Seminary Founder and First President." *The Southwestern Evangel*, March 1929, 162.

Baker, Robert A. "The First Year on the Hill." *Southwestern Journal of Theology* n.s. 8 (October 1965): 89–101.

Beck, Rosalie. "W. H. Whitsitt and Texas Baptists." *Baptist History and Heritage* 33 (Autumn 1998): 42–48.

Brooks, S. P. "Dr. Benajah Harvey Carroll." *Review and Expositor* 12 (April 1915): 193–99.
____. "Dr. Carroll and Baylor University." *Baptist Standard*, 19 November 1914, 2.

Burrows, Lansing. "Dr. Carroll and the Southern Baptist Convention." *Baptist Standard*, 10 December 1914, 6.

Cooper, O. H. "Extracts from the Carroll Memorial Address." *The Southwestern Evangel*, April 1926, 34–36.

Cranfill, J. B. "The Passing of B. H. Carroll." *Baptist Standard*, 19 November 1914, 9, 25, 28–29.
____. "Some Lessons from the Life and Work of B. H. Carroll." *Southwestern Journal of Theology* o.s. 4 (April 1920): 66–82.

Crowder, J. W. "Dr. B. H. Carroll, the Teacher." *Baptist Standard*, 24 December 1914, 11.

Dawson, J. M. "Dr. Carroll, the Pastor." *The Southwestern Evangel*, April 1927, 267–70.

Encyclopedia of Southern Baptists. 4 vols. Nashville: Broadman, 1958–82. Vol. 1. S.v. "Carroll, Benajah Harvey."

Gambrell, J. B. "The Home-Going of President B. H. Carroll—An Appreciation." *Baptist Standard*, 19 November 1914, 1.

Holt, A. J. "Early Ministry of B. H. Carroll." *Southwestern Journal of Theology* o.s. 3 (July 1919): 35–38.

Jester, J. R. "Lessons from a Great Life." *Baptist Standard*, 3 December 1914, 11–12, 29.

Jonas, Glenn. "The Political Side of B. H. Carroll." *Baptist History and Heritage* 33 (Autumn 1998): 49–56.

McConnell, F. M. "B. H. Carroll's Contribution to Preachers." *Southwestern Journal of Theology* o.s. 2 (April 1918): 8–23.

McDaniel, George W. "An Appreciation of Dr. Carroll." *Baptist Standard*, 17 December 1914, 2–3.

Naylor, Robert E. "Southwestern and Evangelism." *Southwestern Journal of Theology* 19 (Fall 1976): 81–94.

Neff, Pat M. "Founder's Day Address." *Southwestern Journal of Theology* o.s. 6 (July 1922): 14–24.

Ray, Jeff D. "B. H. Carroll—Some Side-Lights." *Southwestern Journal of Theology* o.s. 5 (April 1921): 23–35.

_____. "The Preachers' Friend." *Baptist Standard*, 19 November 1914, 9, 32.

Scarborough, L. R. "Dr. B. H. Carroll's Great Prayer Answered." *Baptist Standard*, 5 June 1924, 9–10.

_____. "Dr. Carroll—A Kingdom-Builder." *Baptist Standard*, 19 November 1914, 9.

Segler, Franklin M. "B. H. Carroll: Model for Ministers." *Southwestern Journal of Theology* 25 (Spring 1983): 4–23.

Stubblefield, C. "Doctrine of Election Exemplified in Seminary Founder." *The Southwestern Evangel*, April 1928, 221–22.

Truett, George W. "Funeral Discourse." *Baptist Standard*, 19 November 1914, 4–5, 21.

West, E. P. "Life and Work of B. H. Carroll, Founder of the Seminary." *The Southwestern Evangel*, April 1930, 207–10.

Williams, C. B. "B. H. Carroll, a Prince of Preachers." *Baptist Standard*, 24 December 1914, 24.

_____. "B. H. Carroll's Ideals in Theological Education." *Southwestern Journal of Theology* o.s. 1 (April 1917): 10–21.

Lee Rutland Scarborough
(1870–1945)
Evangelism

Roy J. Fish

BIOGRAPHY

When he was three weeks old, his mother knelt by his crib side and prayed that God would call him to preach. His family always had daily prayer together. His father was a preacher of the gospel whose exemplary life was a constant inspiration to his son. The few books in his home were the writings of great contemporary Christian authors. His parents were so committed to his preaching the gospel with adequate training that money they had saved to build a house went instead to his college education. Growing up in such a context of Christian commitment, it is not difficult to see how God found in Lee Rutland Scarborough the kind of moldable clay he could shape into one of the great Christian leaders of his generation.

Scarborough was born 4 July 1870 in Colfax, Louisiana, the eighth of nine children. His family moved to Texas, and Scarborough grew up as a cowboy experiencing the difficulty and excitement of frontier living. His mother's witness to him at an early age prepared the way for his conversion. At seventeen, after rebuffing his mother's efforts to talk to him about his soul, he spent a restless night. The next day, while walking alone to a revival service in a union meeting in Merkel, Texas, he prayed and was saved. His conversion was not extremely dramatic, though sudden, instant, and sure.

With what was an elementary school education by today's standards, Scarborough entered Baylor Academy in 1888. His dream was to become a lawyer. On graduating from Baylor University in 1892, he entered Yale, taking a prelaw course for which he received an A.B. degree. The fact that he was in Phi Beta Kappa at Yale gives some indication of his intellectual ability. But law was not in the plan of God for Lee Scarborough. During his time at Yale he committed his life to the gospel ministry, and in 1899 he entered Southern Baptist Theological Seminary in Louisville. His seminary education was cut short because of the death of a brother, but while he was at Southern he married Neppie Warren of Abilene, who was to make an immense contribution to his later ministry.

Scarborough's first pastoral ministry was a five-year stint at First Baptist Church of Cameron, Texas. From there he assumed the pastorate of First Baptist Church, Abilene. In Abilene his obvious gift and passion for evangelism surfaced. In his seven-year pastorate, some fifteen hundred people were added to the church, most of whom were received by baptism.

In his fifth year of the Abilene pastorate, Scarborough was approached by B. H. Carroll about becoming professor of evangelism at the new seminary he was starting in Waco. After two years of intense struggle as to what to do about Carroll's invitation, Scarborough saw clearly that it was the will of God at the very time he was preaching a sermon on the will of God. H. E. Dana described it: "A conviction clear, mighty, almost cataclysmic, overwhelmed his heart even as he spoke."[1] Scarborough nailed this decision down in his room that evening, and the two-year struggle was ended. When asked by a friend in Abilene how his decision appeared to him, Scarborough replied, "It looks like this, I can stay here and preach in this great church, perhaps the rest of my life. But if I go to the seminary, I can be preaching in a thousand pulpits after I am dead and gone."[2]

Scarborough's position was an altogether new one in theological education. No other theological seminary had ever offered courses in evangelism and certainly not with a full-time professor. No better choice of someone to fill this "Chair of Fire" could have been made than that of Lee Scarborough. Even after becoming president of the seminary, Scarborough continued his teaching ministry until his retirement in 1942. He taught some eight thousand students during this period of time.

There was no question that Scarborough was Carroll's choice to be the next president of Southwestern. With the challenge from Carroll to "'see to it that every day and hour, every month in every year, every year in the long future, this Seminary is kept lashed to the Redeemer,'"[3] Scarborough took the reins as president of Southwestern Seminary in the fall of 1914. His ministry as professor of evangelism was little hindered by his enlarged responsibility, and his being president gave him a far greater platform. Southwestern Seminary won its way not only into the hearts of Texas Baptists but also of Southern Baptists.

Scarborough displayed his abilities as a denominational statesman in leading the Southern Baptist Convention in the support of denominational causes. His most marked success is usually regarded as his leadership of the 75 Million Campaign, an effort to subscribe at least seventy-five million dollars to Southern Baptist causes. Dana referred to this as Scarborough's "supreme denominational contribution."[4] According to Robert A. Baker, the by-product of the campaign was the adoption of the Cooperative Program in 1925.[5]

In 1942 Scarborough retired from his presidency and in 1945 went to his eternal reward.[6] He preceded his wife in death and was survived by three sons, George Warren, Lawrence Rutland, and William Byron, and three daughters, Euna Lee, Neppie, and Ada Beth.

WRITINGS

Along with his administrative duties as president of Southwestern, his classroom responsibilities, and his extensive preaching schedule, Scarborough found adequate time to leave a legacy of books, journal editorials, and numerous articles for Baptist state papers and other periodicals. He was the author of seventeen books, all of which were either indirectly or directly related to evangelism.

Books on Evangelism

Interestingly enough, Scarborough's first book that dealt exclusively with evangelism, considered his *magnum opus*, was *With Christ after the Lost*, written in 1919. In Dana's words,

> This book has been the main textbook in the department of evangelism in the Southwestern Seminary since it was published. More than six thousand students in the Seminary have taken this course and many have studied it in other seminaries and otherwise throughout the world. It has been the textbook in most of the seminaries of the world and has been published in . . . other languages.[7]

For his course in Evangelism in the Book of Acts, Scarborough wrote *Endued to Win*. He called it "an evangelistic interpretation of the Acts of Apostles, pointing out the primal factors of building a soul-winning church."[8] It deals extensively with the work of the Holy Spirit in the apostolic church.

In 1924 and 1925, Scarborough wrote two smaller books related to evangelism. The first of these was *Christ's Militant Kingdom: A Study in the Trail Triumphant*. It describes the power of the kingdom of God, referring to the kingdom as a great militant force for evangelism.[9] The second of these two, *A Search for Souls,* was written for lay people "in order to help this great body of Christian men and women to become skilled in the work of winning men."[10]

The last of his books, centered wholly on evangelism, *How Jesus Won Men*, was written in 1926 for a course which Scarborough was teaching on the evangelism of Jesus.

Sermons

Scarborough's preaching ministry took him all over the United States and to other parts of the world as well. He preached in twelve to fifteen revivals a year. His messages were in such demand that in 1922 Scarborough published three volumes of sermons. These were *Gospel Messages*,[11] *Prepare to Meet God*,[12] and *The Tears of Jesus*.[13]

The book *Products of Pentecost*[14] was written from a series of messages which Scarborough brought at a Baptist encampment in New Mexico. He prepared them at the encampment with the general theme of what Pentecost is to mean to us in our own spiritual stimulation and power.

The last of these books, *After the Resurrection, What?*[15] is perhaps more of a devotional study than a book of sermons; here Scarborough deals primarily with the forty days between the resurrection and the ascension of Jesus.

Books about Travels

Scarborough wrote two books giving great details about two extended journeys which he took while president of the seminary. The first of these, *Holy Places and Precious Promises*, was written in 1924.[16] It is a record of his travels in the Holy Land with a group of some fifty people led by Dr. and Mrs. A. J. Armstrong of Baylor.

The second, *A Blaze of Evangelism across the Equator*, is a description of 144 days in South America, a trip taken by Scarborough and certain representatives of the Foreign Mission Board (SBC).

Miscellaneous Books

The first book Scarborough ever wrote was *Recruits for World Conquest*,[17] in 1914. It is an encouragement to people to step out into some kind of ministry with particular emphasis on those who are called into vocational Christian service. *Marvels of Divine Leadership*[18] is the story of the Southern Baptist 75 Million Campaign, of which Scarborough was the general director. It is a detailed description of how God worked a virtual financial miracle for the purpose of undergirding Southern Baptist organizations and institutions. One of the significant aspects of the 75 Million Campaign was the revival thrust and great moving of the spirit of evangelism that came out of it. Scarborough wrote: "Everywhere revivals broke out. Hundreds of souls were saved. More than four thousand young people in the churches and around 2,500 in the Baptists schools gave themselves to God's service."[19]

Making use of Christian vocabulary that ends with the word "ship," Scarborough wrote the book *Ten Spiritual Ships* in 1927, using terminology such as stewardship, fellowship, debtorship, and others.[20]

My Conception of the Gospel Ministry[21] was written in 1935. As would be expected, the primary thrust of this book was to encourage pastors to be evangelistic in their ministry, but it actually covers virtually every aspect of the life of a preacher of the gospel.

In 1939 Scarborough wrote the story of Southwestern Baptist Theological Seminary, entitled *A Modern School of the Prophets*.[22] It is a detailed history of Southwestern during its first thirty years.

Scarborough was also the author of more than 175 articles which were published in the *Baptist Standard* and other Baptist papers as well as in *The Southwestern Journal of Theology*. These articles deal with Scarborough's favorite subject, evangelism, along with other crucial issues such as stewardship, theological education, the seminary and its relationship to Baptist people, and the importance of cooperation in kingdom endeavors.

CONTRIBUTION TO AND IMPACT ON SOUTHERN BAPTIST EVANGELISM

From the moment of his conversion Scarborough felt a desire to lead others to accept Jesus as their Savior. Immediately he began to pray for his lost brother, Will, and to plan to win him to Christ. "Out of what Christ put in me when he saved me came a hunger and a passionate longing for the salvation of others."[23] He had no idea where this "passionate longing" would take him, but he stated in 1926: "And now, for nearly forty years, that longing abides."[24] How Scarborough's longing expressed itself in more than a forty-year period is the subject now to be addressed.

There is no question but that his understanding of evangelism as a pastor and professor would fall into the category of the "traditional." If he had a formal definition of evangelism, it would have been "spreading the glad tidings of salvation through Jesus Christ to a lost world."[25] Although Scarborough was called to be a professor of evangelism, and his classes were regarded as classes in evangelism, "soul winning" was his favorite word to describe sharing the gospel. He used it far more frequently in his writings than any other. Scarborough was a product of his time, and the word "evangelism" had not yet come into the widespread usage to which Baptists today are accustomed.

Scarborough's emphasis on the term "soul winning" left an impact on the churches of the Southern Baptist Convention. Soul winning was the reaping aspect of evangelism, and this emphasis on the reaping aspect almost eclipsed the necessity of sowing and cultivating as vital parts of evangelism as well. The constant use of "soul winning" caused people to spotlight the harvester or the reaper, so that the person who was present when someone was "birthed" into the kingdom of God became the hero in personal evangelism. Churches lost sight of the importance of bridge building and the fact that it takes time and often more than one person in the sowing, cultivating, and reaping process. It was not until the 1960s that Southern Baptists began to place emphasis on sowing and cultivating as a vital part of evangelism and ultimately soul winning itself.

The fact that Scarborough's concept of evangelism is regarded as traditional, that is, the sharing of the good news of Jesus with a view to winning people to Him as Savior and Lord, should not be taken for granted. Scarborough's concept of evangelism in his lifetime came under fire from certain Baptists in other parts of our country. About the time that Scarborough came to Southwestern, Walter Rauschenbusch released his book *Christianity and the Social Crisis*,[26] and the Social Gospel movement, which questioned the validity of personal salvation in lieu of social reform, was being promoted by sizeable segments of Protestant churches. The fact that this movement never made serious inroads into churches in the Southern Baptist Convention was due to a large degree to the strong emphasis of Scarborough on personal salvation.

Perhaps Scarborough's unique contribution was simply that he became the first professor of evangelism in the history of theological education. He was confident that this position was altogether new in theological education and referred to B. H. Carroll's establishing this chair of evangelism, the "Chair of Fire," as a distinctive and far-reaching action. Scarborough said that Carroll insisted that the Department of Evangelism was to be as important in the life of the institution as any other classical or biblical professorship.

It became a part of Scarborough's vision in time that every theological seminary should have a strong department of evangelism, and he believed that courses in evangelism should be required of all students in a theological institution. Although it was thirty years after his death that the vision became reality in each of the six Southern Baptist seminaries, the dream reached farther than that. Today, one would be hard pressed to find a theological seminary of Protestant vintage which does not offer some type of course in evangelism. Scarborough's vision has come to fruition.

Among his other contributions, Scarborough was a prime mover in the first state evangelism conference ever held in one of the state conventions affiliated with the Southern Baptist Convention. It is more than mere coincidence that this meeting, which turned out to be a powerful spiritual experience, was held in Cowden Hall on the campus of Southwestern Seminary in 1936.

Scarborough actually had had a vision for conferences of this nature long before. Shortly after the conclusion of the 75 Million Campaign in 1920, he wrote that such conferences should be held under the direction of executive directors of state conventions and should be held on Baptist college campuses. Ultimately every state convention followed the Texas convention in conducting state evangelism conferences. This meeting became, almost without exception, the meeting with the largest attendance of any meeting, including the annual state convention, in every state. In Texas, some twelve to fifteen thousand people attended evangelism conferences when attendance was at its highest point.

One cannot read long in the writings of Scarborough without realizing that he considered evangelism to be the preeminent ministry of the church. He referred to it as the big business in Jesus' life, and he conceived of evangelism as essential for life and growth in churches. "The church without evangelism is an engine dead and lifeless and powerless on the track. A church without the spirit of evangelism is a spiritual corpse, a spiritual refrigerator, a house of death."[27] Scarborough defined a church as *"a group of baptized believers going with Christ after the lost."*[28] Words like "mammoth undertaking," "supreme primacy of soul winning," and "mastering the main thing," are typical expressions of Scarborough in describing the importance of evangelism.

Scarborough had a unique ability in the area of personal evangelism. He insisted that the personal element of seeking the lost face to face or hand to hand is probably the most effective way of leading men to Christ. He believed that every Christian could "bear an effective testimony in personal work in winning the lost to Christ."[29] More than once he referred to personal evangelism as a "fine art," and in his book *A Search for Souls* he subtitled it "the finest of fine arts."

One aspect of Scarborough's emphases perhaps not often mentioned was his emphasis on what he called "soul building." He insisted that churches are responsible not only to win people but to mature them as well. This emphasis, though always there in theory, did not actually take a strong hold among Southern Baptists. It is for this reason that, particularly in the twentieth century, from 40 to 50 percent of church members associated with Southern Baptist churches have been inactive. Scarborough said long ago, "It is not wise to say that soul winning is the main thing or that soul building is the main thing. . . . The entire work of the kingdom of God can be organized along two lines: soul winning and soul building."[30] The Southwestern president referred to these as the Siamese twins of God's gospel.

The present author was surprised to discover that Scarborough was far ahead of his time when it came to an emphasis on what contemporary Christians have called "follow up" or "follow through" with new believers. In discussing this issue as it related to revival meetings, Scarborough said, "There should be special committees appointed whose duty it is to constantly look after those who have made public profession. . . . It is not enough that men should be left to Christ simply. They should be caused to follow on to know the Lord in a larger and more gracious way."[31] He suggested that some method should be used to see that the converts of a meeting are trained to study the Bible and are forming the habit of prayer.

One cannot understand L. R. Scarborough without seeing him primarily as a person of great passion for people who are lost. He not only preached it but he lived it. He regarded passion as the main matter in Christianity, the first thing in the Christian's task. Dana is correct when he suggested that Scarborough's "greatest contribution" to Southwestern Seminary was "the spirit he imparted to the institution and the place he won for it in the hearts of Southern Baptists, and Baptists to the end of the earth."[32]

Thanks to the life and ministry of L. R. Scarborough, the reputation of Southwestern became that of a seminary with a major emphasis on evangelism both at home and around the world. This was the case when other seminaries did not seem to be so interested in this aspect of ministry.

More than once Scarborough is quoted as having said, "'Whatever power I may have at all is due to the fact that any time of the day or night, I can close my eyes and weep for a lost world.'"[33] Scarborough wrote a book, *The Tears of Jesus*, but it would not be difficult to find adequate evidence for authoring a book on the tears of L. R. Scarborough.

BIBLIOGRAPHY

1. Primary

BOOKS

After the Resurrection, What? Grand Rapids: Zondervan, 1942.

A Blaze of Evangelism across the Equator. Nashville: Broadman, 1937.

Christ's Militant Kingdom: A Study in the Trail Triumphant. Nashville: Sunday School Board of the Southern Baptist Convention, 1924.

Endued to Win. Nashville: Sunday School Board of the Southern Baptist Convention, 1922.

Gospel Messages. Nashville: Sunday School Board of the Southern Baptist Convention, 1922.

Holy Places and Precious Promises. New York: George H. Doran, 1924.

How Jesus Won Men. Nashville: Sunday School Board of the Southern Baptist Convention, 1926; rpt.: Grand Rapids: Baker, 1972.

Marvels of Divine Leadership, or The Story of the Southern Baptist 75 Million Campaign. Nashville: Sunday School Board of the Southern Baptist Convention, 1920.

A Modern School of the Prophets. Nashville: Broadman, 1939.

My Conception of the Gospel Ministry. Nashville: Sunday School Board of the Southern Baptist Convention, 1935.

Prepare to Meet God. New York: George H. Doran, 1922.

Products of Pentecost. New York: Fleming H. Revell, 1934.

Recruits for World Conquests. New York: Fleming H. Revell, 1914.

A Search for Souls: A Study in the Finest of Fine Arts—Winning the Lost to Christ. Nashville: Sunday School Board of the Southern Baptist Convention, 1925.

The Tears of Jesus. New York: George H. Doran, 1922.

Ten Spiritual Ships. Nashville: Sunday School Board of the Southern Baptist Convention, 1927.

With Christ after the Lost. Nashville: Sunday School Board of the Southern Baptist Convention, 1919.

      Phephraekhrissasana. Bangkok: Ronghim Thai phathaya Phranakhon, 1963. [Thai]

JOURNAL EDITORIALS AND ARTICLES

"Baptists Facing a Big Task." *Southwestern Journal of Theology* o.s. 3 (July 1919): 3–4.

"Baptists on the Missionary Mount of Observation and Inspiration." *Southwestern Journal of Theology* o.s.7 (October 1923): 9–27.

"The Character Value of the Promises." *Southwestern Journal of Theology* o.s. 6 (October 1922): 93–95.

"Christianity and Our Soldiers." *Southwestern Journal of Theology* o.s. 2 (April 1918): 3–7.

"The Doctrine of Evangelism." *Southwestern Journal of Theology* o.s. 4 (October 1920): 5–8.

"Eternal Matters Involved in the 75 Million Campaign." *Southwestern Journal of Theology* o.s. 3 (October 1919): 3–4.

"The Education of Religious Leaders." *Southwestern Journal of Theology* o.s. 7 (April 1923): 76–79.

"Evangelism in Baptist Schools." *Southwestern Journal of Theology* o.s. 2 (July 1918): 3–8.

"Is Co-operation a New Testament Doctrine?" *Southwestern Journal of Theology* o.s. 6 (April 1922): 92–96; rpt.: *Baptist Standard*, 4 May 1922, 15–16.

"Keeping Up the Morale." *Southwestern Journal of Theology* o.s. 6 (July 1922): 57–61.

"The Militant Church." *Southwestern Journal of Theology* o.s. 1 (October 1917): 3–7.

"The Need of Indoctrination." *Southwestern Journal of Theology* o.s. 4 (April 1920): 3–6.

"Rallying around the Fundamentals." *Southwestern Journal of Theology* o.s. 3 (April 1919): 3–6.

"Redemptive Recruits." *Southwestern Journal of Theology* o.s. 1 (January 1918): 3–10.

"Revival of Doctrinal Preaching and Teaching." *Southwestern Journal of Theology* o.s. 2 (October 1918): 3–6.

"A Serious Educational Matter." *Southwestern Journal of Theology* o.s. 5 (October 1921): 88–90.

"Siding with the Truth." *Southwestern Journal of Theology* o.s. 1 (April 1917): 3–8.
"Some By-Products of the Great Southern Campaign." *Southwestern Journal of Theology* o.s. 5 (January 1921): 6–9.
"Some Editorial Notes on the Union Question." *Southwestern Journal of Theology* o.s. 3 (January 1919): 3–7.
"The Soul-winning Hunger." *Southwestern Journal of Theology* o.s. 1 (July 1917): 3–9.
"Southern Baptists and a Constructive Program." *Southwestern Journal of Theology* o.s. 4 (January 1920): 3–7.
"Summer Evangelism." *Southwestern Journal of Theology* o.s. 8 (July 1924): 3–6.
"Ways to Poison These Fountains." *Southwestern Journal of Theology* o.s. 6 (January 1922): 91–93.
"A Weakening Drift in Education." *Southwestern Journal of Theology* o.s. 5 (July 1921): 3–6.
"Why Southern Baptists Should Achieve a Final Victory in 1924." *Southwestern Journal of Theology* o.s. 8 (January 1924): 3–5.

MISCELLANEOUS ARTICLES

"The Baptist Pot Is Boiling." *Western Recorder*, 4 September 1919, 3–4.
"The Creeds of Dead Hands." *Baptist Standard*, 22 September 1921, 6–7.
"Denominational Co-operation." *The Southwestern Evangel*, May 1927, 279.
"Evangelism in the Pulpit." *The Southwestern Evangel*, April 1925, 33–34.
"The Fruits of Norrisism." [Seminary Hill, Tex.: pvt. ptg.] n.d. Scarborough Collection, File 652, Archives, Roberts Library, Southwestern Baptist Theological Seminary; *Journal of Texas Baptist History* 1 (1981): 89–97; Carson, *Calling Out the Called*, 120–32.
"Going over to Another Gospel." *The Southwestern Evangel*, July 1925, 10, 19.
"Glorifying Christ in Our Lives." *The Southwestern Evangel*, February 1927, 186–88.
"God's Call and Challenge to Southern Baptists." *Baptist Standard*, 13 June 1940, 1–18.
"The Invitations of the Gospel." *The Southwestern Evangel*, February 1925, 14–17.
"Militant Evangelism." *Baptist Standard*, 1 July 1915, 1, 13.
"My Gratitude to God and the Brotherhood of Baptists." *The Southwestern Evangel*, January 1925, 27–29.
"Our Answer to God's Call." *Baptist Standard*, 23 October 1919, 6–7, 30.
"Our Attitude toward Other Faiths." *The Southwestern Evangel*, March 1930, 175.
"The Unfinished Task." *Baptist Standard*, 22 December 1923, 6–7, 22–28.

2. Secondary

Baker, Robert A. "The Cooperative Program in Historical Perspective." *Baptist History and Heritage* 10 (July 1975): 169–76.
_____. *The Southern Baptist Convention and Its People 1607–1972*. Nashville: Broadman, 1974. Pp. 303–4, 336–37, 438.
_____. *Tell the Generations Following: A History of Southwestern Baptist Theological Seminary, 1908–1983*. Nashville: Broadman, 1983. Pp. 25, 126, 139–41, 143, 145, 148–83, 197–240, 245–78, 292–93, 306, 329, 477.
Barnes, W. W. *The Southern Baptist Convention, 1845–1953*. Nashville: Broadman, 1954. Pp. 205–9, 223–24.
Beck, Rosalie. "Lee Rutland Scarborough." *Journal of Texas Baptist History* 1 (1981): 60–62.
Benefield, Leroy. "Lee Rutland Scarborough and His Preaching." Th.D. diss., Southwestern Baptist Theological Seminary, 1970.
Carroll, J. M. *A History of Texas Baptists*. Ed. J. B. Cranfill. Dallas: Baptist Standard, 1923. Pp. 881–82, 886–87, 906, 920, 945, 981–91.

Lee Rutland Scarborough

Carson, Glenn Thomas. *Calling Out the Called: The Life and Work of Lee Rutland Scarborough*. Austin: Eakin Press, 1996.

_____. "Lee Rutland Scarborough: Architect of a New Denominationalism within the Southern Baptist Convention." Ph.D. diss., Southwestern Baptist Theological Seminary, 1992.

Dana, H. E. *Lee Rutland Scarborough: A Life of Service*. Nashville: Broadman, 1942.

_____. "Lee Rutland Scarborough." In *Ten Men from Baylor*, ed. J. M. Price. Kansas City, Kan.: Central Seminary Press, 1945. Pp. 145–59.

Dawson, J. M. "The Apostolate of L. R. Scarborough." *The Southwestern Evangel*, January 1925, 41–44.

_____. "L. R. Scarborough: Chair of Fire." *Baptist Standard*, 30 March 1957, 6–7.

Encyclopedia of Southern Baptists. 4 vols. Nashville: Broadman, 1958–82. Vol. 2. S.v. "Scarborough, Lee Rutland."

Evans, Perry F. "L. R. Scarborough: Biographical Sketch." In *Southwestern Men and Their Messages*, ed. J. M. Price. Kansas City, Kan.: Central Seminary Press, 1948. Pp. 119–21.

Fletcher, Jesse C. *The Southern Baptist Convention: A Sesquicentennial History*. Nashville: Broadman and Holman, 1994. Pp. 111–12, 117–19, 134–36, 140, 155–56, 165–66, 174, 177.

Foreman, A. D., Jr. "The Evangelistic Thrust of L. R. Scarborough." *Southwestern Journal of Theology* n.s. 7 (October 1964): 54–61.

Hawley, Michael Mark. "A Critical Examination of Lee Rutland Scarborough's Concept of Evangelism." Th.D. diss., New Orleans Baptist Theological Seminary, 1992.

Maston, Thomas B. "Dr. Scarborough Memorialized." *Southwestern News*, May 1945, 1–8.

Miles, Delos. *L. R. Scarborough: Shaper of Evangelism*. Shapers of Southern Baptist Heritage. Nashville: Historical Commission of the Southern Baptist Convention, 1987.

Walter Thomas Conner
(1877–1952)
Theology

James Leo Garrett, Jr.

3

BIOGRAPHY

W. T. Conner, Southwestern's theologian for four decades, was, according to his own account, "brought up in the dire poverty of the South after the Civil War."[1] Born on 19 January 1877, in Cleveland County, Arkansas, as the second son to Mississippi-born parents, Walter moved twice in his boyhood with his family to other locations in southern Arkansas.[2] His early education consisted of attending "ungraded country schools on an average of three or four months a year and some years practically none."[3]

In 1892 the Conner family moved to a farm in Taylor County, Texas, southwest of Abilene.[4] Although he had encountered the appeal of the gospel in Arkansas churches, Conner's conversion occurred at the age of seventeen in a Methodist revival service. He recalled it as giving up the load of the conviction of sin rather than an emotional experience.[5] No sooner had Conner been baptized and received into Harmony Baptist Church, Caps, Texas, than he experienced a call to preach the gospel.[6]

Walter Conner was licensed to preach in 1895, but his determined pursuit of education for his ministry was impeded by the death of his father in 1896. For two years he was enrolled intermittently at Simmons College (now Hardin-Simmons University), and in 1898 he entered Baylor University. For the next eight years he attended Baylor at intervals and served as pastor of various Texas Baptist churches, having been ordained at Caps in 1899, in order to pay his debts and help his brother John to continue his studies at Baylor. In 1906 Walter received his B.A. degree, as did Miss Blanche Ethel Horne of Albany, Texas, who in June 1907 became Mrs. W. T. Conner.[7] Continuing his studies at Baylor Theological Seminary, he received the Th.B. degree in 1908 just after the seminary had been chartered as Southwestern Baptist Theological Seminary and simultaneously the M.A. degree from Baylor University. Having been encouraged to prepare for the teaching of theology in the new seminary, Conner studied in Rochester (N.Y.) Theological Seminary, for two years (1908–1910), receiving the B.D. degree.[8]

In 1910 Conner began to teach theology at Southwestern, just after its removal to Fort Worth. During 1914 he spent a leave of absence studying at Southern Baptist Theological Seminary and received therefrom the Th.D. degree in 1916. By writing a second thesis for Southern, Conner received the Ph.D. degree in 1931.[9] Conner's tenure at Southwestern spanned the presidencies of B. H. Carroll, L. R. Scarborough, and E. D. Head.

Conner's basic discipline was systematic theology, but at times he also taught English New Testament, biblical theology, and Greek New Testament exegesis.[10] A native Irish wit, a keen sense of the proper use of anecdote, and his concern to apply theological concepts combined to make Conner an interesting classroom teacher.[11] He, along with other Southwestern employees, suffered dire economic conditions prior to and during the Great Depression,[12] especially with the college education of the six Conner children.[13] Interim pastorates, Bible conferences, summer assemblies, and professional society meetings filled his schedule, and his writings were directed to pastors and laypersons more than to scholars.

Conner suffered a stroke in 1949, which led to his retirement. He died on 26 May 1952 and was buried in Mount Olivet Cemetery, Fort Worth.[14]

SEQUENCE OF WRITINGS

In "Theodore Parker's Theological System," Conner's critique of the Unitarian included Parker's denial of special revelation, atonement, human depravity, the deity of Christ, Jesus' resurrection, the new birth, and eternal punishment. Parker held to a "semi-pantheism," but "the cardinal defect" of his system is its denial of the radicality of sin. Parker's system and "orthodox Christianity," according to Conner, are "utterly irreconcilable." "The Formal Factor in Christianity" (1916) dealt with its "sacred places, times, persons, customs or institutions." Less important than the vital and the doctrinal factors, the formal is not to be identified with Christianity but is designed to express and deepen Christian experience, as in proper observance of baptism and the Lord's Supper. Conner's 1916 Th.D. thesis on "Pragmatism and Theology" focused on the philosophical movement led by C. S. S. Peirce, William James, and F. C. S. Schiller. Defining pragmatism as "the method of testing the meaning of a proposition by its practical consequences" (p. 4), Conner found in it some positive features for Christian theology but even more some serious negatives.

Conner authored thirteen articles for the *Southwestern Journal of Theology* during its first series (1917–24). In "The Fundamental Baptist Principle" he argued that such principle was none other than the fundamental principle for all Christians, namely, the Lordship of Jesus Christ. In "Human Nature in the Light of the Incarnation" he contended for the centrality of the incarnation in Christianity and argued that Protestant theology had given too little attention to the incarnation and too much to the fall of man in formulating its doctrine of human nature. In "Is Christian Science Christian?" Conner answered negatively on the basis of its denial of the Christian doctrines of revelation, God, the world, sin and suffering, Christology, atonement, salvation, and the Holy Spirit. "A man can not be a Christian and an Eddyite at the same time" (p. 53).[15] In "The Nature of the Authority of the Bible" the Southwestern theologian affirmed that the Bible's authority is religious, takes into account its popular language, fosters human freedom, complements conscience, is that of grace and requires faith, and is none other than the authority of Christ. In "The Call to the Work of the Ministry" the call to preach is said not to depreciate the spiritual gifts of all Christians but to be communicated more directly by God. Baptists have been slow to recognize human agency in "calling out the called."

In "The Relation of the Work of the Holy Spirit to the Person and Work of Christ" Conner taught that Pentecost "was the vindication of Christ" as begun in his resurrection and the "manifestation" of his redemptive power. Receiving Christ is receiving the Spirit.

There can be post-regenerational reception of the Spirit for consecration. In "The Significance of Baptism" Conner contended that baptism is "not a condition of salvation" and positively interpreted it as a confession of Jesus Christ as Savior and Lord, a reminder of his death and resurrection for our salvation, a symbol of the believer's death to sin and resurrection to newness of life, and a "forward reference" to eschatological resurrection. According to "The Glorified Christ" the glorification of Christ was preceded by his preincarnate life and his life on earth and occurred both in his death and in his resurrection and ascension. Rom. 8:28 was the text expounded in "God's Purpose and Providence." God's providence is "all inclusive," for, contrary to modern naturalism, "all things" "*energise*" and "*synergise*" for the good of God's children; the "good," contrary to modern materialism, is conformity to Christ; and providence is "grounded in God's eternal purpose of grace." In "The Essentials of Christian Union" Conner explicated the "essential conditions" as "spiritual unity" growing out of a common relation to Jesus as Lord and Savior, "doctrinal unity" on the "great fundamental doctrines," and "symbolic unity," involving church organization and the ordinances, but he rejected any "territorial or national or world-wide organization" that governs the local church. Instead churches can cooperate to extend God's kingdom. According to "Christ's Death and Our Redemption" his death is a "revelation" of God's love for sinful humans, a "demonstration" of God's righteousness, and "the ground" of human salvation. In "Jesus and the Gospel" Conner presented Jesus both as sinless human-example-teacher and as divine Messiah-Savior-Lord.

Conner's first book, 576 pages and designed for textbook usage, *A System of Christian Doctrine*,[16] was published in 1924. Its introduction and seventeen chapters were grouped under four "parts" (revelation, Christ-God-the Spirit, world and man, salvation). Beginning with the question, "Can Man Know God?" the author treated the personal, redemptive, and final revelation of God in Christ before considering the revelation to Israel and through nature and worldviews contrary to the Christian. He concluded with the Bible as the "God-inbreathed" and authoritative record of special revelation in Christ. Part two included the person of Christ (incarnation, two natures, preexistence, virgin birth, temptation, growth, resurrection, ascension), God's attributes (personal, spiritual, righteous, love, holy, absolute), the Holy Spirit (person, relation to Jesus Christ, work), and the Trinity (nature, work, immanent eternality). Under part three Conner discussed God and the world (creation, preservation, governance and miracles), the origin and nature of man, and sin (origin, nature, original sin, penalty). Part four embraced God's purpose of redemption (election), the atoning work of Christ (atonement as penal substitution, false or inadequate theories, intercession of Christ), becoming a Christian (repentance, faith, union with Christ, forgiveness, justification, reconciliation, adoption, regeneration, sanctification, assurance), the Christian life (the Christian's mission, providence, prayer, perseverance, growth), and the consummation of salvation (kingdom of God, death, second coming—interpreted postmillennially, resurrection, judgment, heaven, and hell).[17]

Gospel Doctrines (1925), designed for members of Southern Baptist churches, consisted of chapters on the New Testament as the "gospel source book," Jesus Christ, God the Father and the Holy Spirit, man as person and as sinner, the work of Christ, salvation, Christian character, a gospel church (membership, offices, government, mission), the two ordinances (with a defense of close communion), and the gospel hope. In *The Resurrection of Jesus* (1926), Conner first treated the facticity and the nature of Jesus' resurrection and then explored its significance for the doctrines of God, Christ, salvation, the future life, and the coming of the kingdom of God. *The Teachings of Mrs. Eddy* (1926) drew from Conner's earlier articles on Christian Science, and *The Teachings of "Pastor" Russell* (1926), although written during the presidency of Joseph F. Rutherford, interfaced with the teachings of the founder of Jehovah's Witnesses as to eschatology, soteriology, and Christology, while charging the movement with the lack of "moral depth," the absence of missionary "dynamic," the neglect of social reform, and novelty of teaching.

Turning to the Johannine writings, Conner first wrote an exposition, *The Epistles of John* (1929). Accepting apostolic authorship and identifying the adversarial heresy as Cerinthian Gnosticism, he stated the theme of the First Epistle as: *"The character of God as revealed in Jesus Christ and the spiritual qualities of those who become the children of God by faith in Jesus"* (p. 27). Then in his Ph.D. dissertation, "The Idea of the Incarnation in the Gospel of John," Conner affirmed that the incarnation is the theme of this gospel according to its stated purpose (20:31) and its prologue (1:1–18). Part One defined the incarnation by examining titles applied to Jesus. Part Two recognized the attestations to the incarnation through the witness of disciples, Jesus' claims concerning himself, and his miracles as signs, chief of which is his resurrection. Part Three related the incarnation to the doctrines of God, faith, sin, the Holy Spirit, atonement, eternal life, and union with Christ.

Revelation and God (1936) was a revision of the first half of *A System of Christian Doctrine*. A new chapter on "Man a Religious Being" was inserted. The chapter on revelation through nature now preceded the chapter on biblical revelation, and the latter was followed by the chapter on the revelation of God in Christ. The chapter on "God and the World" (1924) was now placed under the doctrine of God. *Christian Doctrine* (1937) was a condensation and simplification of *A System of Christian Doctrine* designed for college classes and a general readership. The treatments of knowing God and of revelation through nature and in Israel were omitted, chapters on the person of Christ, sin, and atonement were rewritten, and chapters on the church and the ordinances from *Gospel Doctrines* were inserted. The Southwestern theologian insisted that infant baptism not only was not taught in the New Testament passages claimed as its basis but also was not to be inferred from the New Testament. Arising in the third century and depending on the doctrines that the child is born sinful and that baptism regenerates and washes away sin, infant baptism has been defended by Roman Catholics on the basis of original sin and baptismal regeneration, by Presbyterians on the basis of the covenant of grace, and by Methodists as infant dedication calling for parental responsibility. According to Conner, it destroys "the voluntary element" in Christianity, destroys the "spiritual character" of the church, and jeopardizes the "salvation of its recipients." In *Personal Christianity* (1937) one finds fourteen sermons on diverse topics, and in *The Christ We Need* (1938) fourteen of the fifteen sermons are on Jesus.

The aim of *The Faith of the New Testament* (1940) was "to set out the meaning of the main events of the history as well as the main types of teaching found in the New Testament," allowing each to "throw light on the other." "Faith" Conner interpreted both subjectively and objectively, and both Christocentrism and unity/diversity he found in the New Testament. The twenty-nine-chapter book's structure followed the types of New Testament literature: Synoptics, Jewish Christian writings (early Acts, James, 1 Peter, Hebrews), Paul, and John. Especially noteworthy are his treatment of Jesus' baptism and wilderness temptations and of Jesus' teaching on prayer and use of "Son of man" and of Paul's doctrine of sin, wherein Conner affirmed depravity and denied imputation of original guilt.

During the 1940s seven articles by Conner appeared in *Review and Expositor*. In "The Importance of Ecclesiology to Baptists" he called on Baptists, who are not "an ecclesiastically minded people," to rethink their ecclesiology. He argued that "spiritual democracy" helps to preserve the gospel in purity, is the only polity "consistent with the absolute lordship of Jesus," and rests on divine grace, the indwelling of the Holy Spirit, and the "laws of personality." "The Throne and the Lamb," based on Rev. 5:6, expounded the theme that "creative power alone does not interpret the world" but only the slain Lamb can do so. Hence "sovereign power and redemptive love meet in God," and Conner here was favorable to the suffering of God. In "Is Paul's Doctrine of Justification Forensic?" he continued to argue that Paul's doctrine had been misinterpreted by Protestant authors both "orthodox and liberal" by their setting forensic justification over against regeneration and sanctification. Paul "used a legal term" but not "in a legal sense," rather putting "a new meaning into the term." In Romans 5 Paul passes from forensic terms to terms expressive of union with Christ and life "without . . . hesitation," and Romans 6–8 is "not something in addition to justification, but what is involved in justification." Conner agreed with James Denney that "justification is a regenerative transaction" and held that in some sense believers are "made righteous" as well as being "declared righteous." In "Theology, a Practical Discipline" Conner celebrated the resurgence of theology and its emancipation from bondage to the sciences and asserted that theology was not designed to supply speculative knowledge but rather practical knowledge that affects conduct and life.

The Gospel of Redemption (1945) was a revision of the second half of *A System of Christian Doctrine*. The chapter on "The Redemptive Work of Christ" was rewritten to reflect a favorable attitude toward the Christ as Victor theory, repentance and faith were now treated after, not before, the terms indicative of what God does in our becoming Christians, a section on the church, but not the ordinances, was added to the chapter on "The Christian Life," and amillennialism rather than postmillennialism was espoused. Jesus' death as that of the suffering Messiah who preferred to call himself "Son of Man" (Synoptics), his death "for our sins according to the Scriptures" as both justification and propitiation (Paul), and his death as that of the Melchizedekan High Priest who offered a once-for-all offering for human sins (Hebrews) were delineated in "Three Types of Teaching in the New Testament on the Meaning of the Death of Christ." Then in "Three Theories of the Atonement" the Fort Worth theologian critiqued the penal theory as having a one-sided view of God's justice as mandatory righteousness and the moral influence theory as having a one-sided emphasis on divine love and more favorably expounded the Christ as Victor theory, particularly noting how it unites the incarnation and the cross, the life and the death, and the death and the resurrection of Jesus and is so readily applicable to the Christian life. Finally in "Theories of Atonement" Conner noted how theories have been built on biblical analogies, how theories have at times misinterpreted biblical texts, how the New Testament does not present a theory, how each theory has an element of truth but none has the full truth, and that "an ounce of spiritual insight is worth tons of theory."

What Is a Saint? (1948) briefly refuted the Roman Catholic view that limits saints to the canonized ones in heaven, R. R. Byrum's definition of sanctification as cleansing, to which Conner offered the alternative definition of dedication, and Wesleyan perfectionism. In *The Work of the Holy Spirit* (1949) Conner explicated the teachings about the Holy Spirit as found in the various types of New Testament writings, while supplying an introductory chapter on the Old Testament and two concluding chapters on the relation of the Spirit to human powers and on the Spirit as personal. There was no direct interaction with Pentecostal teaching and practice. In *The Cross in the New Testament* (1954), posthumously published, the Southwestern theologian, using the method of New Testament theology and including a chapter that reviewed and critiqued various theories of the atonement, gave final expression to his embrace of the Christ as Victor theory in a chapter entitled "The Inevitable Cross."

SUMMARY OF TEACHING

Inasmuch as the author has recently published[18] a systematic summary of Conner's teaching and in view of the space limitations for this chapter, the reader is referred to that chapter.

EVALUATION AND INFLUENCE

Conner's theology has numerous elements of *strength* that can be recognized five decades after his work ended.[19] For him Christian theology is to be closely related to Christian experience and is not primarily speculative. His writing style, marked by simplicity and an Anglo-Saxon vocabulary, made his teachings available to pastors and lay people, although scholars might have preferred more technical precision and detailed documentation. Conner gave emphasis to the doctrine of revelation when it was receiving much attention from Protestant theologians but did not embrace the Barthian denial of general revelation. God's attributes were interpreted in a quest for the moral self-consistency of God, and the doctrine of God was framed in the light of Jesus Christ. Conner was increasingly concerned with the doctrine of the Holy Spirit, especially the Spirit's work. A human being is not worthy of salvation yet is worth saving and is personally responsible for sin, and hence theories of imputation are not needed. Late in life Conner was capable of making a major shift from penal substitution to Christ as Victor. His departure from Protestant orthodoxy concerning sanctification is probably more persuasive than his departure concerning justification.

Weaknesses in the theology of Conner are also identifiable. Certain major topics treated by other theologians during the nineteenth and twentieth centuries were bypassed or treated only slightly by the Southwestern theologian; for example, theories about the divine inspiration of the Bible, the biblical doctrine of the image of God in man, and the relation of the doctrine of the creation of humans to evolutionary science. Some readers of Conner's books today may be inclined to want to press questions upon him. Have you mistakenly fused general revelation and theistic arguments for God's existence? Are there no clearer conclusions to be drawn concerning Chalcedonian Christology and kenoticism? Is not the Trinity more important than your treatment

41

would suggest? Does not theology need to "grapple seriously" with great contemporary issues confronting church and society?[20]

Those who would identify Conner as a fundamentalist will fall short of proving their case,[21] and those who would reckon him as a full-blown Synod of Dort Calvinist must face the fact that he clearly taught only two (election and perseverance) of the "five points."[22] Clearly he was a Southern Baptist theologian. Probably he can also be identified with conservative or constructive evangelicalism.

Conner's *influence* was almost exclusively limited to Southern Baptists, although some of his books were translated into Spanish, Portuguese, Chinese, Japanese, and Korean. Four decades of students were shaped in his Southwestern classroom, for the same period Conner's theology and Southwestern's theology were almost synonymous, and his books were widely circulated until the 1960s. Those who taught theology with him at Southwestern in his later years and those who taught theology at Southwestern after his retirement were deeply influenced by Conner's theology. In the 1980s and 1990s, his theological work has been found to be relevant to the issues confronting Southern Baptists and a field for intensive research.

BIBLIOGRAPHY

1. Primary

THESIS AND DISSERTATIONS

"The Idea of the Incarnation in the Gospel of John." Ph.D. diss., Southern Baptist Theological Seminary, 1931.

"Pragmatism and Theology." Th.D. diss., Southern Baptist Theological Seminary, 1916.

"Theodore Parker's Theological System." Thesis offered for fellowship, Rochester Theological Seminary, 1909.

BOOKS

Christian Doctrine. Nashville: Broadman, 1937.
  Doctrina Cristiana. Trans. Adolfo Robleto. El Paso: Casa Bautista de Publicaciones, 1962. [Spanish]
  Kidokgyo Kyori. Trans. Oh Kap Kwon. Seoul: Baptist Publications, 1962. [Korean]
  Kiri Suto Kyo Kyo Ri. Trans. Shuichi Ozaki. Tokyo: Jordan Press, 1952. [Japanese]
The Christ We Need. Grand Rapids: Zondervan, 1938.
The Cross in the New Testament. Ed. Jesse J. Northcutt. Nashville: Broadman Press, 1954.
The Epistles of John: Their Meaning and Message. New York: Fleming H. Revell Co. 1929; Nashville: Broadman, 1957.
The Faith of the New Testament. Nashville: Broadman, 1940.

Xin Yue Zhi Xing Yang. Trans. L. H. Chow and Wei-Yuan Siao. Hong Kong: Baptist Press, 1953. [Chinese]

La Fe del Nuevo Testamento. Trans. Lemuel C. Quarles, Alfredo C. Müller, Carlos Ramirez L., José Rivas G. Quizás, and Alfredo Lerin. El Paso: Casa Bautista de Publicaciones, 1951. [Spanish]

Gospel Doctrines. Nashville: Sunday School Board of the Southern Baptist Convention, 1925.

The Gospel of Redemption. Nashville: Broadman, 1945.

O Evangelho de Redenção. Trans. David Gomes and Jabes Torres. Rio de Janeiro: Casa Publicadora Batista, 1950. [Portuguese]

El Evangelio de la Redención. Trans. Lemuel C. Quarles. El Paso: Casa Bautista de Publicaciones, 1954. [Spanish].

Jiu Shu Zhi Fu Yin. Trans. Wei-Yuan Siao and L. H. Chow. Hong Kong: Baptist Press, 1954. [Chinese]

Personal Christianity. Grand Rapids: Zondervan, 1937.

The Resurrection of Jesus. Nashville: Sunday School Board of the Southern Baptist Convention, 1926.

Revelation and God: An Introduction to Christian Doctrine. Nashville: Broadman, 1936.

La Revelación y Dios. Trans. Adolfo Robleto. El Paso: Casa Bautista de Publicaciones, n.d. [Spanish]

A System of Christian Doctrine. Nashville: Sunday School Board of the Southern Baptist Convention, 1924.

The Teachings of Mrs. Eddy. Nashville: Sunday School Board of the Southern Baptist Convention, 1926.

The Teachings of "Pastor" Russell. Nashville: Sunday School Board of the Southern Baptist Convention, 1926.

What Is a Saint? Nashville: Broadman, 1948.

Que é um Santo? Trans. Almir S. Gonçalves. Rio de Janeiro: Casa Publicadora Batista, 1949. [Portuguese]

¿Que es un Santo? Trans. Arthur R. Dailey. El Paso: Casa Bautista de Publicaciones, n.d. [Spanish]

The Work of the Holy Spirit. Nashville: Broadman Press, 1949.

Shen Lin Zhi Gong Zuo. Trans. Samuel Y. C. Tang. Taipei, Taiwan: Taiwan Baptist Theological Seminary, 1957. [Chinese].

A Obra do Espírito Santo: Tratado sôbre a Doutrina Bíblica do Espírito Santo. Trans. Waldemar W. Wey. Rio de Janeiro: Casa Publicadora Batista, 1961. [Portuguese]

Sei Rei No Hatara Ki. Trans. Goki Saíto and ed. Shuichi Ozaki. Tokyo: Jordan Press, 1966. [Japanese]

CONTRIBUTIONS TO BOOKS

"Theological Education." In *Fourth Baptist World Congress: Record of Proceedings*, ed. W. T. Whitley, 286–91. London: Kingsgate Press, 1928.

"Infant Baptism." In *Re-thinking Baptist Doctrines*, ed. Victor I. Masters, 61–80. Louisville: Western Recorder, 1937.

"Autobiographical Sketch" and "The Place of Prayer in the Christian Life." In *Southwestern Men and Messages*, ed. J. M. Price, 41–43, 44–51. Kansas City, Kan.: Central Seminary Press, 1948.

JOURNAL ARTICLES

"The Call to the Work of the Ministry." *Southwestern Journal of Theology* o.s. 3 (July 1919): 48–56.

"Christ's Death and Our Redemption." *Southwestern Journal of Theology* o.s. 7 (October 1923): 58–67.

"Eddyism vs. Christianity." *Southwestern Journal of Theology* o.s. 6 (October 1922): 3–13.

"The Essentials of Christian Union." *Southwestern Journal of Theology* o.s. 7 (April 1923): 47–55.

"The Formal Factor in Christianity." *Review and Expositor* 13 (January 1916): 38–52.

"The Fundamental Baptist Principle." *Southwestern Journal of Theology* o.s. 1 (April 1917): 26–29.

"Fundamentalism vs. Modernism." *Social Science* 2 (Feb.-Mar.-Apr. 1927): 101–6.

"The Glorified Christ." *Southwestern Journal of Theology* o.s. 5 (January 1921): 56–66.

"God's Purpose and Providence." *Southwestern Journal of Theology* o.s. 7 (January 1923): 36–49.

"Human Nature in the Light of the Incarnation." *Southwestern Journal of Theology* o.s. 1 (October 1917): 72–82.

"The Importance of Ecclesiology to Baptists." *Review and Expositor* 37 (January 1940): 13–22.

"Is Christian Science Christian?" *Southwestern Journal of Theology* o.s. 2 (April 1918): 47–53.

"Is Paul's Doctrine of Justification Forensic?" *Review and Expositor* 40 (January 1943): 48–53.

"Jesus and the Gospel." *Southwestern Journal of Theology* o.s. 8 (January 1924): 11–20.

"The Nature of the Authority of the Bible." *Southwestern Journal of Theology* o.s. 2 (October 1918): 11–17.

"The Relation of the Work of the Holy Spirit to the Person and Work of Jesus Christ." *Southwestern Journal of Theology* o.s. 4 (January 1920): 26–33.

"The Significance of Baptism." *Southwestern Journal of Theology* o.s. 4 (April 1920): 49–60.

"Theology, a Practical Discipline." *Review and Expositor* 41 (October 1944): 350–60.

"Theories of Atonement." *Review and Expositor* 44 (July 1947): 301–11.

"Three Theories of Atonement." *Review and Expositor* 43 (July 1946): 275–90.

"Three Types of Teaching in the New Testament on the Meaning of the Death of Christ." *Review and Expositor* 43 (April 1946): 150–66.

"The Throne and the Lamb." *Review and Expositor* 39 (April 1942): 206–12.

2. Secondary

Allen, Arthur Lynn. "A Comparative Study of the Person of Christ in Selected Baptist Theologians: Augustus H. Strong, William N. Clarke, Edgar Y. Mullins, and Walter T. Conner." Th.D. diss., New Orleans Baptist Theological Seminary, 1979. Pp. 2, 4, 24–29, 147–99, 201, 204–9, 216, 220–23.

Basden, Paul Abbott. "Theologies of Predestination in the Southern Baptist Tradition: A Critical Evaluation." Ph.D. diss. Southwestern Baptist Theological Seminary, 1986. Pp. 13, 173, 204–29, 231, 244–48, 312.

Carroll, Raymond Evans. "Dimensions of Individualism in Southern Baptist Thought." Th.D. dissertation., New Orleans Baptist Theological Seminary, 1995. Pp. 69, 105–26, 142, 144, 146, 174, 176–82, 183–84.

Draughon, Walter D., III. "A Critical Evaluation of the Diminishing Influence of Calvinism on the Doctrine of Atonement in Representative Southern Baptist Theologians: James Petigru Boyce, Edgar Young Mullins, Walter Thomas Conner, and Dale Moody." Ph.D. diss., Southwestern Baptist Theological Seminary, 1987. Pp. 9, 137–95, 237,241–43, 245, 246.

Garrett, James Leo, Jr. "The Bible at Southwestern Seminary during Its Formative Years: A Study of H. E. Dana and W. T. Conner." *Baptist History and Heritage* 21 (October 1986): 29–43.

_____. "Conner, Walter Thomas." *Encyclopedia of Religion in the South*. (Macon, Ga.: Mercer University Press, 1984), 184.

_____. "Conner, Walter Thomas." *Encyclopedia of Southern Baptists* (4 vols., Nashville: Broadman, 1958), 1:310.

_____. "Conner, Walter Thomas." *Twentieth-Century Dictionary of Christian Biography* (Grand Rapids: Baker Book House, 1995), 108.

_____. "The Theology of Walter Thomas Conner." Th.D. diss., Southwestern Baptist Theological Seminary, 1954.

_____. "W. T. Conner: Contemporary Theologian." *Southwestern Journal of Theology* 25 (Spring 1983): 43–60.

_____. "W. T. Conner: People's Theologian," *People* 1 (November 1970): 34–37.

Gray, Elmer Leslie. "The Ultimate Purpose of God." Th.D. diss., Southwestern Baptist Theological Seminary, 1951.

Hunt, William Boyd. "Southern Baptists and Systematic Theology." *Southwestern Journal of Theology* n.s. 1 (April 1959): 43–49.

Hurst, Clyde, J. "The Problem of Religious Knowledge in the Theology of Edgar Young Mullins and Walter Thomas Conner." *Review and Expositor* 52 (April 1955): 166–82.

McClendon, James William, Jr. *Pacemakers of Christian Thought*. Nashville: Broadman, 1962. Pp. 54–60.

Moody, Dwight Allan. "Doctrines of Inspiration in the Southern Baptist Theological Tradition." Ph.D. diss., Southern Baptist Theological Seminary, 1982. Pp. 5, 8, 18–28, 153–78, 205, 207–18.

Morgan, Darold Hugh. "Traditional Supernaturalism and the Problem of Evil." Th.D. diss., Southwestern Baptist Theological Seminary, 1953.

Newman, Stewart Albert. "W. T. Conner: Reason and Freedom, Not Inerrancy." In *The Unfettered Word: Confronting the Authority-Inerrancy Question*, ed. Robison B. James, 125–35, Macon, Ga.: Smyth and Helwys Publishing, Inc., 1994.

_____. *W. T. Conner: Theologian of the Southwest*. Nashville: Broadman, 1964.

Northcutt, Jesse James. "Walter Thomas Conner: Theologian of Southwestern." *Southwestern Journal of Theology* 9 (Fall 1966): 81–89.

Parks, Robert Keith. "A Biblical Evaluation of the Doctrine of Justification in Recent American Baptist Theology: With Special Reference to A. H. Strong, E. Y. Mullins, and W. T. Conner." Th.D. diss., Southwestern Baptist Theological Seminary, 1954. Pp. 35, 122–57, 188–89.

Shurden, Walter B. "The Priesthood of All Believers and Pastoral Authority in Baptist Thought." In *The Priesthood of All Believers*, ed. Walter B. Shurden, 146–47. Proclaiming the Baptist Vision. Macon, Ga.: Smyth and Helwys Publishing, Inc., 1993.

Youngblood, Clark Richard. "The Question of Apostasy in Southern Baptist Thought since 1900: A Critical Evaluation." Ph.D. diss., Southern Baptist Theological Seminary, 1979. Pp. 2, 5, 10–11, 67–73, 98–120, 242, 295–99.

William Wright Barnes

(1883–1960)
Church History

4

Harry Leon McBeth

W illiam Wright Barnes served as professor of church history at Southwestern Baptist Theological Seminary from 1913 to his retirement in 1953. At different times he also functioned as chairman of the faculty, registrar, librarian, and interim president during the frequent and lengthy absences of President Lee R. Scarborough. Barnes brought to the infant seminary a dedicated scholarship, an abiding sense of who Baptists are and can be, and a delightful and congenial spirit. He published two books and innumerable articles and spoke frequently at seminaries, churches, conventions, and other Baptist gatherings.

BIOGRAPHY

Born on 28 February 1883, in tiny Toisnot (later named Elm City), Wilson County, North Carolina, young Will Barnes attended the rural schools of the area. He was one of six children born to Wright Barnes and Perneta "Nettie" Bridgers. His ancestors on both sides migrated from the Isle of Wight to Virginia before 1650.[1] His father's people had been Universalists, but his mother's family were Anglicans. Under the influence of the First Great Awakening, both lines had embraced Baptist views. Shortly after 1740 their search for land led them to Edgecombe County, North Carolina. One of Will's ancestors established the first Baptist church in the western part of the county in 1757. Barnes liked to say that he had been a Baptist for two hundred years.

The Barnes family valued education. Both Will's father and older brother were physicians in rural North Carolina. Barnes's mother was valedictorian of her graduating class at Chowan College. Will began school in a one-room building near the village of St. Lewis in Wilson County with one teacher who taught every subject. Barnes remembered that, whether they knew it at the time or not, they used the English tutorial method, with older students assigned to help the younger ones. In addition to the usual subjects, the students also studied higher mathematics, Latin, German, and advanced work in history, in addition to the Morse Code for those who wanted it.

Will and his siblings did not have opportunity to attend Sunday Schools, and only sporadically were they in church services. In 1898, when he was fifteen years of age, Will was converted and baptized into the membership of the Elm City Baptist Church. Within a few years Will had served as song leader, Sunday School teacher, Sunday School superintendent, and janitor and returned one summer to serve as supply preacher. He later said that he had served in every elective office in the church except WMU president. Barnes's teaching career began at the tender age of nine, when he was assigned to tutor a younger student in mathematics. In 1900 he enrolled at Wake Forest College, where he earned both the Bachelor of Arts and the Master of Arts degrees by 1904.

Upon graduation, Barnes went to Cuba as tutor for the children of two American missionary families. He returned in 1905 to North Carolina, where he served for a year as principal and teacher in a rural school. In 1906, despite the reluctance of the school to give him up, Barnes resigned to enter Southern Baptist Theological Seminary in Louisville, Kentucky. He never again lived in North Carolina. He earned the Th.M. degree in 1909. Barnes married Ethel Dalrymple on 20 October 1909, and they had two sons, William Wright, Jr., and Arch Dalrymple. Barnes and his new wife then returned to Cuba in 1909 so that he might be director of the El Colegio Cubano-Americano in Havana, under the Home Mission Board of the SBC. This was his first experience in theological education. He returned to Southern Seminary in 1912 and received the Th.D. degree with a major in church history in 1913.

On the night before his graduation in 1913, Professor B. H. DeMent of Southern Seminary received a telegram from B. H. Carroll, offering young Barnes a professorship at the new seminary in Fort Worth if he could sign the New Hampshire Confession of Faith. After conference with DeMent and W.J. McGlothlin, Barnes agreed that he could sign. He arrived in Fort Worth on 18 June 1913. The campus had only one building, Fort Worth Hall, with no plants or shrubs, and Fort Worth was in the midst of a severe drought and heat wave. Barnes worried that his wife, who had remained with her parents until he could get settled, might be disappointed. Met by L. R. Scarborough and J. B. Gambrell, the thirty-year-old Barnes was taken directly to the home of B. H. Carroll. Barnes remembered that Carroll asked no questions about his doctrinal views, on the New Hampshire Confession of Faith, on Baptist successionism, or on the millennial question. It appears that Barnes assumed his post before any action by the Board of Trustees. After a return to North Carolina, Barnes arrived back in Fort Worth on 12 July, to make his home. He bought a house just north of the campus and made plans to "batch" until Mrs. Barnes arrived weeks later. But Mrs. B. H. Carroll would not hear of this; she prevailed upon young Will to take meals in their home. In those weeks, Barnes remembered, he became well acquainted with the Carrolls.

Over the years Barnes served as a tactful connection between Southwestern Baptist Theological Seminary and its older sister school in Louisville. He was invited many times to speak in Louisville. Barnes related an earlier conversation between John A. Broadus and John R. Sampey, in which Broadus had said, "'It will not be long before another theological Seminary will be founded among Southern Baptists, and it will probably be in Texas.'" He then added to his young colleague one significant remark: "'When the new Seminary comes, it ought to be with the good will of the Southern Seminary.'" Sampey added, "'It has been for me a real pleasure to follow the hint of my great teacher, and encourage the closest cooperation between the two seminaries.'"[2]

Barnes retired from the Southwestern faculty in 1953, died on 6 April 1960, and was buried in Greenwood Cemetery, Fort Worth.

WRITINGS

Robert Andrew Baker, who studied with Barnes at Southwestern Seminary and knew him well, regarded it as "almost inconceivable that when he died he had published simply one principal book."[3] Barnes also published a small handbook in 1934, plus numerous articles for various scholarly journals. He spoke regularly at conferences and conventions, and some of these speeches later found their way into print. All who knew Barnes recognized that he was a mine of historical knowledge. According to Baker, "He was careful, accurate, suspicious of undocumented tradition, and possessed a fine style of writing." The press of other demands prevented his completing several books which he had planned. The debilitating debt of Southwestern Seminary, which necessitated Barnes's frequent absences to serve as interim pastor of churches, interrupted the time that he might have devoted to writing. He was incessantly called on for other duties at the seminary. These included serving as chairman of the faculty (the equivalent of dean today), preparing catalogues, evaluating transcripts, functioning as librarian, enforcing student discipline, and serving as registrar. He was also busy in SBC affairs, serving as chairman of the Committee on the Basis of Representation, as chairman of the Committee on the National Baptist Memorial Church, Washington, and as a member of the Textbook Commission. He was also dean of the summer school held each summer at the Ridgecrest Baptist Assembly. For ten years (1914–1924) he was moderator of Tarrant County Baptist Association. His correspondence shows that he was well acquainted, often on a first-name basis, with most Baptist leaders in the South during his lifetime.

Books

Barnes published privately in 1934 his first book, *The Southern Baptist Convention: A Study in Ecclesiology.*[4] It was a small handbook on the origin and development of the Southern Baptist Convention, especially its developing ecclesiology. In this provocative volume Barnes demonstrated from history the changes which had occurred in the SBC since 1845 as to denominational structure. Barnes traced two distinct Baptist concepts of the church, the "local church" and "general church" and showed that the Southern Baptist Convention had moved to embrace the latter view.

Barnes was commissioned by the SBC Executive Committee to prepare the official centennial history of the Southern Baptist Convention. The volume, _The Southern Baptist Convention, 1845–1953_,[5] which was to have been published in 1945, represented the mature scholarship of Barnes. Several factors delayed its publication. Dislocations of World War II, the serious illness of Mrs. Barnes and their two sons, and the illness of Barnes himself prevented the book from being completed on time. In 1953 Porter W. Routh added a chapter to cover the period since 1945, and the book was published in 1954. It reveals Barnes's careful scholarship, his insistence on using primary sources, and his drawing conclusions from the sources. One feature of the book is its large dependence on the periodical literature of the times.

Articles

Barnes frequently published articles in _Review and Expositor_, _Southwestern Journal of Theology,_ and _The Chronicle_ (now _The American Baptist Quarterly_). He also published in Baptist state papers across the South.

In two articles[6] published in 1926, first delivered as lectures at Southern Baptist Theological Seminary, Barnes identified and traced principles which he associated with Baptists. Although he specifically repudiated the idea that one can trace organized _groups_ during these pre-Reformation years as Baptists, he did show that Baptist _principles_ (one or more held at various times by different groups) had continued.

Barnes's 1938 article on "The Development of Nationalism among American Baptists"[7] traced the trend from independency to a cooperative stance among various Baptist groups in America. He felt that the growth in a national spirit and a denominational structure among Baptist churches closely paralleled the growth of a national spirit in America generally. The First Great Awakening helped to draw Baptists together as did the two major confessions, the Philadelphia and New Hampshire. The first call for a national gathering of Baptists in America was issued by the Warren Baptist Association in 1776, that is, a call for a "Continental Association" (cf. the Continental Congress in political life).[8] The American Revolution prevented that meeting, and when national organization eventually came, it was on a different basis.

"In the history of American Baptists there are two well-defined theories of the church." With this provocative sentence, Barnes began his article on "American Baptist Ecclesiology."[9]

One concept emphasized independence, regarding the church as a local body only. The other concept, equally ancient in Baptist literature, agreed that each local church is complete and autonomous but also taught that all the churches together make up one spiritual body under Christ. These are often referred to as the "particular church" and the "general church." Barnes cited from various confessions of faith to show that both ideas were prevalent in Baptist thought and that one or the other came to the fore according to circumstances.

The New Hampshire Baptist Confession of Faith originated as an effort to harmonize diverse strands of Baptist ecclesiology, according to Barnes.[10] It was framed just after the New England branch of the Freewill Baptists, founded by Benjamin Randall of New Durham, New Hampshire, had reacted to the strict Calvinism then so prevalent. The Freewills took a decidedly corporate view of the church, as did some mainline Baptists. J. Newton Brown, according to Barnes, drew up the new confession so skillfully that those who held to a general view of the church and those holding to the strict local view could both accept it.

"Why the Southern Baptist Convention Was Formed"[11] was the title of a 1944 article by Barnes, who acknowledged that slavery was the *occasion* for the division of 1845 but denied that it was a fundamental *cause*. He affirmed that two basic causes led to that schism: different views of ecclesiology and differences in the home missions operation. Baptists in America held to distinct views of the church, identifiable as the "local church" and the "general church." Baptists in the North preferred the former, while Baptists in the South, for reasons which need not be enumerated here, preferred the latter. The second reason for the separation, according to Barnes, was the alleged neglect of the Southern field by the American Baptist Home Mission Society.

Barnes's 1947 Founders' Day address at Southern Baptist Theological Seminary on "The Theological Curriculum of Tomorrow in the Light of the Past,"[12] seems almost mistitled. In this article Barnes gave the majority of space to a careful history of the beginnings and development of Baptist theological education in the South. He did not come to changing curricula until near the end of the article. "The content of the curriculum has been determined by the current emphases, the problems of the time and the apparent direction of the intellectual life of the day."[13] Barnes then traced the rise of courses in "pedagogy" (religious education) to advances in public school education, courses in social ethics to the Social Gospel movement, and courses in sacred music to rising standards in that field. He predicted that more changes would come in the future for "the needs of the time call for it."[14]

In his last published article, "The Dimensions of the Home Mission Task,"[15] Barnes traced the work of the Home Mission Society (North) and the Home Mission Board (South). He showed that, despite various territorial or boundary agreements between them, both have fostered from the first a national field of work.

THOUGHT

Barnes was the product of an open and free-thinking rural North Carolina. His mind was further stretched by four years at Wake Forest College. His two tours of duty in Cuba further broadened his outlook, and at Southern Seminary he studied with such outstanding scholars as B. H. DeMent, William J. McGlothlin, and William O. Carver. His thought shows especially the mark of McGlothlin, one of the greatest church historians in America.

Importance of Heritage

Barnes was deeply committed to the concept that Christian life and thought are shaped by historical developments. We do not approach the Scriptures with complete objectivity; instead we read through the haze of nineteen centuries of thought that preceded us. The way we believe, our style of worship, and the structures of our church life are conditioned by our time and place. In his article on the "Progress of Baptist Principles from Jesus and Paul to Constantine," Barnes found it necessary to "take a look at the world into which these principles came and in which their progress will be traced."[16] He then traced the elements of that pre-Christian world, including Jewish monotheism, Greek philosophy, and aberrations like the Gnostics and Docetists.

Barnes said that the "Roman conceptions of the State aided in the development of the Medieval Church. Rightly did that Church come to be called Roman." To Barnes, "the ideas of the pre-Christian world" were aptly "illustrated in the spiritual aristocracy of the Jew, the intellectual aristocracy of the Greek and the political aristocracy of the Roman."[17] Against the backdrop of this heritage, Barnes drew his description of the Christian religion, not as the *result* of this cultural contribution but as influenced and shaped by that culture.

Barnes was equally conscious of the influence of social, cultural and political factors in shaping the Baptist mind set. One who is unaware of the historical background is ill-equipped to understand himself and his religious faith.

Origin of Baptists

While Barnes was growing up in North Carolina, the Whitsitt Controversy was raging. William Heth Whitsitt, scholarly historian and president of Southern Seminary, had studied in Britain and Germany, where he had encountered primary documents which led him to conclude that Baptists, as they are known today, emerged in England during 1640-1641. At that time they emerged from the Puritan-Separatist tradition in England and recovered from the Bible the practice of believer's baptism by immersion. Whitsitt utilized the famous "Kiffin Manuscript" to form his views. He published an unsigned article in *Johnson's Universal Cyclopedia in* 1886 on the subject and came out in 1896 with a book, *A Question in Baptist History*.[18] In this book Whitsitt maintained that Baptists could trace their continuous existence back only to the early 1640s. This was in direct conflict with the older Landmark view that Baptists had originated with Jesus and the apostles in the New Testament era and had continued under various names with unbroken succession to the present.

The controversy over Whitsitt's book was immediate and intense. The opposition was led by Benajah Harvey Carroll, pastor of the First Baptist Church, Waco, Texas, and chairman of the Southern trustees. He later founded the Southwestern Baptist Theological Seminary in Fort Worth. Whitsitt was forced to resign 1899, but even this did not calm the controversy.

When Barnes entered Wake Forest College in 1900 and when he later enrolled in Southern Seminary first in 1906, the controversy still swirled. McGlothlin, Barnes's church history professor, was a devotee of Whitsitt, and of course Barnes got detailed training in the new understandings of Baptist origins.[19] B. H. Carroll held the Landmark view; his younger brother, J. M. Carroll, published many years later the infamous *The Trail of Blood*, which embodied that view.

It would be fair to say that Carroll's view was widely held in Texas and throughout the Southwest. Barnes must have felt some trepidation about coming to Texas. But, Barnes recalled, Carroll did not question him about his views of Baptist origins. The reason for the vacancy in church history was that Carroll had dismissed the first professor, Albert Henry Newman, for a variety of reasons, including his view of Baptist origins. Similarly, Carroll was an avid postmillennialist in eschatology, but Barnes to the extent he embraced any position was more amillennial. But Carroll did not pursue that question either.

At a time when Baptists in the South were undergoing a transformation of their views of their own history, Barnes embraced the latest, most scientific view of Baptist origins. He was tactful and did not push these views in a harmful way. But it is clear that Barnes represented the latest scientific and documentary view of Baptist origins.

Baptist Ecclesiology

It is clear from his writings that Baptist ecclesiology was a subject of keen interest to Barnes. His first book and several articles dealt with that subject. Barnes contrasted two doctrines of the church, the "local church only" and the "general church as well as the local church" and showed that historic Baptist thought had contained elements of each. The Landmark faction preferred the local church view, while mainline Baptists tended to combine the local with the general view. Barnes's major contention was that, over the years, Baptists had moved more toward the larger view of the church as denominational structures were developed.

Historic Baptist Principles

In his two articles on Baptist principles, Barnes identified several principles, such as salvation by grace alone, a gathered or believers' church, and religious liberty as Baptist principles.[20] In his later controversies with J. Frank Norris and Selsus E. Tull, Barnes held firmly to what he regarded as historic Baptist teachings.

Priority of Primary Sources

As a historian, Barnes remained suspicious of hearsay and secondary evidence. He insisted upon the priority of primary sources. His major book on the Southern Baptist Convention draws extensively from original or primary sources for his major conclusions. The Barnes Collection at Southwestern Seminary includes drawers of cards on which Barnes laboriously recorded notes from various primary sources. Time has dimmed the pencil notes until they are sometimes hard to read, but the emphasis on primary sources remains clear.

TENABILITY OF THOUGHT

As a twentieth-century historian, Barnes was, of course, a child of his time and place. Certain idiosyncracies of his views are evident, but on balance his thought has endured well. While his strict Baptist principles are not as universally appreciated by some Southern Baptists today, the majority of his views still endure.

BIBLIOGRAPHY

1. Primary

DISSERTATION
"The Place of Peter in the Early Church, up to A.D. 451." Th.D. diss., Southern Baptist Theological Seminary, 1913.

BOOKS
The Southern Baptist Convention: A Study in Ecclesiology. Seminary Hill, Tex.: pvt. ptg., 1934; rpt.: Paris, Ark., Baptist Standard Bearer, Inc., 1997.
The Southern Baptist Convention, 1845–1953. Nashville: Broadman, 1954.

JOURNAL ARTICLES
"American Baptist Ecclesiology." *Review and Expositor* 37 (April 1940): 133–40.
"Baptists and Religious Liberty in the United States, 1755–1790." *Quarterly Review* 15 (April–May–June 1955): 4–8.
"Churches and Associations among Baptists." *Review and Expositor* 52 (April 1955): 199–205.
"The Development of Nationalism among American Baptists." *The Chronicle* 1 (July 1938): 110–14.
"The Dimensions of the Home Mission Task." *Southwestern Journal of Theology* n.s. 2 (April 1960): 49–54.
"Doctor Jesse Mercer." *The Chronicle* 16 (January 1953): 43–54.
"George Washington Truett, 1867–1944." *The Chronicle* 7 (October 1944): 183–85.
"The New Hampshire Confession of Faith: Its Origin and Use." *Review and Expositor* 39 (January 1942): 3–8.

"Progress of Baptist Principles from Jesus and Paul to Constantine." *Review and Expositor* 23 (July 1926): 303–18.

"Progress of Baptist Principles from Constantine to Luther and the Anabaptists." *Review and Expositor* 23 (January 1926): 44–62.

"Retrospect and Prospect." *Southwestern Journal of Theology* n.s. 1 (October 1958): 8.

"Sandy Creek: The Holy Land of Baptists." *The Chronicle* 19 (April 1956): 69–72.

"The Theological Curriculum of Tomorrow in the Light of the Past." *Review and Expositor* 44 (April 1947): 135–57.

"Why the Southern Baptist Convention Was Formed." *Review and Expositor* 41 (January 1944): 3–17.

MISCELLANEOUS

"Autobiographical Sketch." In *Southwestern Men and Their Messages*, ed. J. M. Price, 17–19. Kansas City, Kan.: Central Seminary Press, 1948.

"Balthasar Hubmaier, Hero and Martyr to Truth." *The Southwestern Evangel*, April 1928, 241–44.

2. Secondary

Baker, Robert A., "William Wright Barnes." *Baptist History and Heritage* 5 (July 1970): 144–46.

Baker, Robert A., "William W. Barnes and Southwestern Baptist Theological Seminary." *Southwestern Journal of Theology* 18 (Fall 1975): 72–81.

Williams, Michael. "Enduring Legacy: William Wright Barnes and Church History at Southwestern Baptist Theological Seminary." *Baptist History and Heritage* 37 (Winter 2002): 6–27.

John Milburn Price
(1884–1976)
Religious Education

5

William A. (Budd) Smith

BIOGRAPHY

"Expect great things [from God], attempt great things [for God]." Those inspiring words from the great pioneer of modern foreign missions, William Carey, could easily have come from the heart and the lips of the pioneer of Southern Baptist religious education, John Milburn Price. Price was the founder, director, and dean of the School of Religious Education of Southwestern Seminary. He ministered as a school teacher, pastor, seminary professor, author, and administrator.

Price, a native of the pioneering state of Kentucky, was born in 1884, the youngest of eight children, in a log cabin near the community of Fair Dealing. It became more than the name of his birthplace; it became a way of life for him. When Price was born, he was known for several weeks simply as "the baby." His mother took him to a preaching service at Cap Springs School house, where a traveling preacher, J. H. Milburn, brought a powerful message. His mother was converted that night. She gave her life to the Lord and the preacher's name to her small son. He was always called Milburn by the family and was converted at fourteen.

Two things Price learned growing up in his home were courage and tenacity—courage from his father, and tenacity from his mother. His father, John Powers Price, had fought in the battles of Shiloh and Vicksburg during the Civil War. His father was a wonderful storyteller, and Price himself became known as a great storyteller. His mother, Elizabeth McCloud Price, was a tireless worker with incalculable energy. L. R. Scarborough once commented on the fact that Price had the same tenacity as his mother. He said that when Price came into his office to ask for something for the School of Religious Education, he might as well give it to him. Even if he turned him down, Price would sooner or later get what he wanted.

It was a rule of J. M. Price's life to be sure he was right about something first and then never quit trying to bring it about. He lived by two axioms. The first was written by him as a child on the wall of his school room. It read, "I resolve to be diligent, for by diligence and patience the mouse bit in two the cable." It remained on the wall for many years. The second he quoted frequently, "I would be true, for there are those who trust me."[1]

Price was educated first in a country school at Maple Springs, Kentucky, and was awarded the common school diploma. His higher education included the B.S. degree from Western Kentucky State College; the B.A. degree from Baylor University; the M.A. degree from Brown University; the Th.M., Th.D. and the Ph.D. degrees from Southern Baptist Theological Seminary. Also, Baylor University conferred upon him the honorary LL.D. degree, and California Baptist College conferred upon him the honorary Litt.D. degree.

Price first taught in a public school in Kentucky. Soon the words of J. B. L. Soule, "Go west, young man," sounded like sound advice. He became the principal of a school at Marlow in what was then called "Indian Territory" (later Oklahoma). He later returned to pastorates in both Kentucky and Rhode Island. He was also the first salaried associational worker in the South. While still in Indian Territory, he met a student by the name of Mabel Faulk. Eleven years later (1916), after becoming a member of the faculty at Southwestern, he and Mabel were married. They had four children; one daughter, Mabel Elizabeth; and three sons, John Milburn Jr., Joseph Wayne, and James Otis.

Price moved in 1907 to Texas and Baylor University because of B. H. Carroll, a gigantic man of tremendous mind and spirit. Carroll had been teaching theology and Bible at Baylor since before Price was even born. Only two years before, Carroll had organized the Baylor Theological Seminary that later became Southwestern Baptist Theological Seminary.

While a Marston Scholar at Brown University, Price was inspired by the thought that he should train lay men and women to become Sunday school teachers. He wanted to popularize Bible study among the masses. In less than three years, while completing his theological training at Southern Seminary, the door of opportunity was opened through which he might realize the achievement of his life's dream. In 1915, L. R. Scarborough, the newly elected president of Southwestern Seminary, wrote to Price, "It is now our purpose to establish a School of Christian Pedagogy. I think we have hold of the small end of a big proposition. We will have to do pioneer work and break new ground."[2] He asked Price to move to Southwestern and organize the school. Price accepted the call with only one regular student enrolled in his department.

By 1921, the department had grown to 121 students. This was the year when the Department of Religious Education was organized into the School of Religious Education.

In 1925, Price had drawn plans for a new building to house the School of Religious Education, but it was twenty-three years later before a formal groundbreaking for the building took place on 6 October 1948. While directing the School of Religious Education in Fort Worth, Price also served as the pastor of Webb Baptist Church in Webb, Texas. He retired from the church in 1949 after twenty-one years of service. When Price reached the age of seventy-one in 1956, he decided that it was time to retire from Southwestern as well. By the time of his retirement, he had headed the Department or School of Religious Education for forty-one years.

WRITINGS

The writings of Price were primarily an outgrowth of classroom teaching in religious education at Southwestern Seminary and of addresses delivered to Sunday school workers in churches and associational meetings and at state and SBC assemblies and clinics. Most of his writings came under the designation of study course books. His first book, *Christianity and Social Problems* (1928), dealt with Christian aspects of society and was dedicated "To the memory of my father, my first and finest example of Christian citizenship."

Under the auspices of the Association of Southern Baptist Teachers of Bible and Religious Education, Price, leading a committee of three, became the general editor of a series of small textbooks intended as introductory texts for colleges and seminaries. *An Introduction to Religious Education* (1932) focused on a survey of the entire field of religious education. This was followed by the co-authored *A Program of Religious Education* (1937) in the field of administration and by *A Survey of Religious Education* (1940), which was limited almost exclusively to the local church. The target group for these texts included pastors and educational directors as well as teachers in schools.

Price's next book, *Personal Factors in Character Building* (1934), was a study course book for local church members. It was later revised and rewritten under the title *Formative Factors in Christian Character* (1959). This was a psychological approach to character building and met with instant and enthusiastic response. This was of great encouragement to Price as he, along with many of his colleagues, was suffering great financial hardship as a result of the Great Depression. At one point the seminary was a full year behind in salaries.

It was at the beginning of the difficult and troubled World War II years that Price published *Vital Problems in Christian Living* (1942). This book considered physical, mental, moral, vocational, and social needs of Christians and was timely encouragement for local churches during a period of enormous change and conflict.

The next year Price edited the book *Baptist Leaders in Religious Education* (1943). The Southern Baptist Convention was approaching its centennial year, and Price wanted to bring attention to twenty leaders who had envisioned a program of religious education. Ironically, he was not included in the group given tribute.

The following year was another milestone in that Baylor University was celebrating its centennial. To mark the occasion, Price edited *Ten Men from Baylor* (1945), a book that focused attention on ten former students of the university whom he regarded as notable examples of Christian citizenship. Five were ministers and five were laymen.

Three years later when Southwestern Seminary was celebrating its fortieth anniversary, Price edited *Southwestern Men and Their Messages* (1948). This book was on the same order as his earlier work for Baylor University but differed in that short biographies or autobiographies of twelve men were given, followed by sermons, addresses, or articles from each. Once again he was not included in the group so recognized.

The most notable of all of Price's writings is *Jesus the Teacher* (1946), a study of Jesus as master teacher and his methods. It has been translated into Spanish, Portuguese, Arabic, Indonesian, and Korean.

Following his retirement from Southwestern, Price maintained an office in the building named for him. There he finished three more manuscripts. The first, *Mastering Life's Problems* (1958), he considered his finest writing. This psychological approach to problems of living had stirred his mind for some time. Also, as mentioned before, he did a revision of an earlier work under the title *Formative Factors in Christian Character* (1959). His final work, *The Unfolding Life* (1963), was a life span study of student development.

INTERPRETATION

Focus on the Laity

Most of Price's writings were not an attempt at scholarly presentations. Rather the purpose was to draw from life and teaching those principles that would give vision, motivation, and training to the rank and file of lay Sunday school teachers in the local church. Believing that Sunday school teachers were the greatest force in the church and that they worked under serious difficulties and discouragement, Price wrote tirelessly to their need for inspiration as well as information for the tasks. Most of his writings, therefore, were included in the Sunday School Training Course prepared by the Sunday School Department of the Sunday School Board (SBC). The six sections of the course included studies in Bible, doctrines, evangelism, Sunday school leadership and administration, teaching, age group studies, and special studies. Lay leaders were awarded diplomas on the completion of a series of studies.

Curriculum Design Architect

When given the opportunity of starting a new department (eventually to become a school) of religious education at Southwestern, Price faced a great challenge. How does one chart the course? Price's greatest contribution to Southwestern and to religious education in general was not as a writer but rather as curriculum design architect for the school.

Religious education is not a static subject. Christian educators and curriculum developers are forced continually to relate the Christian faith to a changing world. But how does one do that without losing all that is fundamental and orthodox to the Christian faith? Throughout history, and particularly in recent years, Christian educators have struggled with the debate between curriculum models that focus on fundamental, orthodox, subject-matter designs and those that focus on dynamic, active, process-oriented designs.

Price was no stranger to this debate. In fact the era in which Price grew up and received his own education (both public and theological) was one of the most turbulent times for this debate within all educational circles. The struggle centered between two major contemporary theories of educational curriculum design: the traditional approach and the progressive approach.

For the more traditional theories of educational thought, the preferred curriculum design focused on subject matter and emphasized formal methods of instruction, mental discipline, and mastery of certain basic content. The method took the form of conscious and deliberate transmission of the teacher's view of truth and reality to the pupil. This method was teacher-centered. Politically, this approach to education usually limited accessibility of education to the few who had the ability, time, and resources to master the content.

In contrast to the traditionalists, the progressives were more concerned with the processes of learning than with subject matter. The progressives put the pupil at the focal point of education. They sought to develop a curriculum and teaching method that grew out of students' needs, interests, and initiatives, which led them to activity, experiences, and problem-solving undertakings. Progressivism became the dominant approach in American education from the turn of the century to the 1950s. Politically, it had an appeal for teaching the masses and preparing them for practical living. This approach, however, often emerged as weak in the mastery of content.

There is always some injustice involved in putting a man such as Price into a school of thought. It too quickly identifies him with certain points of view that he might, in fact, repudiate. Therefore, I will in no way attempt to associate him with any particular philosophy or school of educational curriculum design. Rather I will attempt to show that in the context of Christian education he saw the necessity of blending both sides of the debate for the sake of theory and practice. This blending process, in fact, became one of his greatest contributions to Christian education in general and to the training of young men and women for the Christian ministry in particular.

Because teaching is a moral enterprise, it requires the careful blending of both theory and practice. Theory without practice is insufficient; practice unguided by theory is aimless. Therefore, Price suggested that teaching has both a reflective and an active dimension as theory and practice are blended together.[3]

In the same vein, theology without practice is futile, and practice without theology is mindless and devoid of soul. It is often said that it is not what a man believes but rather what he does that is important. This is a dangerous half-truth. For Price the blending of these two interrelated polarities is of vital importance in the Christian faith. He pointed out that Christlike action is always based on a proper theological foundation.

> Proper knowledge is necessary to proper living. One cannot live much better than he knows. Right conduct is rooted in right understanding. Whoever, therefore, fashions the ideals of people, determines in a large measure their destiny. . . . In these days when emphasis is being given to problem solving and the life-situation approach in teaching, let us not forget the value of implanting divine truths in the minds of pupils and building life ideals. Major ideals or sentiments are necessary for unifying life. . . . [4]

But theological thinking is not an end in itself as some would have it. Price was quick to point out that theological thinking, from the Christian viewpoint, is to be lived out and to result in Christlike action.

> Jesus did not stop with imparting knowledge about spiritual and moral matters. He knew very well the inadequacy of information alone to overcome instinctive urges and evil environment. . . . So the Teacher sought to deepen conviction as well as to implant truth. . . . [H]e recognized the necessity of arousing feeling and developing attitudes. His ultimate aim was the will. He recognized, as we do, that there must be warmth as well as light for truth to be most effective. . . . [P]upils should go away from our classes with a keen realization of the value of the thing about which they have studied, and also a firm resolution to do something about it. [5]

Price labored tirelessly in the early years at Southwestern to fashion the curriculum of the new School of Religious Education in a way that would blend the mastery of content, reflected in academic excellence, with a practical approach that would result in application of ministry in the Christian faith. This would eventually tend to filter down in some way to every member of every Sunday school in every church in the Southern Baptist Convention.

While retaining a strong commitment to high academic standards (reflected in the number of academic degrees behind his own name), he constantly emphasized in every book, public address, or class lecture the necessity of framing an application curriculum that would result in character development within learners.

Jesus' aims did not stop with securing a formal response to his teachings or even with meeting specific problems. He sought to go further and develop in his followers those graces which would enable them to overcome their weaknesses and vices and grow into strong, integrated Christian characters. . . . He was more concerned about quality than quantity, about weighing people than counting them, about permanent results than temporary ones. And if we are to follow his example, we must realize that it is more important to secure a genuine [rather] than an immediate response, that our work has barely begun when a pupil is converted, and that our task is to develop him to "mature manhood, to the measure of the stature of the fullness of Christ" (Eph. 4: 13).[6]

Summarizing Philip Briggs's dissertation, Joe Davis Heacock said that Price "looks at religious education as a true light and not simply education coated with religion. He believes in religious education as a preparation for citizenship in the kingdom of God."[7]

Modeling

Price was often characterized as a man ahead of his times. W. L. Howse wrote of Price, "One of his great contributions is that he has lived within and yet beyond his generation. He has been years ahead in his planning and preparation for the demands of church and denominational life."[8] Not only did he reach far beyond the curriculum design debates of his day to formulate a functional, blended approach to Christian education that was truly Christian but also he carried throughout his writings a primary theme of the modeling role of Christian teachers. Many educational theorists have dealt with this concept, but his was a primary theme long before modeling became a popular contemporary theme for education in general. He often suggested, "The most important element in the qualification of any teacher is what he is himself."[9] In listing the qualities of a good teacher he said:

One example is worth a hundred exhortations. . . . The best binding for the Gospels is not Morocco, but human skin. It was this fact that led . . . Emerson to remark that "the important thing is not what you learn but with whom you learn." . . . This is so because truth is caught more than taught. . . . Therefore the Sunday school teacher must be something as well as say something.[10]

Price not only taught this but also modeled it within himself. His biographer, Clyde Merrill Maguire, has said of him:

... Price is always a man of action, but a man whose actions are directed by God. Lord Rosebery wrote some words about the saintly Thomas Chalmers that could be appropriately used of J. M. Price: "It should be said that his saintliness was not that of an anchorite brooding in religious solitude. Here was a man bustling, striving, organizing, speaking and preaching with the dust and fire of the world on his clothes, but carrying his shrine with him everywhere."[11]

INFLUENCE

J. M. Price was a visionary leader whose goal was to equip men and women to share an unchanging gospel of Christ with a rapidly changing world. The School of Educational Ministries at Southwestern continues the legacy of that vision, including the blending of the traditional and the progressive in curriculum design and the blending of academic excellence and practical application in teaching.

Starting with that one student in 1915, God gave Price a pioneering vision that looked down the corridor of time to see thousands of students from across America and from around the globe who would respond to God's calling to fulfill the Great Commission of Christ. These students would attend the oldest continuing school of religious education in the world to make preparations to meet the needs for their generation and the generations to come.

When Price retired in 1956, a long list of "firsts" was read. Some of these were: first school among Baptists to offer vocational training in religious education; first school in America to offer a doctoral degree with a major in religious education; first school to offer special seminary courses for non-college graduates; first building in America designed exclusively for teaching religious education; first school of religious education among Southern Baptists to be accredited; and the list goes on.[12]

Price died on 12 January 1976 at the age of ninety-one and was buried in Laurel Land Cemetery, Fort Worth. He was of slight physical build, a man only five feet eight inches tall, and was extremely proud of the fact that at one time he had finally tipped the scales at 150 pounds. Ralph Waldo Emerson once said, "An institution is the lengthened shadow of one man." The School of Religious Education is certainly a lengthened shadow of J. M. Price. He started it, developed it, and made it into a school recognized around the world. For a man short in stature, he certainly has cast a long shadow.

BIBLIOGRAPHY

1. Primary

DISSERTATIONS

"The Catholic Parish School in the United States." Ph.D. diss., Southern Baptist Theological Seminary, 1930.

"The New Birth: A Psychological Study." Th.D. diss., Southern Baptist Theological Seminary, 1919.

BOOKS

(ed.) *Baptist Leaders in Religious Education*. Nashville: Broadman, 1943.

Christianity and Social Problems. Nashville: Sunday School Board of the Southern Baptist Convention, 1928.

Formative Factors in Christian Character. Nashville: Convention Press, 1959.

    Factores en la Formacion del Caracter. Trans. Alfredo C. Müller and Emma Z. de Villaseñor. El Paso: Casa Bautista de Publicaciones, 1963. [Spanish]

(gen. ed.) *An Introduction to Religious Education*. New York: Macmillan, 1932.

Jesus the Teacher. Nashville: Convention Press, 1946; rev. ed.: Nashville: Sunday School Board, Southern Baptist Convention, 1954.

    Jesus Guru Agung. Trans. Jachin Karuniadi. Bandung: Penerbitan Geredja^2 Baptis, 1968. [Indonesian]

    Jesus el Maestro. Trans. O. S. D. de Lerín. El Paso: Casa Bautista de Publicaciones, 1950. [Spanish]

    Jesus, o Mestre por Excelência. Trans. Waldemar W. Wey. Rio de Janeiro: Casa Publicadora Batista, 1958. [Portuguese]

    Sunsaeng Yesu. Trans. Yung Rok Park. Seoul: Baptist Publications, 1968. [Korean]

    Yasū' al-Mu'allim al- 'aḏḥīm. Beirut: Baptist Publications, 1960. [Arabic]

Mastering Life's Problems. Nashville: Convention Press, 1958.

Personal Factors in Character Building. Nashville: Sunday School Board of the Southern Baptist Convention, 1934.

(coauth.) *A Program of Religious Education*. New York: Fleming H. Revell, 1937.

(ed.) *Southwestern Men and Their Messages*. Kansas City, Kan.: Central Seminary Press, 1948.

(coauth.) *A Survey of Religious Education*. New York: Thomas Nelson and Sons, 1940; New York: Ronald Press, 1940; 2d ed. 1959.

    Zong Jiao Jiao Yu Zong Lan. Trans. Wayne Wei-yuan Siao. Kowloon, Hong Kong: Baptist Press, 1956. [Chinese]

(ed.) *Ten Men from Baylor*. Kansas City, Kan.: Central Seminary Press, 1945.

The Unfolding Life. Nashville: Convention Press, 1963.

Vital Problems in Christian Living. Nashville: Sunday School Board of the Southern Baptist Convention, 1942.

ARTICLES

"After the Revival, What?" *Southwestern Journal of Theology* o.s. 1 (October 1917): 83–85.

"Baptists and Education." *Southwestern Journal of Theology* o.s. 4 (October 1920): 17–21.

"Christ the Ideal Teacher." *The Sunday School Builder*, October 1946, 16.

"Christianity and Childhood." *The Baptist Training Union Magazine*, April 1935, 5, 11.

"Christ's Emphasis on Teaching." *The Sunday School Builder*, August 1945, 12.

"Christ's Purpose in Teaching." *The Sunday School Builder*, November 1945, 8.

"Christ's Use of Objects and Dramatics." *The Sunday School Builder*, June 1946, 15.

"Christ's Use of Question and Discussion." *The Sunday School Builder*, August 1946, 17.

"Christ's Use of Stories and Lectures." *The Sunday School Builder*, July 1946, 18.

"Christ's Use of the Scriptures in Teaching." *The Sunday School Builder*, February 1946, 15.

"The Contribution of the Sunday School to Missions." *The Sunday School Builder*, October 1950, 17.

"Country Church through the Sunday School." *The Home Field*, February 1914, 14–16.

"Divine Power for Teaching." *The Baptist Training Union Magazine*, September 1951, 6–7.

"A Double Standard." *Baptist Standard*, 22 November 1961, 8.

"Educational and Spiritual Power." *The Baptist Training Union Magazine*, August 1956, 8–9.

"The Educational Task of a Baptist Church." *The Sunday School Builder*, June 1945, 8.

"Improving Conditions in Religious Education." *The Southwestern Evangel*, February 1929, 137–38.

"An Interpretation of Religious Education from a Southern Baptist Point of View." *The Southwestern Evangel*, July 1931, 297–300.

"Leadership Life: Convictions Underlying Religious Education." *The Teacher*, January 1941, 17, 64.

"Let's Teach Them, As We Win Them." *The Sunday School Builder*, October 1953, 3.

"Making Education Christian." *Southern Baptist Home Missions*, March 1940, 8–9.

"Method in Jesus' Teaching." *The Baptist Training Union Magazine*, March 1959, 4–5.

"The Next Step in Christian Education." *Southwestern Journal of Theology* o.s. 2 (April 1918): 54–57.

"A Penny Saved." *Baptist Standard*, 17 July 1963, 9.

"The Place of the Sunday School Teacher in the World's Reconstruction." *Southwestern Journal of Theology* o.s. 5 (October 1921): 46–48.

"The Present Crisis." *Biblical Recorder*, 10 April 1940, 7–9.

"Procedure in Christ's Teaching." *The Sunday School Builder*, May 1946, 19.

"Religious Education as a Life Work." *Southwestern Journal of Theology* o.s. 1 (April 1917): 55–57.

"Save the Rural Churches . . . Beginners Need Them." *The Sunday School Builder*, July 1949, 35.

"Some Great Christian Teachings." *The Teacher*, April 1935, 3–4.

"Soul Winning: Psychologically Considered." *Southwestern Journal of Theology* o.s. 4 (October 1920): 61–74.

"Trends in Christian Education." *Southern Baptist Home Missions*, February 1940, 14–15.

"Two Years After." *The Home Field*, May 1915, 21–22.

"Underlying Principles in Christ's Teaching." *The Sunday School Builder*, March 1946, 12.

"Visual Aids in the Bible." *Audio-Visual Aids*, February 1958, 1, 3, 6.

"Where is the Bible?" *The Teacher*, October 1943, 7.

2. Secondary

Briggs, Philip Henry. "The Religious Education Philosophy of J. M. Price." D.R.E. diss., Southwestern Baptist Theological Seminary, 1964.

Heacock, Joe Davis. "J. M. Price: Trailblazer in Religious Education." *Southwestern Journal of Theology* 17 (Fall 1974): 83–94.

Kathan, Boardman W. "Six Protestant Pioneers of Religious Education: Liberal, Moderate, Conservative." *Religious Education* 73 (spec. ed., September–October 1978): 138–50, esp. 143–45.

Maguire, Clyde Merrill. *J. M. Price, Portrait of a Pioneer*. Nashville: Broadman, 1960.

Marsh, Leon. "J. M. Price: Pioneer in Religious Education." *Southwestern Journal of Theology* 25 (Spring 1983): 61–75.

Harvey Eugene Dana
(1888–1945)
New Testament

6

Mark E. Taylor

arvey Eugene Dana was born on 21 June 1888 in a rural setting just south of Vicksburg, Mississippi. He was the third child of two boys and two girls. His parents, Charles and Eva Dana, were hard-working, devout Christians and active members of the Antioch Baptist Church, located about five miles from the family farm. From these humble beginnings emerged one of Southern Baptists' most significant and influential New Testament scholars.

Dana is well known in New Testament circles for his intermediate Greek grammar, a book coauthored with Julius R. Mantey[1] that is still in print more than half a century after his death. His influence, however, extended far beyond his contribution to Greek syntax. Dana was a beloved professor, a prolific writer, a gifted communicator, a pastor-evangelist, a diligent scholar, a devoted husband, and a seminary president. Franklin M. Segler, a close friend and colleague, noted, "As one of Southern Baptist's [*sic*] most creative scholars, H. E. Dana was fifty years ahead of his time in New Testament scholarship."[2] This brief essay will attempt to describe the influences that shaped the life, the mind, and the career of Dana and his contribution to the field of New Testament studies.

BIOGRAPHY³

Dana's formative years were defined by a simple routine of home and church life. His mother was a Sunday School teacher, and his father served as a deacon. Dana's conversion occurred at the age of twelve in a revival meeting at the Antioch Baptist Church. Eight years later, in 1908, he was ordained to the gospel ministry and called to be the pastor of his home church while attending Mississippi College. Between his sophomore and junior years, Dana married his childhood sweetheart, Tommie Pettit.⁴ They were parents of two daughters, Elizabeth and Elsie Marie.

Dana's academic interests and abilities were recognized by his elementary school teacher, who often gave him extra books to read. His uncle, a Methodist minister, gladly allowed young Harvey to borrow books from his library, perhaps prompting theological interests and ideas that would bear fruit years later. Dana's academic pursuits began to take on a more definitive form when he enrolled in Mississippi College in 1906. He was an excellent student and graduated in 1911 with the Bachelor of Philosophy degree.

Dana spent several years in the pastorate before enrolling in 1915 in Southwestern Seminary, where he was shaped by conservative theology, a passion for evangelism, and a love for the local church. Men like L. R. Scarborough, James S. Rogers, Charles B. Williams, and W. T. Conner had a lasting impact upon the young scholar.⁵ Although Dana began his studies in the fields of Old Testament and archaeology, he changed his major to Greek and New Testament at the request of President Scarborough, who recognized Dana's abilities and needed someone to teach in that field. In five brief years Dana completed all requirements necessary for the Master of Theology and the Doctor of Theology degrees. His thesis was entitled "The Ecclesia in the New Testament and Early Christian Literature."

Dana's academic pursuits continued after his reception of the Th.D. degree. He spent all or part of five summers at the University of Chicago and studied under men such as E. J. Goodspeed, E. D. Burton, C. R. Bowen, E. C. Colwell, and C. W. Votaw.⁶ He also studied at the University of Dubuque in Iowa and the Universität Heidelberg in Germany. During his postgraduate studies, the scholarship of Dana matured. He maintained his conservative theology and approach to the Bible while at the same time developing an appreciation for the emerging historical-critical methods of biblical interpretation. According to Ray Bennett, Dana's theology was formed at Southwestern and his methodology was developed at the University of Chicago.[7]

The depth and breadth of Dana's life and ministry extended well beyond academic pursuits. During his tenure as a Southwestern professor (1919–1938), Dana continued to serve churches through weekly preaching engagements and numerous interim pastorates. He was a much sought after speaker for youth assemblies and revival meetings. The Southwestern professor was popular in the classroom as well, showing versatility, a genuine interest in others, and patience and sympathy with students. Some of his lectures were reportedly so popular that former students would return from long distances to hear them again.[8] Segler described Dana in the following way:

> The first impression a student had upon coming into his class was the light of confidence and joy which seemed to glow in the face of this attractive man. There was an undeniable magnetism about him, a sort of zeal bubbling up from an experiential faith in the living Lord.[9]

Dana's career at Southwestern ended in 1938 when he accepted the position of president and professor of New Testament at the Kansas City (later Central) Baptist Theological Seminary in Kansas City, Kansas, an institution serving both Northern and Southern Baptists.[10] He continued in that role until his premature death of a heart attack on 17 May 1945 at the age of fifty-six. He was buried in Kansas City.

WRITINGS

Dana, a productive author, began to publish early in his career and continued to write until the time of his death. A bibliography of Dana's works reveals some thirty titles and numerous journal articles. His writings embraced the entirety of the New Testament and focused on issues related to historical background, criticism, canon, hermeneutics, exposition, apologetics, and theology. Following Ray Bennett's chronological and thematic approach, Dana's writings can be organized into four categories: his earliest writings (1920–1924), books on the historical-critical method of interpretation (1924–1932), books written from a more matured scholarship and for a wider audience of pastors, informed laymen, and New Testament students (1932–1945), and works related to the nature and authority of the church written over the whole of his ministry.[11]

The seminary classroom provided the impetus for many of Dana's contributions. Several of his works have their own history, beginning as class notes and then maturing on to publication, revision, and expansion. For the purpose of briefly reviewing Dana's books, Bennett's categories provide a useful working outline.

Earliest Writings (1920–1924)

Dana's earliest writings revealed interests that would stay with him throughout his career, namely, the nature, authority, and interpretation of Scripture. His first book, *The Authenticity of the Holy Scriptures: A Brief Story of the Problems of Biblical Criticism*, was published in 1923. The book was compiled from three papers, all prepared for different occasions.[12] President Scarborough wrote the introduction in order to introduce the new professor and perhaps to ward off the skepticism of some due to the call from Dana for conservatives to take up the methods of biblical criticism.[13]

Other works following soon thereafter demonstrated Dana's lifelong interest in the necessity of a solid foundation for the proper interpretation of Scripture. *The Historical Background of the New Testament* was also published in 1923. A year later a comprehensive response to the attack of radical criticism on the New Testament appeared in *New Testament Criticism: A Brief Survey of the Nature and Necessity, History, Sources, and Results of New Testament Criticism*. Also in 1924, Dana began teaching a course in New Testament criticism and privately published *An Introduction to the Critical Interpretation of the New Testament* for use in his classes. Finally, among Dana's earliest contributions was his role in *A Manual for the Study of the Greek New Testament* (1923), which was later published in 1927 as *A Manual Grammar of the Greek New Testament*. The book is still in use today as a textbook in intermediate level Greek courses.

The Historical-Critical Method (1924–1932)

Dana saw the need among Southern Baptists for conservative yet scholarly books on the historical-critical method of interpreting the New Testament. Several of his publications that sought to fill this demand were originally prepared for use in the seminary classroom.

During 1925–1926 he published *The New Testament Message*, a four-volume set of expository outlines and comments on the entire corpus of the New Testament. *The New Testament World* first appeared in 1926 and 1928 and was later expanded in 1937. In it Dana focused on the historical, political, social, moral, and religious background of the New Testament, both in Judaism and in Hellenism. *A New Testament Manual* appeared in 1929. It also consisted of historical background information along with a brief summary of contents. *The Science of New Testament Interpretation*, published in 1930, furthered Dana's interpretive concerns raised in the 1924 monograph, *An Introduction to the Critical Interpretation of the New Testament*. Both were combined, expanded, and revised in 1936 with the publication of *Searching the Scriptures: A Handbook of New Testament Hermeneutics*. A second edition was under revision at the time of Dana's death and was published posthumously in 1946 by Robert H. Russell. R. E. Glaze completed the revision and in 1961 published *Interpreting the New Testament*. According to Bennett, this was the first book written by a Southern Baptist that addressed the issue of hermeneutics.[14]

Mature Scholarship (1932–1945)

From 1932 to 1945 Dana's target audience broadened from the seminary classroom to pastors, informed laymen, and New Testament students.[15] During this time Dana's writing was more comprehensive in scope than in previous years. In addition to revised editions of previous works, Dana published books of an expository nature that included the Gospels, Acts, Paul, the General Epistles, and Revelation.[16] Other works of a more theological nature also appeared, such as *Christian Sabbath*[17] and *The Holy Spirit in Acts*.[18] Additionally, Dana wrote on the process of canonization in the 1934 publication of *A Neglected Predicate in New Testament Criticism*, in which he tried to answer questions related to how and why the New Testament books were preserved and the interests of the church in preserving them. One of Dana's more significant works appeared in 1940, *The Ephesian Tradition*, the first major application of form criticism to the Gospel of John by a Southern Baptist author. According to Bennett, this book was the only one directed toward other New Testament scholars and in some ways manifested the historical, grammatical, and literary concerns developed by Dana over his career.[19]

Nature and Authority of the Church

Throughout his career Dana wrote on ecclesiology, beginning with his 1920 dissertation.[20] This was followed by *Christ's Ecclesia* in 1926 and *A Manual of Ecclesiology* in 1941. The latter was revised by L. M. Sipes and published under the same title in 1944. Dana was concerned for a proper understanding of the term ἐκκλεσία in the New Testament. He traced the concept of the church from the New Testament writings to early Christian writings and through church history to modern denominationalism. Dana advocated a congregational form of church government as "the most faithful reproduction of the real New Testament idea of the church."[21] Segler judged Dana's contribution on the subject to be "one of the soundest interpretations of the church ever produced by Baptists."[22]

INTERPRETATION OF THOUGHT

Capturing the essence of the thought of one who wrote so extensively and ministered in various capacities is a difficult assignment. As one studies the life and career of Dana, however, several common threads of emphasis emerge. These include his contributions to Greek grammar, a concern for history, and a passion for the proper interpretation, exposition, and application of the Word of God. Throughout his career Dana always emphasized an openness and honesty in scholarship, never fearing the truth and confident that the Scriptures would stand the test of intense scrutiny.

Dana the Grammarian

From the very beginning of his writing career Dana emphasized a concern for the original languages of Scripture. This is obviously manifested in his classroom textbook, *A Manual Grammar of the Greek New Testament*, a work composed in the tradition of A. T. Robertson of Southern Baptist Theological Seminary in Louisville. Dana's commitment to language marks his lifetime of publishing, from his works on the church to his contributions to New Testament hermeneutics.[23]

Dana the Historian

In addition to an emphasis on language, Dana also consistently demonstrated a devotion to a full and accurate knowledge of history. In Dana's view one could not do theology or properly interpret the Bible apart from historical considerations.[24] He argued that the authenticity of Scripture must be viewed in light of its historical origin.[25] He approached ecclesiology from a historical perspective.[26] He wrote books solely devoted to the historical conditions and events bearing on the New Testament. His 1934 treatment of the canon of the New Testament was concerned with history, that is, how and why the New Testament books were preserved. His application of form criticism to the Fourth Gospel was inherently historical in application.[27] Finally, Dana's numerous works on hermeneutics consistently advocated a grammatical-historical approach.

Dana's preaching and teaching also exuded his love for history. According to Segler, he was able to make the New Testament come alive with vivid "historical imagination."[28] Dana was well known for his lecture on Paul, Onesimus, and Philemon as well as the one on James, the half brother of Jesus. His ability to describe people and events warmed the hearts of his audience and faithfully communicated biblical truths.[29]

Dana the Interpreter and Expositor

Dana used the terms "conservative" and "evangelical" to describe his beliefs and approach to the Scriptures.[30] As an interpreter of the Bible, he insisted on both the divine and the human elements of the text. For Dana, this twofold character of the New Testament necessitated principles of exegesis faithful to both[31] and meant that the correct interpretation of Scripture must be the one that explains all of the facts satisfactorily.[32] Dana advocated honesty rather than orthodoxy as the criterion for interpretation, although he did not necessarily view the two as being in conflict with one another.[33]

Dana's view of inspiration also defined his principles of interpretation. He viewed inspiration primarily as a result and not a method.[34] Inspiration included the historical situation, God's oversight of the lives of individuals in their training and abilities, and the direct supervision of the Holy Spirit to insure infallibility.[35] Inspiration, however, did not preclude difficulties.[36] Dana contended, "When God uses human agency He allows it to remain human, and does not deprive it of its essential character because divinely employed."[37]

Closely related to Dana's commitment to proper interpretation was the emphasis on exposition that characterized his work. His writings covered the entirety of the New Testament in this regard, giving evidence of his devotion to the practical result of interpretation, "applying the truth of God's word to human conduct and experience."[38] For Dana, hermeneutics was a historical, theological, and practical endeavor.[39] His works on exposition grew out of classroom teaching and found expression in his published writings and extensive preaching engagements.[40]

TENABILITY OF THOUGHT AND INFLUENCE

Dana wrote during a time when many conservatives were hesitant to take up the methods of biblical criticism. He demonstrated, however, that one can maintain scholarly integrity and hold conservative convictions and a high view of Scripture. Today, his approach to interpretation and methods of exegesis would find acceptance among Southern Baptists and the broader evangelical world.[41] Dana's book on Greek syntax is still in print, although most of the recent intermediate level grammars have opted for the five-case system rather than the eight-case model advocated by Dana.

The influence of a man like Dana who assumed numerous and diverse roles is difficult to measure. His greatest influence was very likely upon his students at Southwestern Seminary who absorbed his love for truth, devotion to the church, scholarly and balanced approach to the Scriptures, and passion for the accurate exposition and application of the Word of God. According to Bennett, Dana wrote primarily to prepare seminary students, local pastors, and church leaders to interpret correctly the New Testament.[42] "His real influence was the personal communication from his own life and lectures to the lives of his seminary students."[43] Dana modeled the pastor/evangelist/scholar combination that has marked the history of Southwestern's faculty.

BIBLIOGRAPHY

1. Primary

DISSERTATION
"Ecclesia in the New Testament and Early Christian Literature." Th.D. diss., Southwestern Baptist Theological Seminary, 1920.

BOOKS
The Authenticity of the Holy Scriptures: A Brief Story of the Problems of Biblical Criticism. Nashville: Sunday School Board of the Southern Baptist Convention, 1923.

Christian Sabbath. Nashville: Sunday School Board of the Southern Baptist Convention, 1934.

Christ's Ecclesia. Nashville: Sunday School Board of the Southern Baptist Convention, 1926.

The Ephesian Tradition: An Oral Source of the Fourth Gospel. Kansas City, Kan.: Kansas City Seminary Press, 1940.

The Epistles and Apocalypse of John: A Brief Commentary. Dallas: Baptist Book Store, 1937.

An Expositor's Harmony of the Synoptic Gospels. Kansas City, Kan.: Central Seminary Press, 1943.

An Expository Survey of the Synoptic Gospels. Seminary Hill, Tex.: Seminary Mimeographers, 1931.

An Expository Survey of the Four Gospels. Fort Worth: Seminary Book Store, 1936.

The Heavenly Guest: An Expository Analysis of the Gospel of John. Nashville: Broadman, 1943.

The Historical Background of the New Testament: A Brief Survey of Events and Conditions Bearing on the Study of the New Testament. Fort Worth: pvt. ptg., 1923.

The Holy Spirit in Acts. Kansas City, Kan.: Central Seminary Press, 1943. 2d. rev. ed., 1946.

(coauth.) *Interpreting the New Testament*. Nashville: Broadman, 1961.

    Shinyak Saegye Ipmun. Seoul: Taehan Yesukyo Changnohoe Ch'onghoe Kyoyukpu, 1979. [Korean]

An Introduction to the Critical Interpretation of the New Testament: A Handbook of Hermeneutics Prepared for Use in the Class of Greek New Testament Exegesis in the Southwestern Baptist Theological Seminary. Seminary Hill, Tex.: pvt. ptg., 1924.

The Jewish Christian Message. Fort Worth: Seminary Book Store, 1934.

Jewish Christianity: An Expository Survey of Acts I to XII, James, I and II Peter, Jude and Hebrews. New Orleans: Bible Institute Memorial Press, 1937; Kansas City, Kan.: Central Seminary Press, 1955.

Lee Rutland Scarborough: A Life of Service. Nashville: Broadman, 1942.

The Life and Literature of Paul. Dallas: Baptist Book Store, 1937.

A Life of Christ. Philadelphia: Judson, 1945.

(coauth.) *A Manual for the Study of the Greek New Testament: A Brief Survey of the Grammatical Principles of the Greek New Testament in the Light of the Best Modern Scholarship*. Fort Worth: Taliaferro Printing Co., 1923.

(coauth.) *A Manual Grammar of the Greek New Testament*. New York: Macmillan Co., 1927, 1957.

    Manual de Gramática del Nuevo Testamento Griego. Trans. Adolfo Robleto, Catalina H. de Clark, and Stanley D. Clark. El Paso: Casa Bautista de Publicaciones, 1975, 1979. [Spanish]

A Manual of Ecclesiology. Kansas City, Kan.: Central Seminary Press, 1941.

(coauth.) *A Manual of Ecclesiology*. 2d rev. ed. Kansas City, Kan.: Central Seminary Press, 1944.

    Manual de Eclesiologia. Trans. Adolfo Robleto et al. El Paso: Casa Bautista de Publicaciones, 1987. [Spanish]

A Neglected Predicate in New Testament Criticism. Chicago: Blessing Book Stores, 1934.

(coauth.) *The New Testament: An Introductory Study: An Elective Course for Use by Sunday School and Leadership-Education Classes*. Rev. and enl. by H. E. Dana. Philadelphia: Judson, 1942.

*New Testament Criticism: A Brief Survey of the Nature and Necessity, History, Sources and Results of
New Testament Criticism.* Fort Worth: World Co., 1924.
    *El Nuevo Testamento ante la Crítica: Breve Estudio de la Naturaleza, Necesidad, Historia,
Orígenes y Resultados de la Crítica al Nuevo Testamento.* Trans. D. E. H. Ed. Alfredo
Lerín and Frank Patterson. El Paso: Casa Bautista de Publicaciones, 1953. [Spanish]
A New Testament Manual. Fort Worth: Southwestern Press, 1929.
The New Testament Message. 4 vols. Fort Worth: Pioneer Publishing Company, 1925–26.
New Testament Times: A Brief Introduction to the Historical Background of the New Testament. Kansas City, Kan.: Kansas City Seminary Press, 1938; Central Seminary Press, 1946.
The New Testament World: A Brief Sketch of the History and Conditions which Composed the Background of the New Testament. Fort Worth: Southwestern Press, 1926.
The New Testament World: A Brief Sketch of the History and Conditions Which Composed the Background of the New Testament. 2d rev. ed. Fort Worth: Pioneer Publishing, 1928.
The New Testament World: A Brief Sketch of the History and Conditions Which Composed the Background of the New Testament. 3rd rev. ed. Nashville: Broadman, 1937.
    *El Mundo del Nuevo Testamento: Breve Esquema de la Historia y las Condiciones que
Constituyeron el Fondo del Nuevo Testamento.* Trans. Ildefonso Villarello. El Paso: Casa
Bautista de Publicaciones, 1956. [Spanish]
    Shinyak Sungsuh Saegye. Trans. Jong Sun Kwon. Taejon: Korea Baptist Theological College, 1985,
1992. [Korean]
Notes on New Testament Lectures. Cooper, Tex.: Roy L. Johnson, 1929.
The Science of New Testament Interpretation. Fort Worth: Southwestern Mimeographers, 1930.
Searching the Scriptures: A Handbook of New Testament Hermeneutics. New Orleans: Bible Institute
Memorial Press, 1936; rev. ed. compl. by Robert H. Russell. Kansas City, Kan.: Central Seminary
Press, 1946.
    Escudriñando las Escrituras: un Manual de las Hermenéuticas del Nuevo Testamento. Trans.
W. Q. Maer. El Paso: Casa Bautista de Publicaciones, 1960. [Spanish]
(coauth.) *Student's Harmony of the Synoptic Gospels.* Seminary Hill, Tex.: Seminary Mimeographers,
1930.
A Syllabus on the Critical Problems of the New Testament. Fort Worth: pvt. ptg., 1937.

JOURNAL ARTICLES
"Authenticity of the Holy Scriptures." *Southwestern Journal of Theology* o.s. 5 (April 1922): 40–78.
"The Bearing of Luke's Preface upon the Doctrine of Inspiration." *Southwestern Evangel* 11 (February
1927): 193–96.
"Beginnings of Church Federation in America." *Southwestern Journal of Theology* o.s. 7 (October
1923): 68–73.
"Christian Unity as Taught in the New Testament." *Southwestern Journal of Theology* o.s. 8 (January
1924): 29–36.
"The Church Idea as Reflected in New Testament Life." *Southwestern Journal of Theology* o.s. 7 (April
1923): 24–37.
"The Church Idea in the Reformation." *Southwestern Journal of Theology* o.s. 8 (April 1924): 17–25.
"The Divine Names in the Old Testament." *Southwestern Evangel* 13 (November 1928): 41–42.
"The Doctrine of Regeneration in the Light of Scientific Research." *Review and Expositor* 38 (January
1941): 39–43.
"Historical Evidence of the Ascension." *Biblical Review* 14 (April 1929): 191–209.
"History of the Word 'Church.'" *Southwestern Journal of Theology* o.s. 6 (July 1922): 52–56.
"The Holy Spirit in Acts." *Southwestern Journal of Theology* o.s. 5–6 (January, April, July 1921; January
1922): 43–47; 36–42; 75–79; 79–83.

"The Influence of Baptists upon the Modern Conception of the Church." *Southwestern Journal of Theology* o.s. 6 (October 1922): 95–99.

"Jesus' Use of the Old Testament." *Biblical Review* 16 (July 1931): 389–99.

"The Lord's Supper." *Southwestern Journal of Theology* o.s. 4 (April 1920): 61–65.

"A New Testament Church of the Twentieth Century." *Southwestern Journal of Theology* o.s. 7 (July 1923): 48–54.

"New Testament Evidence for Ascension." *Southwestern Evangel* 13 (May 1929): 244–46.

"The Old Testament in the Apostolic Age." *Biblical Review* 17 (April 1932): 227–43.

"Paul's Version of Human Personality." *Southwestern Journal of Theology* o.s. 4 (January 1920): 15–20.

"Peculiarities of the View of Christ in the First Epistle [of John]." *Southwestern Evangel* 9 (March 1925): 12–13.

"The Preface to Luke's Gospel." *Southwestern Journal of Theology* o.s. 8 (July 1924): 33–42.

"Some Neglected Principles of Biblical Research." *Review and Expositor* 35 (April 1938): 176–84.

"The Stratification of Tradition in the Fourth Gospel." *Journal of Religion* 17 (January 1937): 62–75.

"The Supreme Need of the Hour for Southern Baptists." *Southwestern Journal of Theology* o.s. 6 (January 1922): 84–85.

"Where Did Paul Persecute the Church?" *Anglican Theological Review* 20 (January 1938): 16–26.

"The Word 'Ecclesia' as Used in the New Testament Writings." *Southwestern Journal of Theology* o.s. 7 (January 1923): 65–85.

2. Secondary

Bennett, Ray Earl. "The Contribution of H. E. Dana to the Southern Baptist Understanding of the Historical-Critical Method of New Testament Interpretation." Ph.D. diss., Baylor University, 1974.

Encyclopedia of Southern Baptists. 4 vols. Nashville: Broadman, 1958–82. Vol. 1. S.v. "Dana, Harvey Eugene."

Garrett, James Leo, Jr. "The Bible at Southwestern during Its Formative Years: A Study of H. E. Dana and W. T. Conner." *Baptist History and Heritage* 21 (October 1986): 29–43.

Hensley, J. Clark. *In the Heart of the Young*. Kansas City, Kan.: Central Seminary Press, 1952.

Ozment, Wayne. "The Hermeneutics of Harvey Eugene Dana." Th.D. diss., New Orleans Baptist Theological Seminary, 1972.

Phillips, Charles D. "The Southern Baptist View of the Church as Reflected in the Thought of J. L. Dagg, E. C. Dargan, and H. E. Dana." Th.M. thesis, Southern Baptist Theological Seminary, 1957.

Segler, Franklin M. "Harvey Eugene Dana: Lights and Shadows." *Southwestern Journal of Theology* 13 (Fall 1970): 67–75.

Thomas Buford Maston

(1897–1988)
Christian Ethics

William E. Goff

BIOGRAPHY

From small, rural beginnings few would imagine the enormous influence that the son of a sharecropper would be able to have, but through a consistent and courageous written and spoken Christian witness much was accomplished. Thomas Buford Maston was born and reared in eastern Tennessee. His home was characterized by hymn singing and pious conversations. Maston was heard to comment that he had learned more about the Christian life from his father at the end of a corn row than he did from many of his teachers. In his late teens, Tom Maston made a profession of faith in the local Baptist church and soon also felt a call to some form of ministry, although he never felt a call to be a pastor. Concerning his conversion and his call, Maston recalled that his father laughed and cried at the same time as he witnessed his son make these decisions.[1]

Maston graduated from Carson-Newman College in 1920 and then entered Southwestern Baptist Theological Seminary, along with his fiancée, Essie Mae McDonald, also a graduate of Carson-Newman. A year later they married. He graduated with an M.R.E. degree in 1923, and in 1925 he earned the first D.R.E. degree awarded by the seminary. He was invited to teach religious education, especially recreation, even before he finished the doctorate. In 1927 he also completed an M.A. degree in sociology at Texas

Christian University. Then in 1939, after a battle with pneumonia, he completed his Ph.D. degree at Yale University under H. Richard Niebuhr, Roland H. Bainton, and D. C. Macintosh. His studies at Yale led him definitively to move more toward teaching Christian ethics, which he determined would be best taught in the School of Theology at Southwestern.[2]

Maston, who became known for his writing and speaking skills, was always attempting to address pressing social and ethical matters in the context of the nation or of the Southern Baptist denomination. He wrote more than a hundred articles for Baptist papers and periodicals, including numerous series of Sunday School lessons. He was a frequent speaker at denominational camps and assemblies and even addressed on several occasions the annual meeting of the Southern Baptist Convention. He was instrumental in beginning and then serving in the organization which became the Christian Life Commission of the Baptist General Convention of Texas. Maston is credited with being responsible for developing the "social conscience of Southern Baptists."[3]

The Mastons had two sons, Thomas McDonald (lovingly called Tom Mac), who was born in 1925, and Harold Eugene, born in 1928. Both boys had severe difficulties being born. Tom Mac became an invalid at birth, and Mrs. Maston almost died giving birth to Gene. Nevertheless, both of the Mastons took untiring care of the boys, especially of Tom Mac, who required their personal attention for his every need all of his life.[4]

Maston retired from teaching at Southwestern in 1963, and a review of his writing reveals that he increased considerably his production of books and other published materials during retirement. He died on 2 May 1988 and was buried in Laurel Land Cemetery, Fort Worth.

WRITINGS

Handbook for Recreational Leaders (1937) was written as a textbook for Maston's teaching this subject in the School of Religious Education.

Of One (1946) called for an end to racial discrimination and segregation in public schools, making it the most controversial of all of his writings. It was published eight years before the United

States Supreme Court declared public school segregation unconstitutional in 1954.[5]

The Christian and the Modern World (1952) was Maston's earliest effort to address the issues confronted by Christians trying to live by their biblically based faith.

Right or Wrong? (1955) was written to give guidance to young people in their decision making on issues of personal morality.

Christianity and World Issues (1957) was Maston's first published work on social issues from an evangelical perspective.

The Bible and Race (1959) created a firestorm of reaction from Southern Christians, including Baptists, because Maston called for a biblically based understanding and equitable treatment of Black people.

Segregation and Desegregation: A Christian Approach (1959) challenged Southern Christians in particular to move beyond the cultural and legal limitations imposed on the Black peoples of the United States.

Isaac Backus: Pioneer of Religious Liberty (1962), an abridgement of his Ph.D. thesis at Yale, dealt with an important New England Baptist.

God's Will and Your Life (1964), Maston's first publication during retirement, was aimed at youth to enable them to make sound decisions at the major turning points of their lives.

Biblical Ethics: A Biblical Survey (1967), an effort to survey the whole Bible for its ethical themes and principles, has been used extensively to teach Christian ethics from a biblical perspective.

Suffering: A Personal Perspective (1967) reflects not only the Maston family experience of personal suffering but also the redemptive dimensions of suffering from the perspective of the cross.

The Christian, the Church and Contemporary Problems (1968) was a typical effort by Maston to design a textbook for a popular course which he frequently taught on the Bible and moral issues. He presented the biblical concepts for ethical orientation needed by Christians and churches and then applied those concepts to family, racial, and political concerns.

The Conscience of a Christian (1971) dealt with the often troubling issue of "following one's conscience" in decision making.

The revised edition of *Right or Wrong?* (1971), coauthored with William M. Pinson Jr., was an updating of some of the data and language in the first edition but did not alter its basic outline or content.

Why Live the Christian Life? (1974) was Maston's textbook for basic Christian ethics courses for Christian colleges and seminaries.

In *Real Life in Christ* (1974) one finds a series of devotional messages setting forth the guidelines for a maturing, obedient Christian who practices the Christian way of life.

The Bible and Family Relations (1983), coauthored with William M. Tillman Jr., is the textbook which is the fruit of Maston's many years of teaching one of his favorite subjects.

To Walk as He Walked (1985), Maston's last book, was his effort to describe what it means to live by 1 John 2: 5–6, which was his life motto.

INTERPRETATION OF THOUGHT

Foundations of Maston's Evangelical Ethics

Maston rightly belongs in the evangelical tradition due primarily to his efforts to bring Baptists in particular and conservative Christianity in general toward a more biblically based social conscience in their evangelism and social practice. Vance Kirkpatrick has observed that diverse theological streams, such as liberal, neoorthodox, and contextual ethics, converge in Maston's arguments, but the dominant one is conservative biblical scholarship.[6] Maston's insistence on balancing evangelism and social concern resonates with the emphases of Carl F. H. Henry, Billy Graham, and other leaders of the post-World War II evangelical movement, particularly their insistence on being more racially inclusive in their practices and teachings.

Biblical Ethics

Even a cursory reading of Maston's works leaves a clear impression of his devotion to the Scriptures. His text, *Biblical Ethics*, is a living testament to the continuing impact of his biblical teaching, since it is the one of his books that continues to be in print, primarily because it is so often used in conservative Christian colleges and seminaries for teaching Christian ethics.

Maston's typical methodology for dealing with moral issues was to use scriptural prooftexting, punctuating his thoughts with biblical references and illustrations. He often insisted on the validity and abiding relevance of the Scriptures for dealing with all of life's issues. One of his characteristic teaching practices was that of using biblical principles, especially when he was dealing with a contemporary moral problem for which there was no direct biblical teaching.[7]

Theology and Ethics

Maston's book, *Why Live the Christian Life?*, deals with basic or foundational Christian ethics, which is essentially the theological and philosophical framework for Christian ethics. Maston's theology is thoroughly evangelical, being based on a conservative interpretation of the Scriptures, which he considered to be completely authoritative and abidingly relevant for the Christian and the church. He saw the Christian faith and Christian morals as inseparable.

To understand further Maston's foundational ethic, one must take into consideration two unique elements: his theological perspective of the cross and his use of constructive tension as a Christian strategy for relating Christians and churches to the world.

The Cross

One of the primary elements of Maston's ethical system is the place which he gives to the cross as the "unifying symbol" of the Christian faith and enterprise. He stressed the two-dimensional aspect of the cross, with its vertical piece symbolizing the need for a right relationship with God and the horizontal piece representing the need for right relationships with other human beings. Maston indicated that Christ not only died on the cross but also lived a cross-like life. Thus the cross is recognized not only as the means by which salvation is brought to humankind but also as the guiding symbol for living an authentic Christian life. Such a life involves for the Christian the crucifixion of self with its selfish ambition and purpose as well as the demonstration of his redemptive love to others.[8]

Constructive Tension

For Maston, the strategy of the Christian and for the church to be moral change agents is formed by the tension created by following God's ideals and his sovereign purposes as they live in a real world of sin and moral failure. It is that tension which contributes to growth, causing Christians to desire the changes for the higher and greater good. It is a healthy, constructive tension which redeems. In this light, Maston was heard at times to say, "It is easy to please God, but next to impossible to satisfy Him."[9]

His often-used visual aid of stretching a rubber band illustrated his point. The tension can pull the opposing forces upward, but if stretched too far, the tension can cause breakdowns. So there has to be some reducing of the tension at times, because if the church maintains too great a tension, it might lose all opportunity to minister to the world that it is seeking to help. Unfortunately, Maston noted, some churches have so made their peace with the world that there is no redeeming tension created, resulting in the church's loosing its power to lift the world toward God's purposes for it.[10]

Balanced Methodology

Maston had a balanced approach to his thinking that took two basic forms. One was a "dyadic" teaching style which expressed "a balance between opposites or counterparts of a common theme." "Conservatism and liberalism, civil obedience and disobedience, order and justice, local and state responsibilities . . . and the relationship between church and state" are all elements to be kept in balance so that neither should be neglected, and when necessary, "conciliation rather than conflict should be the dominant, overriding theme." Maston thus strove to stimulate thinking on both sides of an issue and yet demonstrate love for all participants.[11]

Browning Ware believes that Maston had a second kind of balance which was that of a "dialectician."

> . . . Maston maintains tension between differing expressions of a thought in order to expose both their error and truth. All positions, including his own, stand under the greater tension of the sovereignty of God and its expression as the will of God. The dynamic tension between God's ideal and the human situation is the key to understanding all of Maston's thought.[12]

It would be fair to suggest that not only did Maston use these elements in his teaching and writing but also they found expression in his personal ministry and Christian leadership. He at times appeared to be quite paradoxical in his approach to moral issues, as Ralph A. Phelps has pointed out. While holding conservative theological views, he would sound like a theological liberal in his emphasis on love.

In times of war, he taught peace and the ideal of nonretaliation. In an era of exploitive racial segregation, he taught the oneness of all mankind and the moral imperative of ending segregation in all its degrading forms. . . . At a time when monopolistic capitalism was upheld by many in his own denomination as God's ideal for mankind. . ., he emphatically declared that Christianity was not dependent on any economic system and that no single system was the embodiment of Christ's teachings.[13]

For his various positions taken, he was often accused of being "a liberal, a radical, a socialist, or [even] a Communist,"[14] to which charges Maston never lost his composure but rather continued to demonstrate a sensitivity and a care for all parties and positions taken.

UNIQUE CONTRIBUTIONS ON SELECTED ETHICAL CONCERNS

Maston wrote extensively, especially in articles and pamphlets, on personal ethical concerns such as alcoholism, gambling, drugs, and the decision-making dynamics for Christian youth. He did make some significant contributions to personal ethical guidelines through his teaching on the will of God and marriage and family. In the social ethics realm, however, Maston made more contributions especially in race relations, political involvement and influence of Christians, economics, and war and peace.

The Will of God
An often quoted principle of T. B. Maston on the will of God is that "God wants to start with each one of us where we are and guide us to where he wants us to go."[15] God's will is authoritative for the Christian because it is tied to the very nature of God. Thus Maston concluded that since God is sovereign over the totality of our lives, he has a will for every decision. Maston was careful to indicate that God has both an "intentional or perfect will" for responding to every human problem and a "circumstantial will" that leads us to do the best we can do in difficult situations. When we respond obediently to God's circumstantial will, Maston interpreted, we often find ourselves moving toward God's perfect will for us.[16]

Marriage and Family

For Maston the most basic of all human institutions is the home. From creation, Maston believed, most of the other institutions (school, church, and state) evolved historically out of the home. The home is basic to the development of persons "socially, spiritually, and morally." He believed the home is to be more important to the religious development of persons than the church, because the home is where the Christian experience must be lived out day after day. Primary to the functions of the Christian home is the guiding of the children to accept Christ as Savior and the developing of their Christian faith, their system of values, and their driving motivation and life purpose.[17]

For his day, Maston had some rather innovative elements in his teaching on marriage and the family. He emphasized having a democratic style of leadership, care for the aged, "the home" as "an extension of the kingdom of God," and family life existing in the tension between the ideal and the real. He also used a case-study method for teaching on the family. Nevertheless, Maston tended to be so positive on the family that he did not always deal adequately with problematic issues such as "conflict and anger."[18]

Race Relations

Jase Jones has pointed out that Maston published three books that dealt exclusively with racial issues and then wrote about it in parts of six other books. Maston considered *Segregation and Desegregation* as "his major scholarly work on race." *The Bible and Race* "has been his most influential book" on that subject. "Woman's Missionary Union chose it as a study book in 1962, and Broadman Press published more than 50,000 copies."[19] Probably in no other moral category did Maston so positively influence American Christianity, including his own denomination.

The Influence and Involvement of Christians in Politics

Maston envisioned that Christians should apply themselves under the lordship of Christ to every area of life, including that of being responsible citizens, concerned for influencing their communities for good and for God. He viewed the task as Christians living as citizens in both sacred and secular realms, being responsible to God and man in both. The Christian faith is to be applied to the totality of life. "[T]he God we worship is the sovereign God of the universe, the God of the street as well as the sanctuary."[20]

Economics

Man's relation to God directly affects the way he relates to other persons. Maston was "convinced that the economic order will function effectively only when people seek and do God's will in relation to economic practice and daily work." God's will for a work ethic is that people must take precedence over what those people produce. All machines, organizations, properties, or products "must be evaluated on the basis of their effects on human life and personal dignity." Maston warned the churches not to "become identified with any particular economic class, system, or program."[21]

War and Peace

According to Maston, "An objective reading of the New Testament will lead one to conclude that there are no specific teachings in it concerning war and the Christian's relation to it. War is not explicitly justified or forbidden." He concedes that both war and pacifism can be supported by New Testament teaching.[22] According to Browning Ware, Maston found "that both Testaments acknowledge war as part of the human situation; however, they do not accept war as God's ultimate intention. At best, war is God's adjustment to man's sin; at worst, war is man's gross sin against God's best."[23]

Maston did support an open stance toward accepting conscientious objectors to war, because he saw himself as one in a limited sense, even during World War II, because he reluctantly accepted that justice at times demanded that war was necessary. Peace played an important role in his ethical system. He saw peace as reflecting God's nature and God's will for human life. Nevertheless, he recognized that peace can only be experienced momentarily and "in process by individuals and groups but never perfectly within history."[24]

IMPACT

T. B. Maston was a gentle giant of a Christian gentleman. He was self-retrained in controversy, handling those who opposed him with grace and respect. He gained the trust of many because of his tireless biblical scholarship and compassionate concern for the least and the lost. He had a missionary vision and heart, as well as a being a knowledgeable person on current events and a wide range of theological perspectives. He was a man for his times in that he saw a "world in travail" and sought to address it.

According to Jimmy Allen, T. B. Maston "has been the catalyst for shaping the principles of the gospel to life" for Southern Baptists. Allen has added that Maston "has been a voice to the conscience" of his denomination "at critical decision-making times" and "has helped Southern Baptists toward strengthening family life."[25] Also, according to Allen, Maston at times played the role of "gadfly," because of "his issue orientation." That would probably be the case in Maston's handling of issues such as war and peace and economics and affluence but would not be the case in his treatment of the racial issue. Allen recalled "the tense moment of decision making in the 1954 Southern Baptist Convention" relative to school integration. "Maston's voice along with that of J. B. Weatherspoon called" Southern Baptists "to responsible support of racial justice. They prevailed. That was not gadfly."[26]

Maston also impacted the lives of numerous students during his forty years in the seminary classroom. His forty-nine Th.D. Christian ethics graduates became pastors and college and seminary professors and presidents as well as foreign missionaries and denominational workers on state and national levels. He was recognized as a pioneer in Christian ethics for Southern Baptists because of his passion for justice. James M. Dunn has observed: "Maston taught ethics to men who became denominational leaders at the front edge of Southern Baptists' most rapid growth. The time was right for maximum impact."[27] Maston became one of the leading moral change agents among Southern Baptists, largely because of the combination of his pastoral and prophetic qualities.[28]

A continuing camaraderie has prevailed among the Maston graduates, especially his Th.D. students, which has resulted during the decade of the 1990s in the organization of the T. B. Maston Foundation. Scholarships are awarded to meritorious doctoral students in Christian ethics in various Baptist institutions. As a lasting tribute to the contributions of this great man of God, the foundation has established the T. B. Maston Chair of Christian Ethics in the Logsdon School of Theology at Hardin-Simmons University.

BIBLIOGRAPHY

1. Primary

DISSERTATIONS AND THESIS

"The Ethical and Social Attitudes of Isaac Backus." Ph.D. diss., Yale University, 1939. Abr. ed.: Rochester, N.Y.: American Baptist Historical Society, 1962.

"The Play Program of the Church." D.R.E. diss., Southwestern Baptist Theological Seminary, 1925.

"A Recreational Survey of the Churches of Fort Worth." M.A. thesis, Texas Christian University, 1927.

BOOKS

(coauth.) *The Bible and Family Relations*. Nashville: Broadman, 1983.

The Bible and Race. Nashville: Broadman, 1959.

Biblical Ethics: A Survey. Cleveland: World Publishing, 1967. Rpt.: Waco, Tex.: Word, 1977. With sub-title: *A Guide to the Ethical Message of the Scriptures from Genesis through Revelation*. Macon, Ga.: Mercer University Press, 1982.

The Christian and Race Relations. Memphis: Brotherhood Commission, Southern Baptist Convention, n.d.

The Christian in the Modern World. Nashville: Broadman, 1952; Nashville: Convention Press, 1955.

The Christian, the Church, and Contemporary Problems. Waco, Tex.: Word, 1968.

  Como Vivir en el Mundo de Hoy. Trans. Rubén Zorzoli. El Paso: Casa Bautista de Publicaciones, 1987. [Spanish]

Christianity and World Issues. New York: Macmillan, 1957.

  O Cristianismo e Problemas Mundiais: A Igreja e o Mundo. Trans. Hélcio da Silva Lessa. Rio de Janiero: Casa Publicadora Batista, 1965. [Portuguese]

The Conscience of a Christian. Waco, Tex.: Word, 1971.

God's Will and Your Life. Nashville: Broadman, 1964.

  Irādatu al-Lah wa Hayātuk. Trans. Tanyus Zakhāri. Beirut: Baptist Publications, 1965. [Arabic]

  Gottes Wille: Antworten auf Fragen junger Menschen. Trans. Alfred Schmidt. Kassel: J. G. Oncken, 1968. [German]

  Kehendak Allah. Trans. Ebbie C. Smith. Semarang: Seminari Theologia Baptis, 1970. [Indonesian]

  A Vontade de Deus e Sua Vida. Trans. Thurmon E. Bryant. Rio de Janiero: Junta de Educacão Religiosa e Publicacoēs, 1977. [Portuguese]

A Handbook for Church Recreation Leaders. Nashville: Sunday School Board of the Southern Baptist Convention, 1937.

  Manual para la Dirección de las Actividades Recreativas de la Iglesia. Trans. Viola Campbell. El Paso: Casa Bautista de Publicaciones, 1969. [Spanish]

How to Face Grief. Waco, Tex.: Word, 1978.

Isaac Backus: Pioneer of Religious Liberty. London: James Clark and Co., 1962.

Of One: A Study of Christian Principles and Race Relations. Atlanta: Home Mission Board, Southern Baptist Convention, 1946.

Real Life in Christ. Nashville: Broadman, 1974.

Right or Wrong? Nashville: Broadman, 1955. Rev. ed. with sub-title: *A Guide for Teeners and Their Leaders for Living by Christian Standards*, coauth. William M. Pinson, Jr. Ibid., 1971.

  (Abr. transl.) *Benar atau salah?* Bandung: Geredja Baptis Bandung, 1958. [Indonesian]

  (Abr. transl. of 1st ed.) *Consejos a la Juventud*. Trans. Hiram F. Duffer, Jr. El Paso: Casa Bautista de Publicaciones, 195?. [Spanish]

  (Compl. transl. of 1st ed.) *Bueno o Malo?* Trans. Hiram F. Duffer, Jr. El Paso: Casa Bautista de Publicaciones, 1957. [Spanish]

Certo ou Errado? Trans. Jose Reis Periera. Rio de Janiero: Casa Publicadora Batista, 1958. [Portuguese]

Sawāb am Khata? Trans. Jiryis Dalli. Beirut: Baptist Publishing House, 1968. [Arabic]

Segregation and Desegregation: A Christian Approach. New York: Macmillan, 1959.

Suffering: A Personal Perspective. Nashville: Broadman, 1967. Under title: *God Speaks through Suffering.* Waco, Tex.: Word, 1977.

To Walk as He Walked. Nashville: Broadman, 1985.

Treasures from Holy Scripture. Nashville: Broadman, 1987.

Why Live the Christian Life? Nashville: Thomas Nelson, 1974.

Etica de la Vida Cristiana: Principios Basicos. Trans. Floreal Ureta. El Paso: Casa Bautista de Publicaciones, 1981. [Spanish]

Words of Wisdom. Nashville: Broadman, 1984.

A World in Travail: A Study of the Contemporary World Crisis. Nashville: Broadman, 1954.

CHAPTERS CONTRIBUTED TO BOOKS

"The Heresy of Orthodoxy." In *Southwestern Sermons*, ed. H. C. Brown, Jr., 150–53. Nashville: Broadman, 1960.

"The Husband and Father." In *J. Howard Williams: Prophet of God and Friend of Man*, ed. H. C. Brown, Jr., and Charles P. Johnson, 8–28. San Antonio: Naylor, 1963.

"Interracial Marriage." In *The Cutting Edge: Critical Questions for Contemporary Christians*, ed. H. C. Brown, Jr., vol. 1, 76–81. Waco, Tex.: Word, 1969.

"The Master Needs Men" and "The Minister's Preaching Ministry." In *Messages for Men: For Laymen and Ministers*, ed. H. C. Brown, Jr., 89–96. Grand Rapids: Zondervan, 1960.

"Reflections regarding Democracy." In *Chapel Messages*, ed. H. C. Brown, Jr., and Charles P. Johnson, 91–105. Grand Rapids: Baker, 1966.

"Six Tough Adjustments." In *Plain Talk about Growing Old*, ed. George W. Knight and John W. Steen, 20–25. Nashville: Convention Press, 1977.

JOURNAL ARTICLES

"Baptists, Social Christianity, and Culture." *Review and Expositor* 61 (Winter 1964): 521–31.

"Biblical Bases for Social Concern." *Southwestern Journal of Theology* n.s. 7 (April 1965): 5–16.

"Christian Living and the Way Ahead." *Quarterly Review* 25 (January–February–March 1965): 47–51.

"The Church, the State, and the Christian Ethic." *Journal of Church and State* 2 (May 1960): 26–36.

"Ethical Content of Job." *Southwestern Journal of Theology* 14 (Fall 1971): 43–56.

"Ethical Dimensions of James." *Southwestern Journal of Theology* 12 (Fall 1969): 23–39.

"The Ground for Christian Social Concern." *The Outlook* 9 (October 1959): 14–22.

"Jeff D. Ray and Southwestern Seminary." *Southwestern Journal of Theology* 10 (Fall 1967): 71–83.

"Law, Order, and Justice." *Review and Expositor* 66 (May Supplement 1969): 89–100.

"Man: His Dignity and Work." *Review and Expositor* 51 (July 1954): 299–311.

"Personal Perspective on Ordination." *Southwestern Journal of Theology* 11 (Spring 1969): 112–14.

"Religion's Contribution to Social Work." *Social Science* 2 (February–April 1927): 158–60.

"Where Are We in Race Relations: An Overview." *Search* 4 (Spring 1974): 19–26.

MISCELLANEOUS

"The Bible and Women." *The Student*, February 1985, 4–6, 47–48.

"Campus Conditions." *The Baptist Student*, October 1952, 14–16; November 1952, 20–23; December 1952, 18–20; January 1953, 12–14, 36.

"The Changeless Needs of the Changing Family." *Home Life*, June 1947, 9–12.

"Christian Men and Race Relations." *Brotherhood Journal*, October–November–December 1961, 31–35.

"'Dancing': Hebrew Word Study." *Southwestern Evangel*, May 1930, 263–64.
Encyclopedia of Southern Baptists. 4 vols. Nashville: Broadman, 1958–82. Vol. 2. S.v. "Pacifism."
"Faith Freely Exercised." *Report from the Capital*, May 1983, 4–5.
"The Impact of Culture on Traditional Concepts of Marriage." *Family Life*, December 1950, 1–8.
"The Individual." *Royal Service*, February 1964, 4–6.
Integration. Nashville: Christian Life Commission of the Southern Baptist Convention, 1956.
"The New Testament Ministry." *The Student*, March 1978, 18–22; May 1983, 10–12.
"The Pornography Problem." *Eternity*, May 1971, 20–22.
"Principles of Racial Understanding." *Home and Foreign Fields*, June 1930, 11–12.
(coauth.) "Right or Wrong?" *The Student*, May 1979, 6–10.
"Southern Baptists and the Negro." *Home Missions*, July 1966, 18–19; August 1966, 23–24; September 1966, 38–42; rpt.: *The Baptist Student*, March 1967, 11–13; April 1967, 32–34; May 1967, 26–29.

ORAL MEMOIRS

Oral Memoirs of T. B. Maston. Interviewer, Rufus B. Spain. Baylor University Program for Oral History. Waco, Tex.: Baylor University Religion and Culture Project, 1973.

2. Secondary

Darnell, Janet. "The Catalytic Influence of T. B. Maston on the Church Recreation Program of the Southern Baptist Convention." M.S. thesis, Mississippi University for Women, 1979.
Fitts, Jean Carlisle. "A Study of the Evidences of the Similarities of the Ethical Thought of T. B. Maston to Contemporary Social Work Practice as Reflected in Certain Social Work Journals." Ed.D. diss., Southwestern Baptist Theological Seminary, 1976.
Kirkpatrick, Vance Crawford. "The Ethical Thought of T. B. Maston." Th.D. diss., Southwestern Baptist Theological Seminary, 1972.
Martin, Earl R. *Passport to Servanthood*. Nashville: Broadman, 1988.
McCullough, Charles Franklin. "An Evaluation of the Biblical Hermeneutic of T. B. Maston." Ph.D. diss., Southwestern Baptist Theological Seminary, 1987.
Pinson, William M., Jr., ed. *An Approach to Christian Ethics: The Life, Contribution, and Thought of T. B. Maston*. Nashville: Broadman, 1979.
Tillman, William M., Jr., ed. *Perspectives on Applied Christianity: Essays in Honor of Thomas Buford Maston*. Macon, Ga.: Mercer University Press, 1986.
Valentine, Foy. "Baptist Polity and Social Pronouncements." *Baptist History and Heritage* 14 (July 1979): 59.
_____. "T. B. Maston: A Conscience for Southern Baptists." *Southwestern Journal of Theology* 25 (Spring 1983): 89–103.
_____. *T. B. Maston: Shaper of Ethics and Social Concern*. Shapers of Southern Baptist Heritage. Nashville: Historical Commission of the Southern Baptist Convention, 1987.

Ray Summers
(1910–1992)
New Testament

J. W. MacGorman

BIOGRAPHY

Ray Summers was born in Allen, Texas, a rural community north of Dallas, on 21 February 1910. He was the second in a family of eight children, numbering five sons and three daughters. His parents, Luther C. and Vertie Alice Summers, were farming people who had come to Texas from Arkansas. Long days of hard work in the fields contributed to a remarkable health and longevity in the family. The father's death at eighty-nine years of age was the first among the immediate kin.

From his earliest days Summers was taken by devout parents to Sunday School and worship services at the Allen Baptist Church. At eight he was converted in revival services in his home church led by Dr. J. B. Tidwell of Baylor University, and during his senior year at Boyd High School in McKinney, Texas, he began to sense a call to the Christian ministry. He preached his first sermon in December 1927, taking as his text the Sermon on the Mount and finishing in ten minutes! He was ordained in his home church in Allen in 1928 and became the teacher of a men's Sunday School class.

Following high school graduation in 1928, Summers enrolled in Burleson College in Greenville, Texas, a Baptist junior college he attended for more than two years. There he met Jester Hilger, a preacher's daughter, who was later to become his wife. Both were active in the student mission program with a particular interest in Brazil.

During his second year at Burleson College, Summers began the first of several Texas pastorates: Clear Lake (1928–29); Rosamond Chapel in Anna (1929–34); Krum (1933–38); Chilton (1934–35); and Sycamore Heights Baptist Church in Fort Worth (1938–41). Some of these were half-time churches, which explains the overlapping dates. The time covered paralleled the years of his education at Baylor University and Southwestern Baptist Theological Seminary.

Transferring from Burleson College to Baylor University during the winter quarter of 1931, Summers worked with Drs. J. B. Tidwell, B. O. Herring, and E. D. Head in the Department of Bible. He became interested in comparative religion and found special challenges in courses in philosophy, psychology, and history.

Ray and Jester Summers were married in Greenville on 20 June 1934, following their graduation from Baylor. While students there, both had been active in the Volunteer Band, continuing to anticipate eventual appointment to Brazil. This goal persisted in 1935 as they enrolled for the Master of Theology degree at Southwestern. Here the teachers who had the greatest influence on Summers were H. E. Dana in New Testament and Walter T. Conner in theology. From the former he learned much about the grammatical-historical approach to the study of the Bible; and he described the latter fondly as "way ahead of his time among Southern Baptists as a theologian."[1]

A crisis developed when the Foreign Mission Board (SBC) asked the Summerses to abandon their plans for Brazil in favor of going to Bucharest, Romania, to establish a Baptist seminary. Then, shortly after they agreed to the change, President L. R. Scarborough of Southwestern confronted Summerses with an invitation to remain at the seminary to teach New Testament.[2] He emphasized the prospect of teaching many students who would go from his classes to the mission fields of the world. This prophetic statement had large fulfillment in the years that followed.

Summers's teaching career lasted forty-two years and enriched three educational institutions. For twenty-one years he taught at Southwestern Baptist Seminary (1938–59) and became the first director of the School of Theology (1949–53). During the next five years (1959–64) he served on the faculty of Southern Baptist Theological Seminary in Louisville, Kentucky, where he became the director of graduate studies in his second year.[3] But in 1964 when Baylor University, his alma mater, invited him to return as chairman of the Department of Religion, he accepted the challenge. The prospect of establishing a program leading to the Doctor of Philosophy degree in religion in a Southern Baptist university made a special appeal to him. He devoted the last sixteen years of his teaching career to the development of this new program at Baylor, leading up to his retirement at seventy years of age in 1980.

Mrs. Summers became an outstanding leader in children's work. She pioneered activity-based Bible teaching in the Sunday Schools of the Southern Baptist Convention and contributed much as a childhood conference leader. She published seven books. Dr. and Mrs. Summers had three children: David Ray, Mary Lois, and Sarah Nell.

The final days of both Dr. and Mrs. Summers were spent in the Geriatric Hospital/Nursing Home facilities of Baptist Memorials in San Angelo, Texas. Then, remarkably, after fifty-eight years together, they died within a few hours of each other on 19 August 1992. Their joint funeral was held in the First Baptist Church of Waco, where a host of family and friends gathered to honor their memory with burial in Oakwood Cemetery, Waco.

WRITINGS

Summers regarded writing as an important part of his teaching ministry, and so through various publications he shared his learning with many who never had the privilege of being in his classes. His publications covered many categories: books or monographs, chapters in books with multiple authors, articles (encyclopedia, journal, and curriculum), book reviews, translated works, and sound recordings. The following presentation will be limited to the seven books that he wrote in the order of their publication.[4]

Four of his books were produced during his years on the faculty of Southwestern Baptist Theological Seminary. The first was *Essentials of New Testament Greek* (1950). In this introductory grammar Summers followed a traditional approach, emphasizing Greek forms and their basic functions. By the end of the year the students were working with the Greek text of First John, in preparation for intermediate and advanced courses of extensive reading in the Greek New Testament.

Next Summers published a commentary on the Book of Revelation entitled *Worthy Is the Lamb: An Interpretation of Revelation* (1951). This book was a revision of his Th.D. dissertation submitted in 1943. He had been reared in a climate of dispensational premillennialism and was teaching in a seminary whose founder, B. H. Carroll, had been a postmillennialist. His "historical background approach," however, emphasized the message of the Book of Revelation to its original readers and led him to the position of amillennialism, or nonmillennial adventism. That is, he believed that the Bible teaches the imminence of Christ's triumphant return to the earth, at which time the resurrection, judgment, and determination of the eternal destiny of all people will take place. He denied that Rev. 20:1–10 teaches two resurrections and judgments, each separated by a thousand years of Christ's millennial rule from an earthly throne in Jerusalem, as maintained by premillennial interpreters.[5]

This amillennial approach was presented systematically in *The Life Beyond* (1959), his third book. Here Summers dealt with the biblical teachings about death, the disembodied state, the resurrection, the second coming, judgment, and eternal destiny.

Ephesians: Pattern for Christian Living (1960) was written while he was at Southwestern but was published after he moved to Southern Baptist Theological Seminary. He regarded Ephesians as a circular letter written by Paul during his first imprisonment in Rome (AD 60–62). Its central theme was redemption, and it answered two basic questions: (1) How are we saved? (1:1–3:21); and (2) How ought the saved to live? (4:1–6:24). He wrote, "As an expression of basic Christianity the epistle to the Ephesians stands near the top in any consideration of doctrine and ethics."[6]

His next three books were written during his final years at Baylor. The first was *The Secret Sayings of the Living Jesus: Studies in the Coptic Gospel according to Thomas* (1968). This book grew out of the Day-Higginbotham Lectures delivered at Southwestern Seminary in 1967. It addressed the scholarly interest engendered by the publication of materials discovered in the Nag Hammadi Gnostic Library in Egypt in 1945–1946. Summers translated the 114 *logia* (sayings) in the Coptic Gospel of Thomas and compared them with similar materials in the Synoptic Gospels in an effort to determine validity in both directions. He concluded that the Synoptic writers did not have access to the Coptic Gospel of Thomas; nor did the compiler of the latter have the Synoptics as we have them. Yet he likely had an independent source which the Synoptists did not have.

His last two books were studies of two New Testament Gospels. The first, *Commentary on Luke: Jesus, the Universal Savior* (1972), was a verse-by-verse exposition of the text, emphasizing the universal aspects of Luke's witness to the Christ-event. By his selection and ordering of the gospel materials, he affirmed that what God had accomplished in Christ was for all people. At the beginning when the infant Jesus was presented in the temple, Simeon's song heralded him as "a light of revelation to the Gentiles" (2:32). At the end, between his resurrection and ascension, Jesus commanded that "repentance for forgiveness of sins should be proclaimed in His name to all the nations, beginning from Jerusalem" (24:47).

The last of his seven books was entitled *Behold the Lamb: An Exposition of the Theological Themes in the Gospel of John* (1979). For this book Summers said that he had been gathering materials for thirty years. It did not follow the usual commentary pattern found in his Lukan study. Instead it was "an exposition of the text of the Gospel of John, organized around the theological motifs, themes, figures, and such. So it is a combination, a Biblical theology and an exposition."[7] He regarded the Lamb (of God) as the organizing concept in both the Gospel of John and the Book of Revelation. In the former writing the term occurs only twice, both times in the proclamation of John the Baptist, "Behold, the Lamb of God who takes away the sin of the world!" (1:29; cf. 1:36). In Revelation, however, Jesus is referred to as the Lamb in many passages but none greater than 5:12, "Worthy is the Lamb that was slain to receive power and riches and wisdom and might and honor and glory and blessing." In the Gospel Jesus, the Incarnate Word, is the Paschal Lamb, thus emphasizing his redemptive role. In Revelation, having died, been resurrected, and ascended to the right hand of the throne of God in heaven, Jesus is the enthroned Lamb who has conquered sin and death. He will return to deliver his people in triumph.

THOUGHT

Foundation: A Broad Cultural Base

Those who have read Summers's books and articles, and especially those who have sat in his classes, recognize a broad cultural base as a foundation for his ministry. He had the good fortune of having competent teachers, beginning in the public schools. For example, he attributed an early serious interest in grammar to a good English teacher in grade seven. He memorized great poetry and often quoted it in his messages. He also developed a special interest in foreign languages during his high school years. At Burleson College he received training in Latin and began to read classical literature. Later, while teaching at Southwestern Seminary, he studied French and German in evening courses at Texas Christian University in preparation for sabbatical study in European universities.

Sole Authority of the Bible: The Written Word of God

In his 1979 Founder's Day address at Southwestern Baptist Seminary entitled "Truth Be Thy Mission," Summers emphasized two facets of truth in the divine revelation: (1) Truth and the Incarnate Word: Jesus Christ; and (2) Truth and the Written Word: the Bible. Appealing to John 1:1–18, he magnified Jesus Christ, the Eternal Word who became flesh, as the perfect revelation of God. Moreover, we learn about the Incarnate Word in the Written Word, the Bible, our sole authority in religious faith and conduct.[8]

He noted historically two tendencies in efforts to phrase statements about the authority of the Bible: (1) one regarded such statements as creedal dogma, mandatory for all who held membership in the body; and (2) another regarded them "as consensus statements as good guides which pointed *toward truth* rather than *toward error*, but were not to be regarded as mandatory or creedal."[9] Summers placed Southern Baptists historically in the second category. He cited statements in the preambles of the 1925 and 1963 editions of the Baptist Faith and Message as evidence that Southern Baptists never intended that such confessional formulations were to be regarded or applied as a creed.

Summers took exception to those who based the authority of the Bible on claims of inerrancy and infallibility in the original autographs, for the simple reason that we do not have them. Since we have no means of verification, all claims regarding the original autographs, positive or negative, can never be anything more than a faith assumption or dogma. Thus he concluded:

> So I do have a quarrel with you if you try to make your view creedal, impose it on others as sole truth, and so brand as heretic any who disagree. I will cut out my tongue before I will deny the inspiration, authenticity, integrity, and authority of the Scriptures. And I will cut off my foot before I will march to any man-made creedal drum.[10]

Method of Interpreting the Bible
The Grammatical-Historical Approach

Summers regarded the Bible as the Word of God, the sole authority for religious faith and practice. His doctrine of inspiration emphasized the role of the Holy Spirit in the production, preservation, and interpretation of the biblical texts. But what method of interpreting the Bible will yield the most adequate understanding of the text?

Unequivocally Summers affirmed the grammatical-historical approach. The interpreter should have competence to work with the texts in their original languages. He must probe all avenues of meaning in the texts: the words used, grammatical constructions, syntactical relationships, comparative studies, and literary genre. He must ask questions about the author, his readers, their historical context, and any special needs addressed. This is exegesis, the digging out of the meaning of a passage as the basis for sound exposition.

The opposite of the grammatical-historical approach to the interpretation of the Bible is the dogmatic-theological approach, in which one brings a dogmatic formulation to the Bible and looks for supporting texts. Summers insisted that biblical exegesis must control biblical theology, and not the reverse.

In addition he stated, "A basic principle of interpretation of the Scripture at all places is that the difficult and obscure passage must be interpreted in the light of the clear passages."[11] On the basis of this principle Summers ruled out all premillennial and postmillennial interpretations of Rev. 20:1–10, regarding the passage as unique and highly symbolical. In passages like John 5:28–29 he found evidence more in keeping with the rest of the New Testament for a general resurrection and judgment.

INFLUENCE

Diversity of Ministry

Any consideration of the influence of Summers must take into account the many avenues of his ministry. To be sure, he was primarily a theological educator, who during forty-two years on the faculties of two seminaries and one university touched the lives of thousands of students. He magnified his calling as a teacher. Many students whose doctoral studies he supervised now serve on university and seminary faculties. Going through mission albums, he numbered hundreds of his students serving on home and foreign fields, and he himself accepted many mission assignments. Literally thousands of his students have served on church staffs, in denominational agencies, and in many branches of the chaplaincy.

The scholarly honors bestowed upon him and his memberships in professional societies were numerous. Furthermore, *Festschrift* and *Gedenkschrift* volumes compiled in his honor attest to the esteem in which he was held by former students, colleagues, and international contributors.

But Summers was also a churchman, having served many congregations, large and small, as pastor or interim pastor. He was much in demand on conference platforms and provided a steady stream of articles on a variety of subjects for Baptist publications. He affirmed denominational loyalty at both the national and state levels, fulfilling the seminary ideal of an evangelical scholar who was actively engaged in the ministries of the churches he served. Regarding his theological stance, Summers said, ". . . I think of myself as conservative, but open to the truth."[12]

Impact of Writings

At Southwestern, Summers inherited a strong tradition regarding the importance of studying the Bible in its original languages: Hebrew, Aramaic, and Greek. From the seminary's beginning in 1908 Charles B. Williams, who taught from 1908 to 1919, had established this emphasis. Eventually Williams published a translation of the New Testament under the title: *The New Testament: In the Language of the People.*[13]

Williams was succeeded by H. E. Dana, who taught at Southwestern from 1919 to 1938. Along with Julius R. Mantey he co-authored an intermediate Greek grammar, *A Manual Grammar of the Greek New Testament.*[14] Summers contributed to this inheritance with the publication of an elementary Greek grammar, *Essentials of New Testament Greek*, which was widely used in other institutions.

The rationale for this emphasis is that graduate theological education should equip students to work with the *primary sources* of the Christian faith. Indeed this is an important feature of the legacy of Southwestern, which has found continuing expression in the grammatical publications of more recent colleagues: Huber L. Drumwright, Jr., Curtis Vaughan and Virtus E. Gideon, James A. Brooks (jointly with Carlton Winberry of Louisiana College), Lorin L. Cranford, and G. Lacoste Munn and R. Bruce Corley.

An even more dramatic impact was made by Summers in his two books on eschatological issues: *Worthy Is the Lamb* and *The Life Beyond*. Both were translated into foreign languages and enjoyed wide distribution. He wrote them at a time when and in an area where dispensational premillenialism was the dominant view regarding the prophetic writings of the Old and New Testaments. Both Dallas Theological Seminary in the tradition of C. I. Scofield and Lewis Sperry Chafer and Bible Baptist Seminary of Fort Worth under the leadership of J. Frank Norris were strong centers of dispensationalism.

It came as a surprise to many who were uninformed or had been misinformed that anyone outside dispensationalism actually believed in the second coming of Jesus Christ. Such were regarded as "Modernists who don't believe the Bible"! Yet in his publications Summers stated his firm belief in the personal, triumphant return of Jesus Christ to the earth. Furthermore, unlike other approaches, premillennial or postmillennial, he believed in the *imminence of the Lord's return* in the sense that it could happen today. Dispensationalism believes in the imminence of the rapture of the church but not in the imminence of the visible return of Christ to the earth, which is to follow the rapture by seven years. Even historical premillennialism rejects "any-moment expectancy" and prefers the terms "impending" to "imminent." It may happen in our generation, but it could not happen today. Obviously postmillennialism has no doctrine of imminence, because the Lord does not return to the earth until after the millennium. Today alternative eschatological systems find it more necessary to deal with the issues raised by Summers and other amillennialists.

Christian Example
Claiming the privilege of a personal tribute to his beloved mentor and friend, this writer testifies that the Lord used Summers's invitation to teach New Testament in Southwestern Baptist Seminary to change the direction of his ministry from the pastorate to theological education. From May 1948 until his resignation from Southwestern's faculty in 1959, I served under his able leadership and guidance. But nothing that he taught in the classroom exceeded what he taught by his daily example.

Unfortunately the Lord's servants often suffer their greatest hurts at the hands of those from whom they have every right to expect their greatest understanding and encouragement. It was not otherwise for Ray Summers. The same internal strife that led E. D. Head to resign as president of Southwestern Seminary in 1953 also led Summers to resign as the first director of the School of Theology. He did not leave Southwestern for service elsewhere until 1959. During the intervening years I often marveled at the great personal dignity and faith that he revealed in rising above an unpleasant, even embarrassing, situation. He cooperated fully with his successor as director (later dean), and continued to serve as chairman of the Department of New Testament with his usual excellence. Had he departed, some who were majoring in New Testament would have been left without a supervisor in doctoral studies.

Since no servant of the Lord ever manages to fulfill his calling apart from some painful experiences, the example of leaders who are thoroughly Christian in their response to hurt fulfills a large need. Ray Summers exemplified this fundamental Christian ideal better than anyone I have ever known.

BIBLIOGRAPHY

1. Primary

BOOKS

Behold the Lamb: An Exposition of the Theological Themes in the Gospel of John. Nashville: Broadman, 1979.

Commentary on Luke: Jesus, the Universal Savior. Waco, Tex.: Word, 1972.

Ephesians: Pattern for Christian Living. Nashville: Broadman, 1960.

Essentials of New Testament Greek. Nashville: Broadman, 1950. Rev. and ed. Thomas Sawyer. Nashville: Broadman and Holman, 1995.

    Essentials of New Testament Greek. Braille edition. 5 vols. Transcribed by Harry E. Baldwin, Jr. Midland Park, N.J.: National Braille Association, 1973.

    Gli elementi essenziali del Greco del Nuovo Testamento. Trans. Robert D. Shackelford. Florence: Florence Bible School, 1969. [Italian]

The Life Beyond. Nashville: Broadman, 1959.

    al Hayat Warā'al Qabr. Trans. Virginia Cobb. Beirut: Baptist Publications, 1966. [Arabic]

    Kehidupan di balik kubur. Trans. Jachin Karuniadi. Semarang: Seminari Theologia Baptist Indonesia, 1969. [Indonesian]

    Lai Sheng Lun. Trans. Wayne Wei-Yuan Siao. Hong Kong: Baptist Press, 1966. [Chinese]

    A Vida no Além. Trans. A. Ben Oliver. Rio de Janeiro: Casa Publicadora Batista, 1971. [Portuguese]

The Secret Sayings of the Living Jesus: Studies in the Coptic Gospel according to Thomas. Waco, Tex.: Word, 1968.

Worthy Is the Lamb: An Interpretation of Revelation. Nashville: Broadman, 1951.

    Digno é o Cordeiro: Uma Interpretação do Apocalipsis. Trans. Waldemar W. Wey. Rio de Janeiro: Casa Publicadora Batista, 1957; 2d ed., 1972. [Portuguese]

    Digno es el Cordero: Una Interpretación del Apocalipis. Trans. Alfredo Lerin. El Paso: Casa Bautista de Publicaciones, 1954; 2d ed., 1966. [Spanish]

    Mustahiqqun huwa al-Kharūf. Trans. Virginia Cobb. Beirut: Baptist Publications, 1963. [Arabic]

CONTRIBUTIONS TO BOOKS

"Born of Water and Spirit." In *The Teacher's Yoke: Studies in Memory of Henry Trantham*, ed. E. Jerry Vardaman and James Leo Garrett, Jr., 117–28. Waco, Tex.: Baylor University Press, 1964.

"Christian Stewardship in the Light of Redemption." In *Resources Unlimited*, ed. William L. Hendricks, 21–36. Nashville: Stewardship Commission of the Southern Baptist Convention, 1972.

"Contemporary Approaches in New Testament Study." In *The Broadman Bible Commentary*, ed. Clifton J. Allen, vol. 8, *General Articles; Matthew-Mark*, 48–58. Nashville: Broadman, 1969.

"God's Will for You." In *Southwestern Sermons*, ed. H. C. Brown, Jr., 189–95. Nashville: Broadman, 1960.

"Jude." In *The Broadman Bible Commentary*, ed. Clifton J. Allen, vol. 12, *Hebrews-Revelation; General Articles*, 232–39. Nashville: Broadman, 1972.

"1 Peter." In *The Broadman Bible Commentary*, ed. Clifton J. Allen, vol. 12, *Hebrews-Revelation; General Articles*, 141–71. Nashville: Broadman, 1972.

"2 Peter." In *The Broadman Bible Commentary*, ed. Clifton J. Allen, vol. 12, *Hebrews-Revelation; General Articles*, 172–87. Nashville: Broadman, 1972.

"The Revelation of John." In *The New Testament from 26 Translations*, ed. Curtis Vaughan, 1196–1237. Grand Rapids: Zondervan, 1967.

JOURNAL ARTICLES

"The Christ of John's Gospel." *Southwestern Journal of Theology* n.s. 8 (October 1965): 35–43.

"The Death and Resurrection of Jesus, John 18–21." *Review and Expositor* 62 (October 1965): 473–81.

"An Exegetical Approach to the Eschatology of Mark." *Southwestern Journal of Theology* n.s. 1 (October 1958): 42–51.

"First Corinthians: An Exposition." *Review and Expositor* 57 (October 1960): 398–421.

"The Johannine View of the Future Life." *Review and Expositor* 58 (July 1961): 331–47.

"Matthew 24–25: An Exposition." *Review and Expositor* 59 (October 1962): 380–87.

"One Message—Redemption." *Review and Expositor* 60 (Fall 1963): 380–87.

"The Plan of Matthew." *Southwestern Journal of Theology* n.s. 5 (October 1962): 7–16.

"Revelation 20: An Exposition." *Review and Expositor* 57 (April 1960): 176–83.

"Setting the Parables Free." *Southwestern Journal of Theology* 10 (Spring 1968): 7–18.

"Teaching Outline of Ephesians." *Review and Expositor* 60 (Fall 1963): 372.

ENCYCLOPEDIA ARTICLES

Encyclopedia of Southern Baptists. 4 vols. Nashville: Broadman, 1958–62. Vol. 1. S.v. "Jesus Christ: Virgin Birth," "Jesus Christ: Baptism," "Jesus Christ: Temptation," "Jesus Christ: Transfiguration," and "Jesus Christ: Resurrection."

ORAL MEMOIRS

Oral Memoirs of Ray Summers (11 August 1980–29 August 1980). Interviewer, Daniel B. McGee. 2 vols. Texas Baptist Oral History Project. Waco, Tex.: Baylor University Institute for Oral History, 1984.

2. Secondary

Garrett, James Leo, Jr. "The Writings of Ray Summers." In *Chronos, Kairos, Christos II: Chronological, Nativity, and Religious Studies in Memory of Ray Summers*, ed. E. Jerry Vardaman, 21–42. Macon, Ga.: Mercer University Press, 1998.

Hilburn, Glenn O., comp. "Publications by Ray Summers." In *New Testament Studies: Essays in Honor of Ray Summers in His Sixty-Fifth Year*, ed. Huber L. Drumwright, Jr., and Curtis Vaughan, 177–95. Waco, Tex.: Markham Press Fund of Baylor University Press, 1975.

_____, comp. "Published and Unpublished Works by Ray Summers." In *Chronos, Kairos, Christos II: Chronological, Nativity, and Religious Studies in Memory of Ray Summers*, ed. E. Jerry Vardaman, 43–58. Macon, Ga.: Mercer University Press, 1998.

Robert Andrew Baker

(1910–1992)
Church History

Stephen M. Stookey

Forty-one years of teaching at a single institution; courted by seminaries, colleges, and pulpit committees of prominent Baptist churches; guest lecturer in the United States; active participant in professional societies and denominational consultations; popular interim and supply preacher in Texas Baptist churches; and author or coauthor of fourteen books and contributor to texts, journals, and newspapers—Robert Andrew Baker was widely recognized as the dean of Southern Baptist historians during the third quarter of the twentieth century. Preaching, teaching, research, writing, and denominational service were all directed toward one specific arena in Robert Baker's ministry—teaching.

BIOGRAPHY

Born in St. Louis, Missouri, 22 December 1910, the second of three boys born to William Baker and Grace Hartman,[1] and reared in Kansas City, Kansas, Baker as a youth knew the reality of sacrifice. Robert Baker was two years old when his father died.[2] Bob, as he was known to family and friends, admired his mother, a woman of dignity and culture. Following William Baker's death, Grace Hartman Baker moved her family to Kansas City. The Baker children all pitched in to help the family make ends meet; Bob delivered newspapers and worked at the YMCA. Family financial needs necessitated that Baker drop out of high school after his junior year. He returned to finish high school a year later at the insistence of his mother. After graduating from high school in 1929, Baker entered secretarial school to learn court reporting and shorthand, skills later put to use as a historian.[3]

The Baker children attended Immanuel Baptist Church,[4] while their mother remained a lifelong Methodist. Bob was actively involved at Immanuel, particularly in BYPU activities. Immanuel was affiliated with the Northern Baptist Convention, and Baker admitted to having no knowledge of the Southern Baptist Convention's existence until he was eighteen or nineteen.[5] Upon his profession of faith and baptism at age twelve, Baker felt a call to Christian ministry. Family financial needs delayed plans to enter the ministry.[6]

Baker's career before entering the ministry demonstrates a commitment to excellence. In June 1932, Baker accepted an office position with the Treasury Department's Secret Service division. The appointment doubled his salary as a legal secretary, but it required a move to Oklahoma City. Baker had not abandoned his call to ministry, but the fiscal needs of his mother and siblings took priority. Shortages in the Oklahoma City office took Baker from his desk to unofficial work as a field operative. Baker's innate skills to investigate and close cases with convictions led to an unexpected and unprecedented promotion to operative.[7] Baker excelled in the Secret Service, gaining experience in counterfeiting schemes, a task which required a keen eye for minute details—a skill Baker evidenced in his historical research.[8]

Baker was actively involved at First Baptist Church, Oklahoma City, and his potential skills as a minister were noticed, nurtured, and encouraged by pastors Thomas Luther Holcomb and William Richardson White.[9] White urged Baker to lay aside all distractions and dedicate all his energies to ministerial preparation. Baker had been taking night classes at the University of Oklahoma. With his siblings now able to care for his mother's needs, Baker resigned from the Secret Service in December 1936 to prepare for vocational ministry. At the urging of White, Baker enrolled in Baylor University.[10]

Maturity and urgency of calling compelled Baker to waste no time at Baylor. He was a committed student, excelling in the classroom. The former undercover agent carried trays at Luby's Cafeteria to earn his meals. He gained practical ministry experience as assistant pastor/music director at Bell Mead Baptist Church.[11] Fred A. McCaulley, pastor of Bell Mead, mentored the former Secret Service agent turned ministerial student. Baker completed his B.A. degree in 1939. The third of June 1939 was a busy day for Baker; graduation in the morning was followed by matrimony in the afternoon to Fredona McCaulley, the oldest daughter of Pastor McCaulley.[12]

Resigning from Bell Mead shortly after graduation, Baker and his bride moved to Fort Worth so that he could attend Southwestern Baptist Theological Seminary. Baker's intellectual abilities caught the attention of W. T. Conner and W. W. Barnes, the godfathers of faculty selection. Serving as pastor to two half-time churches as a student, Baker entered his second year at Southwestern with the added responsibility of teaching night classes for African-American students.[13]

As graduation approached in 1941, Baker wrestled with his future in ministry—the pulpit or the classroom. First Baptist Church, Hillsboro, Texas, offered Baker far more salary to serve as its pastor than Southwestern could offer Baker to continue teaching adjunctively while pursuing a Th.D. degree. Conner and Barnes, each looking for an heir, extolled the virtues of a ministry in theological education. Further encouraged by new faculty member Stewart A. Newman, Baker entered Southwestern's Th.D. program.[14]

When Baker accepted a faculty position at Southwestern in 1943, he did not relinquish pulpit ministry. He served as pastor of Highland Baptist Church, Dallas, from 1946 to 1952—a church with a resident membership between twenty-five hundred and three thousand and a regular Sunday School attendance of between seven hundred and eight hundred. Interim pastorates and supply preaching marked the remainder of Baker's ministry from Southwestern.[15]

Baker could have joined any department in the School of Theology. His early course offerings included Greek, church history, and missions.[16] Baker's full teaching attention soon turned to church history.[17] Why church history? First, Baker enjoyed the factual aspect of history. Second, Baker saw history as a discipline of wide perspective, helping one better to understand life in the present. Third, Baker admired W. W. Barnes. Impressed by the refined Barnes, Baker hoped that the study of church history would help him to become a Christian gentleman and scholar like Barnes. Barnes and Baker developed a father-son relationship. Baker learned all he could from Barnes, revering the respected historian's grasp of the details of history as well as the breadth of context.

Completing his Th.D. in 1944, Baker had the unexpected opportunity to pursue a Ph.D. at Yale University during 1945–46. Baker thrived at Yale, studying "church history with [Kenneth Scott] Latourette, European history with Roland Bainton, American Christianity with Luther Weigel, and history of doctrine with Robert Calhoun."[18] Latourette had great influence on Baker, impressing him with his grasp of bibliographic resources and broad understanding of historical context. After only one year of course work, Baker passed his doctoral exams with honors. Baker's Yale dissertation, completed in 1947, is a remarkable example of thorough primary and secondary source research. Employing investigative skills honed in the Secret Service, Baker analyzed in detail the American Baptist Home Mission Society's financial records and field reports so as to disprove the South's contention that during the 1840s there had been disproportionate low returns in services rendered for contributions to the "northern society." He demonstrated that the South actually received more than its fair share in missionaries and services. Written while Northern Baptist-Southern Baptist relationships were strained, the even-handed treatment of the issues present in the research became a trademark of Baker's career as an interpreter of Baptist life.[19]

During his tenure at Southwestern, Baker emerged as a respected leader on campus and within Southern Baptist life. In 1952 Baker assumed responsibility for Southwestern's Th.D. (later Ph.D.) program, and for the next twenty-nine years he guided its development. He was an active participant in the work of the SBC Historical Commission and the Texas Baptist Historical Society.[20] A severe heart attack in 1972 curtailed Baker's activities beyond Southwestern, but it did not significantly impair his research or teaching. Baker retired from the faculty of Southwestern in 1981 but continued his research and writing. Death claimed Robert A. Baker on 15 November 1992, and he was buried in Laurel Land Cemetery, Fort Worth. He was survived by his wife, Fredona, daughter Colleen Kay, and son Robert A., Jr.

CLASSROOM

Why is Robert Baker revered by his former students? The answer lies in his abilities as professor, pastor, author, and interpreter of Baptist life. In all of these areas he was a teacher, instilling in his audience a passion for the past and its impact on the present.

Baker was not an electrifying lecturer; he could easily be described as the Joe Friday of church history— "Just the facts, ma'am." His lectures focused on the facts, the stuff of history. He systematically worked through the assigned texts, supporting the day's topic with readings from primary sources—figures from the past summoned to provide eyewitness testimony. His application of history to contemporary life and ministry were subtle, allowing the drama of history to accomplish the task.

Baker's classes were not devoid of humor; Baker's dry, subtle wit found its way into the classroom. He bantered with his "back row boys" and blew the dust off resource documents onto the students seated in the front row. He employed self-deprecating humor, telling classes, "I can repeat the definition of Chalcedon, but still I don't understand what it means." The statement was then followed by a detailed and insightful exegesis of the council's decision. There was no question among students that Baker knew well his discipline.[21]

Baker was not an easy professor. He expected his students to be students. He often wrote ancient creeds on the blackboard in Latin and/or Greek, with no apologies to the undereducated.[22] Exams were essay and tested the students' grasp of historical facts. He expected much of his students, and they delivered.

Remembered as a caring professor, Baker was not one to share personal stories in class. His life experiences were certainly present in his lectures but in very subtle ways, woven into the fabric of the class and separated from personal identification, so as not to draw attention to self. He modeled ministerial and academic excellence, and the students took note. Without hype or flash, Baker used the facts of history to help students to interpret the past, understand the present, and prepare for the future. Baker treated all people—past and present—with fairness; he avoided labeling people or groups and refused to judge another's experience with Christ. Primary sources read to the class allowed the players in the historical drama to defend and/or incriminate themselves. These encounters with "history friends"—worthy men and women of the past—were meant to inspire students toward faithful ministry, emboldened by "the historical evidence of the living Lord marching through the pages of Christian history."[23]

The lessons of history, however, were not privileged information for seminarians. Baker appealed to a wider audience through the written word. Baker's classroom emphasis on a clear presentation of the facts of history provided the backbone for his literary pursuits.

WRITINGS

Robert Baker's writings—for the guild and the laity—reveal a deep reliance on primary sources and a thorough knowledge of secondary sources. He reflected the best of his mentors, Latourette and Barnes; both men possessed broad historical vision and wrote and taught from the excess of extensive research and an intimate knowledge of source material. Baker approached historical inquiry like an investigation, combing the mass of primary documents, collecting testimony from the players, and scrutinizing the minutiae of history for the critical matter for accurate historical understanding. Accurate historical interpretation could not be built on circumstantial evidence.

Baker's first two publications, *J. B. Tidwell Plus God* (1946) and *Relations between Northern and Southern Baptists* (1948), set the pattern for the remainder of his writing career. Biography became a staple of Baker's approach to history, both in the classroom and in texts. Baker's biography of Baylor's popular professor evidences an eye for detail and an ability to connect the reader with the personality. Biographic vignettes pepper Baker's texts, bringing a personal dimension to historical events. Detailed research, thoughtful analysis, and well-developed conclusions mark *Relations between Northern and Southern Baptists*.[24]

A decade passed before the issuance of Baker's next book, but the interim was filled with Sunday School lessons and articles in journals and newspapers.[25] A pair of texts closed out the 1950s: *The Baptist March in History* (1958) and *A Summary of Christian History* (1959). Designed for the laity, *The Baptist March in History* acquainted lay readers with the place of Baptists in the flow of church history. Well received by lay readers, this text has been translated into Spanish, Arabic, and Korean. Classroom need led to the production of *A Summary of Christian History*. Intended to be a "temporary make-shift until a suitable text could be located," *A Summary of Christian History*, became the text for a generation of seminarians and college students. In 1994 it was revised and updated for a new generation of students.[26]

The 1960s brought a rapid succession of books and articles. *Survey of Christian History* (1964) and *The First Southern Baptists* (1966) continued Baker's efforts to make history accessible to lay people. Baker's detailed research in Kittery, Maine, documented the residency of William Screven, Sr., from 1682 to 1696. Previous scholars had relied on speculation and circumstantial evidence to locate Screven; such evidence would not suffice for Baker.[27]

A Baptist Source Book, with Particular Reference to Southern Baptists (1966) allowed students access to 241 primary source documents with brief introductions highlighting context and relevance. The content bears witness to Baker's emphasis on primary sources as the building blocks for accurate historical understanding. Baker closed the 1960s with two institutional histories: *The Story of the Sunday School Board* (1966) and *The Thirteenth Check: the Jubilee History of the Annuity Board of the Southern Baptist Convention, 1918–68* (1968). Alongside the five books published during the 1960s, Baker found time to publish articles and contribute chapters to texts.

Baker continued his prolific schedule of research and writing during the 1970s in spite of a severe heart attack in 1972. *The Blossoming Desert* (1970) regaled Texas Baptists with their efforts to fulfill Z. N. Morrell's dream of a blossoming Baptist witness in the Lone Star state. Written to fill a need for a text, *The Southern Baptist Convention and Its People, 1606–1972* (1974) is hailed as Baker's "greatest contribution to his denomination." Baker transcended Barnes's earlier history of the SBC,[28] which had focused on the broad sweep of Southern Baptist experience. Baker told the story of the SBC by emphasizing the stories of its constituencies, specifically state conventions. The text contains an impressive array of statistical data for each state. While extremely useful, the abundance of statistical analysis obscures Baker's traditional style of writing, thus creating a dry account of Southern Baptist history. Baker readily acknowledged the perceived shortcomings of the text created by editorial limits, the bane of Baker's writings projects.

> I almost went mad trying to chop out—I cut out the fat, to start with, and then I cut out the lean, and then I cut out some of the bones, and the thing that's left is barely a skeleton. And it's been gnawed on quite a bit. It's almost dry bones now.[29]

Baker would have much preferred the luxury of Latourette's multi-volume style.

Baptist History and Heritage, Quarterly Review, and *Southwestern Journal of Theology* were the recipients of the overflow of Baker's research and cut material from *The Southern Baptist Convention and Its People, 1606–1972*. Typical of Baker's articles in the 1970s was a series of six articles in *Quarterly Review* which introduced readers to six "Big Little-Known Baptists."[30] Baptist virtues, both in distinctive beliefs and practical ministry, were highlighted in these and similar vignettes.

Baker penned two local church histories, *Her Walls before Thee Stand* (1977), the centennial history of First Baptist Church, Texarkana, and the coauthored *Adventure in Faith: The First 300 Years of First Baptist Church, Charleston, South Carolina,* (1982). Both works exhibit Baker's reliance on detailed research and engaging prose.

Retirement from Southwestern in 1981 did not bring an end to Baker's literary pursuits. In 1983 Baker published *Tell the Generations Following: A History of Southwestern Baptist Theological Seminary, 1908–1983*. Baker previewed Southwestern's history in the months preceding publication with a series of vignettes in *Southwestern News*.

COMMENTARY

Reared by a Methodist mother, nurtured in a Northern Baptist church, educated at Baylor University, Southwestern Seminary, and Yale University, Robert Baker was not a provincial Southern Baptist. Baker's lectures, sermons, and writings display an intimate knowledge of the breadth and depth of Baptist life. His unfolding of the past helped students in the classroom, people in the pew, and interested readers to understand the essentials of

Baptist life. Key Baptist distinctives—authority of the Bible, local church autonomy, priesthood of all believers, missions/evangelism, and religious liberty—were modeled and taught by Baker in the classroom and through his writings.

Causation was Baker's primary concern as a historian.[31] A keen intellect, an eye for detail, and a broad understanding allowed Baker to demonstrate how the present came to be—true to the facts of history. Baker's emphasis on primary source research allowed those in the present to "dialogue with the ancients" and gain insight into present conditions.[32] Baker refused to play the role of prophet, focusing on history's practical application in the present.[33]

Baker's eye for detail, evidenced in his Yale dissertation, defined Baker as a historian. Baker's statistical data in *The Southern Baptist Convention and Its People, 1606–1972* is a valuable resource to the serious student of Baptist history.[34] Footnotes and bibliography in Baker's writings are an invaluable guide to resource material. Baker was the beneficiary of W. W. Barnes's research, receiving Barnes's library and research notes. Baker's ability to speed-read and his court reporting skills allowed him to work through vast quantities of material with detailed notes. Baker's research files multiplied and outstripped the research of Barnes. Baker believed that the research files of the Barnes-Baker collection would easily fill fifteen to twenty volumes. Baker's files evidence that he left no stone unturned.[35]

Baker refused to treat history as a sensationalist tell-all memoir. Baker's Christian character would not allow him to label, libel, or lampoon another person. Baker did not tell everything found in his research. Extremely controversial episodes in denominational or institutional life were given summary, professional treatment; the essentials and not the excess were conveyed.[36] Baker's reluctance to tell all raises important questions about the role of a historian. Is a historian obligated to tell everything found in the course of research? Or is it the historian's responsibility to tell only that which conveys the essence of the story? Baker employed editorial restraint, especially when key participants in controversies were still alive or when the unflattering details distracted from the essentials of historical inquiry. Jesse Fletcher observed, "[Baker] will say everything

117

vital to a point and write all the background needed to draw a conclusion, but he disdains anything more than is required for either."[37]

Baker sought to make history relevant and practical.[38] Baker frequently utilized biography to accomplish these goals. Baker's first book, *J. B. Tidwell Plus God*, established Baker's emphasis on biography as a window to the past. Virtues of self-sacrifice, humility, devotion, Christian character, and Baptist identity were common themes in Baker's biographic studies. For example, Baker's biographic vignettes in the *Southwestern News* (1982–1984) reminded the Southwestern family of the institution's commitment to academic excellence and effective ministry. Baker did not have to force application on the reader; the witness of the lives highlighted provided the application.

When asked about the process of identifying writing projects, Baker replied, "I either wrote to fill teaching needs or in response to a request."[39] Through Baker's literary pursuits a generation of Baptists became intimately acquainted with those individuals and organizations who nurtured and preserved the Baptist witness. Baker's students, infected with his passion for church history and academic excellence, interpreted Christian history and the Baptist experience from pulpits, on mission fields, at denominational agencies, and in the classrooms of seminaries and colleges.[40] The Baptist histories produced by H. Leon McBeth and Jesse Fletcher evidence Baker's emphasis on causation as explained through detailed primary source research.[41] William R. Estep and Leon McBeth continued Baker's tradition of excellence in historical research, writing and teaching at Southwestern and in turn passing on the Barnes-Baker tradition to a new generation of students.

Baker valued diversity in Southern Baptist life, reminding audiences: "There are no first lieutenants among Baptists; they are all generals."[42] He emphasized cooperation over independency, diversity over creedalism, and love over antagonism. These lessons, subtly woven throughout Baker's writings, sermons, and lectures, achieved a forceful emphasis in Baker's final years. In his 1985 Hobbs Lecture at Oklahoma Baptist University, "Divided We Stand," Baker succinctly analyzed the divisions present within the SBC, demonstrated with clarity and precision the emergence of creedalism in Southern Baptist life, provided insight into the present, and suggested a remedy for the future.[43] He berated no person or group; he stood as a objective observer, allowing the facts of history to speak. Baker concluded that Southern Baptists were not moving toward creedalism; they had long since arrived.

Jesse Fletcher correctly concluded his biographical survey of Robert Baker's life with the observation that "[t]he spectacular is not his thing; accuracy is."[44] In final analysis, however, be it in the classroom, behind the pulpit, or through the written word, Baker's accuracy as a historian had a spectacular impact.

BIBLIOGRAPHY

1. Primary

DISSERTATIONS

"The American Baptist Home Mission Society and the South, 1832–1894." Ph.D. diss., Yale University, 1947.

"An Introduction to the Study of the Development of Ecclesiology." Th.D. diss., Southwestern Baptist Theological Seminary, 1943.

BOOKS

(coauth.) *Adventure in Faith: The First 300 Years of First Baptist Church, Charleston, South Carolina.* Nashville: Broadman, 1982.

The Baptist March in History. Nashville: Convention Press, 1958.

    Los Bautistas en la Historia. Trans. and adapt. R. Cecil Moore. El Paso: Casa Bautista de Publicaciones, 1965. [Spanish]

    Chimryegyo Baljunsa. Trans. Keen Huh. Seoul: Baptist Publications, n.d. [Korean]

    Sayru al-Ma'madāniyīn fi al-Tārikh. [Beirut]: al-Manshūrāt al-Ma'madaniyat, 1961. [Arabic]

A Baptist Source Book, with Particular Reference to Southern Baptists. Nashville: Broadman, 1966.

The Blossoming Desert: A Concise History of Texas Baptists. Waco, Tex.: Word, 1970.

The First Southern Baptists. Nashville: Broadman, 1966.

Her Walls before Thee Stand: Centennial Story, First Baptist Church, Texarkana, Texas. [Texarkana, Tex.]: n.p., [1977].

J. B. Tidwell plus God. Nashville: Broadman, 1946.

(coauth.) *Pulling Together!* Nashville: Broadman, 1987.

Relations between Northern and Southern Baptists. Fort Worth: pvt. ptg., 1948. 2d ed., ibid., 1954.

The Southern Baptist Convention and Its People, 1607–1972. Nashville: Broadman, 1974.

The Story of the Sunday School Board. Nashville: Convention Press, 1966.

A Summary of Christian History. Nashville: Broadman, 1959. Rev. ed. by John M. Landers. Nashville: Broadman and Holman, 1994.

    Compendio de Historia Cristiana. Trans. Francisco Almanza G. El Paso: Casa Bautista de Publicaciones, 1974. [Spanish]

    Ji Du Jiao Shi Lue. Trans. Wayne Wei-yuan Siao. Hong Kong: Baptist Press, 1961. [Chinese]

Tell the Generations Following: A History of Southwestern Baptist Theological Seminary, 1908–1983. Nashville: Broadman, 1983.

The Thirteenth Check: The Jubilee History of the Annuity Board of the Southern Baptist Convention, 1918–68. Nashville: Broadman, 1968.

CHAPTERS CONTRIBUTED TO BOOKS

"Baptist Sacramentalism." In *Chapel Messages*, ed. H. C. Brown, Jr. and Charles P. Johnson, 23–28. Grand Rapids: Baker, 1966.

"Baptists and Religious Liberty in the Revolutionary Era." In *The Lord's Free People in a Free Land: Essays in Baptist History in Honor of Robert A. Baker*, ed. William R. Estep, 75–85. Fort Worth: School of Theology, Southwestern Baptist Theological Seminary, 1976.

"Divided We Stand." In *The Fibers of Our Faith*, ed. Dick Allen Rader, 146–58. Franklin, Tenn.: Providence House, 1995.

"The Nature of Sin." In *Southwestern Sermons*, ed. H. C. Brown, Jr., 7–13. Nashville: Broadman, 1960.

"The Seminary President." In *J. Howard Williams: Prophet of God and Friend of Man*, ed. H. C. Brown, Jr., and Charles P. Johnson, 85–99. San Antonio: Naylor, 1963.

"A Significant Development in Baptist Ecclesiology." In *The Teacher's Yoke; Studies in Memory of Henry Trantham*, ed. E. Jerry Vardaman and James Leo Garrett, Jr., 274–86. Waco, Tex.: Baylor University, 1964.

"Southern Baptist Convention: Historical Summary," and "Southwestern Baptist Theological Seminary." In *Baptist Advance: The Achievements of the Baptists of North America for a Century and a Half*, ed. Davis Collier Woolley, 261–72, 350–52. Nashville: Broadman, 1964.

JOURNAL ARTICLES

"Baptists and the American Revolution." *Baptist History and Heritage* 11 (July 1976): 149–59.

"Baptist Heritage—Religious Liberty." *Quarterly Review* 23 (April–May–June 1963): 5–10.

"Big Little-Known Southern Baptists: Adiel Sherwood." *Quarterly Review* 37 (January–February–March 1977): 17–22.

"Big Little-Known Southern Baptists: Ann Graves." *Quarterly Review* 37 (April–May–June 1977): 20–24.

"Big Little-Known Southern Baptists: John G. Landrum." *Quarterly Review* 38 (January–February–March 1978): 20–25.

"Big Little-Known Southern Baptists: Joseph Cole Stalcup." *Quarterly Review* 38 (April–May–June 1978): 18–23.

"Big Little-Known Southern Baptists: Lewis Lunsford." *Quarterly Review* 37 (October–November–December 1976): 18–22.

"Big Little-Known Southern Baptists: Zacharius N. Morrell." *Quarterly Review* 38 (October–November–December 1977): 20–25.

"The Contributions of South Carolina Baptists to the Rise and Development of the Southern Baptist Convention." *Baptist History and Heritage* 17 (July 1982): 2–9, 19.

"The Cooperative Program in Historical Perspective." *Baptist History and Heritage* 10 (July 1975): 169–76.

"Factors Encouraging the Rise of Landmarkism." *Baptist History and Heritage* 10 (January 1975): 1,2,18.

"The First Year on the Hill." *Southwestern Journal of Theology* n.s. 8 (October 1965): 89–101.

"The Forgiveness of Sin." *Review and Expositor* 41 (July 1944): 224–35.

"The Independence of Baptist Churches." *Review and Expositor* 53 (October 1956): 525–35.

"The Magnificent Years (1917–1931)." *Baptist History and Heritage* 8 (July 1973): 144–57, 167.

"Norman W. Cox: Good and Faithful Servant." *Baptist History and Heritage* 4 (January 1969): 3–7.

"The North Rocky Mount Baptist Church Decision." *Review and Expositor* 52 (January 1955): 55–62.

"Organization of the Southern Baptist Convention, 1845." *Quarterly Review* 15 (April–May–June 1955): 30–35.

"Organizational Difference between Northern and Southern Baptists in the Nineteenth Century." *The Chronicle* 15 (April 1952): 68–75.

"The Presidency and the Roman Catholic Church." *Journal of Church and State* 2 (November 1960): 112–16.

"Profile of a Baptist Historian [Morgan Edwards]." *Baptist History and Heritage* 1 (August 1965): 5–7, 26.

"Recollections of B. A. Copass." *Southwestern Journal of Theology* 11 (Fall 1968): 104–10.

"Reflections on the Southern Baptist Convention."?*Southwestern Journal of Theology* n.s. 6 (April 1964): 15–25.

"Reflections on *The Southern Baptist Convention and Its People, 1609–1972*." *Baptist History and Heritage* 9 (October 1974): 223–29, 236.

"The Retirement of President Robert E. Naylor." *Southwestern Journal of Theology* 20 (Spring 1978): 6–14.

"Southern Baptist Beginnings." *Quarterly Review* 44 (April–May–June 1984): 70–76. A slight elongation of the article by the same title in *The [Baptist] Student*.

"The Southern Baptist Convention, 1845–1970." *Review and Expositor* 67 (Spring 1970): 125–39.

"The Story of the Southern Baptist Foundation." *Baptist History and Heritage* 21 (January 1986): 40–47.

"William Hillary McIntosh: Home Mission Board Secretary." *Baptist History and Heritage* 23 (January 1988): 4–12.

"William W. Barnes and Southwestern Baptist Theological Seminary." *Southwestern Journal of Theology* 18 (Fall 1975): 72–81.

"William Wright Barnes." *Baptist History and Heritage* 5 (July 1970): 144–46.

ENCYCLOPEDIA ARTICLES

Encyclopedia of Southern Baptists. 4 vols. Nashville: Broadman, 1958–82. Vol. 1. S.v. "Baptist Movements, Recent Minor." Vol. 2. S.v. "Lord's Supper, Requisites to," "Premillennial Baptist Groups," "Relations between Northern and Southern Baptists," "Society, The Baptist," "Southwestern Journal of Theology, The," and "Williams, Charles Bray." Vol. 3. S.v. "Barnes, William Wright," "Texas, Baptist General Convention of," and "Tidwell, Josiah Blake."

MISCELLANEOUS ARTICLES

"A. H. Newman Qualified as World-Class Scholar." *Southwestern News*, May 1984, 2.

"Baptists and the Trail of Buffalo," *Baptist Record*, 10 November 1955, 16.

"Barnes' Knowledge Impressed Students, Colleagues." *Southwestern News*, October 1983, 2.

"Conner's Mind Greatest Asset." *Southwestern News*, May 1983, 3.

"Copass Looked like Isaiah." *Southwestern News*, December 1983, 4–5.

"Danger Ahead!" *Baptist Standard*, 11 July 1962, 6–7.

"Dilday, like Timothy, Nurtured in Christian Household of Faith." *Southwestern News*, July 1983, 8.

"H. E. Dana Showed 'Historical Imagination' in Teaching." *Southwestern News*, February 1984, 2.

"I. E. Reynolds Exemplifies Spirit." *Southwestern News*, June 1983, 5.

"J. W. Crowder Earns Bible Degree, Respect." *Southwestern News*, January 1984, 2.

"Jeff Ray, Carroll, Close Friends." *Southwestern News*, February 1983, 5.

"Jeff Ray Remembers First Seeing Carroll." *Southwestern News*, September 1982, 5.

"King Remembered as Seminary's Olympic Hero." *Southwestern News*, March 1984, 2.

"L. R. Elliott Transformed Seminary Library into Full-fledged Academic Support System." *Southwestern News*, October 1982, 9.

"McKinney Left Music Legacy of 263 Hymns." *Southwestern News*, April 1984, 2.

"Naylor Directed Southwestern through Large Growth Period." *Southwestern News*, March 1983, 4.

"President E. D. Head a Technical Scholar." *Southwestern News*, December 1982, 5.

"Price Forges Path of 'Firsts.'" *Southwestern News*, April 1983, 5.

"Relations between Northern and Southern Baptists," *Baptist Standard*, 10 June 1948, 1,5; 17 June 1948, 2–3; 24 June 1948, 6; 1 July 1948, 3; 8 July 1948, 6; 15 July 1948, 3.

"Scarborough Weathers War, Norris as President." *Southwestern News*, November 1982, 22.

"She Put Her Golden Years into Southwestern's Beautification." *Southwestern News*, July–August 1984, 12.

"The Significance of Christian History." *Adult Teacher*, November 1961, 6–8, 37.

"Southern Baptist Beginnings." *The [Baptist] Student*, June 1981, 40–43, 48.

"Students Remember E. L. Carlson's Zeal." *Southwestern News*, November 1983, 4.

"Versatile Ball Realized Dreams." *Southwestern News*, September 1983, 2.

"Williams Brought Compassion to Office." *Southwestern News*, January 1983, 6.

"Williams: Talented Bible Translator." *Southwestern News*, June 1984, 2.

ORAL MEMOIRS

The Oral Memoirs of Robert A. Baker: A Series of Interviews Conducted September 21, 1977 through October 19, 1997. Interviewer: Tom J. Nettles. Texas Baptist Oral History Consortium. Dallas: Baptist General Convention of Texas, 1981.

2. Secondary

"Commencement." *Southwestern News*, May 1944, 2.

Crutcher, Mary. "Summer Sketchbook." *Fort Worth Press*, 27 August 1964.

"Faculty Addition." *Southwestern News*, May 1943, 2.

"Four Professors on Sabbatic Leave." *Southwestern News*, July 1962, 8.

The Lord's Free People in a Free Land: Essays in Baptist History in Honor of Robert A. Baker. Ed. William R. Estep. Fort Worth: School of Theology, Southwestern Baptist Theological Seminary, 1976. Esp. Jesse C. Fletcher, "A Pen Portrait: Robert Andrew Baker" (1–7) and Keith C. Wills, "A Bibliography of Published Writings of Robert Andrew Baker" (195–98).

"News Briefs." *Southwestern News*, April 1981, 12.

"Retired Professor Renews Vision of Seminary for Trustees." *Southwestern News*, November–December 1990, 5.

"Robert A. Baker: 1910–1992." *Southwestern News*, January–February 1993, 14–15.

"Robert Baker Award Jointly Established." *Southwestern News*, December 1977, 7.

"Robert Baker Honored with First Festschrift." *Southwestern News*, July 1976, 3.

"Southwestern's Ph.D. to Reflect Quality." *Southwestern News*, October 1974, 1.

Stanley, Robert L. "Baker's 24th Year Is Year of Publications." *Southwestern News*, March 1966, 7.

John (Jack) William MacGorman
(1920–)
New Testament

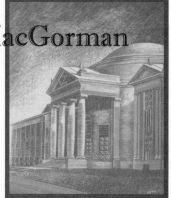

Siegfried S. Schatzmann

BIOGRAPHY

B orn on 26 December 1920 in Amherst, Nova Scotia, as the eldest of six siblings, John William was raised as a "preacher's son" in a devout Christian family. He attributes his own early exposure to Christlikeness to his English-born mother whose prayer-centered life and acted Christlikeness became indelibly imprinted on his own life. Perhaps one of the greatest tributes he pays to his "Baptist preacher dad" is that he instilled in him such a profound sense of awe of the God who called him to lifelong service that the very thought of ever bringing disrepute on his name elicits abhorrence and its avoidance continues to be his consuming passion.

His father's acceptance of a call to a church in Waterville, Maine, in 1927 meant an inevitable relocation for young MacGorman at the delicate age of seven. When the family faced another move, this time to Caribou, Maine, in 1934, just before Jack was to enter high school, he did not take kindly to the involuntary uprooting from his home and friends and chose to react to the new situation with rebellion. Although continuing the practice of regularly reading the Bible, he allowed the influence of new companions to plunge him into the currents of uncharted waters of behavior. This downward spiral was complicated by his worsening physical condition, when at the age of eighteen (5 May 1939) he had to undergo surgery for

125

what was wrongly diagnosed as a case of emphysema. On 20 May of the same year he was advised to move to the Northern Maine Sanatorium for a one-month period of observation. Instead of his health improving, it deteriorated to the point that the hospital staff advised his father to come to prepare his son for death.

Having already come to the lowest point of his life as an eighteen-year old, staring death in the face, and, at least initially, quarreling with God over the unfairness of what had been allotted to him, he began to cry out to God anew. Like the freshness of the morning dew after a protracted drought, MacGorman recalls God's gentle encounter in the words of Jesus to Martha: "I am the resurrection and the life. He who believes in me will live, even though he dies; and whoever lives and believes in me will never die" (John 11:25–26, NIV). Thus the seed of hope was planted, as was the unshakeable confidence that God would restore him to health. Although the battle with ill-health was by no means over as yet—indeed he was diagnosed with bronchiectasis, ordered to submit to more surgery, but then discharged as inoperable in June 1941, he was now prepared to work with the Lord with dogged determination to regain his strength. The alternation of success and failure in this pursuit caused doubts about his future to resurface; these too, however, were dispelled when he heard the Lord say: "You have trusted me thus far; why don't you let me have you the rest of the way?" Earlier he had come face to face with Christ as Lord over death; now he acknowledged his lordship in life.

These life-and-death struggles of body, soul, and spirit have shaped MacGorman more than any other single experience or person. He was now willing to do whatever it took to pursue life. Upon the advice of his doctors he undertook to move to a drier climate in Arizona but only made it as far as Austin, Texas. There he completed his B.A. in 1945 at the University of Texas and in 1947 married Barbara Ruth Stephens. They were blessed with six children of their own (Donald Ray, Stephen Ross [deceased 1984], Robert Scott, Linda Ruth, Deborah Kay, and John Michael). Having completed a B.D. at Southwestern Baptist Theological Seminary in 1948, he began his teaching career there in New Testament the same year. His studies culminated with a Th.D. from Southwestern in 1956 and a Ph.D. from Duke University in 1965. MacGorman was named the first Wesley Harrison Professor of New Testament in 1981, was named distinguished alumnus of Southwestern in 1986, and retired from full-time teaching in 1992. His teaching career—or teaching ministry, as he prefers to call it—was brought to a conclusion after fifty-three years of undiminished devotion to God's calling and enablement in the summer of 2001.

WRITINGS

MacGorman's literary contributions are generally clustered around the Letter of James, the Pauline writings in general and Paul's letters to the Galatians, Romans and (1) Corinthians in particular. Late in his career he also wrote on Acts.

In his 1956 Th.D. dissertation, entitled "A Comparison of the Book of James with the Jewish Wisdom Literature," MacGorman soberly concluded that James bears marks of both continuity and discontinuity with Jewish wisdom literature. His initial publishing venture (1969), an article dealing with introductory matters on the book of James, reflects his convictions on its authorship, readers, date and purpose, all of them based on existing scholarly analysis, as well as contextual and exegetical findings.

Most of his writings have engaged the Pauline writings, however, beginning with the Duke Ph.D. dissertation of 1965, wherein he examined the Pauline corpus (apart from Ephesians and the Pastoral Epistles) for the possibility that Paul's eschatology might have developed from an early form of Parousia-consciousness (1 Thessalonians) to a later abandonment of the same (2 Corinthians). According to MacGorman's assessment of the textual and critical data, the claims of a change in Pauline eschatology are neither compelling nor persuasive. Interestingly, he has not revisited this issue again in his subsequent writings, probably because he has considered the matter settled.

The Southwestern professor contributed a commentary each for the January Bible Studies on Romans (1976) and Acts (1990), as well as the volume on Romans and 1 Corinthians in the Layman's Bible Book Commentary series. Although his treatment of Galatians in the Broadman Bible Commentary reflects a more critical engagement, the penchant for perceptive exegesis is also evident in the volumes intended for the nonspecialists on the local-church level. All of the articles in journals and festschriften reflect cutting-edge discussions of difficult texts, as well as crucial issues and concepts arising in the principal letters of Paul.

THOUGHT AND METHOD

The Holy Spirit and His Gifts

One of the significant features in MacGorman's writings is the importance of the Holy Spirit in the life of the believer and the Christian community. Fundamentally the very confession "Jesus is Lord" is enabled by the Spirit and, for MacGorman, the Holy Spirit's ultimate task is to "plant" this confession "at the center of every man's being." He further observes that "the confession 'Jesus is Lord' is not just the initial phase of the work of the Spirit in one's life. There is no subsequent stage at which the Spirit points beyond Jesus to himself."[1] The sovereign role of the Spirit is acknowledged in his bestowing and making effective every charismatic gift given to the believer on the one hand,[2] and in producing in him the fruit that expresses the demand for ethical behavior characteristic of life in the Spirit on the other.[3] The same dynamic also expresses the work of the Spirit in Acts, in terms of the apostles living a Spirit-filled life and of empowering believers for witness and proclamation of the gospel to all nations.[4]

The Place of Scripture

Embedded in all of MacGorman's literary contributions is a profound sense of awe for the Bible as the Word of God and an unflinching commitment to its being the sole authority. This stance is presuppositional rather than combative, regardless of whether he addresses the scholarly guild or the denominational constituency, especially through the January Bible Studies (Romans, Acts). Consequently, MacGorman's stance on *sola Scriptura, sola fide* left him little alternative but to regard signing any statement of authority other than the text of Bible itself as a betrayal of the latter. Thus he submitted a signed copy of the Bible to the Southwestern Seminary administration to authenticate his commitment to the truth and trustworthiness of the Bible but refused to sign any lesser confessional formulation.[5]

His commitment to the text itself, as well as to sound grammatical-syntactical exegesis, is also demonstrated in his daring to confront popular theological assumptions. For one, concerning the place of Israel in the gospel of God's righteousness (Romans 9–11), he does not subscribe to various forms of spiritualizing "Israel" but allows "all Israel" to be understood as the counterpart to "the full number of the Gentiles."[6] For another, on exegetical grounds he dismisses the notion of cessationism with regard to the place and purpose of charismata (1 Corinthians 12–14, esp. 13:8–12). He observes, "the context suggests that the return of Christ and the establishment of the eternal order will mark the terminus for all the charismatic gifts."[7]

Similarly, his high view of Scripture compels him to address Galatians 5:2–4—perhaps the most difficult passage in this Pauline letter—by allowing the syntax of the clauses to suggest the meaning. In this case Paul sets up the argument by means of a conditional clause in v. 2 and concludes it in v. 4 with a stern warning with pastoral intent. He wisely points out that both over-interpretation and under-interpretation are to be avoided because they equally misinterpret the Word of God.[8] Conversely he dares to express his personal bias on the date of the Letter of James, suggesting that it may have been written "near the end of the first century," a view that was much more common a generation ago but will find few advocates among recent interpreters.[9] In other words, matters of provenance are here clearly distinguished from the text; whereas the former is a matter of opinion, the latter is part of God's Word through James.

The Function of the Mosaic Law

Nowhere does Paul clarify the function of the Mosaic law with reference to the believer's life more clearly that in Galatians, especially in 3:24–25. Here Paul adduces the analogy of the *paidagōgos* to shed light on the matter. MacGorman masterfully places Paul's teaching in its appropriate context and delineates the problem of interpreting this concept in a contextually sensitive manner. He correctly questions such educative notions as "tutor," "instructor," or "pedagogue" to capture the intended meaning and instead prefers a more custodial term, such as "guardian" or "custodian."[10] Paul is clearly stressing the transitional nature of the law's function, as 3:23 and 24 demonstrate. Any other alternative, MacGorman concludes, "was to nullify the grace of God and to render meaningless to death of Christ on the cross (Gal. 2:21).[11]

129

Witness, Evangelism, and Missions

To speak of the work of the Spirit, for MacGorman, without at the same time also expounding on the proclamation of the good news of Jesus Christ means to misconstrue both. Concerning the purpose of the Holy Spirit in Acts he writes: "the greatest evidence of the Holy Spirit's presence and power is bold witnessing to God's redemptive achievement through Jesus Christ, His Son."[12] Far from merely harnessing what the texts which he exegeted said concerning the various dimensions of communicating the gospel, MacGorman devoted himself to evangelism and missions at home, in North America, as well as on the continents of Latin America, Africa, Asia and Australia. He practiced and modeled what he believed and taught.

EVALUATION

For this writer and perhaps for countless thousands of others of his students over the fifty-three years of Jack MacGorman's career as professor of New Testament at Southwestern, he stands out as a model of uncompromising commitment to Jesus Christ and of interpreting the Word of God with integrity. He personifies scholarship clothed in humility. He may not have written any tomes by which posterity will remember him, but he invested himself in the thousands of students who cherished exegetical and theological challenges and in the midst of that pursuit sensed God's powerful presence and his transforming work by his Spirit.

BIBLIOGRAPHY

1. Primary

DISSERTATIONS

"An Analysis of the Factors Which Relate to the Possibility of Tracing Development in Pauline Eschatology." Ph.D. diss., Duke University, 1965.
"A Comparison of the Book of James with the Jewish Wisdom Literature." Th.D. diss., Southwestern Baptist Theological Seminary, 1956.

BOOKS

Acts: The Gospel for All People. Adult January Bible Study. Nashville: Convention Press, 1990.
The Gifts of the Spirit. Nashville: Broadman, 1974.
Romans, 1 Corinthians. Layman's Bible Book Commentary, vol. 20. Nashville: Broadman, 1980.
Romans: Everyman's Gospel. January Bible Study. Nashville: Convention Press, 1976.

CHAPTERS CONTRIBUTED TO BOOKS

"The Convincing Work of the Holy Spirit." In *Southwestern Sermons*, ed. H. C. Brown Jr., 143–49. Nashville: Broadman, 1960.

"The Discipline of the Church." In *The People of God: Essays on the Believer's Church*, ed. Paul A. Basden and David S. Dockery, 74–84. Nashville: Broadman, 1991.

"Galatians." In *The Broadman Bible Commentary*, ed. Clifton J. Allen. Vol. 11, *2 Corinthians—Philemon*, 77–124. Nashville: Broadman, 1971.

"The Law as Paidagōgos: A Study in Pauline Analogy." In *New Testament Studies: Essays in Honor of Ray Summers in His Sixty-fifth Year*, ed. Huber L. Drumwright, Jr., and Curtis Vaughan, 99–111. Waco, Tex.: Markham Press Fund of Baylor University Press, 1975.

JOURNAL ARTICLES

"An Exposition of James 3." *Southwestern Journal of Theology* 29 (Fall 1986): 31–36.

"Glossolalic Error and Its Correction: 1 Corinthians 12–14." *Review and Expositor* 80 (Summer 1983): 389–400.

"Introducing the Book of James." *Southwestern Journal of Theology* 12 (Fall 1969): 9–22.

"Problem Passages in Galatians." *Southwestern Journal of Theology* 15 (Fall 1972): 35–51.

"Romans 7 Once More." *Southwestern Journal of Theology* 19 (Fall 1976): 31–41.

MISCELLANEOUS

"Paul's Unplucked Thorn." *Baptist Standard*, 6 June 1984, 12–13.

2. Secondary

"After 44 Years, Jack MacGorman Can't Find a Biblical Basis for Retirement." *Southwestern News*, January–February 1992, 11.

Alford, Chip. "MacGorman: 40 Years in Seminary Classroom." *Baptist Standard*, 1 February 1989, 12.

Bird, Craig. "MacGorman's Weakness Has Been a Strength." *Baptist Standard*, 13 August 1986, 18.

"MacGorman Dream Alive in Students." *Southwestern News*, June 1986, 5, 9.

"New Testament Model: Lessons Are More Than Book Learning for MacGorman." *Southwestern News*, January 1989, 12.

Smith, Brian. "Driving Force." *Southwestern News*, Winter 1997, 22–23.

"Warner, Greg. "MacGorman—New Testament: Synonymous!" *Southwestern News*, November 1980, 21.

James Leo Garrett, Jr.
(1925–)
Theology

Paul A. Basden

11

BIOGRAPHY

James Leo Garrett, Jr. has been a part of the Southwestern family for more than thirty-five years and a part of the larger Southern Baptist family for his entire life. He was born on 25 November 1925 in Waco, Texas, to James Leo Garrett, Sr., a certified public accountant, and Grace H. Jenkins, the daughter of a Baptist pastor-teacher who had graduated from Southern Baptist Theological Seminary in 1895. Leo professed his faith in Christ at nine and was baptized into Seventh and James Baptist Church. The valedictorian of his class in Waco High School, he graduated from Baylor University in 1945 with a major in English and as permanent president of his class. Licensed and ordained by First Baptist Church, Waco, Leo enrolled in Southwestern Seminary, where he came under the tutelage of Dr. W. T. Conner and others and where he met Myrta Ann Latimer of Garrison, Texas, whom he married in 1948. To their union were born three sons: James Leo, III, Robert Thomas, and Paul Latimer. Garrett received his B.D. degree from Southwestern (1948), his Th.M. from Princeton Theological Seminary (1949), his Th.D. from Southwestern (1954), and a Ph.D. from Harvard University (1966). He has served as pastor of three churches and interim pastor of ten.

Garrett began teaching theology at Southwestern in 1949, remaining on faculty there for a decade. In 1959, he accepted an

133

invitation to move to Louisville, Kentucky, to teach at Southern Baptist Theological Seminary following a major faculty crisis in that institution. Garrett remained at Southern until 1973, when he returned to Baylor to direct the J. M. Dawson Studies in Church and State and to be professor of religion. In 1979, he returned to Southwestern as professor of theology, where he was still teaching in 2001 as distinguished professor of theology, emeritus.

WRITINGS

Garrett has written, cowritten, edited, or coedited thirteen books, produced two dissertations and one thesis, contributed chapters or essays to sixteen books, authored forty-five journal articles and editorials, and penned nine major encyclopedia articles. His master's thesis at Princeton in 1949 was on the subject of "Thomas Aquinas' Doctrine of Penance: A Critical Analysis," and his doctoral dissertation at Southwestern in 1954 was entitled "The Theology of Walter Thomas Conner." Revealed in these choices were two subjects that claimed much of his attention throughout his career as a teacher and author: Baptist theology and theologians, and Roman Catholic theology and practice.

In the late 1950s and early 1960s, Garrett began to show interest in the meaning of church for Baptists, first in *The Nature of the Church according to the Radical Continental Reformation* (1957). This was followed by "Seeking a Regenerate Church Membership" in 1961, *Baptist Church Discipline* in 1962, and *Evangelism for Discipleship* in 1964. Each of these writings suggested that current Baptist churchmanship did not measure up to the ideals of Baptist life and polity.

Beginning in the mid-1960s, Garrett started to write about Roman Catholic thought. In 1963, he issued an article on "Polemic, Conversion, and/or Dialogue: Baptist Postures toward the Church of Rome," which he expanded into book form in 1965 as *Baptists and Roman Catholicism*. In 1965, he combined three of his favorite subjects into one essay entitled "Religious Liberty, Vatican Council II, and Baptists." These writings led to the completion in 1966 of Garrett's Harvard dissertation. In 1971 he wrote "The Shifting Foci of the Protestant-Roman Catholic Confrontation: Peter, Mary, and the Sacraments," and in 1972 he penned brief works out of his dissertation research on *Reinhold Niebuhr on Roman Catholicism* and "John A. Mackay on the Roman Catholic Church."

Garrett shifted gears somewhat when he became director of Baylor's J. M. Dawson Studies in Church-State Studies, delving into matters directly related to religious liberty. What he had begun in 1965 with a paper for the Baptist World Alliance on "The Biblical Basis of Religious Liberty," he continued in 1974 with an essay on "'Civil Religion': Clarifying the Semantic Problem"; in 1975 with twin articles on "The 'Free Exercise' Clause of the First Amendment" and "The 'No Establishment' Clause of the First Amendment"; in 1976 with "Religious Freedom: Why and How in Today's World" and with "Does Church-State Separation Necessarily Mean the Privatization of Religion?"; in 1977 with a two-part article on "The Dialectic of Romans 13:1–7 and Revelation 13"; and in 1979 with "Bureaucratic Governmental Regulation of Churches and Church Institutions."

Concurrent with the doctrinal controversy in the Southern Baptist Convention that marked the 1970s and 1980s, Garrett stepped up his writings on Baptist views on the Bible. He addressed the thorny question of biblical authority in 1972 in an article entitled "Biblical Infallibility and Inerrancy according to Baptist Confessions of Faith." He offered a companion piece in 1974, "Representative Modern Baptist Understandings of Biblical Inspiration." In 1978 Garrett wrote "Sources of Authority in Baptist Thought." He followed up with two more articles in 1979, the year the denominational controversy began: "Doctrinal Authority, 1925–75: A Study in Four Representative Baptist Journals" and "Biblical Authority according to Baptist Confessions of Faith." As the debate heated up, Garrett kept writing on matters related to the Bible. In 1986 he wrote "The Bible at Southwestern Seminary during Its Formative Years: A Study of H. E. Dana and W. T. Conner." In 1987 he contributed to the Conference on Biblical Inerrancy an article on "The Teachings of Recent Southern Baptist Theologians on the Bible." In 1999 Garrett continued to address biblical authority in a lengthy article entitled "The Authority of the Bible for Baptists."

One of the highlights of Garrett's writings during the SBC controversy was his discussion of the relation of Baptists to Evangelicals. He initiated the dialogue in a 1983 article, "Southern Baptists as Evangelicals." That same year he was a coauthor with E. Glenn Hinson and James E. Tull of *Are Southern Baptists "Evangelicals"?*.

A decade later he made several observations on the status of that debate in "Are Southern Baptists 'Evangelicals'? A Further Reflection" (1993).

Throughout his career Garrett endeavored to make historical theology more acceptable and understandable to Southern Baptists. Early he introduced the subject to his constituency with two articles: "Historical Theology: 1945–1965" (1965) and "The History of Christian Doctrine: Retrospect and Prospect" (1971). Garrett found himself particularly drawn to patristic theology. He wrote three companion articles on the early history of the doctrine of the priesthood of believers: "The Biblical Doctrine of the Priesthood of the People of God" in 1975, "The Pre-Cyprianic Doctrine of the Priesthood of All Christians" in 1979, and "The Priesthood of All Christians: From Cyprian to John Chrysostom" in 1988. He also wrote "A Reappraisal of Chalcedon" in 1974 and "New Dimensions in Patristic Theology, 1980–1995" in 1998. His love for Reformation theology may be seen in his 1964 essay on "Luther's Developing Doctrine of Baptism," in a bibliographical essay written in 1967 on "Studies of the Sixteenth Century Protestant Reformation: The Literature in English, 1946–1966," and in his 1980 edited work entitled *Calvin and the Reformed Tradition*.

But Garrett's favorite subject in the history of doctrine was Baptist theology. He contributed two related articles to *Encyclopedia of Southern Baptists*: "Theology, History of Baptist" (1958) and "Theologians, Baptist" (1971). In 1974 he explored Baptists and ecumenism in an edited volume called *Baptist Relations with Other Christians*. In 1984–85 Garrett completed one of the most fully documented histories of a Baptist congregation ever published.[1] He evaluated the ordinance of baptism in 1986 in "The Theology and Practice of Baptism: A Southern Baptist Perspective," and again in 2001 in "Baptists concerning Baptism: Review and Preview." He tackled the topic of the church in 1989 in "Understanding the Church: A Southern Baptist Perspective." Garrett sought to summarize Baptist theology in "Major Emphases in Baptist Theology" (1995), in "The Distinctive Identity of Southern Baptists *vis-à-vis* Other Baptists" (1996), and in the Baptist World Alliance book he edited in 1999, *We Baptists*. He delighted to bring to the attention of younger Baptists the contributions of his theological mentor W. T. Conner, first in his 1954 dissertation, then in a 1983 article entitled "W. T. Conner: Contemporary Theologian," and again in 1990 and 2001 in chapter form ("Walter Thomas Conner," in *Baptist Theologians* and *Theologians of the Baptist Tradition*).

As Garrett neared retirement from full-time faculty status at Southwestern, he published his magnum opus, *Systematic Theology: Biblical, Historical, and Evangelical* (1990, 1995). He revised both volumes in 2000 and 2001. Here we find Garrett's mature interpretation of significant theological themes, organized systematically and historically.

INTERPRETATION

Who Are Baptists?

Baptist Distinctives

One of Garrett's chief concerns has been to state succinctly exactly who Baptists are and what they believe. In a 1995 address, Garrett summarized a lifetime's reflections on "Major Emphases in Baptist Theology."[2] Speaking to Eastern Orthodox theologians in Istanbul, Turkey, he first noted the considerable areas of agreement between Baptists and "the wider or worldwide company of Christians." Then he focused on "that which is unique to or at least peculiarly emphasized by Baptists,"[3] namely, "congregations gathered around believer's baptism by immersion,"[4] religious liberty and church-state separation, and the responsibility of all churches and Christians to practice evangelism and missions. Although they may not be fully appreciated or understood, "[T]here still exists a *raison d'être* for Baptist Christians."[5]

Garrett also defined Southern Baptists vis-à-vis other Baptist groups,[6] noting seven peculiar characteristics of Southern Baptists: the coalescing of the Charleston and Sandy Creek traditions, the defense of slavery and later of racial segregation, the acceptance of Landmarkism, the adoption of "the convention method of denominational work instead of the society method,"[7] the impact of Southern culture, the unifying and organizing influence of the Sunday School Board, and the increasingly "multi-ethnic character"[8] of Southern Baptist congregations. Garrett then concluded by showing how Southern Baptists are now changing with respect to these characteristics.

Baptists and Other Christians

Garrett was one of the pioneer ecumenists among Southern Baptists. He once wrote: "Baptist Christians tend to be known for their sectarian separatism more than for their cooperation with other Christians and their devotion to Christian unity." Despite that reputation, however, "Baptists have often participated in and even given leadership to expressions of Christian togetherness, cooperation, and unity that transcend denominational lines."[9] Garrett himself has been such a participant and leader.

Believers' Churches

Garrett identified believers' churches as "that segment of the Protestant Christian heritage which is distinct both from Classical Protestant and from Catholic . . . understandings of the church by its insistence on the indispensability of voluntary churchmanship with its many implications."[10] Wanting to explore Baptists' "next of kin," Garrett presided over a large family reunion in Louisville in 1967 called the Conference on the Concept of the Believers' Church, the first of its kind. The 150 nonelected participants represented over two dozen separate denominations that claimed affiliation with the broader Christian family known as the Believers' Church, including Baptists of various stripes, Mennonite bodies, Brethren groups, Assemblies of God, Churches of Christ, Disciples of Christ, and others. Garrett edited the thirteen conference addresses in a subsequent book, *The Concept of the Believers' Church.*[11]

Christians within the believers' churches share several distinctives. First, Garrett asserted that "particular congregations of Baptists are supposed to be composed only of those who have given and do continue to give evidence of having been 'begotten' or 'born anew' or 'born from above' by the Holy Spirit."[12] He suggested a careful reconsideration of the church discipline practiced by the Philadelphia and Charleston Baptist associations and lamented the fact that "Baptists in the United States, and Southern Baptists in particular, are giving meager evidence of having today an ordered, disciplined churchmanship."[13]

Next, Garrett warned Baptists not to transmute the doctrine of the priesthood of all believers into radical egalitarianism or rugged individualism in which the priesthood means only unhindered

138

access to God.[14] He asserted that the biblical meaning of the doctrine "is the offering of 'spiritual sacrifices' such as in worship, witness, stewardship, and service (ministry)."[15]

Third, Garrett addressed religious liberty. Commenting on the "No . . . Establishment" clause of the First Amendment, he stated that it "should continue to safeguard excessive entanglement of government and religions so as to give opportunity for those religious expressions to which the 'free exercise' clause more directly speaks."[16] Reflecting on the "Free Exercise" clause, he wrote: "The freedom of religious beliefs . . . is to be upheld. The freedom to propagate one's religious beliefs . . . must also be protected. . . . But there are limits to 'free exercise'. . . ."[17] Garrett was not naive, however, about the power of government. He knew that while Romans 13:1–7 teaches that Christians should obediently submit to the government because it comes from God and is intended for our good, Revelation 13 reveals that when the government persecutes Christians because of their faith, it is being "authorized and empowered by *Satan*."[18]

Evangelicals

In 1983, Garrett and E. Glenn Hinson entered into "a fraternal debate" about Southern Baptists and Evangelicals which was intended to "enlighten and strengthen" rather than "divide or disrupt."[19] But because Garrett and Hinson approached the topic so differently and reached such opposite conclusions, the dialogue got a little testy.

Garrett first identified "Evangelicals" as "the less strict heirs of Fundamentalism" with roots in the earlier awakenings. He observed that Evangelicals generally agree on four primary Christian doctrines: Scripture, Jesus Christ, being born anew or justified by grace through faith, and evangelism and missions.[20] Finally, Garrett identified Southern Baptists as moderately Calvinistic, missionary-minded, broadly denominational, conservative theologically, denominationally cooperative but not ecumenical, and proponents of a historical rather than symbolic approach to the Bible. His conclusion: "*Southern Baptists are denominational Evangelicals*."[21]

Roman Catholics

Garrett has long nurtured a deep interest in the Roman Catholic Church. Late in 1965 he was a guest of the Secretariat for Promoting Christian Unity at Vatican Council II in Rome. The next year he completed his doctoral dissertation at Harvard University on American Roman Catholicism. During this time, Garrett produced a brief monograph entitled *Baptists and Roman Catholicism*,[22] the thesis of which was that Baptists had historically adopted one of three "postures toward the Church of Rome."[23] The first, polemical controversy, has included several varieties.[24] The second Baptist posture has been evangelization, assuming that some Roman Catholics are unbelieving non-Christians who need to be converted.[25] The third and final approach has been "dialogue or fraternal discussion and interchange."[26]

What Do Christians Believe?[27]

In the early 1990s, Garrett produced his *Systematic Theology*: a two-volume work with ten sections, eighty-seven chapters, and over fifteen hundred pages![28] It treats all of the major Christian doctrines as thoroughly as possible. Garrett's method is that of a historical theologian who has also appropriated the work of twentieth-century biblical theologians. He reviews Christian theology through the lens of Christian history, bringing all of the pertinent historical development of a doctrine to bear upon his final formulation. Historical consciousness is the great gift he gives to Baptists interested in theology. *Systematic Theology* is distinguished by its theological conservatism. Garrett never attempts to write "new theology" but is content to comment on Christian doctrine as it has been given to the church through the Ecumenical Councils and the Protestant Reformers. Nevertheless, he has not shied away from tackling some of the thorniest questions facing Baptists and other Christians.

The Bible

Garrett's discussion of the Bible is the fullest in many years from a Baptist theologian.[29] Concerning *biblical inspiration*, he warns against uncritically embracing "extremes in respect to the divine and the human associated with the Bible."[30] Concerning *biblical criticism*, Garrett cautiously accepts the need for historical and scientific analysis of the Bible but questions "'the assured results of biblical criticism'" and encourages "'the criticism of criticism.'"[31]

Garrett saves some of his wisest counsel for the topic of biblical inerrancy, which he calls the "*dependability or truthfulness of the Bible.*"[32] Steering between "errancy" on the one hand and "inerrancy" on the other, he concludes that "none of the problems or difficulties connected with specific biblical texts and posed in relation to dependability/trustworthiness/infallibility/inerrancy . . . jeopardizes any basic Christian doctrine unless it should be inerrancy."[33]

Concerning *biblical authority,* Garrett argues that the Bible is authoritative "primarily as a book of religion or of divine revelation. It is not a textbook on the natural sciences or a record of all ancient history." Moreover, its authority derives from the authority of God, an insight which can keep modern Christians from falling into the trap of "bibliolatry." Finally, its authority depends on its proper interpretation, which centers in Jesus Christ.[34]

God
In a day when the Fatherhood of God has come under frequent attack, Garrett affirms the traditional, orthodox view of *God as Heavenly Father*. Radical feminist theology calls for the feminization of God and affirms the motherhood of God. While acknowledging that "there are some biblical texts . . . in which maternal features are ascribed to God,"[35] Garrett emphasizes that we can and should maintain our understanding of God as Father, without falling into the trap of an uncritical paternalism or patriarchy.[36]

Jesus Christ
Although fully human, Jesus is also the sinless Son of God, who is the Savior of the world and "provides the only effectual salvation for humankind."[37] But how far does this salvation extend when it comes to the unevangelized? Garrett rejects pluralism, which claims that salvation can come through many religions and saviors, as wells as inclusivism, which argues that Jesus is only the ontological savior of the world. He opts for exclusivism, which asserts that salvation occurs solely through personal, conscious faith in Jesus Christ. Garrett prefers a modified exclusivism by stating, "It would seem that the church's proclamation should be exclusivist so as not to promise salvation outside the conscious acceptance of Jesus and the

gospel but that in God's sovereign freedom he may effectively work outside the boundaries of exclusivism."[38]

The Holy Spirit

While Baptists are typically squeamish about the Holy Spirit, Garrett boldly addresses *gifts of the Spirit*, especially charismatic "sign gifts." While accepting that the gift of tongues is still operable in today's world, Garrett recognizes that the gift's practice has led to many abuses. He encourages "non-tongues-speakers" to "ask tongues-speakers not to elevate this gift above all others . . . or to look upon non-tongues-speakers as inferior or second-class Christians." He also encourages those who do not speak in tongues not to "exclude or disfellowship those who exercise tongues-speaking within the Pauline perimeters." Finally, he gratefully acknowledges Pentecostals and Neo-Pentecostals for their "clear witness to the dynamic agency and the sovereign lordship of the Holy Spirit in today's world."[39]

The Christian Life

In the historic debate over election, Garrett argues that belief in God's election of the elect does not require belief in God's equal "nonelection of the nonelect." He seems to favor the view that God's election of humans rests on a conditional decree that does not deny human accountability, and he does stress that the corporate aspect of election needs more emphasis.[40] Garrett treats in detail some topics not discussed by earlier systematic theologians: for example, discipleship, stewardship, prayer, and missions.[41]

The Last Things

Garrett believes in one universal resurrection at the second coming of Jesus Christ and an intermediate state, critiques dispensationalism as a system and prefers amillennialism, and affirms dual eternal destiny vis-à-vis eschatological universalism and annihilationism.[42]

EVALUATION

In evaluating Garrett's theology, one must first identify his purpose in writing. His goal is not to present a finely honed thesis and then to argue and prove that thesis, but to let his readers in on an intergenerational discussion of the cardinal truths of Christianity.

His aim is not to offer essay-like opinions on every controversial doctrinal subject, but to provide differing opinions and contrary arguments related to the controversial issues facing the church, so that readers can make up their own minds.

This impacts the long-term value of Garrett's work. For future theologians who want to see the historical development of virtually every Christian doctrine, from the biblical materials to current debates, Garrett's work will be their best source. Future readers who want a systematic theology which offers them brevity or personal opinion or in-depth biblical exposition will likely look elsewhere.

The writer predicts that future generations will regard Garrett as a "gentleman theologian" who sought to illuminate theological controversy rather than agitate those with whom he differed. Also he will likely be seen as Baptists' finest historical theologian. Finally, he may be remembered as the last Baptist theologian of the twentieth century to grapple with Christian doctrine from a "modern" viewpoint. The future of Baptist theology may well be in the hands of younger "postmodern" theologians who see life and interpret the Bible and think about doctrine very differently. But Garrett's work will stand as long as Christians seek to understand Evangelical and Baptist theology as seen through twentieth-century eyes.

BIBLIOGRAPHY

1. Primary

DISSERTATIONS AND THESIS

"Protestant Writings on Roman Catholicism in the United States between Vatican Council I and Vatican Council II: An Analysis and Critique in View of the Contemporary Protestant Roman Catholic Confrontation." Ph.D. diss., Harvard University, 1966.

"The Theology of Walter Thomas Conner." Th.D. diss., Southwestern Baptist Theological Seminary, 1954.

"Thomas Aquinas' Doctrine of Penance: A Critical Analysis." Th.M. thesis, Princeton Theological Seminary, 1949.

BOOKS

(coauth.) *Are Southern Baptists "Evangelicals"?* Macon, Ga.: Mercer University Press, 1983.

Baptist Church Discipline. Broadman Historical Monographs. Nashville: Broadman, 1962.

(ed.) *Baptist Relations with Other Christians.* Valley Forge, Pa.: Judson, 1974.

Baptists and Roman Catholicism. Broadman Historical Monographs. Nashville: Broadman, 1965.

(ed.) *Calvin and the Reformed Tradition.* Christian Classics. Nashville: Broadman, 1980.

(ed.) *The Concept of the Believers' Church: Addresses from the 1967 Louisville Conference.* Scottdale, Pa.: Herald, 1970.

Evangelism for Discipleship. Louisville: pvt. ptg., 1964.

Living Stones: The Centennial History of Broadway Baptist Church, Fort Worth, Texas, 1882–1982. 2 vols. Fort Worth: Broadway Baptist Church, 1984, 1985.

Reinhold Niebuhr on Roman Catholicism. Louisville: Seminary Baptist Book Store, 1972.

Systematic Theology: Biblical, Historical, and Evangelical. 2 vols. Grand Rapids: Eerdmans, 1990, 1995.

> *Teologia Sistematica: Biblica, Historica y Evangelica*. Vol. 1, trans. Nancy Bedford de Stutz. El Paso: Casa Bautista de Publicaciones, 1996. Vol. 2, trans. Nancy Bedford de Stutz, Daniel Stutz, and LaNell W. de Bedford. Ibid., 2000. [Spanish]

Systematic Theology: Biblical, Historical, and Evangelical. 2d ed. 2 vols. North Richland Hills, Tex.: BIBAL Press, 2000, 2001.

(coed.) *The Teacher's Yoke: Studies in Memory of Henry Trantham*. Waco, Tex.: Baylor University Press, 1964.

(ed.) *We Baptists*. Franklin, Tenn.: Providence House for the Baptist World Alliance, 1999.

CHAPTERS CONTRIBUTED TO BOOKS

"Are Southern Baptists 'Evangelicals'? A Further Reflection." In *Southern Baptists and American Evangelicals*, ed. David S. Dockery, 218–23. Nashville: Broadman, 1993.

"Authority for the Christian World Mission." In *Christ for the World*, ed. G. Allen West, 73–82. Nashville: Broadman, 1963.

"Basic Theological Differences" and "Man, Sin, and Redemption." In *Revolt and Commitment*, ed. Stuart P. Garver, 28–30, 40–46. Sea Cliff, N.Y.: Christ's Mission, Inc., 1960.

"The Biblical Basis of Religious Liberty." In *The Truth That Makes Men Free: Official Report of the Eleventh Congress, Baptist World Alliance, Miami Beach, Florida, USA, June 25–30, 1965*, ed. Josef Nordenhaug, 280–87. Nashville: Broadman, 1966.

"The Biblical Doctrine of the Priesthood of the People of God." In *New Testament Studies: Essays in Honor of Ray Summers in His Sixty-Fifth Year*, ed. Huber L. Drumwright, Jr., and Curtis Vaughan, 137–49. Waco, Tex.: Markham Press Fund of Baylor University Press, 1975.

"Christian Knowledge and Conviction." In *Book of Proceedings: Child Life Conference, January 31–February 3, 1961*, 74–86. Nashville: Baptist Sunday School Board, 1961.

"A Christian View of Material Things." In *Resource Unlimited*, ed. William L. Hendricks, 83–96. Nashville: Stewardship Commission, Southern Baptist Convention, 1972.

"Does Church-State Separation Necessarily Mean the Privatization of Religion?" In *Readings on Church and State*, ed. James E. Wood, Jr., 141–48. Waco, Tex.: J. M. Dawson Institute of Church-State Studies, 1989.

"Free Church Architecture: Its History and Theology." In *Proceedings of Church Buildings and Architecture Conference, March 15–16, 1960*, 123–35. Nashville: Baptist Sunday School Board, 1960.

"God's Loving-Giving Nature." In *Witnessing Giving Life*, 56–68. Nashville: Stewardship Commission, Southern Baptist Convention, 1988.

"Luther's Developing Doctrine of Baptism." In The *Teacher's Yoke: Studies in Memory of Henry Trantham*, ed. E. Jerry Vardaman and James Leo Garrett, Jr., 203–14. Waco, Tex.: Markham Press Fund of Baylor University Press, 1964.

"New Dimensions in Patristic Theology, 1980–1995." In *New Dimensions in Evangelical Thought: Essays in Honor of Millard J. Erickson*, ed. David S. Dockery, 69–91. Downers Grove, Ill.: InterVarsity Press, 1998.

"The Pre-Cyprianic Doctrine of the Priesthood of All Christians." In *Continuity and Discontinuity in Church History: Essays Presented to George Huntston Williams on the Occasion of His 65th Birthday*, ed. F. Forrester Church and Timothy George, 45–61. Studies in the History of Christian Thought, vol. 19. Leiden: E. J. Brill, 1979.

"The Teaching of Recent Southern Baptist Theologians on the Bible." In *The Proceedings of the Conference on Biblical Inerrancy, 1987,* 289–315, 546–53. Nashville: Broadman, 1987.

"The Writings of Ray Summers." In *Chronos, Kairos, Christos II: Chronological, Nativity, and Religious Studies in Memory of Ray Summers,* ed. Jerry Vardaman, 21–42. Macon, Ga.: Mercer University Press, 1998.

"Walter Thomas Conner." In *Baptist Theologians,* ed. by Timothy George and David S. Dockery, 419–33. Nashville: Broadman, 1990. Revision in *Theologians of the Baptist Tradition,* ed. Timothy George and David S. Dockery, 202–15. Nashville: Broadman and Holman, 2001.

JOURNAL ARTICLES AND EDITORIALS

(coauth.) "Amin's Uganda: Troubled Land of Religious Persecution." *Journal of Church and State* 19 (Autumn 1977): 429–36.

"The Authority of the Bible for Baptists." *Southwestern Journal of Theology* 41 (Spring 1999): 4–40.

"Baptists concerning Baptism: Review and Preview." *Southwestern Journal of Theology* 43 (Spring 2001): 52–67.

"The Bible at Southwestern Seminary during Its Formative Years: A Study of H. E. Dana and W. T. Conner." *Baptist History and Heritage* 21 (October 1986): 29–43.

"Biblical Authority according to Baptist Confessions of Faith." *Review and Expositor* 76 (Winter 1979): 43–54.

"Biblical Infallibility and Inerrancy according to Baptist Confessions of Faith." *Search* 3 (Fall 1972): 42–45.

"Bureaucratic Governmental Regulation of Churches and Church Institutions." *Journal of Church and State* 21 (Spring 1979): 195–207.

"'Civil Religion': Clarifying the Semantic Problem." *Journal of Church and State* 16 (Spring 1974): 187–95.

"The Dialectic of Romans 13:1–7 and Revelation 13: Part One." *Journal of Church and State* 18 (Autumn 1976): 433–42; "Part Two." *Journal of Church and State* 19 (Winter 1977): 5–20.

"The Distinctive Identity of Southern Baptists *vis-à-vis* Other Baptists," *Baptist History and Heritage* 31 (October 1996): 6–16.

"Doctrinal Authority, 1925–1975: A Study in Four Representative Baptist Journals." *Foundations* 22 (January–March 1979): 3–12.

"Evangelism and Social Involvement." *Southwestern Journal of Theology* 12 (Spring 1970): 51–62.

"The 'Free Exercise' Clause of the First Amendment: Retrospect and Prospect." *Journal of Church and State* 17 (Autumn 1975): 393–98.

"Forum" [Response to Three Evaluators of *Systematic Theology*, volume 1]. *The Theological Educator* no. 45 (Spring 1992): 49–57.

"Historical Theology, 1945–1965." *Southwestern Journal of Theology* n.s. 7 (April 1965): 77–82.

"The History of Christian Doctrine: Retrospect and Prospect." *Review and Expositor* 68 (Spring 1971): 245–60.

"John A. Mackay on the Roman Catholic Church." *Journal of Presbyterian History* 50 (Summer 1972): 111–28.

"Joseph Martin Dawson: Pastor, Author, Denominational Leader, Social Activist." *Baptist History and Heritage* 14 (October 1979): 7–15.

"The Kingdom of God according to Baptist Theology." *Southwestern Journal of Theology* 40 (Spring 1998): 53–68.

"Major Emphases in Baptist Theology." *Southwestern Journal of Theology* 37 (Summer 1995): 36–46.

"Missions and Baptist Systematic Theologies." *Baptist History and Heritage* 35 (Spring 2000): 67–71.

"The Nature of the Church according to the Radical Continental Reformation." *Mennonite Quarterly Review* 32 (April 1958): 111–27.

"The 'No Establishment' Clause of the First Amendment: Retrospect and Prospect." *Journal of Church and State* 17 (Winter 1975): 5–13.

"Polemic, Conversion, and/or Dialogue: Baptist Postures toward the Church of Rome." *Review and Expositor* 60 (Summer 1963): 319–42.

"The Priesthood of All Christians: From Cyprian to John Chrysostom." *Southwestern Journal of Theology* 30 (Spring 1988): 22–33.

"A Reappraisal of Chalcedon." *Review and Expositor* 71 (Winter 1974): 31–42.

"Religious Freedom: Why and How in Today's World." *Southwestern Journal of Theology* 18 (Spring 1976): 9–24.

"Religious Liberty, Vatican Council II, and Baptists." *Review and Expositor* 62 (Spring 1965): 175–85.

"Representative Modern Baptist Understandings of Biblical Inspiration." *Review and Expositor* 71 (Spring 1974): 179–95.

"Restitution and Dissent among Early English Baptists: Part One." *Baptist History and Heritage* 12 (October 1977): 193–210, 251; "Part Two: Representative Late Sixteenth and Early Seventeenth Century Sources." *Baptist History and Heritage* 13 (April 1978): 11–27.

"Retrospect: Twelve Milestones in Catholic Education in the United States." *Quarterly Review* 22 (April–May–June 1962): 70–74.

"Solzhenitsyn: Literary Prophet for the Human Conscience." *Journal of Church and State* 16 (Winter 1974): 5–9.

"Seeking a Regenerate Church Membership." *Southwestern Journal of Theology* n.s. 3 (April 1961): 25–36.

"The Shifting Foci of the Protestant-Roman Catholic Confrontation: Peter, Mary, and the Sacraments." *Review and Expositor* 68 (Winter 1971): 29–41.

"Sources of Authority in Baptist Thought." *Baptist History and Heritage* 13 (July 1978): 41–49.

"Southern Baptists as Evangelicals." *Baptist History and Heritage* 18 (April 1983): 10–20.

"Studies of the Sixteenth Century Protestant Reformation: The Literature in English, 1946–1966." *Review and Expositor* 64 (Spring 1967): 207–25.

"The Theology and Practice of Baptism: A Southern Baptist Perspective." *Southwestern Journal of Theology* 28 (Spring 1986): 65–72.

"A Theology of Prayer." *Southwestern Journal of Theology* 15 (Spring 1972): 3–17.

"Understanding the Church: A Southern Baptist Perspective." *The Theological Educator* no. 39 (Spring 1989): 60–66.

"W. T. Conner: Contemporary Theologian." *Southwestern Journal of Theology* 25 (Spring 1983): 43–60.

"Waco Baptist Association, 1860–1985: A Worthy Model for Texas and Southern Baptists." *Texas Baptist History* 6 (1986): 23–35.

"What's Happening in Theology Today." *Search* 2 (Fall 1971): 44–52.

"Why Build for Worship?" *Quarterly Review* (October–November–December 1972): 9–20.

"Why Systematic Theology?" *Criswell Theological Review* 3 (Spring 1989): 259–81.

ENCYCLOPEDIA AND DICTIONARY ARTICLES

Dictionary of Christianity in America. Ed. Daniel G. Reid. Downers Grove, Ill.: InterVarsity Press, 1990. S.v. "Justification."

Disciple's Study Bible: New International Version. Nashville: Holman, 1988. S.v. "History of the Doctrine of Prayer."

Encyclopedia of Early Christianity. Ed. Everett Ferguson. New York: Garland, 1990. S.v. "Image of God" and "Satan."

Encyclopedia of Southern Baptists. 4 vols. Nashville: Broadman, 1958–82. Vol. 2. S.v. "Millennium," "Prayer," and "Theology, History of." Vol. 3. S.v. "Theologians, Baptist."

New Twentieth Century Encyclopedia of Religious Knowledge, 2d ed. Ed. J. D. Douglas. Grand Rapids: Baker, 1991. S.v. "Liberty, Religious."

MISCELLANEOUS

Baptists and the Awakenings of Modern History. Fort Worth: pvt. ptg., 1959.

"Crisis in Theological Education." *The Southern Baptist Educator*, February 1967, 6–9.

"Ecclesiology: The Crucial Issue." *Baptist Standard*, 14 October 1954, 6–7; 21 October 1954, 8.

"Foundations for Christian Citizenship." *Baptist Standard*, 8 December 1982, 14–15; rpt.: *The [Baptist] Student*, December 1983, 47–79.

(co-auth.) *Environment: A Southern Baptist and Roman Catholic Perspective*. Atlanta: Interfaith Witness Department, Home Mission Board, SBC; Huntington, Ind.: Our Sunday Visitor, 1993.

"Is Anything Sacred?" *Baptist Student*, May 1955, 12–15.

The Nature of the Church according to the Radical Continental Reformation. Fort Worth: pvt. ptg., 1957.

"Recovering My Priesthood." *Home Missions*, February 1965, 14–15.

"'Salvation': A Babel of Answers." *Baptist Student*, February 1961, 8–12.

"Seeking to Understand Baptist Theology." *Baptist Standard*, 18 August 1993, 8–10.

"Should Southern Baptists Adopt the Synod of Dort?" *Baptists Today*, 26 June 1997, 18–19.

"Theology Professor Examines Background to Statement's Changes," *Baptist Standard*, 29 May 2000, 10–12.

"Who Are the Baptists?" *The Baylor Line*, June 1985, 11–15.

2. Secondary

Basden, Paul A. "James Leo Garrett, Jr." In *Theologians of the Baptist Tradition*, ed. Timothy George and David S. Dockery, 297–316. Nashville: Broadman and Holman, 2001.

_____ and David S. Dockery, eds. *The People of God: Essays on the Believers' Church*. Nashville: Broadman, 1991. Note esp. ix-xii, 236–37, 243–46, 325–26, 333–34, 351.

Burkhalter, Frank E. *A World-Visioned Church: Story of the First Baptist Church, Waco, Texas*. Nashville: Broadman, 1946. Pp. 259–60.

Bush, L. Russ, III, and Thomas J. Nettles. *Baptists and the Bible: The Baptist Doctrines of Biblical Inspiration and Religious Authority in Historical Perspectives*. Chicago: Moody, 1980. Pp. 392–95. 2d ed. rev.: *Baptists and the Bible*. Nashville: Broadman and Holman, 1999. Pp. 356–58, 380–81.

Dockery, David S. "Looking Back, Looking Ahead." In *Theologians of the Baptist Tradition*, 358, 359, 409.

Estep, William R., Jr. "Law and Gospel in the Anabaptist-Baptist Tradition." *Grace Theological Journal* 12 (Fall 1991): 189, 213–14.

Freeman, Curtis W. "The 'Coming of Age' of Baptist Theology in Generation Twenty-Something." *Perspectives in Religious Studies* 27 (Spring 2000): 25, 28, 30, 33–34.

McNeal, Reggie. "The Priesthood of All Believers." In *Has Our Theology Changed? Southern Baptist Thought since 1845*, ed. Paul A. Basden, 207, 220–21. Nashville: Broadman and Holman, 1994.

Moody, Dwight A. "The Bible." In *Has Our Theology Changed? Southern Baptist Thought since 1845*, 10–11, 13–14, 19–21, 28–30,36–40.

[Pattillo, Wesley M. (Pat).] "Garrett . . . Ecumenical Baptist," *The Tie*, September 1970, 5.

Pitts, William L. "The Priesthood of All Christians in the Baptist Heritage." *Southwestern Journal of Theology* 30 (Spring 1988): 41–42.

_____. "The Relation of Baptists to Other Christians." In *The People of God: Essays on the Believers' Church*, 235–50.

Spivey, James T. "The Millennium." In *Has Our Theology Changed? Southern Baptist Thought since 1845*, 251.

Ralph Lee Smith
(1918–1999)
Old Testament

Rick L. Johnson

12

BIOGRAPHY

The academic contributions of Ralph L. Smith reflect the dedication of a man committed to making the Word of God known to ministers and laity alike. He was a teacher who wrote for the church. Born on 10 September 1918, he earned a B.Ed. degree from the University of Southern Illinois in 1942. While attending Southwestern Baptist Theological Seminary, he met and married fellow student Dorothy Frances Means of Independence, Missouri. Their four children are Frances Lee, Ruth Ann, Carolyn Sue, and Franklin Bennett.

In 1947 Smith took a position as Bible teacher and secretary of the Baptist Student Union at Texas A. and I. College in Kingsville, Texas. In 1949 he received his Th.D. degree and joined the faculty of Southwestern. He retired formally in 1989 but continued teaching through spring 1996. He died on 23 July 1999 and was buried in Laurel Land Cemetery, Fort Worth.

Students of Ralph Smith remember him as the master of Old Testament theology. He taught many different courses in Hebrew and the Old Testament. At times he led the doctoral seminars on Old Testament criticism and the poetical literature. His primary interest, however, was Old Testament theology, having written his dissertation on "The Doctrine of God in the Psalms." He offered for many years the master's degree course and the doctoral seminar on Old Testament theology.

The major influences on his thinking can be found in his voluminous reading. His writings show thorough awareness of the world of Old Testament scholarship. He studied or carried out research at Harvard University, Perkins School of Theology, the University of Chicago, Oxford, Cambridge, and Edinburgh. In 1957 he spent a brief sabbatical in Palestine in connection with New York University.

His ministry included preaching and teaching in churches and other Baptist settings. Harry Hunt has noted that in earlier years Ralph Smith frequently supplied in pulpits, served as interim pastor and evangelist, and taught Bible studies in churches.[1] During 1977–1978 he continued in these roles while teaching at the Taiwan Baptist Seminary. He wrote many articles for Sunday School literature, state Baptist papers, and study Bibles and worked on the New American Standard Version of the Bible.

In recognition of his accomplishments, the regional Society of Biblical Literature elected him president in 1968. The Baptist Bible Teachers Association elected him president in 1969. Southwestern Baptist Theological Seminary honored him by naming him Distinguished Professor of Old Testament and Hebrew in 1987. The *Southwestern Journal of Theology* dedicated its Summer 1990 issue to him.

WRITINGS

This survey will only consider the books and scholarly articles that are significant for understanding Smith's thought, especially on Old Testament theology. The earliest was "Interpretation of Scriptures—Principles of Interpretation" (1958). Here he defined six principles essential to correct understanding of the Bible: establishing the original text, identifying the historical background, interpreting the grammatical sense, considering the literary context, listening to the Holy Spirit, and applying the Scriptures to the present. He stated clearly the guiding presuppositions that can be found throughout all of his later work. "God has spoken through various authors," and interpreters must "understand the thoughts of the men through whom he wrote." Smith's commitment to evangelical truth rings clear. "Because the Bible is a divine Book as well as a human Book, its spiritual truths must be spiritually discerned. One must be a member of the redeemed community before he can correctly interpret the Word of God."

The next year Smith offered a survey and evaluation of the reemergence of Old Testament theology in "The Revival of Old

Testament Theology." He briefly explained the reasons for the death and rebirth of the discipline and gave five characteristics of the new work. It used historical criticism, appropriated biblical categories for its organization, recognized the importance of revelation, and emphasized the uniqueness of Israel's faith and the unity of the Bible. Smith applauded the renewed attention to revelation and its demand for commitment. He warned, however, that overemphasis on theology at the expense of historical critical exegesis could lead to a new rationalism and dogmatism.

Smith contributed several articles to *Southwestern Journal of Theology*. Most of them treated the book chosen for the Winter Bible Study (formerly, the January Bible Study) in the Southern Baptist Convention. The *Journal* also published his essay "Old Testament Concepts of Stewardship" in 1971.

The civil rights movement in the 1960s led to the collection of essays on race in the first volume of *The Cutting Edge* (1969). Smith wrote "The Race Issue in the Old Testament," demonstrating the unity of humanity and refuting purported biblical bases for racism.

In 1970, Convention Press published Ralph Smith's book, *Israel's Period of Progress*, as volume four of the Bible Survey Series. His book, *Job: A Study in Providence and Faith*, written as the Church Study Course book for the January Bible Study, appeared in 1971. He wrote the commentary on Amos for *The Broadman Bible Commentary*.

The *Wycliffe Bible Encyclopedia* appeared in 1975. Sponsored by Moody Press, it adhered to "Christian orthodoxy, the fundamentals of the faith generally accepted by believers of conservative, evangelical persuasion."[2] Smith wrote eighteen entries for this work and collaborated on another. He wrote four articles for the *Baker Encyclopedia of the Bible* and six for the *Holman Bible Dictionary*.

The first of Smith's major publications appeared in 1984, his Word Biblical Commentary volume on the minor prophets from Micah through Malachi. The design of the series called for an original translation of the biblical texts, a bibliography, an introduction, and commentary on technical, linguistic, historical, formal, and theological concerns. The editors chose authors whom they considered evangelical "in its positive, historic sense of a commitment to scripture as divine revelation, and to the truth and power of the Christian gospel."[3] The related series, Word Biblical Themes, presented Smith's companion volume.

In 1993, Broadman and Holman published the crowning achievement of Smith's career, his *Old Testament Theology: Its History, Method, and Message*, addressing "students, pastors, and interested lay people."[4] Written for use as a textbook and using voluminous quotations from other theologians, it led readers into deeper knowledge of the message of the Old Testament and of the history of Old Testament theology. It is the principal source for his thought.

CONTRIBUTION TO OLD TESTAMENT STUDIES

An assessment of Ralph Smith's views of the Old Testament requires an understanding of his conclusions about methodology. On that basis it is possible to explain his positions on the reliability of the Old Testament record, the origin of the books, and their message in the past and the present.

Critical Methodology

Smith's use of the critical disciplines of Bible study derived from his commitment to the Bible itself. His estimation of it as the Word of God appears repeatedly in his writings.[5] It is not merely an assertion secondary to his purpose. Instead, it motivated his life. He wrote to make the Bible accessible to others. His respect for its truth even appears in his touching tribute to his wife Dorothy.[6]

In principle, Smith considered it mandatory for responsible Christian interpretation to use critical disciplines.[7] Since the Bible in the first instance is God's Word to humanity at particular times and places, it is necessary to use historical investigation. God spoke through particular people to their contemporaries. The proper way to read the resulting texts is first to ask what they meant when they were produced. Consequently, Smith used not only textual criticism and grammatical exegesis but also source criticism, form criticism, history of traditions, historical criticism, and canonical criticism.[8]

The other side of Smith's reception of the Bible as divine and human required dependence on the Holy Spirit for understanding. Just as the Spirit worked through the writers in history to produce the books, so also the Spirit works through the disciplines of reading and historical investigation to enlighten minds today.[9] His previously mentioned claim that interpreters must be redeemed people fits his later claim that Old Testament theology is a Christian discipline.[10]

The historical movement begun in the Old Testament finds its fulfillment in Jesus Christ.

History of Israel

Smith's confidence in the reliability of the biblical record led him to
conservative conclusions about history. He used historical criticism
to weigh the significance of archaeological discoveries for interpreting the Bible. While some scholars at the end of the twentieth century denied the historical trustworthiness of anything in the Old
Testament before the eighth or ninth centuries BC, Smith confi-
dently accepted the veracity of the traditions about the patriarchs,
Moses, the Exodus, the Sinai covenant, the conquest of Canaan, the
battle of Jericho, David, and Solomon.[11]

When extracanonical evidence conflicted with traditional interpretations of the Bible, Smith practiced caution. Often he post-
poned firm conclusions until more evidence was available. On the
long day in Joshua 10, he surveyed various theories but did not state
his preference.[12] He handled similarly the questions about the number of Israelites in the Exodus and the account of the battle at Ai in
Joshua 7–8.[13] He preferred to date the Exodus late, allowing archaeological evidence to influence the understanding of the biblical
text.[14] He granted that the site of the crossing of the sea was
unknown but appears to have favored a central location based on
biblical evidence.[15] In none of these cases, however, did he doubt
the historicity of the events.

Composition of Old Testament Literature

The cautious conservatism which Smith exhibited in historical conclusions also governed his views of the writing of Old Testament
books. On the Pentateuch, he warned against assigning all of it or
none of it to Moses, recommending instead a respect for biblical
claims and an openness to different interpretations of them.[16] Since
he apparently accepted the existence of the Yahwist (J) in the tenth
century BC, it seems likely he would have accepted the existence of
all four traditions J, E, D, and P.[17] On the other hand, he recognized
the subjective and provisional nature of the history of traditions
method and rejected it as a basis for constructing Old Testament
theology.[18] He considered the text of the Bible itself to be the
authoritative basis.

Since Smith did not write on every part of the Old Testament, it
is not possible to know his views about every book. But his general

approach can be gleaned from what he did write. He treated the prophetic books as substantially from the men whose names appear over them, while also granting that later editors and preservers of tradition had a hand in supplementing and shaping them. It is common to deny that hopeful passages stem from preexilic prophets. But, although Smith left the question open, he thought it likely that Amos wrote the hopeful end to his book.[19] Similarly, he granted that Micah had words of hope and stood behind the whole of his book, even though parts of it could come from later hands.[20] He concluded that Zechariah 7–8 was from Zechariah but was edited at a later time. He thought it was impossible to determine the original setting of Zechariah 9–14.[21]

Smith treated the wisdom books as products of tradition. The book of Proverbs resulted from a collection of Solomonic material being expanded until perhaps the fifth century BC. Job likely passed through several hands before being shaped as a unity by a single person in the sixth century BC. The author of Ecclesiastes lived in the fourth or third century BC. Smith supported these conclusions on the basis of linguistic and internal evidence.[22]

Aside from questions of date and authorship, Smith thought it important to identify the genre and, if possible, the situation in life (*Sitz im Leben*) of the books and individual passages. Like most contemporary scholars, he recognized that the key to the book of Psalms lies not in identifying the author of each one but in asking how it was used in Israel's worship. Form criticism provides essential clues. Since it is the final form of the text that is Scripture, Smith also accepted the validity of redaction criticism, literary criticism, and canonical criticism. He insisted, however, on testing their results against the text itself.

Old Testament Theology

Smith's contribution to Old Testament theology appears not only in his textbook but also in the numerous essays on the theology of various parts of the Old Testament and on particular doctrines. His approach remained remarkably consistent throughout his career.

In defining the discipline of Old Testament theology, Smith resisted a merely cognitive approach.[23] Knowledge of God in the biblical sense is experiential and requires commitment. But Smith also resisted a definition of the discipline as normative in a way leading to sectarianism. The normativity of Old Testament theology is limited by its pre-Christian status. It is "valid as far as it goes" and is descriptive in that it deals with events in the Old Testament.[24] "Old Testament theology is a 'reflection on,' a 'construal,' and a 'construct' of the theological materials in the Old Testament that are relevant to us."[25]

Although the traditional systematic organization had fallen out of favor, Smith continued to use it for several reasons. Whatever organizational principle a theologian might use will always be a foreign schema imposed on the text. No thematic center is sufficiently comprehensive for the Old Testament. Tradition history is too uncertain. The "key-word" approach lacks cohesiveness and falsely assumes that individual words have theological content. Secondly, the systematic approach is appropriate for an exercise interested in theological content. Theology is constructive work, and the systematic approach identifies materials suitable for religious purposes beyond those envisioned by the biblical authors. Furthermore, it facilitates the appropriation of results by students.

Accordingly, Smith's treatment included the following doctrines: knowledge of God (revelation), election and covenant, the nature of Yahweh, the nature of humanity, sin and redemption, worship, the obedient life, death and resurrection, and the consummation. In each area Smith introduced both the biblical materials and the most important modern discussions, including definitions of biblical and modern vocabulary.

A dialectical posture dominates the chapter on the knowledge of God. Such knowledge is relational and involves both words and acts of God, who reveals and hides himself. The commitment demanded by such "knowledge" extends to the modern question of verifiability. Historical confirmation is important if God's actions occurred in the real world, but judgments about it require subjective faith dispositions. Even the revelation of the name Yahweh bears this dialectical, relational nature. God commits himself to his people but remains free from coercion.

God's commitment immediately includes election, which grows out of his sovereignty and issues in mission. It does not eliminate the need for human decision, nor does nonelection mean reprobation. The nonelect have different roles than the elect and may even be better than the elect. Their place in God's plan is simply different. The elect receive a covenant from God. Smith rejected the idea of an Adamic covenant and concluded Israel had two covenant traditions, one promissory (Noah, Abraham, David) and one with obligations (Sinai). The prophets, however, rejected any claims of permanent security. The promissory covenant tradition and Jeremiah's new covenant led Smith to discuss views of their relationship to the New Testament, but he concluded that a final answer was beyond the scope of Old Testament theology as a descriptive endeavor. Here, as in his earlier treatments of this question, Smith showed the importance of taking all that the Bible says on a subject rather than isolating proof texts. The covenant was permanently available but always assumed obligations.[26]

Smith organized the doctrine of God by following the historical sequence of the order in which Israel learned about the divine nature. Consequently, God's saving and blessing character precedes creation. The oneness of God comes at the end and leads to a consideration of ties to Trinitarian theology. History-of-religions material appears in several connections.

Smith found no systematic doctrine of humanity in the Old Testament. His outline emphasized creatureliness, the image of God, and the social and unitary character of humans. Relational categories again aid his discussion. The image of God binds people not only to God but to one another. The stress in Genesis on gender deals with "personal encounter, not progeny." "Men and women are human beings on the basis of perfect equality."[27] Smith agreed with many contemporary scholars that biblical anthropology understands human beings to be unitary rather than dichotomous or trichotomous.

Sin is rebellion against God, leads to estrangement at every level of human existence, is without excuse, and is inexplicable. By free choice Adam and Eve disobeyed. God removes sin when the rebellious mind turns around and seeks forgiveness, which is the renewal of relationship. Smith listed many biblical metaphors for removal of sin, including a few instances of propitiation.

On worship, Smith discussed linguistic terms and times, places, and forms. He accepted the historicity of the tabernacle tradition. Old Testament forms of worship were legitimate but ultimately inadequate. An excursus rejected the connection between circumcision and baptism. Smith's chapter on ethics is mainly retrospective and programmatic. He emphasized the inseparability of religion and ethics and also the importance of the covenant. Ethics depends on the will of God.

Accepting a broad definition of Old Testament eschatology as including events surrounding the end of the age, Smith dealt first with individual destiny and then with national and cosmic questions. He explained Israel's slow development of an idea of life after death as possibly related to opposition to pagan religions, to an emphasis on corporate and unitary views of human existence, and to a dominating concern for existence in the present. Only Isa. 26:19 and Dan. 12:2 clearly mention resurrection of the individual, but other passages provide a theological foundation for the belief. The future of Israel and the world included restoration of nature. Since human sin affected the physical order, the coming of the kingdom of God would require a renewal of the cosmic realm. Israel's specific expectations did not include a new universe, but Israel's hopes were reinterpreted in that direction in later Judaism and the New Testament. Jesus fulfilled the hopes for the Messiah, the Suffering Servant in Isaiah, and the Son of Man (Daniel 7), although the Old Testament writers themselves did not foresee how he would do so.

EVALUATION OF THOUGHT AND INFLUENCE

Ralph Smith's contribution to Old Testament studies must be understood primarily as an expression of his Christian faith. His writings repeatedly address the questions of Jesus' fulfillment of Old Testament hopes and the relevance of the Old Testament for contemporary Christians. He wrote for the church. No other present work of Old Testament theology is at once so comprehensive, so accessible for beginning students, and so thorough in surveying scholarship as his book.

Appropriately for modern readers, he insisted on the necessity of a historical understanding of the Bible. The Word of God came first to the ancient Israelites. Smith's insistence on not reading Christian ideas into the text of the Old Testament at times forced him to leave certain exegetical questions unanswered. But his concern to appropriate the significance of the Old Testament in the present led him to address contemporary issues dealt with only minimally or not at all in the Old Testament, such as the Trinity, abortion, homosexuality, and the supposed relationship between circumcision and baptism (he wrote as a Baptist).[28]

The influence of modern discussions can be seen in his choice and ordering of topics. Discussions of revelation, election, and covenant precede the nature of God. One might perceive here a modern concern for epistemology stemming from the Enlightenment.

But one could also argue that Smith allowed Israel's experiences of divine revelation in history to shape his presentation. He answered modern questions in biblical terms. One could see influence from dialectical theology in his emphasis on covenant and relational categories and in his resistance to strict systematic schemes, but he retained too much emphasis on history to be called a dialectical theologian. He used systematic categories but no system. His awareness of the importance of presuppositions made him wary of overconfidence in modernity and critical methodology.

On the whole, Smith was a conservative Baptist Christian Old Testament theologian whose work exudes deep faith and missionary spirit. It would be difficult for anyone to measure the influence which he had in forty-seven years of teaching. His students numbered in the thousands and spread around the world. His doctoral students have taught in many universities and seminaries. Even many of those who were not Old Testament majors remembered his seminar as one of the high points of their education. His witness to the Lord Jesus Christ continues in their lives and work today.

BIBLIOGRAPHY

1. Primary

DISSERTATION
"The Doctrine of God in the Psalms." Ph.D. diss., Southwestern Baptist Theological Seminary, 1949.

BOOKS
Israel's Period of Progress. Nashville: Convention Press, 1970.
Job: A Study in Providence and Faith. Nashville: Convention Press, 1971.
    El Libro de Job: Un Engoque a la Providencia y la Fe. El Paso: Casa Bautista de Publicaciones, 1971. [Spanish]
Micah–Malachi. Word Biblical Commentary, vol. 32. Waco, Tex.: Word, 1984.
    Miga–Mallagi. Inchon: Immanuel, 1991. [Korean]
Micah–Malachi. Word Biblical Themes. Dallas: Word, 1990.
Old Testament Theology: Its History, Method, and Message. Nashville: Broadman and Holman, 1993.

CHAPTERS CONTRIBUTED TO BOOKS
"Amos." In *The Broadman Bible Commentary*, ed. Clifton J. Allen, vol. 7, *Hosea—Malachi*, 81–141. Nashville: Broadman, 1972.
"A City without Walls." In *Southwestern Sermons*, ed. H. C. Brown, 184–88. Nashville: Broadman, 1960.
"The Race Issue in the Old Testament." In *The Cutting Edge: Critical Questions for Contemporary Christians*, ed. H. C. Brown, Jr., 1:32–41. Waco, Tex.: Word, 1969.

JOURNAL ARTICLES

"The Book of Jeremiah." *Southwestern Journal of Theology* 4 (October 1961): 11–32.

"Covenant and Law in Exodus." *Southwestern Journal of Theology* 20 (Fall 1977): 33–41.

"Introduction to the Book of Job." *Southwestern Journal of Theology* 14 (Fall 1971): 5–16.

"Major Motifs of Hosea." *Southwestern Journal of Theology* 18 (Fall 1975): 22–32.

"Old Testament Concepts of Stewardship." *Southwestern Journal of Theology* 13 (Spring 1971): 7–13.

"The Revival of Old Testament Theology." *Southwestern Journal of Theology* 1 (April 1959): 35–42.

"The Shape of Theology in the Book of Job." *Southwestern Journal of Theology* 30 (Fall 1987): 22–27.

"Significant Old Testament Commentaries since 1950." *Southwestern Journal of Theology* 23 (Spring 1981): 30–40.

"Some Theological Concepts in the Book of Deuteronomy." *Southwestern Journal of Theology* 7 (October 1964): 17–32.

"The Theological Implications of the Prophecy of Amos." *Southwestern Journal of Theology* 9 (Fall 1966): 49–56.

"The Use and Influence of the Psalms." *Southwestern Journal of Theology* 27 (Fall 1984): 5–16.

PERIODICAL ARTICLES

"Clues to the Study of Job." *Outreach*, December 1971, 6–7.

"God, Man, Creation: The Biblical View." *Outreach*, April 1978, 38–39.

"A Look at Wisdom Literature." *Outreach*, July 1975, 40–41.

"Pilgrims of Faith." *Outreach*, June 1978, 34–35.

"The Sin Problem." *Outreach*, May 1978, 20–21.

DICTIONARY AND ENCYCLOPEDIA ARTICLES

Baker Encyclopedia of the Bible. Ed. Walter A. Elwell. 2 vols. Grand Rapids: Baker, 1988. Vol. 1. S.v. "Balance, Balances," and "Chronicles, Books of First and Second." Vol. 2. S.v. "Micah, Book of," and "Zechariah, Book of."

Encyclopedia of Southern Baptists. 4 vols. Nashville: Broadman, 1958–82. Vol. 1. S.v. "Copass, Benjamin Andrew" (coauth.), "Interpretation of Scriptures—Principles of Interpretation," and "Crowder, Joseph Wade." Vol. 2. S.v. "Old Testament Literature—The Law." Vol. 3. S.v. "Rossell, William Harvey."

Holman Bible Dictionary. Ed. Trent C. Butler. Nashville: Holman Bible Publishers, 1991. S.v. "Exodus," "Hell," "Malachi," "Pentateuch," "Pit," and "Red Sea (Reed Sea)."

Disciple's Study Bible: New International Version. Nashville: Holman Bible Publishers, 1988. S.v. "Job: An Introduction."

Wycliffe Bible Encyclopedia. 2 vols. Chicago: Moody, 1975. Vol. 1. S.v. "Ark of the Covenant," "Camp," "Captivity," "Cart," "Chariot," "Deborah," "Eliezer," "Gedaliah," "Gehazi," "Gemariah," "Gerizim" (coauth.), "Geshem," "Hallel," and "Haman." Vol. 2. S.v. "Milk," "Psalms," "Ships," "Theocracy," and "Zerah."

2. Secondary

" Ralph Smith: Tribute to a Teacher." *Southwestern Journal of Theology* 32 (Summer 1990).

Henry Clifton Brown, Jr.
(1921–1973)
Preaching

Al Fasol

H. C. Brown, Jr., had an analytical mind, a tenacious personality, a ready smile, and a love for seminary students and was devoted to teaching and writing. His analytical mind is seen in his lecture notes and in his writings. The tenacious personality is testified to by his faculty colleagues. The ready smile is apparent in photographs of him, and in the memories of his family and his students. His love for students is evident in our warm memories of him and our sense of loyalty to him decades after his death. His devotion to writing is evident in the books and articles which he wrote in his twenty-four years on the Southwestern faculty.

Much of Brown's life was dominated by an illness suffered when he was ten years old. This illness was devastating to his self-image. He loved sports, but because of his health problems he could not participate in them. He loved preaching, but because of his illness he was limited in how much preaching he could do, especially in the last ten years of his life. Brown wrote of his health problems in the introductory chapter of his book *Walking toward Your Fear:* "When I was ten years old, I had had rheumatic fever with resulting damage to the aortic and mitral valves of my heart. Since then I had practiced hiding the truth about my heart problems."[1]

His heart problems led to two open heart surgeries, the second of which he did not survive. His heart problems gave to him a constant sense of urgency: about time, how much he had left before he died; and, therefore, about his life, how much he could achieve before his weakened heart muscles brought an end to his teaching and writing.

BIOGRAPHY

Henry Clifton Brown, Jr., was born in Bossier City, Louisiana, on 16 September 1921. His father was employed as a switchman by a railroad company. Brown and his parents and older sister attended the First Baptist Church of Bossier City, where H. C., Jr., was baptized in May 1930.

Brown attended a business school after high school graduation. By this time the nation had been in the Great Depression for ten years. Because of his heart problems, Brown's parents felt that their son should do clerical work. In private conversations, Brown said that his parents, like many parents in the 1930s, wanted their son to work in a bank, where they hoped he would find vocational and financial security.

At that time, Dr. G. Earl Guinn became pastor of First Baptist Church in Bossier City. Guinn had a strong positive effect on the youthful H. C. Brown, Jr. Guinn prayed with him, and through those prayer sessions Brown came to realize that God wanted him in the ministry. Guinn virtually dictated the course of the rest of Brown's life. Guinn told Brown where to go to college and to seminary and later, when Guinn was on the faculty of Southwestern, he was influential in having Brown invited to teach preaching.

Brown enrolled at Louisiana Baptist College in Pineville just as Guinn urged him to do. During his college days Brown was active on the debate team and honed his analytical skills in preparing and responding to other debate teams. In addition to his studies, Brown was pastor of the Mora, Louisiana, Baptist Church, during 1943–44. He also served as president of the Baptist Student Union council, 1944–46, and as state Baptist Student Union president in 1946.

Brown served as associate pastor of the First Baptist Church of Pollock, Louisiana and was ordained there in 1946. While enrolled at Louisiana Baptist, he was married to Dorothy Ruth Ware on 25 May 1945. She majored in English and helped her husband in writing his papers, in preparing his debate presentations, and later in the editing and writing of his first books. Their children were Mary Kathryn, who survives, and Clifton Scott, who died in infancy.

Brown enrolled in the B.D. program at Southern Baptist Theological Seminary in the fall of 1946, again just as Guinn urged him to do. While a student at the seminary, Brown was called to his last pastorate at Pigeon Fork Baptist Church in Waddy, Kentucky. He served there from 1947 to 1949. He graduated with the B.D. in May 1949. That summer he accepted an invitation to teach preaching at Southwestern and would work on his Th.D. His major was Old Testament, and he wrote his dissertation on "Positive Elements in the Preaching of Amos and Hosea," thus combining his major studies with his field of instruction.

WRITINGS

Brown edited, authored, coauthored, and coedited fifteen books. *Southern Baptist Preaching*, published in 1959, is a collection of sermons by selected Southern Baptist preachers. Each preacher wrote a one-page summary of his sermon preparation and selected one of his sermons for publication. Brown used the sermons as models for class discussion.

Southwestern Sermons, published in 1960, is a collection of sermons from the faculty of Southwestern's School of Theology. These sermons were also used as a teaching tool.

Steps to the Sermon was coauthored by Brown and his colleagues in the Department of Preaching, H. Gordon Clinard and Jesse J. Northcutt. This book takes the beginning preacher from a foundational understanding of the nature and task of preaching through sermon preparation and closes with a discussion of sermon delivery. This book has been in continuous publication since 1963 and was revised in 1996.

J. Howard Williams: Prophet of God and Friend of Man is a collection of remembrances of the fourth president of Southwestern Seminary. The book, coedited by Brown and Charles P. Johnson, was published in 1963.

In *More Southern Baptist Preaching,* issued in 1964, Brown returned to the compiling of a collection of sermons. Smarting from criticism that he received for preachers not included in his earlier compilation, Brown published a second book in which selected

Southern Baptist preachers summarized their methods of sermon preparation and selected a sermon to be included in the book.

Chapel Messages is a collection of sermons preached in chapel services at Southwestern. Brown considered hundreds of sermons preached in chapel and chose thirteen for this book, which was published in 1966. Brown said that he wanted to help future chapel speakers to see how other preachers had addressed the student body. Brown also included a two-page listing of criteria for preaching effectively in chapel, which is coupled with the headings "More of Excellence" and "Less of Mediocrity."

A Christian Layman's Guide to Public Speaking is a brief book published in 1966 to do exactly what the title says. Brown summarized his basic preaching courses as a guide for the lay speaker to get a handle on sermon preparation and delivery.

A Search for Strength (1967) was a therapeutic writing exercise. Brown's first wife, Dorothy Ruth, died in 1966. Brown wrote as an impressionist would paint. He described his stages of grief and what he did to cope at each stage.

A Quest for Reformation in Preaching had been in Brown's mind for a long time. The illness and untimely death of Dorothy Ruth had prevented his concentrating on the book. After writing *A Search for Strength,* Brown submitted his manuscript for *Quest* to his doctoral seminars. He asked for and received several suggestions, and the book was published in 1968. Brown was disappointed in it and thought of several revisions which he wanted to make. He had, however, some other writing obligations to fulfill first, and he was becoming warmly acquainted with his editor at Broadman Press. Velma Darbo, an author in her own right, had worked on some of Brown's manuscripts. They were married in 1967.

Quest was published by Word Books. Brown's acquaintance with the editors at Word led to invitations to edit the *Biblical Sunday School Commentary, 1969,* and *1970.*

On several occasions Brown taught a doctoral seminar titled "Preaching on Contemporary Issues." He assigned to his students research on specific ethical issues. From these seminars came a two-volume work entitled *The Cutting Edge,* published by Word in 1969. These volumes are much more related to the study of Christian ethics than they are to preaching. Brown presumed that he could help the busy pastor by supplying information on the ethical issues of the day and the pastor could then apply the principles of sermon preparation taught in his classes and develop his own sermons.

Brown's analytical mind led to *Sermon Analysis for Pulpit Power.* This little paperback, published in 1971, is a series of questions to be asked by the preacher throughout sermon preparation as a way of guiding the preacher to keep the sermon closely related to its text.

Brown had long felt that the principles of sermon preparation could be applied to teaching. Consequently, he and his second wife, Velma Darbo Brown, published *Preparing for Effective Bible Teaching* in 1971.

Walking toward Your Fear was Brown's final book. It was written after Brown learned that he would have to undergo a second heart surgery. Although the writing of this book was therapeutic, Brown deeply hoped that he could encourage others who would undergo any sort of major surgery. Brown reviewed his early feelings related to his heart problem and how his faith was strengthening him in his preparation for his second surgery. The book was published in 1972, the year before he died.

CONTRIBUTIONS

Brown's most significant books were *A Quest for Reformation in Preaching* and *Steps to the Sermon,* of which he was a coauthor. Within these two books, but especially *Quest*, Brown contributed some unique insights to the study of preaching.

In chapter one of *Quest*, Brown expressed an intense dislike for shallow, shoddy, unimaginative, cliché-ridden preaching that sounded religious—even at times sounded Christian—but had little relationship to a biblical text. The opening pages are replete with exclamation points as he made his case for a "Reformation" in preaching: "Why do we have so much poor preaching from Protestant pulpits? *The reason is that Protestant ministers hold inadequate and inferior concepts about the ministry in general and preaching in particular.*"[2] In the preface Brown had written that "homiletical fitness . . . may be secured by a correct understanding of the authentic nature of a sermon. . . . Authentic sermons must be understood in terms of *authority* [italics mine], purpose, and form."[3]

The unique contribution of *Quest* is Brown's emphasis on and description of biblical authority in the sermon. Only a few homiletical books make an allusion to the relationship of the biblical text to the sermon. *Quest* is the only book in the history of homiletical writing that attempts in intricate detail to describe how the relationship between the text and the sermon may be measured. "The reformation of preaching," he wrote, "depends upon the proclamation of sermons saturated with true Biblical authority."[4]

The first category, to Brown, is the highest one. *Direct* biblical authority conveys the central idea of the text, or

> uses Scripture in the message with the same meaning as it has in the text. The direct Biblical sermon employs the natural, grammatical, and historical meaning of the text in a direct, straightforward fashion. Only by moving correctly from the grammatical-historical "then" to the relevant "now" can a sermon be a direct Biblical sermon.[5]

Brown used a "plain vanilla" approach in describing how a *direct* biblical sermon may be prepared. Brown taught that the *direct* biblical sermon employs affirmations and propositions of the Bible, uses negatives and prohibitions of Scripture, and makes use of timeless and eternal truth of Scripture. This last category was to be achieved by writing a central idea of the text, which was to be a simple declarative sentence interpreting what the text meant "then" and that from which a present-tense application of the text could be written.

The next category is the *indirect* biblical sermon. "In one sense the indirect Biblical sermon moves at a tangent from the central idea of the text."[6] Each step away from the *direct* biblical sermon brings on additional room for hermeneutical subjectivity. Brown urged the preacher to exercise caution and to be certain not to misconstrue the text.

The third category is the *casual* biblical sermon. Brown warns that hermeneutical subjectivity can become extreme here. This sermon may be a spiritual essay that has some bare connection to a text, or it may be developed from some idea suggested by the text. His favorite illustration of a rhetorical suggestion is taken from Phil. 4:22 (KJV): "All the saints salute you, chiefly they that are of Caesar's household." The saints in Caesar's household suggest being a Christian in a difficult place.

166

Combination biblical authority may be self-explanatory. Brown had in mind sermons in which major sections may be developed with variations in biblical authority. For instance, there can be a major point which is *direct*, and the other points perhaps either *indirect* or *casual*.

The final category Brown described as the *corrupted* use of Scripture, or sermons in which the eternal truths of the text are set aside and the preacher's own apostate ideas are proclaimed.

Steps to the Sermon was coauthored by Brown, Clinard, and Northcutt. In their introductions to their courses on sermon preparation, Clinard and Northcutt would often admit that Brown was the "captain" of their writing team. They acknowledged his leadership; in fact, the idea of publishing a book on sermon preparation originated with Brown. *Steps* was published five years prior to *Quest* and is still in print today in a revised edition. In the preface, the authors wrote that the purpose of their book was "to define, to explain, and to place in sequence all sermonic parts so that a preacher not only understands *what* he is doing and *how* he is doing it, but he understands *when* he should do it."[7] Thus the book suggests eight chronological steps in preparing a sermon.

Those eight steps begin with a definition and a history of preaching; move to finding an idea for a sermon and relating that idea to a biblical text; interpreting the text; gathering information and illustrations related to the text; maturing the sermon idea; forming the actual sermon; finalizing and polishing the sermon; and delivering the sermon. *Steps* presumes that each sermon will be built on rhetorical outline points. In fact, chapters five, "Maturing the Idea," and six, "Formulating the Structure," include as detailed an analysis of outlining as will be found in any course in rhetoric or in logic. Every intricacy in outlining is illustrated and discussed and borders on being overwhelming to the first-time preacher. The final chapter, "Delivering the Sermon," is a cursory summary of sermon delivery but is a good primer for novice preachers.

Soon, *Steps* will be in its fortieth year of continuous publication. Obviously the book has met a need in the field.

INFLUENCE

When H. C. Brown, Jr., began teaching preaching in 1949, he had been aware that new methods of evaluating sermons were desperately needed. He had determined that the words "expository," "textual," and "topical" were inadequate for describing and evaluating a sermon.

"Expository" had many definitions among preachers, some saying that expository preaching meant discussing every word of a text and others saying that expository meant discussing each verse but not each word of the text. Other preachers scoffed at those definitions and said that expository preaching is simply the exposition of the text no matter what form the sermon takes. "Textual" was defined superficially as a sermon having a text of only one or two verses. "Topical" sermons included several biblical passages all related to a particular topic. Brown, disdaining these terms, sought a method for sermon preparation and for measuring the effectiveness of that method that would help the preacher much more than using words which had varied and superficial meanings.

The *method* came first. Brown decided to put his students through a hermeneutical exercise in which they were to determine the *central idea of the text*. This central idea was to be limited to fifteen to eighteen words, expressing the eternal truth of the text in past tense. Next, the student was to express this idea in a fifteen- to eighteen-word present tense application. Consequently the preaching students first grounded themselves in the "then" of the biblical passage and then moved from the "then" to the "now" by writing a present tense application of the text.

This exercise taught a generation of preachers to begin their sermon preparation with the text. The preaching students learned that the biblical text dictates the development of the sermon, and a strong, clear biblical sermon is the result.

Next came the *measuring stick*. Brown, as noted, was the first homiletics author to provide a way to measure the biblical authority of a sermon. Rather than just asking whether the sermon is expository, textual, or topical, Brown provided a way of measuring the true worth of the sermon by measuring its biblical authority. Although some of his nomenclature is unfortunate, Brown did put the homiletical world on an invaluable track for studying the relationship of a sermon to its biblical text. No other book in the history of homiletics analyzes this subject as thoroughly as does *A Quest for Reformation in Preaching.*

H. C. Brown, Jr., did not preach often; his damaged heart prevented him from doing so. Instead, he became an analyst of preaching and through his writings contributed valuable instruction for those who would and do preach.

BIBLIOGRAPHY

DISSERTATION

"Positive Elements in the Preaching of Amos and Hosea." Th.D. diss., Southwestern Baptist Theological Seminary, 1954.

BOOKS

(ed.) *Biblical Sunday School Commentary, 1969.* Waco, Tex.: Word, 1968.
(ed.) *Biblical Sunday School Commentary, 1970.* Waco, Tex.: Word, 1969.
(ed.) *Chapel Messages.* Grand Rapids: Baker, 1966.
A Christian Layman's Guide to Public Speaking. Nashville: Broadman, 1966.
(ed.) *The Cutting Edge: Critical Questions for Contemporary Christians.* 2 vols. Waco, Tex.: Word, 1969.
(co-ed.) *J. Howard Williams: Prophet of God and Friend of Man.* San Antonio: Naylor Co., 1963.
Messages for Men: For Laymen and Ministers. Grand Rapids: Zondervan, 1960.
(ed.) *More Southern Baptist Preaching.* Nashville: Broadman, 1964.
(co-auth.) *Preparing for Effective Bible Teaching.* Nashville: Broadman, 1971.
A Quest for Reformation in Preaching. Waco, Tex.: Word, 1968.
A Search for Strength. Waco, Tex.: Word, 1967.
Sermon Analysis for Pulpit Power. Nashville: Broadman, 1971.
(ed.) *Southern Baptist Preaching.* Nashville: Broadman, 1959.
(ed.) *Southwestern Sermons.* Nashville: Broadman, 1960.
(co-auth.) *Steps to the Sermon.* Nashville: Broadman, 1963; rev. ed.: Broadman and Holman, 1996.
Sulgyo Bangbupron. Trans. Cheong Hui Lee. Seoul: Jordan Press, 1985. [Korean]
Walking toward Your Fear. Nashville: Broadman, 1972.

ARTICLES

"Power in the Pulpit." *Christianity Today,* 2 January 1961, 7–8.
"Preaching Values in Mark's Gospel." *Southwestern Journal of Theology* n.s. 1 (October 1958): 63–73.
"The Primacy of Preaching." *Southwestern Journal of Theology* n.s. 5 (April 1963): 85–97.

William Curtis Vaughan

(1924–)
New Testament

14

R. Bruce Corley

BIOGRAPHY

Like Caesar's Gaul, Tennessee, stretching 450 miles from the Appalachians to the Mississippi, is divided into three parts. The marshy western third of the state is cotton country, resting on a low, fertile plateau that edges down to the Mississippi, where the high river bluffs hold the state's largest city—the storied port of Memphis. The deep soil of West Tennessee has produced bountiful crops and stalwart people; one of its notable sons is Curtis Vaughan. He was born 30 October 1924 in Humboldt, some eighty miles northeast of Memphis, as the sixth in a family of seven children—two girls, five boys. His father, Benjamin Franklin Vaughan, and mother, Rosa Ileta Bryant, both came from the land, born and reared in farming families. Their struggles with deep poverty and lack of home-place would shape all of Vaughan's childhood.

When Curtis was four years old, his family moved to Memphis, driven on by the Great Depression (1929) that fell on them like an ominous, black cloud. His father, who had been a bookkeeper, lost his job and went to Memphis to eke out a living, working at various odd jobs and moving the family from house to house. Vaughan vividly recalls[1] those difficult times: a father, who never owned a car and could not afford a five-cent ride, walking miles to survival jobs; older siblings leaving school to work for the family; and moves to eleven different rent-houses during childhood. In a word, the Vaughans were poor, "dirt poor." Charity trucks bringing free food were found at their front door, and to his embarrassment Curtis stood each day in a line of school children who reached out needy hands to receive a token for a free lunch. There emerged from these events a young man determined to work hard and to make his life count.

In the grip of hard times, Curtis sensed early on God's hand in his life when, as a four-year old at his mother's knee, he asked her the question that shaped his life, "What is God like?" Near the time he professed faith in Christ as a "Junior boy," his older sister gave him his first book for a Christmas present—a Bible. Since it was his, he read it, and God spoke to him through the Book. In and through reading the Bible, Curtis became absolutely certain that God had called him to preach. Natural shyness (a trait some have mistaken for aloofness!) made it very difficult for him to share his inner feelings with anyone. For example, as a high school student, he found himself unable to recite poetry before the class; so his teacher retained him after school, and with her as the sole audience he recited without a flaw. Only with difficulty had he mustered the courage to walk the aisle of his church and be baptized, but for one so timid the prospect of standing before a church to preach was overwhelming. For a long season the conviction that God had called him lay only in the solitude of his heart.

The senior year of high school in Memphis (1941) brought a dramatic change by an unexpected means. In the aftermath of Pearl Harbor, students were permitted to learn a useful trade in the afternoon. Vaughan, self-described as a "rather mediocre student" (he simply did not study), decided to attend welding school and excelled at it. He was so proficient at running beads of molten steel that he became a model for older workers to imitate. For a year he worked at an iron company on landing barges, where he was the top-rated welder; he outstripped seasoned shipyard workers in production, doing in six days what they did in seven (he would not work on Sunday). Vaughan had worked hard and excelled—a providential and persuasive catalyst for him that a higher task could be done as well. While he was engaged in the welding job, God gave him a compelling sense to share his calling with his family and church. He was soon to be found stepping off a train in Jackson,

Tennessee, walking with pasteboard suitcase in hand to the campus of Union University as a "preacher boy."

At Union University, he applied himself with diligence to academic studies and delivered the initial sermons of what would be a fifty-year preaching ministry. The beginning attempt was rather abrupt; at the small Roellen Baptist Church near Dyersburg, Vaughan's first sermon lasted all of five minutes![2] Soon, however, in a second sermon two weeks later, he reached a milestone in his pulpit career. He determined that, since he was speaking for God, he need not be fearful and timid behind the pulpit. He was there enabled to speak God's word boldly, and from that day forward God blessed him with forthrightness to open the Scriptures to audiences large and small. After preaching regularly in a one-room schoolhouse near Ramer for six months, Vaughan took the pastorate of the Westover Baptist Church near Jackson, where he experienced the joy of a caring and generous people. Two-and-a-half happy years as a college pastor (1943–46) brought him to graduation at Union, where he received the B.A. degree in 1946. Primarily on the advice of R. E. Guy, his mentor and teacher of Bible and Greek (his son, R. Cal Guy, would be a colleague at Southwestern), Vaughan resigned his church and moved to Fort Worth to begin seminary training at Southwestern.

When he came to Southwestern in the fall of 1946, he found a dry, parched ground, withered by an unrelenting south wind. The few trees were scrawny, the grass was brown, and the horizon forlorn. In Vaughan's words, "I thought it was the most desolate-looking place I had ever seen." Even the bus ride to the campus offered a warning. When passengers boarded the bus on Hemphill Street, they did so after hearing the driver call out, "All aboard for Poverty Knob!" Two brief Texas pastorates gave him staying power, Mount Carmel Church (1946–48) near Cleburne and Center Point Church (1948–50) near Weatherford, but all was refreshed by a young lady from West Virginia, Marian Withers, who entered his life at Southwestern. While a student at Southwestern, Marian directed the Baptist Student Union at Texas Wesleyan College. When Vaughan received the B. D. degree (1949), he was asked by Dean Ray Summers to begin teaching in the Southwestern faculty (1950); then shortly thereafter in 1951 he and Marian were married. Under the supervision of Summers, he completed his doctoral program in

1957, and during those years three children were born to the marriage: William Curtis, Jr., 1952, Rebecca Sharon, 1955, and Stephen Withers, 1958. With dissertation done and family intact, Vaughan's career as a Southwestern professor was launched; the 1960s and 1970s would prove to be his most productive years in terms of writing, teaching, and preaching.

It was a good time: church and denominational engagements multiplied; books flowed from his pen; the family flourished; new academic vistas opened. An early sabbatical leave brought Vaughan in contact with Professor F. F. Bruce at the University of Manchester (1961); a year's pastorate in Munich, Germany was a joyous time of ministry and study (1974–75). But at the peak of his ministry, terminal illness struck Marian; her four-year struggle and subsequent death (1980) brought him to a low ebb. Although he continued to teach and carry out duties, brokenheartedness led to deep depression. A sabbatical leave as a pastor in a caring church in West Berlin effected no real change.

In God's time many prayers were answered when Vaughan met Frances Brown, a vivacious Christian from Tulsa, Oklahoma. Her blessing to his well being can hardly be overstated; she brought him back to life. They were married in 1983. Except for a two-year absence (1987–89), Vaughan taught continuously at Southwestern from 1950 to 1995, the year in which he retired as distinguished professor emeritus of New Testament. He and Frances dwell happily together now in Fort Worth.

WRITINGS

The distinctive trait of Vaughan's primary writings is the studied attempt to communicate the meaning of the Bible to the common reader—students, pastors, and laypeople. This accounts for the astounding fact that his books in English have sold more than 1.25 million copies, making him the most widely distributed author in the history of Southwestern.[3] His first published piece, "Gethsemane," a section of a larger contribution by Ray Summers entitled "Jesus Christ" in the two-volume *Encyclopedia of Southern Baptists* (1958), set the tone for much that followed. He was the first Southwestern professor invited to write a convention-wide study guide for the popular January Bible Study series. When he produced *The Letter to the Ephesians* in 1963, he began a writing program that would span twenty-five years (1963–88). Through arrangements with Zondervan Publishing House, Vaughan initiated a series of *Study Guide* volumes for New Testament books, produced for a Southern Baptist readership. Each one of the series, later named *Bible Study Commentary*, exhibits the same features: a brief exposition, a simple outline of the biblical text, and dominant themes and meanings of key words, with the reader encouraged to use an open Bible alongside. These nine volumes[4] represent the heart of Vaughan's written legacy, reflecting his awareness of the need for careful exposition put in a readable, accessible form.

His other writings on the Bible carry the same focus and clarity. The commentary on Colossians in the *Expositor's Bible Commentary* (1978) includes more technical matters but highlights the message of the book. The materials for Sunday School teachers and personal discipleship make practical applications of the Bible for general readers.[5] Vaughan did not view himself as a scholar writing for the academic guild but rather as an expositor of the New Testament providing help for the seeking Christian. His expositions never lose track of the biblical message and never lose sight of the believing church.

Another significant work points in the same direction—the interpretive tool commonly known as *26 Translations*. After initial groundwork by Jack Hamm of Dallas and his Old Testament colleague, William H. Rossell, Vaughan took over general editorship of the project in 1964. The original idea was to produce a multiversion New Testament by printing more recent translations (twenty-six as it happened) of the biblical text alongside the King James Version. These parallel renderings would serve somewhat as a commentary on the older translation and thus clarify the meaning of the scriptural text for English readers. Having gathered an eminent team of biblical scholars, Vaughan produced the New Testament volume in 1967; its positive reception led to a comparable volume on Old Testament poetry (1973), and finally there was issued the entire Bible, entitled *Twenty-Six Translations of the Bible* (1985).[6] This aid to Bible students has proved immensely popular, registering several reprints and selling in the thousands each year up to the present.

The technical side of Vaughan's scholarship lay in the field of Greek grammar; so those writings are of seminal importance for students of the Greek New Testament. His expertise was demonstrated in a doctoral dissertation on the clause structure of Colossians (1957); soon he and Virtus E. Gideon, a colleague in the Department of New Testament, collaborated on a manual workbook for the teaching of syntax (1964). This manual used by many Southwestern students was eventually published as *A Greek Grammar of the New Testament* (1979). In the tradition of the Robertson-Davis and Dana-Mantey intermediate grammars, Vaughan emphasized noun (the eight-case system) and verb syntax, using 1 Thessalonians and 1 Peter as set texts for reading and interpretation. His workbook approach used graphic conventions for the diagramming of Greek sentences, a very helpful feature of his teaching method. Vaughan's latest writings were descriptive notes on Greek morphology and syntax; the two manuals were used in elementary and intermediate courses.[7]

THOUGHT

As it is with many biblical expositors, an analysis of Vaughan's theological outlook will suffer some arbitrary judgments because he left no systematic presentation of his thought. His themes were determined by the texts he engaged, not by a logical development of topics. Such cautions notwithstanding, one can make some headway by asking three questions: (1) What was his primary focus? (2) What was his exegetical method? and (3) What was his theological perspective?

Focus: Hearing the Word of God

First and foremost, Vaughan's life and work display an affection for, a preoccupation with, and a dedication to the Word of God. His early encounters with the Bible were pivotal; he experienced the power of reading God's Word as a child and found there the assurance of his calling in life. His sermons and expositions bear witness to the authority of the Word; he received it, embraced it, and made it his own. He wrote, "To receive the word in the fullest sense is to so open the inner self to the influence of God's Word that its truth is transfused into the heart."[8] Vaughan leaves no doubt about the utter trustworthiness and full truthfulness of the Scriptures; he spoke openly about such matters before it was popular to do so.

The centrality of the Word accounts in large measure for his labor expended in the study of Greek, the preparation of commentaries, the collation of translations, and the delivery of sermons. The latent possibility in God's Word for the hearer brought Vaughan to his tasks with what Charles H. Spurgeon called the "most essential quality" for success in ministry—"earnestness."[9] Earnestness for God's Word, whether before a class, behind a pulpit, or in the words he penned, marked all that Vaughan did.

Method: Syntax and Exegesis

Vaughan based his theology on a sound, constructive approach to the biblical text. He refused all forms of consecrated guesswork and showed critical awareness everywhere in his handling of textual and grammatical issues. A statement like "not supported by the oldest and best manuscripts of this letter" often appears in verse comments where the original reading of the Greek text is in dispute.[10] Historical, chronological, and geographical matters come up for consideration where different views are held, such as the date and recipients of the Galatian letter or the gnostic threat addressed in the letters of John. For alternative interpretations of difficult passages, a list of options is provided and, usually, a preference given.[11] In short, Vaughan's exegesis is balanced, serious, and well-informed; his readings of the New Testament are free of novelty and idiosyncrasy.

It is instructive to note the authors whom he quotes. The best commentators on the Greek and English texts turn up on page after page. The English conservatives of the nineteenth century are well represented: J. B. Lightfoot, F. J. A. Hort, B. F. Westcott, H. C. G. Moule, G. G. Findlay, and James Denney; their tradition leads down to Vaughan's contemporaries like F. F. Bruce, C. F. D. Moule, and C. E. B. Cranfield. He paid special attention to classic Greek works like those of F. W. Beare and E. G. Selwyn on 1 Peter, whether they confirmed his views or not. While appreciative of his Baptist heritage, principally A. T. Robertson, H. E. Dana, and Ray Summers, he freely consulted and learned from a much wider circle.

To say that Vaughan's method is well informed is to say too little. Its most inviting aspect is the uncanny ability to capture the message of the text, or the argument of a book, to sketch the main contours of a writer's thought, or to lay out a theme and its point-by-point development. Part of this is native genius that Vaughan developed as a skill, the art of interpretation. But part is the science of relating word, phrase, sentence, paragraph, and section to each other and then describing the whole for the reader. Vaughan's exegesis grows out of his attention to the syntax of the sentence and beyond. His books carry the reader along in the text; the reader gets the notion that he hears the message of the Bible. The simplicity of Vaughan's written product belies the complexity of what he accomplishes. Many pastors and teachers look in vain for other expositions that get to the heart of the matter in such an effective way.

Perspective: Grace and Piety

The English Puritan tradition played a prominent role in Vaughan's theological outlook. He found a treasure in the old commentaries of Thomas Manton and Robert Leighton; he often alluded to or quoted from John Bunyan's *Pilgrim's Progress*.[12] His favorite resource was Charles H. Spurgeon, the prince of Particular Baptist preachers. Vaughan made a routine of engaging Spurgeon, reading a sermon each day as a devotional exercise. It comes as no surprise then that both contend for the doctrines of grace and that both may be described fairly as Calvinists but not of the "high" variety.

An essential distinction appears in Vaughan's denial of double predestination: election and reprobation are not symmetrical wills of God; divine sovereignty and human responsibility, if mysterious, nonetheless must both be affirmed. On the phrase "chosen in him" (Eph. 1:4), Vaughan quoted the London preacher, "'Do not conceive,' said Spurgeon, 'that some decree, passed in the dark ages of eternity, will save your souls, unless you believe in Christ. Do not . . . fancy that you are to be saved without faith . . . That is a most abominable and accursed heresy, and has ruined thousands. Lay not election as a pillow for you to sleep on, or you may be ruined.'"[13] If such paradoxes, views also espoused by John A. Broadus and B. H. Carroll, make for poor Calvinists, then perhaps Vaughan would better be called a good Paulinist.

INFLUENCE

Vaughan's influence on the shaping of a Baptist generation is immense. His commentaries have reached far and wide. All nine volumes of the *Bible Study Commentary* were translated into Chinese and remain in print; the one on Ephesians was also translated into Spanish and Portuguese. In 1995, under the auspices of the (then) Foreign Mission Board (SBC), the nine Chinese volumes were translated and distributed in Asia, Southeast Asia, and the Pacific from a ministry base in the Philippines. The *Twenty-Six Translations of the Bible* has guided thousands of teachers and preachers to a better understanding of the biblical text. The impact of his basic writings will be felt for generations to come.

His commentary and translation work gave him significant editorial responsibilities: the Executive Review Committee for the *New King James Version* (1979, 1982); the Editorial Advisory Committee of the Zondervan Publishing House; and a general editor for the New American Commentary published by Broadman and Holman. Vaughan was honored as a distinguished alumnus of Southwestern and received the distinguished service award from his alma mater, Union University. He served more than forty Baptist churches as an interim pastor, several more than once. He preached and taught at state conventions and the two assemblies, Glorieta and Ridgecrest. His fifty-year preaching and teaching ministry took him to twenty-five states, Germany, and Switzerland. The platform from Southwestern was effectively used by Vaughan to reach into the lives of untold thousands.

Vaughan's abiding legacy perhaps rests in his students. His elective courses in New Testament were always filled and drew students hungry to hear his expositions. He pioneered the teaching of elementary Greek as a complete course in a single summer term. Most importantly, he taught two successive generations of classes at Southwestern to master and cherish the Greek New Testament. His memoirs are filled with letters of appreciation from his Greek students. Because the course of Greek study carried over two years, many of these students came to know Vaughan at a deeper level. Although some despaired of his rigorous demands, a great number enjoyed him as their favorite teacher. His high expectations were contagious, and his devout earnestness carried great weight with them. The greatest compliment a teacher can receive comes from appreciative students who have taken up the mantle he so ably bore—so it is with Curtis Vaughan.

BIBLIOGRAPHY

DISSERTATION

"A Syntactical Analysis of the Epistle to the Colossians as an Approach to the Study of Subordinate Greek Clauses." Th.D. diss., Southwestern Baptist Theological Seminary, 1958.

BOOKS

Acts: Bible Study Commentary. Grand Rapids: Zondervan, 1974.

    Shi Tu Xing Chuan: Yan Jing Dao Du. Trans. Bao-luo Li. Hong Kong: Tien Dao Publishing House, 1986. [Chinese]

(coed.) *The Biblical Sunday School Commentary*. Waco, Tex.: Word, 1969, 1970.

Colossians and Philemon: Bible Study Commentary. Grand Rapids: Zondervan, 1980.

    Ge Luo Xi Shu, Fei Li Men Shu: Yan Jing Dao Du. Trans. Qi-fen Hu and Yue-ming Feng. Hong Kong: Tien Dao Publishing House, 1995. [Chinese]

Colossians: A Study Guide. Grand Rapids: Zondervan, 1973.

(coauth.) *1 Corinthians: Bible Study Commentary*. Grand Rapids: Zondervan, 1983.

    Ge Lin Duo Qian Shu: Yan Jing Dao Du. Trans. Kang-min Liang. Hong Kong: Tien Dao Publishing House, 1992. [Chinese]

Ephesians: A Study Guide Commentary. Grand Rapids: Zondervan, 1977; rpt. under title: *Ephesians: Bible Study Commentary*. Ibid., 1983?; rpt.: Founders Study Guide Commentary. Cape Coral, Fla.: Founders Press, 2002.

    Comentario y Estudio Biblico: Efesios. Trans. Adolfo Robleto. Miami: Editorial Vida, 1987. [Spanish]

    Efésios: Comentário Bíblico. Trans. Jorge César Mota. Miami: Editora Vida, 1986. [Portuguese]

    Yi Fu Suo Shu: Yan Jing Dao Du. Trans. Si Hui. Hong Kong: Tien Dao Publishing House, 1981. [Chinese]

Galatians: A Study Guide. Grand Rapids: Zondervan, 1972.

    Jia La Tai Shu: Yan Jing Dao Du. Trans. Zhang-ping Shao and Miao-zhen Yin Shao. Hong Kong: Tien Dao Publishing House, 1995. [Chinese]

(coauth.) *A Greek Grammar of the New Testament: A Workbook Approach to Intermediate Grammar*. Nashville: Broadman, 1979.

James: A Study Guide. Grand Rapids: Zondervan, 1969; rpt. under title: *James: Bible Study Commentary*. Ibid., 1985?

    Ya Ge Shu: Yan Jing Dao Du. Trans. Wei-ben Zhao. Hong Kong: Tien Dao Publishing House, 1994. [Chinese]

1, 2, 3 John: A Study Guide. Grand Rapids: Zondervan, 1970; rpt. under title: *1, 2, 3 John: Bible Study Commentary*. Ibid., 1983.

    Yue Han Yi Er San Shu: Yan Jing Dao Du. Trans. Rui-qing He and Jia-bao Yu. Hong Kong: Tien Dao Publishing House, 1996. [Chinese]

The Letter to the Ephesians. Nashville: Convention Press, 1963.

(coauth.) *Master Design: Your Calling as a Christian* [re Ephesians]. Nashville: Sunday School Board of the Southern Baptist Convention, 1986.

(ed.) *The New Testament from 26 Translations*. Grand Rapids: Zondervan, 1967.

(coed.) *New Testament Studies: Essays in Honor of Ray Summers in His Sixty-Fifth Year*. Waco, Tex.: Markham Press Fund of Baylor University Press, 1975.

(ed.) *The Old Testament Books of Poetry from 26 Translations*. Grand Rapids: Zondervan, 1973.

(coauth.) *1, 2 Peter, Jude: Bible Study Commentary*. Grand Rapids: Zondervan, 1988.
    Bi De Qian Hou Shu, You Da Shu: Yan Jing Dao Du. Trans. Hai-lun Liang. Hong Kong: Tien Dao
        Publishing House, 1998. [Chinese]
(coauth.) *Romans: A Study Guide Commentary*. Grand Rapids: Zondervan, 1976; rpt. under title:
    Romans: Bible Study Commentary. Ibid., 1982?
Luo Ma Shu:Yan Jing Dao Du. Trans. Li-zhong Hu. Hong Kong: Tien Dao Publishing, 1984. [Chinese]
(ed.) *Twenty-Six Translations of the Bible*. 3 vols. Atlanta, Ga.: Mathis Publishers,1985. Republished in
    one volume as: *The Word: The Bible from 26 Translations*. Moss Point, Miss.: Mathis Publishers,
    1991.

CHAPTERS CONTRIBUTED TO BOOKS
"The Character of Apostolic Preaching." In *Chapel Messages*, ed. H. C. Brown, Jr., and Charles P. John-
    son, 135–43. Grand Rapids: Baker, 1966.
"Colossians." In *The Expositor's Bible Commentary*, ed. Frank E. Gaebelein. Vol. 11: *Ephe-
    sians-Philemon*, 161–226. Grand Rapids: Zondervan, 1978.
"The Lordship of Jesus Christ." In *Southwestern Sermons*, ed. H. C. Brown, Jr., 196–203. Nashville:
    Broadman, 1960.
"1 Peter," "2 Peter," "1 John," "2 John," "3 John," and "Jude." In *The Teacher's Bible Commentary*, ed.
    H. Franklin Paschall and Herschel H. Hobbs, 785–805. Nashville: Broadman, 1972.
"The Simeon Incident: An Interpretation of Luke 2:25–35." In *New Testament Studies: Essays in Honor
    of Ray Summers in His Sixty-Fifth Year*, ed. Huber L. Drumwright and Curtis Vaughan, 13–26.
    Waco, Tex.: Markham Press Fund of Baylor University Press, 1975.

JOURNAL ARTICLES
"An Exegetical Outline of the Gospel of John." *Southwestern Journal of Theology* n.s. 8 (October 1965):
    21–24.
"The Established Facts of the Gospel (An Outline of Luke)." *Southwestern Journal of Theology* 10 (Fall
    1967): 25–36.

ENCYCLOPEDIA ARTICLE
Encyclopedia of Southern Baptists, 4 vols. Nashville: Broadman, 1958–82. Vol. 1. S.v. "Jesus Christ:
    Gethsemane."

Franklin Morgan Segler

(1907–1988)
Pastoral Ministry

15

C. W. Brister

BIOGRAPHY

What does it take for a person to maintain a sound mind and body over the span of eight decades and to remain a productive member of society? Franklin Morgan Segler discovered the answer, for he lived to celebrate his eighty-first birthday. Born 11 April 1907 at Ardmore, Indian Territory (which became the state of Oklahoma in November of that same year), Segler's forebears were pioneers from Georgia and Alabama who migrated to the "Home of the Redman" by way of Texas. In his personal memoirs, the late pastoral practitioner described his parents—Ada Pearl Gabriel and Samuel M. Segler—as honest and poor sharecropper farmers.

Were we to ask Segler to name key factors in his identity formation, he would likely mention his place in sibling birth order (as the eldest of six surviving children), loss of his father at age nine, love of learning, and adjusting to stepparenting when his mother remarried. Growing up in rural surroundings, Franklin learned to work and assume manly responsibilities at an early age. He worshipped with his family in a one-room schoolhouse at Countyline, Oklahoma, and was converted and baptized at age twelve.

In high school, English was the youth's favorite subject, and he played on the school's baseball and basketball teams. Young Franklin's home life was genuinely religious. Rituals of Bible reading, prayer, and public worship became a way of life. Vocal and choral

183

music appealed to him as a young adult. Later, he would sing in church choirs and lead music in Baptist church worship.

Life choices of a biblical worldview, a vocation in Christian ministry, and lasting personal friendships highlighted his college years at Oklahoma Baptist University. Following a stint of teaching in a consolidated high school near Duncan from 1929 to 1931, he began serving as minister of music and education in Duncan's First Baptist Church. Then from 1933 to 1935 he served in music and education ministries at Capitol Hill Baptist Church, Oklahoma City, where he was ordained to the gospel ministry.

Wedding bells rang for Fannie Mae McCord and Franklin Segler on 11 June 1935 in the depths of America's Great Depression. Their union was blessed with three children: Dana, Samuel (now deceased), and Sylvia. The Seglers' educational, teaching, and pastoral careers carried them to Southwestern Baptist Theological Seminary, where he earned the Th.M. degree in 1938 and the Th.D. in 1945; to pastorates at Carlisle Baptist Church, located fifteen miles west of Henderson, and Garland, Texas; and, in time, to Emmanuel Baptist Church in Alexandria. A key Louisiana church, Emmanuel was poised for growth and major building construction when the Seglers moved from Garland in 1945.

In 1951, the forty-four-year-old Louisiana pastor accepted Southwestern's invitation to begin the work of the Department of Pastoral Ministry. As the founder of a new, practical discipline in the School of Theology, the teacher had to start from "scratch." He developed a basic curriculum consisting of courses in pastoral duties, Christian worship, church leadership, pastoral care and counseling, and ministerial ethics.

Among his strengths and gifts Segler manifested four key attributes as a theological educator: a deep biblical faith tinged with optimism, a strong creative bent as an author, an ability to reach out to others, and the power to endure. Segler had not only to make a place for himself in a growing educational community but also to generate new course materials, serve on committees, and build library resources. In 1957, he was asked to lead the School of Theology while Dean Jesse Northcutt taught in Switzerland. Segler authored seven published works, numerous articles, and several unpublished resources. After retirement from Southwestern Seminary in 1972, he served for ten years as minister of pastoral care at Fort Worth's Broadway Baptist Church.

The veteran pastor-teacher was felled by a fatal heart attack on 30 November 1988 and was memorialized in a worship service co-led by his pastor, Cecil Sherman, and Southwestern Seminary's president, Russell H. Dilday, Jr. He was buried in Laurel Land Cemetery, Fort Worth. In retrospect, Segler enjoyed people and reached out to his colleagues, students, alumni, laypersons in congregations he served temporarily in pastoral capacities, his denomination, and the community. His publications continue to bless readers, and his former students serve in many places in the earth.

WRITINGS

The readers will recall that the Louisiana pastor had begun teaching in 1951. By 1955, Segler had made outlines of his class lectures on "Pastoral Duties" and "Pastoral Ministry" available for sale to his students. Serious research for his first book, *A Theology of Church and Ministry*, was begun during a sabbatical leave, 1957–58, spent in and around Boston. A Sealantic Fund fellowship awarded by the American Association of Theological Schools enabled the Segler clan to profit from a year of study and travel in New England. The Baptist educator absorbed ideas on the church and its ministry from noted scholars at Boston University School of Theology, Andover Newton Theological School, and Harvard Divinity School. That meaningful year of study provided substantial information and inspiration for his remaining lifetime of teaching and writing. During 1964–65 Segler spent a sabbatical leave with his family at the Arab Baptist Seminary in Beirut, Lebanon.

Franklin Segler was fifty-three years of age, well seasoned as a pastor-teacher, when *A Theology of Church and Ministry* was published in 1960 by Broadman Press. It was widely used in colleges and seminaries as the basis for a general course on the life and ministry of the pastor.

His second publication in 1964, *The Christian Layman*, was inspired by a spate of books addressing laypersons by authors of various faith traditions. While scholars in mainline churches produced technical works on the laity, Segler's book was popular in nature. In reflecting on its merits years later, the author noted that the book never received wide publicity or sales and soon went out of print.

Building on his years of pastoral practice, his experiences of leading congregational hymns, and his researching, observing, and planning services of worship, Segler authored *Christian Worship: Its Theology and Practice*, published in 1967. Written as a textbook, the volume is still used in colleges and seminaries as a basic text in courses on worship in the free church tradition. Because of its enduring value and potential for sales, the book was revised by Randall Bradley in 1996.

One of Segler's best-selling works was *The Broadman Minister's Manual* (1968). The author considered it an honor to have the popular book bear the Broadman imprint in its title. The practical pastor's guide offered suggestions for conducting weddings, funerals, ordination services, baptisms, and many other rites and rituals of Baptist worship. Pastors for generations have learned from and leaned on Segler's wisdom.

In the late 1960s and early 1970s, Broadman Press offered readers a plan of twelve value-priced, brief book selections each year. Two of Segler's briefer works appeared during this marketing emphasis: *Your Emotions and Your Faith* in 1970, and *A Pailful of Stars*, an inspirational treatise, in 1972.

Three years after his retirement from Southwestern Seminary, Segler published *Alive! And Past 65!* By then, he was working at Broadway Baptist Church as the minister of pastoral care, maintaining an active speaking schedule, and celebrating the births of grandchildren. It was out of his own life and ministry experiences that he penned guidelines for dealing with the problems of older persons and their families.

Books edited by other persons, to which Segler contributed chapters or portions, were *Southwestern Sermons*, edited by H. C. Brown, Jr., 1960; *J. Howard Williams: Prophet of God and Friend of Man*, edited by H. C. Brown, Jr., and Charles P. Johnson, 1963; *Everyday, Five Minutes with God*, edited by William Cannon, 1969; *Broadman Devotional Annual*, edited also by Cannon, 1972; and *Ideas for Effective Worship Services*, edited by James C. Barry and Jack Gulledge, 1977.

Perhaps the most revealing work by and about the late teacher-preacher was his unpublished autobiography, prepared as a legacy for his family. Titled *Sand Hills, Cockleburs, and Religion; An Oklahoma Pilgrimage: Personal Memoirs of an Oklahoma Farm Boy*, the lengthy manuscript was completed by Fannie Mae Segler after her husband's death. The retired minister learned to use a personal computer given to him by his children and composed the typescript using new technology. His appreciation of the English language is revealed in his detailed, even elaborate, amplification of journal notes made in diary form throughout his lifetime. Segler's faith and fidelity to his Christian calling are revealed in this family-owned, most prized, personal legacy.

INTERPRETATION OF THOUGHT

There are central themes in Segler's life and work that the careful observer notes. His writings reflect the essential elements of effective Christian ministry in his free church tradition. His discourses offer straightforward Baptist beliefs with no attempt to deal with diversionary matters or potentially controversial issues. His fidelity to biblical authority and recommended life responses grew out of his Christian hope. At the deepest level, the man taught and wrote out of who he was—to borrow James S. Stewart's description of the apostle Paul—"a man in Christ."[1] We now consider some basic themes.

Christocentric Vision

The Oklahoma youth, Franklin Segler, bereft of his father at nine, determined early to become an authentic self. That focus was achieved, in part, by his personal faith in Jesus Christ as the incarnate Son of God. His Christ-consciousness provided a focus in a world of rural poverty, hard work, continuous change, and divine provision of a godly mother and a fine stepfather. He became growingly convinced by experience that the Christ was the Alpha and Omega of all existence.

In his treatise on the church and its ministry there are thirty-eight references to Jesus Christ: his authority as the founder and head of the church; the redemptive purpose of Christ's incarnation, servant-style ministry, sacrificial death, resurrection, and promised return; the object of the church's worship; and the empowerer of its work. He held that in many respects the church's ministry is a continuation of Christ's mission on earth.

Congregational Context

Each of Segler's monographs, published articles, and unpublished autobiography focused on aspects of the church's ministry. For him the church's life, worship, and work *is the ministry of Jesus Christ*. While he appreciated the universal church as the ideal body of Christ, this pastor-teacher was far more interested in the church as a functioning institution.

Indications of what troubled the author about contemporary church life lie embedded in surprising places. He was concerned with the church's superficiality and preoccupation with externals (like numbers, buildings, mistaken authority exercised by some religious leaders, and nuances of doctrine); with its lack of solid biblical and theological foundations, and its passionless self-satisfaction. Such problematic considerations he often challenged.

Concern for the Laity

There are numerous references to laypersons in Segler's work, including one book devoted entirely to their vocation: *The Christian Layman*. Had he been writing in today's feminist climate, Segler would have been criticized for being paternalistic. He used the term "women" only once in his 272-page *A Theology of Church and Ministry*, although he does mention the Woman's Missionary Union in Baptist congregations. The author offered a disclaimer in the preface to his treatise on laity: "The term 'laity' as used in these discussions includes the men, women, youth, and children of the church."

Persons who knew the author well affirm his appreciation for and inclusion of women in spirit. He wrote generically of laypersons as *being* the church—in their friendship with and support of the professional clergy, in family life, and as creative missioners for the world. He noted the church's dialogue with the world through the combination of the preacher's and the layperson's voices.

Biblical Foundations

Segler, relying heavily on the New Testament, viewed the church as the people of God's *new covenant* (the OT covenant with Abraham having been superseded by the incarnation of Jesus Christ)—forming a "New Israel." A vast range of biblical references, from Genesis to Revelation, serves to underpin his writings. He viewed the Bible as the "life book" of the church, holding it up as "the record of God's revelation of his own life-giving to his people." "It is not primarily the church's authority because it is the Bible," he wrote in *A Theology of Church and Ministry*, "it is the church's Bible because it is the authority of God" (130). Viewing the Scriptures as a *sourcebook* for the church, he helped church leaders to understand biblical teachings and to affirm their calling and mission in Christ Jesus.

Ministry as Paradox

Persons in ministry occupations soon discover that the local church is, according to the late Dean Samuel H. Miller of Harvard Divinity

School, a unique kind of world. It has its own ethos, sacred scriptures, language, architecture, organization and inner hierarchy, its own code of ethics, sense of divine authority, means of self-justification, and antagonism with the world. Segler understood the fine line of distinction between church health and congregational conflict. Thus he worked and wrote with a sense of the tragic.

There are poignant, even poetic, passages in Segler's works that remind readers of the difficulty a preacher faces as a buffer between church and world. He writes with the wisdom of one who, each week as a pastor, proclaimed the rigor of the gospel to teachable hearers. He called congregants to trust, love, and serve God amid the mystery of human sin, evil, and suffering. The tenor of his written legacy reveals the heart of a man who wrestled with life's mysteries, faced his own demons, and affirmed his Christian certitude in the power of the Spirit of God.

In summary, Segler's written works embrace a holism in Christian ministry. He wisely held individual concerns of religious callings in one hand and multiple complexities of institutional ministry in the other. The wisdom, inclusiveness, and sensitivity of his legacy is not the work of a dilettante. While he remained a humble seeker in reaching out to know and obey God, Segler was a mature, wise, and caring pastor-teacher whose writings have helped many leaders and caregivers along the way.

EVALUATION

Were it possible to converse with the late Franklin Segler and hear a firsthand appraisal of his key contributions as a Christian thinker, he would likely mention two enduring themes: his call for a Christlike ministry in the churches and his plea for congregational faithfulness to the church's prophetic witness. Uppermost in all his writings is his confidence that God has cast creation along redemption lines. It follows that every expression of the Christian ministry must be held in tension with this divine ideal.

Segler's passion was ministerial excellence, although he wrote for both ordained professionals and laypersons. Whatever his subject, he insisted on a theological foundation for church ministry. Segler used "ministry" in two ways—one broad, the other restricted—first, as the church's purpose and mission and, second, as its leadership function in pursuing its God-given purpose. He advocated inclusiveness in ministry—both professional clergy and the work of the entire church membership.

Segler insisted that church leaders move beyond ephemeral goals of success to true effectiveness in Christian mission. His major treatise, *A Theology of Church and Ministry*, challenged church leaders to anchor their calling in biblical revelation and in church history as well as in contemporary contextual needs. He then applied these foundational principles to each functional aspect of a congregation's ministry. His other textbook, *Christian Worship: Its Theology and Practice*, reflected the author's basic ecclesiology, in which the church is both a spiritual fellowship and a missional institution.

Evaluating Segler's work requires, secondly, that he be viewed as a pioneer—the initiator of a new, practical discipline in a historically classical theological curriculum. At mid-twentieth century, Southwestern Seminary named a study committee to enlist suggestions from its School of Theology alumni in order to strengthen its curriculum for more effective ministry performance in the churches. When the aspiring new teacher arrived on the Fort Worth campus, he was presented with titles of a few basic courses for which catalogue descriptions had been suggested: Pastoral Leadership, Pastoral Duties, Pastoral Counseling, The Pastor and Public Worship, The Devotional Life, Parliamentary Procedure, Ministerial Ethics, and Pastoral Care.

The tasks before him in 1951 were (1) to generate library resources to sustain academic research in each subject area; (2) to create course syllabi for a semester's work in each of the above subject areas; (3) to produce lecture materials suitable for use with both undergraduates and baccalaureate degree college graduates; (4) to make a quantum leap from daily pastoral demands into the fast-moving stream of a theological school context; and (5) to catch step through continuing education with major thinkers and writers in the fields of practical theology and pastoral care and counseling. In time, he would be writing in a number of these subject fields.

In addition, Segler had the transitional tasks of staying in touch with his family back in Alexandria, Louisiana, establishing contacts with congregations in Texas that might be inclined to use him in some interim ministry capacity, and interfacing with colleagues and curricula of Southwestern Seminary's School of Church Music and School of Religious Education. Those first years required getting his bearings and shifting identity from a pastoral/preaching occupation to a teaching ministry vocation.

In depicting Segler's legacy, thirdly, we note a sensible practice of linkage. His writing ministry dovetailed with his preaching, teaching, and lecturing tasks. Segler's doctoral dissertation on "Paul's Christian Experience: The Basis of His Theology" (1945) anchored him in the study of theology. His two major treatises on church ministry and worship were profoundly theological as well as functional. His concern for spiritual formation is evidenced in devotional writings like *Your Emotions and Your Faith* and *A Pailful of Stars: Gleams of Hope for a Time of Despair*. His courses in parliamentary procedure and ethical guidelines for the work of ministry issued in *The Broadman Minister's Manual*. In sum, his concern was enhancing ministers' understanding of and preparation for the practice of Christian ministry.

Fourthly, Segler's studies with Paul Johnson at Boston University School of Theology and contacts with Wayne E. Oates of Southern Baptist Theological Seminary in Louisville provided a treasury of resources on caring for persons throughout the human life cycle. Given his own life stage, Segler's particular interests lay in the aging process. While he was realistic enough not to romanticize growing old, he tackled various aspects of aging and eldercare as an adventure. Surviving his near-death experience of a major heart attack at age fifty-six helped Segler to look retirement and death in the face. He gave much thought to how a Christian adapts to elderhood by self-attention and introspection.

He observed how persons mature full circle from childhood and youth to adulthood and then the mature years. From those observations he wrote *Alive! And Past 65! How to Deal with Aging for Families and Church Leaders*. Practical subjects appear for treatment—from health matters, tasks of family caregivers, and how to gain comfort and guidance from the Bible to reflections on the church's role in developing effective ministries with older adults. Having been a patient in a hospital's critical care unit himself, Segler sought supervised experiences in a clinical setting to enhance his understanding of illness, a patient's recovery, and wellness maintenance.

Fifthly, Segler's pathway into old age was marked by the era during which he grew up—a period of competitive individualism—with mottoes like "Do the best you can" and "Pull yourself up by your own bootstraps." Still, he sought to honor people who helped him along the way in his *Sand Hills, Cockleburs, and Religion; An Oklahoma Pilgrimage: Personal Memoirs of an*

Oklahoma Farm Boy. His profound faith in God, enthusiasm for life, and reflective capacities—linked to carefully kept journal entries through his ministry years—enabled Segler to recall times, names, places, and events from the past. His detailed reflections reveal his characteristic penchant to picture past events in the most favorable light possible.

Segler found ways to burnish the life and talent he was given. The transformation of an Oklahoma farm boy into a gifted scholar, productive theological educator, influential denominational statesman, faithful marriage partner, and faithful minister of the Christian gospel is a compelling story. His life is in his writings—words that are carefully chosen, nontechnical in style, biblical in substance, and focused on church life and leadership in the Baptist tradition. Segler was always open to new ideas and new applications. While tolerating doubt and pursuing inquiry for his own growth, he proposed eternal truths for his readers. Indeed, his is a contribution worthy to share.

BIBLIOGRAPHY

1. Primary

THESIS AND DISSERTATION
"Exegesis of the Sermon on the Mount (from the Greek Text)." Th.M. thesis, Southwestern Baptist Theological Seminary, 1938.
"Paul's Christian Experience: The Basis of His Theology." Th.D. diss., Southwestern Baptist Theological Seminary, 1945.

BOOKS
Alive! And Past 65! How to Deal with Aging, for Families and Church Leaders. Nashville: Broadman, 1975.
The Broadman Minister's Manual. Nashville: Broadman, 1968.
The Christian Layman. Nashville: Broadman, 1964.
Christian Worship: Its Theology and Practice. Nashville: Broadman, 1967.
　Yebaehak wonron: Shinhak kwa Siljae. Trans. Jin Hwang Chung. Seoul: Jordan Press, 1978. [Korean]
A Pailful of Stars: Gleams of Hope for a Time of Despair. Nashville: Broadman, 1972.
Pastoral Ministries 133: The Work of the Pastor. Nashville: Seminary Extension Department of the Southern Baptist Convention, 1964; rev. ed., 1972; 1973 supplement.
Sand Hills, Cockleburs, and Religion; An Oklahoma Pilgrimage: Personal Memoirs of an Oklahoma Farm Boy. Fort Worth: pvt. ptg., 1995.
A Theology of Church and Ministry. Nashville: Broadman, 1960.
　Jiao Mu Xue Yao Yi. Trans. Wayne Wei-yuan Siao. Hong Kong: Baptist Press, 1968. [Chinese]
　Koehae wa Mokhweui Shinhak. Trans. Sung Chan Kim. Nashville: Broadman, 1962. [Korean]
　Mokhwehak Geron. Trans. Cheong Hui Lee. Seoul, Korea: Jordan Press, 1977. [Korean]

Understanding, Preparing for, and Practicing Christian Worship. 2d ed., rev. by Randall Bradley. Nashville: Broadman and Holman, 1996.
Your Emotions and Your Faith. Nashville: Broadman, 1970.

JOURNAL ARTICLES
"Areas of Strategic Insight Which Aid Maturity in Ministerial Students." *Southwestern Journal of Theology* n.s. 5 (April 1963): 73–84.
"B. H. Carroll: Model for Ministers." *Southwestern Journal of Theology* 25 (Spring 1983): 4–23.
"The Concept of Ministry." *Review and Expositor* 66 (Spring 1969): 141–53.
"Devotional Values of Isaiah." *Southwestern Journal of Theology* 11 (Fall 1968): 59–72.
"An Evaluation of Modern Worship in the Free Church." *Review and Expositor* 50 (October 1953): 401–20.
"Harvey Eugene Dana: Lights and Shadows." *Southwestern Journal of Theology* 13 (Fall 1970): 67–75.
"A New Understanding of Pastoral Care." *Southwestern Journal of Theology* n.s. 3 (October 1960): 53–60.
"The Pastor and Church Administration." *Southwestern Journal of Theology* n.s. 1 (April 1959): 26–34.
"Theological Foundations for Ministry." *Southwestern Journal of Theology* 29 (Spring 1987): 5–18.

CHAPTERS CONTRIBUTED TO BOOKS
"Conducting the Ordinance of Baptism" and "Observing the Lord's Supper." In *The Practice of Ministry: A Sourcebook*, ed. Doran C. McCarty and George W. Knight, 101–8. Nashville: Seminary Extension of the Southern Baptist Seminaries, 1995.
"Grace Abounding." In *Southwestern Sermons*, ed. H. C. Brown, Jr., 178–83. Nashville: Broadman, 1960.
"The Pastor." In *J. Howard Williams: Prophet of God and Friend of Man*, ed. H. C. Brown, Jr., and Charles P. Johnson, 46–63. San Antonio: Naylor Co., 1963.
"Planning Better Orders of Worship." In *Ideas for Effective Worship Services*, ed. James C. Barry and Jack Gulledge, 10–17. Nashville: Convention Press, 1977.
"Restoring the Glory." In *Everyday, Five Minutes with God*, ed. William S. Cannon, 17–18. Nashville: Broadman, 1969.

2. Secondary
Sewell, Dag William. "A Critical Evaluation of Franklin M. Segler's View of Pastoral Ministry." Ph.D. diss., Southwestern Baptist Theological Seminary, 1995.

Huber Lelland Drumwright, Jr.

(1924–1981)
New Testament

David E. Crutchley

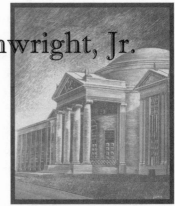

BIOGRAPHY

The dedicatory words in Huber Drumwright's seminary doctoral dissertation in 1957, "to my mother and father who were the first to teach me that the word of God is living and powerful," testify to the godly home of Huber L. Drumwright, Sr., and Rubye Evalyn Lokey, which he entered in Walters, Oklahoma, 1 February 1924. When his parents migrated south to Texas shortly after his birth, the family linked with First Baptist Church in Dallas. Here his life and death interfaced with the history and personalities of this significant community of faith. His father, an executive with the Chevrolet Motor Division of General Motors, taught a Bible class under this steeple in downtown Dallas. Drumwright was led to Christ and baptized by Pastor George W. Truett and was ordained in 1950 under the presiding leadership of Pastor W. A. Criswell, who also preached in his memorial service at Southwestern Seminary after his untimely death in Arkansas in 1981.

Huber attended Baylor University on a debate scholarship in the fall of 1941 until he volunteered for the United States Navy. As a communications officer on a ship in the south Pacific that had no chaplain, he was drafted by the captain to lead services each Sunday. Drumwright wrote of a night during World War II when he knelt on the warm sands along the shore of a small island off the coast of New Guinea and prayed to know the will of God for his life. At the conclusion of the war, he returned to Baylor to continue his major in English and added a religion track to his studies. Drumwright's love of English poetry, particularly that of Robert Browning, is attested by his Bible annotated with literary quotations.

Enrolling as a student at Southwestern in 1947, he received his Th.D. degree in 1957. During his early seminary days, he served as pastor of First Baptist Church of Allen, Texas, and married a pastor's daughter from San Antonio, Minette Williams. He had met Minette on the Baylor campus and recognized her beauty and love for God. This was borne out in her later writings on prayer and the twelve years she invested as director of the international prayer strategy office of the International Mission Board (SBC) in Richmond after her husband's passing. Together they served three other churches: Wilshire Baptist Church, Dallas (1951–55), Oak Grove Baptist Church, Burleson, Texas, (1955–59), and First Baptist Church, Ada, Oklahoma (1959–60).

Drumwright taught New Testament at Southwestern from 1951 to 1959 and from 1960 to 1980, and during this significant chapter of his life he served also as dean of the School of Theology from 1973 to 1980. In 1980 he was elected executive director of the Arkansas Baptist State Convention and moved to Little Rock. The Drumwrights were parents of two: Minette (Meme) and Debbie.

WRITINGS

Drumwright attributed his interest in Hebrews to a Greek New Testament class. His doctoral dissertation, "A Study of the Epistle to the Hebrews with Special Reference to the Hebraic Mind," challenged the tendency of scholarship to focus on the original readership of Hebrews rather than analyzing the author's background and religious heritage. Drumwright claimed that reading Hebrews through the prism of the author's "Hebraic mind" provides a more accurate interpretation of the letter.

In "A Homiletic Study of the Sermon on the Mount: The Ethical Motif in Matthew 5–7," Drumwright proposed that whether this sermon was ever preached as a sermon or not "the unifying thread . . . is found in connection with its ethical import" (66). He drew out the ethical demands of Jesus' iconoclastic sermon proclaimed on a Galilean hillside that continues to shake the very foundations of secular and postmodern society.

Drumwright's contribution, "Appendix to the Fourth Gospel," appears in a work honoring the memory of Henry Trantham, professor of Greek and history at Baylor University from 1910 to 1958. Drumwright declared that "no book in the New Testament gives evidence of greater care at the point of organization than does the Fourth Gospel," and he rejected the practice of some scholars who rearrange and dislocate sections of this gospel text with no manuscript warrant (129). He set aside the question of who authored the appendix and inquired why "fresh material" is added to the gospel. Drumwright found the answer in the personal nature of the material appearing in chapter 21: "The Gospel is an interpretation of Jesus; the Appendix is especially an interpretation of the significance of the two apostles, Peter and John" (134).

In his article, "Re-evaluating the Significance of John's Gospel," Drumwright suggested that three frontiers need exploring if the average interpreter is to find his way. These include the literary integrity of this gospel, recent manuscript discoveries impacting John, and interpretive approaches to the Fourth Gospel.

Drumwright wrote articles for the *Southwestern Journal of Theology* addressing the hermeneutical approaches to "Problem Passages in Luke" (1967) and "Problem Passages in the Johannine Epistles" (1970). He selected passages that pose exegetical difficulties and impact the purpose and design of the author. Drumwright's grasp of hermeneutical issues is reflected in his significant contribution to the *Zondervan Pictorial Encyclopedia of the Bible* entitled "Interpretation." In this article he defined the nature, methods, history, and principles of biblical interpretation.

In Luke, Drumwright focused on the genealogy of Jesus, his rejection at Nazareth, the Sermon on the Plain, and the kingdom of God; these provide clues to the theological intent of the evangelist. In his analysis of the Johannine epistles, Drumwright sought to solve the problems of the prologue, confessing sin, the antichrist, the three witnesses of water, blood, and Spirit, the "elect lady," and the authority of the elder.

Saints Alive! The Humble Heroes of the New Testament captures the spirit of the author who lavished attention on all who crossed his path. He made the humblest student feel important and always took time to stop to visit with a needy heart. This work concentrates not on the lauded New Testament saints but on the anonymous heroes of the faith who walked across the pages of the New Testament. "They are for the most part the unsung infantry in God's mighty army of the faithful, little known men and women who were in the forefront of the action but in the background of the record" (10). Perfection was not their hallmark but their humanity. Drumwright wrote: "Some of them quarrel. Some of them are overly ambitious. Some of them are weak when they ought to be strong" (11). As we rustle through the pages of these living documents, we note the diversity and rich texture of the first-century community of faith.

The Southwestern professor acknowledged in "The Holy Spirit in the Book of Acts" the numerous references to and pivotal role of the Spirit in the structure of the text and narrative of the early church; consequently, some scholars consider Acts the "Gospel of the Holy Spirit."

Drumwright admitted in "A Mosaic of Jesus: John 2:12–4:54" that "all modern commentators would agree that the Johannine tradition has come down to the present time in a skillfully crafted composition with many significant literary distinctives"(55). The section in question stands between two carefully shaped sections—the seven days beginning Jesus' ministry and the four controversies that structurally replicate the same format and explain why Jesus was rejected as Messiah. Drumwright located a unifying purpose in the five vignettes within this section of the gospel.

Prayer Rediscovered shares incisively the different dimensions of a prayer relationship with God. Drumwright stated that "an individual's theology will inevitably determine his belief about prayer and the practice of it" (18). Prayer assumes a number of predicates: its practice is grounded in the very character of God, who is actively and immanently involved in his creation, and humankind is shaped in the *imago dei* with the capacity to have a relationship with God. The Creator invites his human family to participate with him in realizing the objectives of his universe through the gift of prayer that imparts power and guidance.

Ironically, the Greek language provides a bookend for Drumwright's theological pilgrimage. Needing help with a Navy crew, he wrote a young preacher from his Baylor days who was then enrolled at Southern Baptist Theological Seminary. A few months later a package arrived from his friend with two books—J. G.

Machen's *New Testament Greek for Beginners* and a Greek New Testament! Thus began the student's love of Greek. *An Introduction to New Testament Greek* represents Drumwright's last literary work, dedicated to his students and to his Greek teachers: Henry Trantham, John William MacGorman, and Ray Summers. The primer provides a clear and insightful approach that shares the fruit of a language which he loved and taught for twenty-five years.

INTERPRETATION

As a New Testament scholar, Drumwright concentrated on the Johannine writings. He wrote several articles applauding the sophisticated literary design of the Fourth Gospel. He noted the prologue with its seminal concepts of the Word, the Life, and the Light woven into the tapestry of the entire document and the major divisions of Christ's revelation of himself to the world (chaps. 2–12) and to his disciples (chaps. 13–20). Drumwright posited that John 2:12–4:54 reflects a mosaic that skillfully articulates a theological message of the purpose and person of Jesus as Messiah and is not a random series of incidents included because of their absence in the Synoptic Gospels.[1] The stylistic and linguistic differences between chapter 21 and the rest of John's Gospel do not compromise the unity of that gospel or outweigh the similarities. The purpose of the appendix resides in the intimate material that forecasts the life stories of the apostles Peter and John.[2]

Drumwright penned his articles on the Gospel of John when valuable manuscript discoveries required a rethinking of the Johannine landscape. He acknowledged the import of the publication of the John Rylands Library fragment on John in 1935, the discovery of the Dead Sea Scrolls at the Wadi Qumran in 1947, and the location of the Nag Hammadi Coptic Gnostic Library in Upper Egypt in 1945.[3] Drumwright provided a useful synthesis of the major interpretive paradigms of his day that wrestle with the fundamental issue of whether "to hellenize or hebraize" the Gospel of John. These *religionsgeschichtliche* models, including Bultmann's Gnostic paradigm, seem somewhat anachronistic compared with today's New Testament critical agenda besieged with synchronic options.[4]

Keeping an eye on the layman as he wrote, Drumwright assumed responsibility for engaging problem passages in the New Testament. He noted the spiral structure of 1 John and claimed that this literary genre does not fit the traditional letter model. He solved the conundrum posed in texts like 1 John 1:8 and 1 John 3:9 that seem to indicate that a Christian can sin and cannot sin, through analysis of the Greek verb tenses. The term "antichrist" is unique to 1 and 2 John, and the "special heresy" involved "deny[ing] that Jesus was at one and the same time the perfect man and the true God."[5]

Following B. F. Westcott's opinion that the Greek construction allows ambiguity on the identity of the addressee in John's second letter, Drumwright posed the tantalizing possibility that the shortest book in the New Testament spoke to a woman. Third John shares an intriguing cameo of first-century church politics, having appeared as a letter at the dawn of the monarchical episcopate of Ignatius's day. Two conditions contributed to the establishing of the system whereby a bishop had authority over a group of churches in a certain area: an apostolic or sub-apostolic attrition through death, and the need to curb the ambitious and recalcitrant spirit of men like Diotrephes who threatened the harmony of the church.[6]

Problem areas in the Gospel of Luke include wrestling with the irreconcilable differences between the Matthean and Lukan genealogies. Drumwright revealed his methodological support of H. J. Holtzmann's approach to the Synoptic problem and claimed that Luke not only borrowed from Mark but improved the vocabulary and grammar as well. The question of the kingdom of God stands at the epicenter of the New Testament eschatological drama, and in the gospels the reader discovers notions of the present age and the imminent new age coexisting.[7]

Drumwright's article on "The Holy Spirit in the Book of Acts" provides clues to his pneumatology. He mentioned that "filled with the Holy Spirit" and "full of the Holy Spirit" are Luke's favorite designations for describing the believer's involvement with the Spirit and suggest a surrender and drawing near to Jesus on the part of the disciple. The term "baptism in the Spirit" in Acts is always associated with John the Baptist's declaration of what the Messiah would enact, and "baptism of the Spirit" refers to the medium or sphere in which the act of baptism occurs.[8] Drumwright concurred with H. E. Dana's finding that to be "baptized with the Spirit" and "filled with the Spirit" are "'figurative representations of the same essential experience, contemplated from different points of view.'"[9] He also found "no fixed order in Acts as to the relation between baptism, the laying on of hands and the coming of the Spirit."[10]

He reminded the reader that the meaning of Pentecost eclipses the phenomena accompanying the event. Pentecost narrates the birth of the church, the empowering of ordinary men and women for the divine task of mission, and the carrying of the live coals of the gospel to the far corners of the earth.[11] He concluded this article with a practical list of suggestions elicited from the Acts account: the Holy Spirit reveals God's truth and intent, nurtures authentic worship and community, counters falsehood, and protects the inclusiveness of the universality of the gospel.[12]

In his doctoral dissertation on Hebrews, Drumwright explored the impasse between scholars who recognized the Hebraic and those who held to the Hellenistic distinctives of the epistle. He contended that the choice of construct predetermines the interpretation of the book. Drumwright did not hold to Pauline authorship of Hebrews but subscribed to the position that the apologetic that lies behind the text reflects a Jewish audience.

This letter, however, is not a polemic against Judaism. Christianity evolved out of the crucible of Judaism, and one needs to grasp the fact that the converted member of the commonwealth of Israel encountered enormous pressures and theological conflict. What happened to the accoutrements of Judaism—temple, sacrifice, Mosaic Law, and the national consciousness of covenant relationship with God—at conversion? Initially, Jewish Christians remained in the synagogue and temple, notwithstanding their belief in Jesus as the Messiah. As the rift between Judaism and Christianity widened, the Jewish believer faced heartbreak and loss. Converts were alienated from the religion of the fathers, sidelined by the gradual metamorphosis of Christianity into a Gentile religious sect, and disillusioned by the eschatological failure of the Messiah to return to restore the kingdom. No doubt, these issues made them wonder whether they had adopted a sacrilegious alternative and been false to their history. Into this context the Letter to the Hebrews spoke.

The question of the occasion of the Letter to the Hebrews begs for resolution. Advocates who state that the writer addresses apostasy, a deliberate return to Judaism, oppose those scholars who claim that the burden of the letter challenges the ostensible Jewish Christian with a defective faith. Drumwright posited that the author envisions a parallel danger between those who started for the land of promise in the Old Testament, whose bones now lie bleached in the wilderness, and first-century Jewish Christians who stand to miss the realization of God's promises because of a flawed faith in Christ.[13]

Drumwright's scholarship always planted itself in pragmatic soil. He viewed the sermon as a vehicle to elicit response and provoke action and interpreted the function of the Sermon on the Mount as demanding an ethical response. The Beatitudes are not a manifesto of abstract ideals but a reminder that the one who spoke these words embraced them in lifestyle and practice. Drumwright claimed that in Matt. 5:17–48 Jesus did not clash with the religion of the Old Testament or contradict the Mosaic Law but completed the Torah and captured its spiritual significance. He targeted the scribe's legalistic interpretation that obviates the incarnation of the spiritual essence of the law. In Matthew 6 the Rabbi exposes the insincere motives behind the religious practices of Judaism, namely, almsgiving, prayer, and fasting. Drumwright recognized the curse of avarice and anxiety that rules the heart of humanity and erodes enjoyment of life. Jesus concluded his sermon with three metaphors: the "two ways," the "two kinds of fruit," and "the two builders." Drumwright commented with insight: "Here is an ethic unknown and unattainable for the natural man. Only a new quality of life, a life given of God, can bring these ethical tenets to reality."[14]

Prayer marked the life of Huber Drumwright, and it is no surprise that he wrote in the preface to *Prayer Rediscovered* that "the doctrine of prayer is the integrating doctrine of the Bible, though at times it has been treated as an appendix to biblical truth." He defined prayer broadly as communication between the creature and the Creator that might take the form of adoration, thanksgiving, confession, petition, intercession, and other feelings. Drumwright shared simple but useful axioms of prayer that challenge our impoverished spirituality.[15]

In *Saints Alive!* Drumwright revealed his shepherd heart as he scoured the New Testament and found in every nook and cranny an unsung hero and anonymous saint. His message is unambiguous: the life of the Christian disciple counts for God. Drumwright visited a memorial on the island of Panay in the Philippines where eleven missionaries had been executed in 1943 by enemy forces. He cited a poem by one of the martyrs, Dr. Francis H. Rose, and commented, "Dedication to God has always had its price tag . . . There is nothing cheap about the service of God." Drumwright's spirituality touched the core of his being, and that is evident in the wisdom material which he shared regarding the Christ follower.[16]

INFLUENCE AND TENABILITY OF THOUGHT

Huber Drumwright's versatility stands out. In the classroom he could diagram complex Greek sentences and parse irregular verbs with consummate ease. But here was no abstract theologian. Love for the New Testament text confluences with communication of the searching truths of God's word to student and layperson alike. He had an ability to ferret out a profound meaning in a text and transpose it into a provocative life principle. He could walk the hallowed halls with the scholars. He studied textual criticism with New Testament scholar Bruce Metzger at Princeton Theological Seminary on a sabbatical in 1957, and in 1964 he closeted himself by doing postdoctoral research at the American School of Classical Studies in Athens, Greece, for his future Greek grammar.

His legacy as a person perhaps will outlast his literary contribution. The two institutions that shaped most of his life journey recognize his stature. Both Southwestern and Baylor University have a series of annual lectures in his memory. His students fill the Baptist pulpits of this land and occupy significant positions in theological institutions. His colleagues and peers speak of his flamboyance with a golf club, his hunting forays in South Texas in the fall, and his profound pastoral instincts. His students recall lectures that invigorated the mind and took captive their hearts. This dean of theology was easily recognized on campus by all by his driving a beat-up Dodge and wearing a battered straw hat.

The final sermon that he preached in First Baptist Church, Eldorado, Arkansas, on 1 November 1981 centered on the text 2 Cor. 12:9 (RSV, NIV): "My grace is sufficient for you, for my power is made perfect in weakness." One can only muse how differently the consciousness and landscape of Texas Baptist life might be today had someone of the stature of a Huber Drumwright not been taken from us so early. His gravestone in Hillcrest Cemetery in Dallas captures his credo in Greek capitals—ΚΡΙΣΤΟΣ ΕΣΤΙΝ ΚΥΡΙΟΣ— "Christ is Lord."

BIBLIOGRAPHY

DISSERTATION

"A Study of the Epistle to the Hebrews with Special Reference to the Hebraic Mind." Th.D. diss., Southwestern Baptist Theological Seminary, 1957.

BOOKS

An Introduction to New Testament Greek. Nashville: Broadman, 1980.
Prayer Rediscovered. Nashville: Broadman, 1978.
Saints Alive! The Humble Heroes of the New Testament. Nashville: Broadman, 1972.

CHAPTERS CONTRIBUTED TO BOOKS

"The Appendix to the Fourth Gospel." In *The Teacher's Yoke: Studies in Memory of Henry Trantham*, ed. Jerry Vardaman and James Leo Garrett, Jr., 129–34. Waco, Tex.: Baylor University Press, 1964.
"A Mosaic of Jesus: John 2:12–4:54." In *New Testament Studies: Essays in Honor of Ray Summers in His Sixty-fifth Year*, ed. Huber L. Drumwright, Jr., and Curtis Vaughan, 55–67. Waco, Tex.: Markham Press Fund of Baylor University Press, 1975.

JOURNAL ARTICLES

"The Holy Spirit in the Book of Acts." *Southwestern Journal of Theology* 17 (Fall 1974): 3–17.
"A Homiletic Study of the Sermon on the Mount: The Ethical Motif in Matthew 5–7." *Southwestern Journal of Theology* n.s. 5 (October 1962): 65–76.
"Problem Passages in Luke: A Hermeneutical Approach." *Southwestern Journal of Theology* 10 (Fall 1967): 45–58.
"Problem Passages in the Johannine Epistles: A Hermeneutical Approach." *Southwestern Journal of Theology* 13 (Fall 1970): 53–64.
"A Re-evaluation of the Significance of John's Gospel." *Southwestern Journal of Theology* n.s. 8 (October 1965): 7–20.

ENCYCLOPEDIA ARTICLES

Encyclopedia of Southern Baptists. 4 vols. Nashville: Broadman Press, 1958–82. Vol. 1. S.v. "Jesus Christ: The Great Confession."
Wycliffe Bible Encyclopedia. 2 vols. Chicago: Moody, 1975. Vol. 1. S.v. "Decapolis." Vol. 2. S.v. "Saint," "Schools, Hebrew," "Siloam, Pool of," "Synagogue," "Tabor, Mount," "Temple" (coauth.), "Trachonitis," and "Worship" (coauth.).
Zondervan Pictorial Encyclopedia of the Bible. Merrill C. Tenney, gen. ed. 5 vols. Grand Rapids: Zondervan, 1975. Vol. 1. S.v. "Accommodation," "Beauty," "Council, Councillor," "Counsel, Counsellor," and "Crucifixion." Vol. 2. S.v. "Diaspora." Vol. 3. S.v. "Hypocrisy," "Interpretation," "John, The Epistles of," "Lamb, Lamb of God," and "Lawgiver." Vol. 4. S.v. "Madness," "Nazarene," "Nicodemus," "Nicolaitans," and "Nicolaus." Vol. 5. S.v. "Savior," "Sea of Glass," "Seat," "Senate, Senator," "Sermon on the Mount, The," and "Shekinah."

John Paul Newport
(1917–2000)
Philosophy of Religion

Frank Louis Mauldin

J

ohn Paul Newport wove the fabric of his thought and life with colored threads of diverse disciplines, heritages, ministries, and character traits. He practiced the disciplines of philosophy of religion, apologetics, and theology within the biblical, Christian, Baptist, and contemporary heritages. He ministered too as a preacher, a teacher, and an academician. In it all, Newport interlaced the character traits of an abiding faith with reasonableness, an insatiable desire for all knowledge, an ecumenical spirit, and a practical temperament focused in life's ultimate questions. He was likewise a choice friend and a cherished family member.

Each colored thread by itself is a substantial legacy. Each thread, in fact, changed the lives of Newport's students, colleagues, and friends, who served in churches, seminaries, private and state universities, denominational agencies, and missionary posts around the world. But Newport's enduring legacy lies elsewhere in a fundamental pattern that integrated the diversely colored threads into a unity and gave the fabric of his thought its remarkable consistency. Newport spoke of this pervasive pattern as "eschatological-holy history" or as the "already-not yet" stream of redemptive history. He spoke of it too as "a biblical philosophy." The Scriptures, he insisted, contain "a biblical worldview" expressed in such categories as history, covenant, and personalism. Herein was John Newport's genius—and his enduring legacy within the legacy of Southwestern.

BIOGRAPHY

The odyssey of John Newport to a biblical philosophy began with his parents, Marvin Jackson and Mildred Morrow Newport, who placed the highest priority on their evangelical heritage and experiential faith. But Christian belief and experience came vividly to life in a personal way in November 1925, when Newport accepted Jesus Christ as his Savior and Lord and was baptized in a chilly river in Buffalo, Missouri, the town of his birth, on 16 June 1917. Thus began his experimental walk with the total fact of Jesus Christ, which led to a lifetime of proclaiming the gospel in pulpit and podium.[1]

John Newport was not alone in his personal walk and abiding confidence in the validity of experiential Christian faith and calling. In 1941, he married Eddie Belle, daughter of storied Baptists Frank H. and Martha Boone Leavell of Nashville, and their family grew to include Martha Ellen, Frank Marvin, and John Paul, Jr. Newport fittingly described Eddie Belle, who holds B.A. and M.A. degrees from Meredith College and Texas Christian University, as an "enabler, a companion of the years, the love of my life, and the real Baptist in the family with a vital sense of the liberty found in Christ."[2] John and Eddie Belle Newport were active members of Broadway Baptist Church throughout their residence in Fort Worth. Together they conducted numerous study tours to Europe, the Middle East, and Asia.

Upon graduation from William Jewell College (B.A., 1938), Newport pursued his first program of advanced study at Southern Seminary (Th.M., Th.D., 1942, 1944), where he majored in New Testament with Hersey Davis, took his first philosophy of religion course under H. C. Goerner, and was greatly persuaded by the writings of E. Y. Mullins. While a pastor in Clinton, Mississippi, he realized the necessity of relating the Scriptures to contemporary culture and of undergirding the validity of Christianity. He consequently embarked on a second program of advanced study in philosophical theology at Basel and Zurich universities and the University of Edinburgh (Ph.D., 1953) and came under the tutelage of Karl Barth, Emil Brunner, John Baillie, and Oscar Cullmann in matters of revelation and "a metaphysic of subjects." During an Oklahoma pastorate, Newport studied philosophy at the University of Tulsa and would later pursue advanced studies in philosophy at Tulane and Columbia and with Alvin Nelson at Texas Christian University (M.A., 1968).

In a fourth program of sabbatical work (1958–59), he studied at Harvard and Boston universities, where Paul Tillich, John Wild, and G. Ernest Wright influenced his views of culture and history. A fifth era of study at Union Theological Seminary, New York, brought Newport into contact with Abraham Joshua Heschel, Daniel Day Williams, and others.

At Baylor University, Newport offered his first philosophy course in 1949 and then taught at New Orleans Seminary during 1951–52. He then joined the faculty of Southwestern Seminary (1952–76) and became academic vice president and provost (1979–90), after teaching at Rice University (1976–79). Building on the foundation laid by Albert Venting (1921–37) and Stewart A. Newman (1936–52), his predecessors in philosophy at Southwestern, Newport developed a biblical philosophy. He would be joined in the work of Christian philosophy by Professors Milton Ferguson (1959–73) and Yandall Woodfin (1973–94), as well as by fellows in philosophy at Southwestern. Of particular influence in the formation of Newport's biblical philosophy were the studies of J. V. Langmead Casserley, Abraham Joshua Heschel, Otto A. Piper, John Macmurray, H. Wheeler Robinson, Alan Richardson, and Edmond La Beaume Cherbonnier (biblical metaphysics) by Southwestern fellows Dan W. Cochran, Robert E. Clarke, David C. George, Allen A. Denton, Arnold G. Ashburn, Alfred V. Woodard, and F. Louis Mauldin. Of strategic importance too in understanding topics related to Newport's biblical approach to philosophy were the analyses of suffering, biblical language, painting, literature, and Hebraic thinking by Southwestern fellows Clyde R. Majors, Forrest E. Wood, Wallace Roark, James R. Heath, and James W. Bryant. Newport lectured or spoke in more than sixty colleges and universities, including more than twenty on the Staley series. Newport died on 16 August 2000; his funeral was in Broadway Baptist Church, and he was buried in Greenwood Cemetery, Fort Worth.

WRITINGS

As Newport searched for a philosophical direction in the 1950s and early 1960s, he evaluated alternatives in a series of works published privately for classroom use. His four-volume *A Guide to a Christian Philosophy of Religion* was a compilation of views, while his two-volume *Questions People Ask about a Christian Philosophy of*

Religion reflected more of his own thinking on key issues and philosophical perspectives. Newport's volume, *A Guide to Religious Authority and Biblical Interpretation in the Thought of John Calvin*, and the one on *Religious Authority, Biblical Interpretation and the Modern Mind* examined options in epistemology.

A biblical philosophy first appeared in the compilation, *Biblical Philosophy and the Modern Mind*, which contained a 1963 article[3] by the same name. The article signaled Newport's decisive move from an objective philosophical approach and traditional apologetics to a biblical philosophy. The turning point in Newport's mind was occasioned by the realism of G. Ernest Wright of Harvard, who urged him "to develop a distinctively biblical philosophy following the structures of the biblical mind and the centrality of history and covenant." Before the turning point, Newport explained, "I took a neutral, objective approach. After, I began with the Christian faith and biblical key-categories, then turned to dialogue." That is, "I began with history plus existence, then proceeded to revelation and to reason and from reason to dialogue with world religions, art, science, etc."[4]

In research and in teaching, Newport made the move to a biblical philosophy in the early 1960s, but it did not initially yield books in the area. Newport's love of dialogue led him to publish the 1971 (1979) book, *Theology (Christianity) and Contemporary Art Forms*, and the 1972 book, *Demons, Demons, Demons*. He would coauthor in 1974 *Why Christians Fight over the Bible* and produce in 1978 *Christ and the New Consciousness*. Theological interests resulted in two 1984 books, *Paul Tillich* and *What Is Christian Doctrine?*, which explored faith, culture, and historic Christianity. Biblical concerns led to his 1986 commentary on Revelation, *The Lion and the Lamb*.

The demonstration and documentation of the system of a biblical worldview came with the 1989 book, *Life's Ultimate Questions: A Contemporary Philosophy of Religion*. Newport's 1998 book, *The New Age Movement and the Biblical Worldview*, applied biblical philosophy to key areas of life. In both books, Newport preserved the integrity of the biblical tongue and established the viability of a biblical worldview in terms of the ultimate questions raised within the modern-postmodern world.

A BIBLICAL WORLDVIEW

"A renaissance person"—these words well describe John Newport. All knowledge beckoned him. He exploded circles into the future—no possibility eluded him. Dialogue and engagement became ways of thinking. Yet in all things, a biblical worldview gave form and content. Indeed, the essential core, the deep-down bone marrow, of Newport's thought is there, just there, in a biblical worldview centered in synoptic philosophy, eschatological-holy history, historical knowledge, and the principle of complementarity.

Synoptic Philosophy

John Newport was a synoptic philosopher who integrated knowledge in a worldview, or a comprehensive vision of reality which tells us who we are and why we are here. A worldview originates, he contends, in a key category or a faith principle selected from experience. Although it originates in a subjective, convictional basis, a worldview says something about the ways in which objective reality transcends experience, and it does so in terms of models or analogies found within experience. The specific faith-commitment which gives rise to Newport's key category and metaphysic arises from the interaction of revelation, redemption, personal realism, and history found in the Scriptures, which contain a common set of presuppositions—an implicit metaphysic.

Methods must be established for comparing worldviews and for demonstrating the superiority of the biblical worldview in the modern-postmodern world. Newport consequently argued that verification of (1) the basic premise and (2) the system of biblical metaphysics can be obtained. First, he verified the basic premise or key category in the interplay of event and word, of act and interpretation, which together constitute the biblical revelation firmly grounded in history. God entered history in mighty acts, supremely in Jesus Christ, so as to create a people and a redemptive history. God also inspired persons to interpret the significance of the acts. In the interpretation of events, however, inspiration was not solely verbal or subjective. God's self-revelation occurred in "the concrete stuff" of history and in the arena of "historical or public encounters," which enabled the biblical writers to interpret God's acts in such a way that the interpretation could be tested by historical inquiry, facts, witnesses, and probability. Verification of the key category, for Newport, thus centers its case in unique historical events which, when interpreted, hold the clues to meaning.

Second, Newport verified the system of biblical metaphysics and demonstrated its "normativity" by means of criteria applicable to any viable metaphysic. The basic question to ask a worldview is not from what experience does it arise, but whether it measures up to reasonable criteria. It must be rationally coherent and empirically adequate. Then, too, it must be sound existentially and tested pragmatically in terms of ultimate questions that touch on matters basic to life itself. A metaphysic, if true, must also be comprehensive, creative, and subject to comparative testing.

In the modern-postmodern world, Newport entered the marketplace of ideas and shared his deepest conviction about why he thought that the biblical worldview alone furnishes the fundamental pattern for the scattered pieces of the jigsaw puzzle of life. Firmly rooted in the Baptist heritage of liberty, he insisted that God created human variety and wants us to theologize and philosophize in varied ways. He insisted too that sin, finitude, and historical contingency make it impossible for any view to represent absolute truth. Therefore, Newport enjoined, the biblical worldview must be shared by persuasion and incarnation within a context of dialogue, openness, and verification—without abandoning the claim that the biblical worldview is unique, definitive, and normative.

Eschatological-Holy History
A biblical worldview affirms the reality of history and the God of history. It does not, however, make history the ultimate reality. God acts in history but is also other than and beyond history. Still, according to Newport, the Living God is a personal agent who creates and redeems the world and providentially governs it. Life and history, as a consequence, are real and meaningful and serve to reveal God, who plunges into the matrix of history and encounters persons in the particulars of the life-world. In effect, the Living God as Creator, as Redeemer, as Sanctifier, and as Sovereign Lord engages in a constant dialogue with persons in the nitty-gritty of history.

In the biblical epic of history, meaning does not wait for the final curtain; it exists in each line of the script. It literally courses through the whole drama in particular events and persons. Meaning focuses, however, in kairotic or pivotal events, such as the exodus and covenant, and supremely in Jesus Christ, who is the final self-revelation of the Triune God and who forges a fundamentally new reality. Thus, history, particularity, and personality are bound up in a knot of mutual relationships in Jesus Christ. The redemptive line of history, which is the Christ-line, is also eschatological by turn. In fact, for Newport, eschatology is "the key in which everything is set." The kingdom of God is here—a present reality. It has an "already" character. Still, the kingdom has a "not yet" character too. In the "already-not yet" flow of history, God's purposes permeate and unify all creation, redemption, and providence—all events, life, persons, and nature. History is not a given in which God acts. The contemporary Christ and the eschatological purposes embodied in God's acts literally give hope and substance to all of history.

Historical Understanding

Knowing historical realities requires a unique way of understanding. We must adopt, in Newport's view, a holistic perspective which relates the ultimate authority of God's self-revelation in history to the mediating authority of the Scriptures, individual encounter, and faith seeking understanding. These authorities, each brought alive by the vivifying presence and power of the person of the Holy Spirit, are interrelated in historical understanding, which includes objective and subjective elements.

At the center of understanding is God's self-revelation in history. Although God is mystery, God clothed the mystery with meaning by voluntarily accommodating and "disclosing himself" in an incredibly realistic and personalistic fashion. This revelation occurred in specific events, especially in God's decisive act in Jesus Christ, and not in the form of abstract truths. It took the shape of an Event "rooted in the singular," which can be located, dated, identified, and interpreted. Hence, concrete language, dramatic narratives, event symbols, personal models, "empirical-logical" thinking, and historical references dot the pages of the Scriptures. But God's self-disclosure expressed itself in word as well as in event. It took the form of inspired language and created a book—the Scriptures. Significantly, Newport held, God raised up prophetic voices, which interpreted the kairotic events in terms of themselves and their place in holy history, and apostolic voices, which interpreted the

Supreme Event of Jesus Christ. Mystery thus has meaning within the historical milieu and narrative in which it arises, from which it is taken, and to which it is applied.

The Scriptures, which are truthful in that they achieve their purpose of revelation-redemption, confront us with another world and ask if it will become our world. Thus, although grounded objectively in revelation and the Scriptures, historical understanding requires involvement. To know, Newport insisted, is to encounter God's reality within "the personality of the subject," an encounter which draws the subject into the objective reality of God through the event of Jesus Christ and by the Holy Spirit's work. Encounter involves faith, or a relation of personal trust, as well as immersing oneself in the ongoing redemptive story of God's acts well enough to allow a person to interpret and to experience the self, the world, and God in terms of that story. In encounter, understanding begins with faith, Newport added, but faith has continuity with reason and a Christian life, which together flesh out an understanding and a concrete appropriation of revelation, the Scriptures, and a faith encounter in the present stage of the biblical drama.

A Principle of Complementarity

In order to gain a richer, more concrete access to reality by means of synoptic, historical understanding, Newport appealed to a principle of complementarity. The principle appears in his view of the relation of event and word, as well as in the interplay of ultimate and mediating authorities. It can be seen too in his view of science and the Scriptures. The Scriptures raise questions about persons, values, and purpose, whereas science asks about natural phenomena. But, although they occupy different domains and use distinct methods to answer distinct kinds of questions, Newport saw the Scriptures and science as separate maps for the same terrain and hence as complementary. Newport's love of complementarity also surfaces in his hermeneutics. The meaning of the Bible is conditioned by the perspectives of the biblical writers and the interpreters, but it is possible to discover a transcultural meaning in a culturally conditioned text by asking two questions: what the text meant and what it means. Meaning is, after all, a matter of action as well as of reflection; and truth is lived out, not simply thought, in history, wherein the two questions complement each other.

The principle of complementarity also reverberates throughout Newport's apologetics. Newport, more than any Southwesterner, has called for a new encounter of the world's philosophies and religions, an engagement with science, the arts, and the humanities, and a continual interaction with the modern-postmodern world. Nothing short of the free exposure to the truths in all viewpoints and the incorporation of compatible truths in a biblical worldview will suffice, for truth—all of it—is God's truth. All views, however, must be rigorously tested in terms of life's ultimate questions. They must provide the stories through which persons can view reality and address the basic issues of the nature of history, creation, redemption, providence, persons, and God, the ultimate questions of the relations of revelation, language, faith, and reason as well as the basic issues of the meaning of evil/suffering and of moral responsibility and freedom.

CHALLENGE

At the heart of John Newport's legacy lies a paradigm shift—a shift in the questions available for Christian thought and in the standards by which thinkers determine what counts as an admissible problem or as a legitimate solution; a shift to a biblical model that sets rules, methods, language, categories, norms, and applications.

Shortly before his death, Newport spoke with me about the need to carry forward the paradigm shift of biblical philosophy. The unfolding paradigm, which "still has crucial validity," he counseled, must center in historical, relational, and personal categories.[5] It must also address the essence of the past, present, and future, and the way in which they interact with each other and with eternity to form a unity. Other questions surely remain: the nature of historical causality and what it means for God to "act" in history; the relation of truths and truth itself (and the priority of the latter); and the viability of the subject-object dualism, with which Newport struggled but which he never overcame. Biblical philosophy also needs to unpack the meaning of Jesus' words, "I am the truth," in terms of the realism of the gospel and the Baptist heritage of personal truth.

The challenge to the Southwestern community today is that John Newport has set the ancient landmarks of a biblical worldview, but the paradigm is not yet complete, nor should it be. From first to last, biblical philosophy is characterized by continuity and change. It is by turn forward-looking and dynamic, but it develops as it holds true to the ancient landmarks while it is seen in ever fresh ways. This "already-not yet" quality is the key in which biblical philosophy has been bequeathed to us by John Newport, and it is an integral part of the legacy of Southwestern.

BIBLIOGRAPHY[6]

1. Primary

DISSERTATIONS AND THESIS

"The Jewish Messiah of the Apocrypha and Pseudepigrapha." Th.D. diss., Southern Baptist Theological Seminary, 1946.

"An Investigation of Factors Influencing John Calvin's Use of the Linguistic and Historical Principles of Biblical Exegesis." Ph.D. diss., University of Edinburgh, 1953.

"Representative Contemporary Attempts to Establish the Meaningfulness and Uniqueness of Religious and Biblical Language." M. A. thesis, Texas Christian University, 1968.

BOOKS

Christ and the New Consciousness. Nashville: Broadman, 1978.

Cristianismo y Ocultismo: Un Enfrentamiento. Trans. Guillermo Krätzig. Buenos Aires: Junta Bautista de Publicaciones, 1974. [No published English edition.]

Demons, Demons, Demons: A Christian Guide through the Murky Maze of the Occult. Nashville: Broadman, 1972.

    Demonios, Demonios, Demonios: Una Guía Cristiana para la Baraúnda del Ocultisimo. Trans. Arnoldo Canclini. Buenos Aires: Junta Bautista de Publicaciones, 1973; rev. ed.: El Paso: Casa Bautista de Publicaciones, 1987. [Spanish]

    Demonios, Demonios, Demonios. Trans. Talleres Graficos. ?: Argen-Press, 1973. [Spanish]

Life's Ultimate Questions: A Contemporary Philosophy of Religion. Dallas: Word, 1989.

The Lion and the Lamb: The Book of Revelation for Today. Nashville: Broadman, 1986.

The New Age Movement and the Biblical Worldview: Conflict and Dialogue. Grand Rapids: Eerdmans, 1998.

(ed.) *Nineteenth Century Devotional Thought*. Christian Classics. Nashville: Broadman, 1981.

Paul Tillich. Makers of the Modern Theological Mind. Waco, Tex.: Word, 1984.

Theology and Contemporary Art Forms. Waco, Tex.: Word, 1971. Publ. as *Christianity and Contemporary Art Forms*. Waco: Word, 1979.

What Is Christian Doctrine? Layman's Library of Christian Doctrine, vol.1. Nashville: Broadman, 1984.

    ¿Qué es la Doctrina Christiana? Su Valor, Necesidad y Base. Biblioteca de Doctrina Cristiana. Trans. Roberto Gama. El Paso: Casa Bautista de Publicaciones, 1985; 2d ed., 1988. [Spanish]

(co-auth.) *Why Christians Fight over the Bible*. Nashville: Thomas Nelson, 1974.

CHAPTERS CONTRIBUTED TO BOOKS

"Arts from a Conservative Perspective." In *Arts in Society*, ed. Edward Kamarck, 56–57. Madison: University of Wisconsin Extension Division, 1976.

"The Challenge of Recent Literary Approaches to the Bible." In *Beyond the Impasse? Scripture, Interpretation, and Theology in Baptist Life*, ed. Robison B. James and David S. Dockery, 64–90. Nashville: Broadman, 1992.

"Christianity and the Arts." In *At the Edge of Hope: Christian Laity in Paradox*, ed. Howard E. Butt, Jr., 102–16. New York: Seabury, 1978.

"The Church Member." In *J. Howard Williams: Prophet of God and Friend of Man*, ed. H. C. Brown, Jr., and Charles P. Johnson, 121–29. San Antonio: Naylor Co., 1963.

"The Future Church Faces Radical New Religions." In *Future Church*, ed. Ralph W. Neighbour, Jr., 187–205. Nashville: Broadman, 1980.

"Holy Spirit: Empowering for the Living of the Witnessing-Giving Life." In *Witnessing-Giving Life*, 84–101. Nashville: SBC Stewardship Commission, 1988.

"Interpreting the Bible." In *Broadman Bible Commentary*, ed. Clifton J. Allen, vol. 1, 25–33. Nashville: Broadman, 1969.

"The Mystery of Immortality and the Life Beyond." In *the Miracle of Easter*, ed. Floyd Thatcher, 115–23. Waco, Tex.: Word, 1980.

"The Purpose of the Church." In *The People of God: Essays on the Believers' Church*, ed. Paul A. Basden and David S. Dockery, 19–40. Nashville: Broadman, 1990.

"Response" and "Satan and Demons: A Theological Perspective." In *Demon Possession: A Medical, Historical, Anthropological and Theological Symposium*, ed. John Warwick Montgomery, 58–61, 325–45. Minneapolis: Bethany Fellowship, Inc., 1976.

"Understanding, Evaluating, and Learning from the Contemporary Glossolalia Movement." In *Tongues*, ed. Luther B. Dyer, 105–27. Jefferson City, Mo.: Le Roi Publishers, 1971.

"The World: A Tangled Web and a Scarlet Thread." In *Waiting in the Wings*, ed. Porter W. Routh, 117–24. Nashville: Broadman, 1978.

JOURNAL ARTICLES

"America's Continuing Controversy over Humanism." *Liberal and Fine Arts Review* 3 (January–July 1983): 87–98.

"The Arts in Worship." *Review and Expositor* 80 (Winter 1983): 71–83.

"Biblical Interpretation and Eschatological-Holy History." *Southwestern Journal of Theology*. n.s. 4 (October 1961): 83–110.

"Biblical Language and Religious Authority." *Foundations* 17 (January–March 1974): 58–67.

"The Biblical Worldview and Church-Related Colleges." *Southern Baptist Educator* 53 (August 1989): 3–20.

"Facing toward the Millennial Year 2000 under Biblical Guidance with a Focus on the Resurrection." *Ex Auditu* 9 (1993): 109–21.

"God, Man, and Redemption in Modern Art." *Review and Expositor* 61 (Summer 1964): 142–55.

"Guest Editorial: The Musical Heritage of Baptists." *Baptist History and Heritage* 19 (January 1984): 2–3.

"Humanism and the Future: A Tentative Proposal for an American Solution." *Liberal and Fine Arts Review* 4 (January 1984): 53–61.

"Lessons from the Odyssey of an Evolving Baptist Theologian." *Southwestern Journal of Theology* 37 (Spring 1995): 38–42. The NABPR presidential address, November 1992.

"New Developments in New Testament Theology." *Review and Expositor* 49 (January 1952): 41–56.

"Presenting an Authentic Christian Witness in a World of Secularism and Religious Obsession." *Search* 7 (Spring 1977): 46–57.

"The Problem of Demonic Power and the Nature of the Christian Response." *Ogbomoso Journal of Theology* 3 (December 1988): 27–31.

"Questions Ministers Ask about Contemporary Literature and Drama." *Southwestern Journal of Theology* 10 (Spring 1968): 31–47.

"Religion, Architecture and the Arts in the 1980s." *Faith and Form* 13 (Spring-Summer 1979): 10–11, 19–21.

"Representative Contemporary Approaches to the Use of Philosophy in Christian Thought." *Review and Expositor* 82 (Fall 1985): 507–19.

"Representative Historical and Contemporary Approaches to Biblical Interpretation." *Faith and Mission* 3 (Spring 1986): 32–48.

"Secularization, Secularism, and Christianity." *Review and Expositor* 68 (Winter 1971): 81–93.

"Sexuality in the Contemporary Arts." *Review and Expositor* 68 (Spring 1971): 203–15.

"Southern Baptists and the Bible: Seeking a Balanced Perspective." *Southwestern Journal of Theology* 34 (Spring 1992): 31–42.

"The Theology and Experience of Salvation." *Greek Orthodox Theological Review* 22 (Winter 1977): 393–404.

"The Unique Nature of the Bible in the Light of Recent Attacks." *Southwestern Journal of Theology* n.s. 6 (October 1963): 93–106.

"Why Christians Argue over Biblical Interpretation." *Southwestern Journal of Theology* 16 (Spring 1974): 15–29.

ENCYCLOPEDIA AND DICTIONARY ARTICLES

Encyclopedia of Southern Baptists. 4 vols. Nashville: Broadman, 1958–82. Vol. 1. S.v. "Bible, The: Authority of the Bible."

Mercer Dictionary of the Bible. Ed. Watson E. Mills. Macon, Ga.: Mercer University Press, 1990. S.v. "Athens," "Inheritance in the New Testament," and "Savior in the New Testament."

MISCELLANEOUS ARTICLES

"The American Dream: Religion, Religious Liberty and the Public Schools." *Missouri Schools*, October 1985, 22–26.

"Communicating the Gospel through Contemporary Art Forms." *The Journal of the Southern Baptist Church Music Conference* (1962–63): 18–25.

"Satan, the Bible, and the Modern Mind." *Sunday School Lesson Illustrator*, Winter 1975, 25–27.

"Should Christians Be Interested in Contemporary Art Forms?" *[Baptist] Student*, June 1971, 8–13.

"Some Thoughts about Miracles." *Baptist Student*, May 1965, 2–4, 39.

"Speaking with Tongues." *Home Missions*, May 1965, 7–9, 21–26.

"Student Shapers." *Baptist Student*, December 1967, 14–20.

"Updating the American Dream." *Report from the Capital*, January 1986, 4–5, 7.

2. Secondary

Bush, L. Russ, III. "John Paul Newport: A Man for All Seasons." *Southwestern Journal of Theology* 29 (Summer 1987): 5–11.

Bush, L. Russ, III, Joe M. Cooper, Frank Louis Mauldin, Warren McWilliams, Samuel J. Mikolaski, and John P. Newport, "Forum: Reflections on John Newport's *Life's Ultimate Questions*." *Theological Educator* no. 41 (Spring 1990): 35–61.

Cabal, Theodore James. "Problems and Promise in a Biblical Worldview with Special Reference to John Paul Newport." Ph.D. diss., Southwestern Baptist Theological Seminary, 1995.

Dilday, Russell H., Jr. "Practical Apologist: Faith Seeking Understanding." *Southwestern Journal of Theology* 29 (Summer 1987): 12–18.

Ferguson, Milton U. "Revelation, Religious Authority and Biblical Interpretation." *Southwestern Journal of Theology* 29 (Summer 1987): 28–32.

Mauldin, Frank Louis. "John Newport and a Biblical World View." *Southwestern Journal of Theology* 29 (Summer 1987): 33–45.

William Roscoe Estep, Jr.
(1920–2000)
Church History

Paul L. Gritz

18

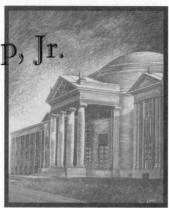

BIOGRAPHY

William Roscoe Estep, Jr., taught church history at Southwestern Seminary from 1954 to 1990 and then adjunctively to 1994. He was a native of Kentucky, receiving his B.A. degree from Berea College (1942) and his Th.M. from Southern Baptist Theological Seminary (1945). His Th.D. came from Southwestern Baptist Theological Seminary (1951). Bill and Edna Alice McDowell were married in 1942. He served as pastor and interim pastor of churches in Kentucky, Texas, and Oklahoma before and after joining the faculty of Southwestern Seminary. The Esteps joined Gambrell Street Baptist Church, Fort Worth. Two children preceded Bill in death, Alice (1947) and Martin (1969). Their other children are Merl, Rhoda, Mary, and Lena.[1]

At Southwestern, where he taught the required courses which surveyed church and Baptist history, Estep's interest centered upon his elective courses and doctoral seminars in the Reformation, especially on the Anabaptists. He led several Reformation study tours in Europe. To equip himself in languages, he studied Spanish in Costa Rica and participated as a research fellow doing Latin and German translations at the summer institute of the Society for Reformation Research in St. Louis.

Estep took his sabbatical leaves abroad at Baptist schools in Colombia (1959–60) and in Rüschlikon, Switzerland (1967–68), where he also studied at the universities of Zurich and Basel; at Madrid and the University of Oxford (1974–75); and after retirement in Hong Kong (1994–95). He served as senior lecturer for the Southwest Commission on Religious Studies (1988–89) and lectured and presented papers at conferences in North America, Latin America, Europe, and Asia. He participated in the Believers' Church Conferences, the Conference of Faith and History (president, 1983–84), the American Society of Church History, the Southern Baptist Historical Society, and the Texas Baptist Historical Society.

WRITINGS

In the classroom, from the pulpit, and through his writings, Estep advocated the distinctive positions of the believers' church heritage, especially the Baptist expression of it. He challenged his students and readers to understand the circumstances and beliefs shaping their churches and themselves. A survey of his writings will show the various areas of historical study to which he made important contributions and will provide a broad framework for appreciating his thought.[2]

Ecumenical Studies

Estep did his doctoral research at Southwestern on the emergence of the World Council of Churches.[3] He summarized his findings in "A Historical Sketch of the World Council" (1955). With "Baptists and the Ecumenical Movement" (1964) he surveyed divergent postures toward ecumenism ranging from Northern (American) Baptist involvement to Southern Baptist aloofness. His *Baptists and Christian Unity* (1966) allowed him to collate and expand his previous discussions.[4]

Based on his historical research, Estep had assessed negatively the Roman Catholic Church's approaches prior to the Reformation with "John XXIII and the Papacy" (1958). In "Church and Culture in Latin America" (1962), Estep described the militantly anti-Protestant character of Spanish Roman Catholicism and its effect on Latin America. He wanted Baptists and the larger evangelical community to take a guarded stance toward renewed Catholic efforts to be viewed favorably. With "El Concilio Vaticano II y Los Papas Posteriores" (1984), however, he did sketch the steps which

Popes Paul VI and John Paul II had taken to implement conciliatory policies toward other Christians in light of Vatican II.[5]

On behalf of the Baptist World Alliance (BWA) in 1986, Estep drafted "A Response to *Baptism, Eucharist, and Ministry: Faith and Order Paper No. 111.*" The *BEM* document by the World Council of Churches had been proposed in 1982 as a means of unifying various church traditions. Estep pointed out the problems for Baptists in the ecumenical movement's efforts to bring agreement among people with vastly different views about the Bible's teachings on issues such as the sacraments and episcopal polity.[6]

Anabaptist and Reformation Studies

The Anabaptist Story (1963) stands out as the book which established Estep's scholarly reputation.[7] With "Our Anabaptist Heritage" (1956), however, he had already begun to examine the formative role of the Anabaptists.[8] In his book, Estep elaborated on themes from his earlier articles and added biographical portrayals of early Anabaptist leaders, their characteristic beliefs, and their specific legacy to Baptists and other believers' churches. Later in "A Believing People: Historical Background" (1969), he set forth again his view that Baptists had emerged because of the influence of the Anabaptist vision on key leaders of English Separatism in the early 1600s.[9] He expanded on this controversial thesis with "Anabaptists and the Rise of English Baptists" (1968, 1969). Through these various writings about Anabaptist influence, Estep had rekindled the debate over the sources of the distinctive beliefs which have characterized Baptists.

Estep wanted to show today's Baptists and others the relevance of Anabaptist thinkers such as Balthasar Hubmaier (c. 1480–1528). One of the areas on which Estep focused attention was how Hubmaier and the Anabaptists were the first ones in the Reformation era to speak out for complete religious liberty and church-state separation. The theological and biblical principles undergirding Hubmaier's position the Southwestern professor explicated in "*Von Ketzern und Iren Verbrennern*: a Sixteenth-Century Tract on Religious Liberty" (1969). He later elaborated on the scholarly discussion of the Anabaptists' views on church and state with "Anabaptists as Subversives in the Sixteenth Century" (1971).[10]

Providing Hubmaier's writings in an accessible English translation became part of Estep's larger endeavor to promote the importance of this Anabaptist leader who had anticipated the views of later Baptists. In 1976, he published a source book, *Anabaptist Beginnings (1523–1533)*. It contained eighteen documents, nine of which he had translated from German into English. Important works by Hubmaier such as his defense of believers' baptism, "On the Christian Baptism of Believers," were included in this volume along with documents from other early leaders in the movement.[11] In 1979 some of the source book materials, especially the translations of Hubmaier's writings, were included in the volume which Estep edited, *The Reformation: Luther, the Anabaptists*.[12] When the volume on Hubmaier's writings in the Classics of the Radical Reformation series was planned by Mennonites, the editors approached Estep about joining the project. He declined due to differences between Baptists and Mennonites over how to describe and assess Hubmaier's importance for the development of Anabaptism.

Estep championed the significance of Hubmaier by cotranslating and editing the definitive biography by Torsten Bergsten, *Balthasar Hubmaier: Anabaptist Theologian and Martyr* (1978).[13] To counter the way some historians had minimized his significance, Estep outlined in "Balthasar Hubmaier: Martyr without Honor" (1978) the writings by which this Anabaptist Reformer had shaped the theology of the movement. Since some medieval, catholic, and nominalist motifs in Hubmaier's writings on man's free will had been noted, Estep responded with "The Anabaptist View of Salvation" (1978) to show Hubmaier's consistently evangelical position. Presenting the Anabaptists as the pivotal and logical expression of the Reformation became a crucial project for Estep.

In his textbook, *Renaissance and Reformation* (1986), Estep noted the individuals of the 1400s and 1500s who shaped Europe's cultural and church life.[14] Although both Luther and Zwingli received two chapters each, Estep focused one chapter on the Swiss Reformation and another on Zwingli and his students, their disagreement with him over the nature of the church, and their formation of the first Anabaptist congregation at Zurich in 1525. The next chapter sketched the early Anabaptist leaders with Hubmaier receiving major attention for his role in shaping the theological outlook of the movement. Clearly for Estep the two movements, Reformed and

Anabaptist, which sprang from the Swiss context, held center stage in the drama of the Reformation.[15]

In *The Anabaptist Story*, Estep had described the distinctive theological emphases of Anabaptism. With "The Ecumenical Implications of Menno Simons' View of the Church" (1988), he expanded on his earlier treatment. He showed that Menno's teaching about the celestial flesh of Christ (even with its deviation from ancient conciliar orthodoxy) arose from his view that the true church had to be completely different from the world. The centrality of God in Christ giving to believers new life Menno believed had to be expressed in the actual holiness of the church and its members. This belief led Menno to practice strict church discipline and separation from the world's ways. With "The Reformation Anabaptist Style" (1993), Estep reiterated how Anabaptists focused on identifying with Christ and how their characteristic beliefs arose from such a commitment.

Studies on the Origins of Baptists

With his paper, "On the Origins of English Baptists" (1987), Estep returned to his earlier contention that an Anabaptist influence had shaped English Baptists.[16] He argued for a dual-heritage approach in understanding Baptist distinctives because it held in tension both a Puritan-Separatist strain of theology and a strain influenced by Anabaptism. With "Anabaptists, Baptists, and the Free Church Movement" (1993), the Southwestern professor presented in detail John Smyth's arguments against the Separatists' covenantal understanding of the Bible and the reasons why he had embraced instead an Anabaptist interpretation. Estep proposed, however, that it had been Thomas Helwys who had expressed the Baptist approach by synthesizing Smyth's Christocentric views with their congregation's original Separatist heritage. Helwys did so, however, without embracing all Mennonite views with regard to Christology or the necessity of pacifism. In an innovative step, Helwys had declared that a believer could be a magistrate but could not use his "sword" or power to enforce religious worship. The first position departed from Mennonite Anabaptism, but the second sided with it. Helwys had in effect revitalized Hubmaier's stance that Christians could participate in civil government, a view which the majority of Anabaptists had rejected. Helwys had outlined the approach which Baptists would follow in understanding church-state relations and also in other hallmark beliefs.

Estep made the case for a continuity of biblical interpretation from the evangelical Anabaptists to English and American Baptists with "Law and Gospel in the Anabaptist/Baptist Tradition" (1991). He expanded on the nature of an Anabaptist-Baptist approach to the Bible in "Sixteenth-Century Anabaptism and the Puritan Connection: Reflections upon Baptist Origins" (1993). The Anabaptist and Baptist governing principle remained the lordship of Christ as revealed in the New Testament. Their mutual insistence on believer's baptism and church-state separation showed how this principle distinguished both groups from Magisterial Reformers such as Luther and Calvin. In *Why Baptists? A Study of Baptist Faith and Heritage* (1997), the native Kentuckian reviewed Baptist beginnings and emphasized that even the Particular or Calvinistic Baptists developed their unique confessional outlook not so much from a modified Reformed position as from the theological framework of Anabaptism.[17]

Religious Freedom Studies

For Estep, the Anabaptist-Baptist hermeneutic found its clearest expression in the advocacy of complete religious liberty. As he often reiterated in lectures and publications, the Anabaptists insisted that faith cannot be coerced but results from a voluntary response to the gospel. In *Revolution within the Revolution: The First Amendment in Historical Context, 1612–1789* (1990), Estep lamented the Religious Right's disparaging of church-state separation and fostering instead the notion of a "Christian" America. Consequently, he surveyed the Anabaptist and early Baptist understanding of the necessity of religious freedom.[18] In "Civil Religion and Revolution within the Revolution" (1993), Estep contrasted the espousal of civil religion by high-profile, contemporary Baptists with the stand for church-state separation which George W. Truett had proclaimed in the early twentieth century.

Baptist Confessional and Controversial Studies

As a response to the controversy among Southern Baptists over the place of the Bible, Estep discussed how historic Baptist confessional statements had regarded the Scriptures. In "Biblical Authority in

Baptist Confessions of Faith, 1610–1963" (1987),[19] he cited the specific articles of those documents in which early English General and Particular Baptists focused on how Scripture pointed to Christ. They emphasized that the Bible had its authority through illumination by the Holy Spirit and obedience to it by believers. The Bible, especially the New Testament, was their sole rule for faith and practice. Baptists in Colonial America, including predestinarian Regulars (Particulars) and revivalistic Separates, made similar affirmations. Only the 1677 Second London (and later Philadelphia) Confession, which was based on the Reformed Westminster Confession, seemed to give the Bible itself a preeminent status. Estep noted that the less Calvinistic New Hampshire Confession (1833) had replaced the 1677 document as the most widely used belief statement among Baptists in America. Its articles served as the basis for the 1925 and the 1963 statements of the Baptist Faith and Message by the Southern Baptist Convention. According to Estep, even the 1963 amendment to the 1833 statement's first article ("On the Scriptures") had actually restored the Christ-focused viewpoint of the Bible which Baptist confessions had always emphasized before 1677.

In "Was Calvin Wrong? Doctrines Lead to 'Dunghill,' Prof Warns" (1997), Estep stirred up a vigorous reaction. *The Founders Journal* (Summer 1997) reprinted his article along with several rebuttals.[20] His opponents objected to Estep's assertions that Calvinism was a man-made system, not a biblical one; its God appeared to be like Allah of Islam and not the loving Father of Christ; human responsibility was stripped away by talk of absolute, divine predestination; intolerance of opponents was fostered; and an anti-missions/anti-effort orientation was encouraged.

Baptist Church and Denominational Studies

Estep always considered himself to be a servant of the churches. In this regard he assisted several Texas Baptist congregations by writing their histories.[21] To honor the contributions of his colleague, Robert A. Baker, Estep edited a collection of articles by Baker's friends and former students, *The Lord's Free People in a Free Land* (1976). Their articles addressed the historical background of various dimensions in Baptist life. In the chapter, "Southern Baptists in Search of an Identity" (1976), Estep himself described the component elements of and the controversies which he believed had

molded Southern Baptists.[22] Estep's own passion for gospel proclamation prompted him to participate in as well as to write about
Baptist mission efforts and the challenges confronting them. His
description of the work in *Colombia: Land of Conflict and Promise*
(1968) grew out of his teaching experience in Colombia while on a
sabbatical leave.[23] In "Latin America" (1974), he surveyed the expansion of the witness of Baptists throughout Latin America, the persecution which they had encountered from Roman Catholics, and the
relationship of Baptists with other Evangelicals on the continent.

The Foreign (now International) Mission Board of the Southern Baptist Convention recruited Estep to tell its story from 1845 to
1995. In *Whole Gospel—Whole World* (1994), he outlined in a three
chapter-prologue the pioneering efforts by Baptists in the modern
missions movement. The remaining ten chapters portrayed the
struggle and advance of this global agency and its missionaries.[24] Of
all his publications, Estep considered this one to be his most significant contribution to the cause of Christ.

INTERPRETATION

Certain themes appeared repeatedly in what Estep emphasized
with his publications. For Estep the evangelical Anabaptists like
Hubmaier were committed to Christ and his teachings as expressed in the New Testament. Telling their stories and presenting
their insights allowed Estep to advocate a vision for Christians as
they witness to their world. He was convinced that "a study of the
sixteenth-century Anabaptists can be instructive for those of us
who seek to follow Christ in obedient discipleship."[25]

In fact, Estep stated that Baptists' indebtedness to the Anabaptist heritage "has largely shaped the nature of the Baptist witness in
the world today."[26] He pointed out that both Anabaptists and Baptists insisted on a new birth experience of conversion, believer's
baptism as a declaration of one's faith, following completely Christ
as Lord, gathering congregations of committed believers, voluntary
action based on an unhindered response to God's word and the
work of the Holy Spirit, the Supper as a symbol not a sacrament,
mutual accountability in church discipline, and the practice of love
for others. Their convictions led them to witness vigorously and to
act self-sacrificially, and in the case of the Anabaptists to embrace
nonresistance and even to expect martyrdom. Estep observed that

strict adherence to the Scriptures enabled Anabaptists and Baptists to break from state-church traditions, especially infant baptism as retained by most mainline Protestants.

By its undergirding their shared cluster of beliefs Estep saw an Anabaptist-Baptist hermeneutic at work. Specifically, the Anabaptists had seen and relied on a distinction between the work of God's Spirit within a person's heart as described in the New Testament and the outward obedience to sacramental or covenantal patterns of behavior as prescribed in the Old Testament. In other words, the coming of Christ and the activity of the Holy Spirit in the lives of believers marked a major change in the way God was carrying out his redemptive plan. The Southwestern professor noted that this same distinction about God's plan appeared in the confessional statements of the seventeenth-century by both the English General (free will type) and the Particular (predestinarian type) Baptists. It also represented the viewpoint of most influential Baptist writers during the eighteenth, nineteenth, and twentieth centuries.

A distinct understanding of the Scriptures, which differed from a Reformed or covenantal viewpoint, Estep believed, had led Anabaptists and Baptists to advocate positions such as complete religious freedom and church-state separation. In the latter case, they agreed that spiritual means such as preaching the word and prayer were God's way to make believers. The civil state could use its "sword" to punish criminals but not to promote true religion. By thinking that the civil means could be used in spiritual matters, many Protestant Reformers and their heirs had effectively denied the significance of Christ's incarnation and his method of bringing people to know him in a saving way. For Estep, then, the Anabaptists and Baptists advocated a viewpoint which should guide all believers.

If one should keep in mind Estep's convictions about the importance of the common beliefs and biblical perspective of Anabaptists and Baptists, then the diversity of his publications and activities demonstrates an essential coherence. For him, an Anabaptist-Baptist approach provided the most consistent way to live as a Christian. It had to be understood and embraced by each generation of Baptists if they were to uphold their heritage and calling.

EVALUATION

The tenability of Estep's writings and viewpoint arises from the profound influence that he exerted on his students and readers not only at Southwestern Seminary but across the globe. His prodigious writings gained for him recognition far beyond Southern Baptist circles. His effectiveness in sharing the vision of the believers' churches resulted from several factors.

First, Estep focused on communicating to students and lay people rather than engaging in the intricacies of discussion carried on among specialists on the Reformation. Second, as a Baptist scholar he participated in a wider circle of church historians who were instrumental in the renaissance of Anabaptist studies. Third, Estep was not afraid of swimming against the stream in historical interpretation among scholars by calling for a reexamination of the possibility of Anabaptist roots for Baptists. By doing so he stepped beyond the confines of the English and American scene and addressed issues crucial for Baptists from cultures across the world. That *The Anabaptist Story* has been translated so widely and used in other countries attests to this fact. Fourth, Estep believed that Baptists were part of a distinct and rapidly growing expression of Christianity—the believers' church tradition—and that Baptists should understand this and make a contribution to others. In several of these factors Estep seems to have played for Baptists in the latter half of the twentieth century the role that Albert Henry Newman, Southwestern's first church history professor, performed in the latter nineteenth and early twentieth centuries.[27]

Any limitations on Estep's impact may result from his intensely personal identification with the Anabaptist and Baptist leaders about whom he wrote. Estep had his heroes and villains. In many ways his biases reflected the conflicts of the Reformation era. His Anabaptist and Baptist heroes were the advocates of religious freedom who relied on the proclamation of the gospel itself to advance Christ's church. His villains were their persecutors—Roman Catholics, Magisterial Reformers, or others who relied on coercion to enforce their views on others. In particular, Estep found it difficult to acknowledge much value in the Reformed tradition, and he opposed vigorously any effort to collapse Baptists into a subset of Calvinism. He was so adamant in finding connections between

Baptists and Anabaptists that he sometimes downplayed the dissimilarities between them. He also focused so much on the evangelical Anabaptists as the normative expression of the tradition that he treated mystical, unorthodox, apocalyptic, and revolutionary spokesmen as unimportant variations when in fact these individuals were historically significant to the Radical Reformation.

In the final analysis, Estep exemplified the strength of Southwestern's legacy. He tied together excellence in awareness and involvement in his academic discipline with a commitment to show the application and relevance of historical issues for Christian believers today.

BIBLIOGRAPHY

1. Primary

DISSERTATION

"A Historical Study of the Ecumenical Movement." Th.D. diss., Southwestern Baptist Theological Seminary, 1951.

BOOKS

(ed.) *Anabaptist Beginnings (1523–1533): A Source Book*. Nieuwkoop, Netherlands: B. de Graaf, 1976.
The Anabaptist Story. Nashville: Broadman, 1963; 2d ed. Grand Rapids: Eerdmans, 1975; 3d ed. with sub-title: *An Introduction to Sixteenth-Century Anabaptism*. Grand Rapids: Eerdmans, 1996.
Istina je neuništiva. Trans. Rut Lehotsky. Novi Sad: Baptistička Teološka Škola, 1977. [Serbo-Croatian]
Jaechimryegyodoui Yuksa. Trans. Soo Young Chung. Seoul: Jordan Press, 1985. [Korean]
Příběh křtěncu̇: radikálové evropské reformace. Trans. Artur Jerśak and Milena Přecechtělová, with bibliography by Petr Macek. Prague: Evangelickém nakladatelství, 1991. [Czech]
Revolucionarios del Siglo XVI: Historia de los Anabautistas, Trans. W. R. Estep. El Paso: Casa Bautista de Publicaciones, 1975. [Spanish]
La Verità è Immortale: una vivace presentazione del Movimento Anabattista e del suo significato per il mondo moderno, Trans. Piero Bensi and Amato Billour. Rome: Casa Editrice Battista, 1971. [Italian]
And God Gave the Increase: The Centennial History of the First Baptist Church of Beaumont, Texas, 1872–1972. Beaumont, Tex.: First Baptist Church, 1972.
Baptists and Christian Unity. Nashville: Broadman, 1966.
Colombia: Land of Conflict and Promise. Nashville: Convention Press, 1968.
La Fe de los Apostoles: Un Resumen de la Historia del Periodo Apostólico, 30–100 d. de J.C. El Paso: Editorial Verdad, [1960?]. [Spanish]
A Fé dos Apóstolos: um Resumo da História da Era Apostólica, 30–100 d.c. Trans. Elisabeth Tammerik. Rio de Janeiro: Casa Publicadora Batista, 1961. [Portuguese]
The Gaston Story: The First Hundred Years, 1887–1987. Dallas: Gaston Avenue Baptist Church, 1987.
An Introduction to the Historical Development of Baptist Church-State Relations, 1612–1833. [Oak Bend, Ill.:] Christian Legal Society, 1983.

(ed.) *The Lord's Free People in a Free Land: Essays in Baptist History in Honor of Robert A. Baker*.
Fort Worth: School of Theology, Southwestern Baptist Theological Seminary, 1976.
A New Chapter in the Gaston Story. Dallas: Gaston Oaks Baptist Church, 1993.
The Reformation and Protestantism: Church History, Second Course. Student Learning Activities by
Gayle Hogg. El Paso: Carib Baptist Publications, 1983.
(ed.) *The Reformation: Luther, the Anabaptists*, Christian Classics. Nashville: Broadman, 1979.
Religious Liberty: Heritage and Responsibility. North Newton, Kan.: Bethel College, 1988.
Renaissance and Reformation. Grand Rapids: Eerdmans, 1986.
Revolution within the Revolution: The First Amendment in Historical Context, 1612–1789. Grand
Rapids: Eerdmans, 1990.
*Whole Gospel-Whole World: The Foreign Mission Board of the Southern Baptist Convention,
1845–1995*. Nashville: Broadman and Holman, 1994.
Why Baptists? A Study of Baptist Faith and Heritage. Dallas: Baptist Distinctives Committee, Baptist
General Convention of Texas, 1997.

BOOK COTRANSLATED
(cotrans. from German and ed.) *Balthasar Hubmaier: Anabaptist Theologian and Martyr*, by Torsten
Bergsten. Valley Forge, Pa.: Judson, 1978.

CHAPTERS CONTRIBUTED TO BOOKS
"Anabaptists as Subversives in the Sixteenth Century." In *God and Caesar: Case Studies in the Relationship between Christianity and the State*, ed. Robert D. Linder, 29–43. Longview, Tex.: Confer-
ence on Faith and History, 1971.
(coauth.) "Baptists: A Global Community of Faith." In *We Baptists*, ed. James Leo Garrett, Jr., 1–18.
Franklin, Tenn.: Providence House for the Study and Research Division, Baptist World Alliance,
1999.
"Baptists and the Ecumenical Movement." In *Baptist Advance: The Achievements of the Baptists of
North America for a Century and a Half*, ed. Davis Collier Woolley et al., 459–71. Nashville:
Broadman, 1964.
"A Believing People: Historical Background." In *The Concept of the Believers' Church: Addresses from
the 1967 Louisville Conference*, ed. James Leo Garrett, Jr., 35–58. Scottdale, Pa.: Herald, 1969.
"Biblical Authority in Baptist Confessions of Faith, 1610–1963." In *The Unfettered Word: Southern Bap-
tists Confront the Authority-Inerrancy Question*, ed. Robison B. James, 155–76. Waco, Tex.:
Word, 1987; rpt.: with subtitle: *Confronting the Authority-Inerrancy Question*. Macon, Ga.:
Smyth and Helwys, 1994.
"Church and State." In *The People of God: Essays on the Believers' Church*, ed. Paul A. Basden and
David S. Dockery, 267–76. Nashville: Broadman, 1991.
"Contrasting Views of the Lord's Supper in the Reformation of the Sixteenth Century." In *The Lord's Sup-
per: Believers Church Perspectives*, ed. Dale R. Stoffer, 46–62. Scottdale, Pa., and Waterloo, Ont.:
Herald, 1997.
"The English Baptist Legacy of Freedom and the American Experience." In *Pilgrim Pathways: Essays in
Baptist History in Honour of B. R. White*, ed. William H. Brackney, Paul S. Fiddes, and John H. Y.
Briggs, 263–81. Macon, Ga.: Mercer University, 1999.
"Latin America," In *Baptist Relations with Other Christians*, ed. James Leo Garrett, Jr., 131–45. Valley
Forge, Pa.: Judson, 1974.
"The Negro and American Christianity in Historical Perspective." In *The Cutting Edge: Critical Questions
for Contemporary Christians*, ed. H. C. Brown, Jr., 1:42–56. Waco, Tex.: Word, 1969.
"The Place Called Calvary [Luke 23:33]." In *Southwestern Sermons*, ed. H. C. Brown, Jr., 77–82. Nash-
ville: Broadman, 1960.

"Respect for Nonconformity Permeates the Baptist Conscience." In *Defining Baptist Convictions: Guidelines for the Twenty-first Century*, ed. Charles W. Deweese, 78–85. Franklin, Tenn.: Providence House, 1996.

"A Response to *Baptism, Eucharist, and Ministry: Faith and Order Paper No. 111.*" In *Faith, Life and Witness: The Papers of the Study and Research Division of the Baptist World Alliance, 1986–1990*, ed. William H. Brackney, 2–16. Birmingham, Ala.: Samford University Press, 1990.

"Sixteenth-Century Anabaptism and the Puritan Connection: Reflections upon Baptist Origins." In *Mennonites and Baptists: A Continuing Conversation*, ed. Paul Toews, 1–38. Winnipeg, Manitoba, and Hillsboro, Kan.: Kindred, 1993.

"Southern Baptists in Search of an Identity." In *The Lord's Free People in a Free Land*, 145–69.

JOURNAL ARTICLES

"A. H. Newman and Southwestern's First Faculty." *Southwestern Journal of Theology* 21 (Fall 1978): 83–98.

"The Anabaptist View of Salvation." *Southwestern Journal of Theology* 20 (Spring 1978): 32–49.

"Anabaptists and the Rise of English Baptists." Part 1, *Quarterly Review* 28 (October–November–December 1968): 43–53; and Part 2, 29 (January–February–March 1969): 50–62.

"Anabaptists, Baptists, and the Free Church Movement." *Criswell Theological Review* 6 (Spring 1993): 303–17.

"Balthasar Hubmaier: Martyr without Honor." *Baptist History and Heritage* 13 (April 1978): 5–10, 27.

"A Baptist Reappraisal of Sixteenth Century Anabaptists." *Review and Expositor* 55 (January 1958): 40–58.

"The Baptist Struggle for Freedom in the Historical Context." *Southwestern Journal of Theology* 31 (Spring 1989): 42–48.

"Baptists and Authority: The Bible, Confessions, and Conscience in the Development of Baptist Identity." *Review and Expositor* 84 (Fall 1987): 599–615.

"The Changing Ecumenical Scene: A Baptist Perspective." *Quarterly Review* 28 (January–February–March 1968): 52–59.

"Church and Culture in Latin America." *Southwestern Journal of Theology* n.s. 4 (April 1962): 27–47.

"Civil Religion and Revolution within the Revolution." *Fides et Historia* 24 (Fall 1992): 42–52.

"El Concilio Vaticano II y Los Papas Posteriores." *Dialogo Theologico* no. 23 (April 1984): 21–33.

"Course-changing Events in the History of the Foreign Mission Board, SBC, 1845–1994." *Baptist History and Heritage* 29 (October 1994): 5–13.

"The Ecumenical Implications of Menno Simons' View of the Church." *Mennonite Quarterly Review* 62 (July 1988): 356–67.

"A Historical Sketch of the World Council." *Review and Expositor* 52 (April 1955): 216–26.

"Law and Gospel in the Anabaptist/Baptist Tradition." *Grace Theological Journal* 12 (Fall 1991): 189–214.

"The Making of a Prophet: An Introduction to Charles Haddon Spurgeon." *Baptist History and Heritage* 19 (October 1984): 3–15.

"The Nature and Use of Biblical Authority in Baptist Confessions of Faith, 1610–1963." *Baptist History and Heritage* 22 (October 1987): 3–16.

"On the Origins of English Baptists." *Baptist History and Heritage* 22 (April 1987): 19–26.

"Our Anabaptist Heritage." *Quarterly Review* 16 (April–May–June 1956): 54–60.

"Reflections on Eighty Years of Theological Education at Southwestern." *Southwestern Journal of Theology* 37 (Summer 1995): 14–19.

"The Reformation Anabaptist Style." *Criswell Theological Review* 6 (Spring 1993): 195–206.

"Religion in the Lone Star State: An Historical Perspective." *International Review of Mission* 78 (April 1989): 180–86.

"The Significance of the Reformation." *Quarterly Review* 27 (October–November–December 1967): 49–54.

"Southern Baptist Global Evangelism, 1950–1994: Strategies, Tensions, Achievements." *Baptist History and Heritage* 30 (January 1995): 14–22.

"Thomas Helwys: Bold Architect of Baptist Policy on Church-State Relations." *Baptist History and Heritage* 20 (July 1985): 24–34.

"*Von Ketzern und Iren Verbrennern*: A Sixteenth Century Tract on Religious Liberty." *Mennonite Quarterly Review* 43 (October 1969): 271–82.

DICTIONARY AND ENCYCLOPEDIA ARTICLES

Brethren Encyclopedia. 3 vols. Philadelphia and Oak Brook, Ill.: Brethren Encyclopedia, 1983. Vol. 1. S.v. "Baptists."

Dictionary of Baptists in America. Ed. Bill J. Leonard. Downers Grove, Ill.: InterVarsity, 1994. S.v. "Baptism, Baptist Views," "Carey, William," "Clarke, John," "Gospel Mission Controversy," "Johnson, William Bullein," "Leland, John," "Mullins, Edgar Young," "Sampey, John Richard," "Southern Baptist Convention," "Toy, Crawford Howell," "Whitsitt, William Heth," and "World Council of Churches, Baptist Participation in."

Dictionary of Christianity in America. Ed. D. G. Reid et al. Downers Grove, Ill.: InterVarsity, 1990. S.v. "Clarke, John," "Leland, John," "Mullins, Edgar Young," "Southern Baptist Convention," and "Whitsitt, William Heth."

Encyclopedia of Southern Baptists. 4 vols. Nashville: Broadman, 1958–82. Vol. 1. S.v. "Ecumenical Movement, The." Vol. 3. S.v. "Baptists and Ecumenism," and "Ecumenical Movement, The."

Encyclopedia USA: The Encyclopedia of the United States of America Past and Present. 33 vols. Ed. R. A. Lee, A. P. MacDonald, and D. W. Whisenhunt. Gulf Breeze, Fla.: Academic International Press, 1983–2000. Vol. 4. S.v. "Asbury, Francis."

Evangelical Dictionary of Theology. Ed. W. A. Elwell. Grand Rapids: Baker, 1984. S.v. "Strong, Augustus Hopkins" and "Teresa of Avila."

Mennonite Encyclopedia. 5 vols. Ed. H. S. Bender, C. H. Smith, C. J. Dyck, and D. D. Martin. Scottdale, Pa.: Mennonite Publishing House, 1955–1959, 1990. Vol. 5. S.v. "Hubmaier, (Huebmör), Balthasar."

New 20th-Century Encyclopedia of Religious Knowledge. 2d ed. Ed. J. D. Douglas. Grand Rapids: Baker, 1991. S.v. "Southern Baptist Convention (SBC)."

MISCELLANEOUS

"A Baptist Chapter of Texas History." *Baptist Standard*, 12 January 1957, 4–5,12.

"Conflict over the Sacraments in the Reformation." "Zwingli," and "Smyth." *The Canadian Baptist*, May 1983, 4–8, 8–11, 11–13.

"John XXIII and the Papacy." *Baptist Standard*, 10 December 1958, 4–5, 12, and 17 December 1958, 6–7. Reprinted with three appendixes in booklet form: Fort Worth: Deering, 1958.

"Separation as Sedition: America's Debt to the Anabaptists." *Christianity Today*, 21 May 1976, 8–10.

"Was Calvin Wrong? Doctrines Lead to 'Dunghill,' Prof Warns." *Baptist Standard* 26 March 1997, 12. Reprinted in *Founders Journal* no. 29 (Summer 1997): 6–9.

ORAL MEMOIRS

Oral Memoirs of William Roscoe Estep, Jr., 19 May 1981—25 February 1982. Interviewer, Rosalie Beck. Texas Baptist Oral History Project. 2 vols. Waco, Tex.: Baylor University Institute for Oral History, 1985.

2. Secondary

Ascol, Tom. "Do Doctrines Really Lead to Dunghill?" *Founders Journal*, no. 29 (Summer 1997): 1–5.

"Baptist History Has Been Estep's Guide for Today." *Southwestern News*, July/August 1990, 9, 11.

Davis, Lori and Russ Williams. "Southwestern Baptist Theological Seminary and the Production of Instructional Television Courses." M.A. in Comm. thesis, Southwestern Baptist Theological Seminary, 1985. Use of videotape of Estep's instructional television course in Baptist history and interviews with Estep.

Gritz, Paul L. "William R. Estep, Jr.: Advocate for the Free Church Heritage." *Southwestern Journal of Theology* 36 (Summer 1994): 5–9.

Hailey, Cory J. "Baptist Historian W. R. Estep Dies of Cancer." *Scroll*, 17 July 2000, 1–2.

Mohler, R. Albert. "The Reformation of Doctrine and the Renewal of the Church: A Response to Dr. William R. Estep." *Founders Journal*, no. 29 (Summer 1997): 10–13.

Nicole, Roger. "An Open Letter to Dr. William R. Estep." *Founders Journal*, no. 29 (Summer 1997): 14–16.

"Professors Write to Help Baptists Know Themselves." *Southwestern News*, January 1988, 3.

Quimby, Betty. "Getting to Know You: Bill and Edna Estep." *Saints Alive!* (Newsletter for Senior Adults at Gambrell Street Baptist Church, Fort Worth, Tex.) December 2001.

"William R. Estep: Baptist History Maker, Influencing History." *Baptists Heritage Update*, Winter 1996, 2.

C. W. Brister

(1926–)
Pastoral Ministry

Nathan Larry Baker

19

rom a windswept hilltop "where the West begins," C. W. Brister—a man from the pine hills and cypress-studded bayous of Louisiana—invested more than half a lifetime as a professor in the Southwestern Seminary School of Theology. He joined Franklin Segler and Carl Clark in the Department of Pastoral Ministry in 1957 and plunged into the field of pastoral care and the art of caring when the department was only six years old. For forty-four years, C. W. Brister called clergy and laity alike to the practice of Christian care.

BIOGRAPHY

The Things He Brought with Him

The Things They Carried with Them: A Work of Fiction[1] is a novel about Vietnam that reminds readers that everyone carries something with him—by necessity, choice, or circumstance. Like the characters in Tim O'Brien's novel, Brister brought much with him to his task.

Brister brought a profound personal faith in Jesus Christ with him to his ministry in pastoral care. Like Timothy, who had been nurtured by the faith of mother and grandmother, he had been nourished by the faith of parents and extended family. C. W. made public and demonstrated that faith through baptism in 1935 in First Baptist Church, Pineville, Louisiana. His faith supported him through the tragedy of his father's death, guided him during adolescence, and anchored him during young adulthood. Brister's personal faith and his biblical understanding anchored his approach to pastoral ministry. In *People Who Care*, Brister linked evangelism and encouragement, a reflection of his faith story.

Brister brought churches with him to his classroom. The first of those was First Baptist Church, Pineville, Louisiana.[2] The church traced its birth to 1911, and its vigorous life towered above the Central Louisiana region during Brister's childhood and youth.

Brister brought other churches with him. Three he served as pastor: two rural churches in Louisiana and a fledgling suburban church in Fort Worth. Further, his "pastoral relationship with people was begun in an inner-city church in New Orleans" where he and his wife, Gloria, "called upon apartment residents in a large urban renewal project which formed the church setting."[3]

Throughout his career, Brister stayed connected with the church. He maintained membership in University Baptist Church, Fort Worth, where he gave his best energies in support of the church and in its ongoing activities.

Brister brought strong educational credentials to his faculty assignment: premedical studies in Louisiana College; officer's school during World War II; graduate work in business administration at Louisiana State University; a theology degree from New Orleans Baptist Seminary; and a doctorate in Christian ethics from Southwestern. Additionally, he completed his first unit of Clinical Pastoral Education in 1952–53 in Baptist Hospital, Alexandria, Louisiana, under the tutelage of a supervisor trained by Richard Young and Wayne E. Oates.

Throughout his career Brister immersed himself in continuing education. Sometimes he focused on clinical pastoral education. Other times involved postdoctoral studies at Princeton Theological Seminary and Union Theological Seminary. Yet others took him to Regent's Park College, Oxford University, and American summer institutes in Switzerland. Additionally, Brister plunged into the study of family systems theory.

Firsthand experience with suffering and struggle accompanied Brister to the teaching of pastoral care. In the Great Depression era, the Brister family lost its home, and his father lost his business. When C. W. was nine years of age, his father was killed in an automobile accident.

The professor of pastoral ministry came to his task equipped with direct contact with a cross section of human experience. The man grew up in a pine-covered river town planted on rolling hills, where the conventional culture of North Louisiana bumped up against the Cajun culture of South Louisiana, in a time when Baptists and Catholics maintained little more than an uneasy peace. His adolescent years spanned a time when military bases dominated the region and overran his quiet hometown with people with strange accents and stranger ways. Before he reached the seminary faculty, he had worked for a summer on the *Sweet William*, a tugboat on the Mississippi River, as a broadcaster for a Baton Rouge radio station, as a teaching fellow in economics at Louisiana State University, and as an officer in the U.S. Merchant Marines.

The young Brister was drawn early toward internationalism. In New York he attended a church that was ecumenical, interracial, and international. By the time he was eighteen, he had been uprooted from the provincial and parochial world of Central Louisiana and dropped into overseas settings; he was in England while V-2 bombs were dropping.

Brister brought an appreciation for and love of language with him to his tasks. A high school English teacher, Annie Laurie Peters, spawned in him a love for words, language, and expression and a profound appreciation for a literary legacy. C. W.'s mother, herself a teacher of history at Louisiana College, deepened Brister's love of language.

The young professor brought a partner in ministry with him to his calling: his wife, Gloria. The man who planted the word "care" at the heart of his ministry and on the hearts of his students married Gloria Nugent, a classmate at Louisiana College, in 1946. All of Brister's books point in some way to Gloria's significant place in his life and ministry. The Bristers welcomed a son, Mark Allen, into their family in 1951.

An Investment Multiplied

Like the astute servant in Jesus' parable, Brister invested wisely "the things he brought with him" and multiplied them for kingdom causes. Elected to the faculty in 1957, Brister made major contributions to Southwestern. For example, he introduced clinical pastoral education to the seminary and made it an integral part of his department. During his tenure Brister bade farewell to Segler and Clark, who retired, and welcomed five others who taught alongside him for various tenures: Gerald E. Marsh, N. Larry Baker, George H. Gaston III, Douglas M. Dickens, and Steve M. Lyon.

During his faculty years Brister taught students at every level—diploma, master's, and doctoral—and guided the work of fifty Ph.D. candidates and many others who completed Master of Theology and Doctor of Ministry degrees. Additionally, he gave himself to the ongoing work of the seminary and as a representative of the school throughout Southern Baptist life. Brister has administered the Warren C. Hultgren Chair of Pastoral Care from its inauguration in April 1997 until the present time. The chair is designed to foster wholeness, strength, and usefulness for ministers and their families through its Center for Ministry Empowerment.

Brister's contributions extended beyond the seminary. Brister was professionally active—in the American Association for Marriage and Family Therapy, the Association for Clinical Pastoral Education, the Society for Pastoral Theology, and Family Systems Ministries International. He was active in the Baptist World Alliance and chaired its Commission on Church Leadership from 1995 to 2000. He and Gloria traveled, taught, and ministered in sixty countries, helping both nationals and missionaries and their children.

WRITINGS

Although his calling was the classroom, Brister gave himself to writing as well as teaching and speaking. Upon retirement, Brister had published eleven books, contributed to four others, and penned numerous articles.

"The Liberation of Life"[4] is both the title of a sermon and of Brister's first published work; it might also serve as a central theme in Brister's thought. Brister preached the sermon in the seminary chapel soon after joining the faculty; it was published afterward in a collection of faculty sermons.

Pastoral Care in the Church was Brister's second published work, a major one produced by an influential publisher, Harper and Row. The book was written during Brister's first sabbatical, was released in 1964, was revised twice (1977, 1992), and remained in print until 1993. Additionally, the volume was translated into Spanish in 1974.

Five smaller volumes followed. The five began with *People Who Care* in 1967 and concluded with *Take Care* in 1978; three others came in the years between: *Dealing with Doubt*, 1970; *It's Tough Growing Up*, 1971; and *Life under Pressure: Dealing with Stress in Marriage*, 1976.

The five books shared two commonalties: all were designed for laypersons, and each dealt with a crucial concern in everyday living—doubt, adolescence, marriage, how to live the life of faith in a faithless and fragmented world. The dedication pages and the prefaces to the volumes witnessed to the range of clergy, laypersons, and students to whom Brister related and who put him in touch with the needs of persons and churches.

A second major work was published in 1978: *The Promise of Counseling*. This, like Brister's 1964 book, was published by the venerable Harper and Row. Also, like the earlier work, this volume followed the completion of a sabbatical from seminary responsibilities.

Four volumes followed: *Becoming You: A Young Person's Guide for Living*, 1980; *Beginning Your Ministry*, 1981; *Caring for the Caregivers*, 1985; and *Change Happens*, 1997. In *Becoming You*, Brister revisited *It's Tough Growing Up*. *Beginning Your Ministry* and *Caring for the Caregiver* both resulted from Brister's lifetime involvement in the training of ministers. In the first, Brister and his coauthors set out "to dramatize the young minister's move from campus to congregation."[5] *Caring for the Caregivers*, like two of his earlier works, followed a sabbatical. In this work, Brister expressed "concern for persons who invest their whole lives in Christian mission and ministry."[6]

In 1997, Brister published his eleventh volume: *Change Happens: Finding Your Way through Life's Transitions*. Early in his ministry Brister encountered and was influenced by Lewis J. Sherrill's *The Struggle of the Soul*. That book dealt with life's unfolding epochs, from birth to death, in theological perspective. With his volume, Brister offered the current generation a similar gift.

In an article twice published in *Southwestern Journal of Theology*, first after delivery as a convocation address on Southwestern's seventy-fifth anniversary in 1983 and again in 1995, Brister wrote about "The Making of a Southwesterner." "Brister," observed William M. Tillman, Jr., the journal's editor, "with an intriguing visionary bent, provided thirteen years ago a vision of the current Southwestern student demographics."[7]

INTERPRETATION

Writing Down the Bones
In a book entitled *Writing Down the Bones*, Natalie Goldberg declares, ". . . I want students to be 'writing down the bones,' the

essential, awake speech of their minds."[8] Had Brister studied with Goldberg, he would have stood at the head of the class; he ably wrote down the themes that guided his journey through four decades of ministry.

First, Brister immersed himself in defining and delineating pastoral care for ministers and laity, for congregations and individuals. His perspective, approach, and methodology set him apart from and alongside the towering twentieth-century figures in Protestant pastoral care—Wayne Oates at Southern Baptist Theological Seminary and Seward Hiltner at Princeton Theological Seminary, for example.

In *The Promise of Counseling*, Brister built upon such understandings as he had developed in his first major work. Therein he wrote, "My *Pastoral Care in the Church* discusses how the church and its community provide a comprehensive context for pastoral care. The full breadth of a Christian congregation's concerns for its members is described. . . . Here, my purpose is . . . to clarify counseling in a biblical perspective."[9]

In his approach, Brister brought the Bible, Christian theology, psychology, and pastoral practice together in a manner that permitted the reader to scan the landscape for the "big picture" and to focus in depth on pastoral tasks. Brister understood that the "pastoral task" is not the exclusive domain of the pastor but belongs to the church as well. At the heart of Brister's understanding of pastoral care is the conviction that "the Christian *koinonia*, by its very nature, implies a shared ministry by the pastor and one's people."[10] Nevertheless, Brister's understanding would not permit the pastor to function half-heartedly or in a slipshod manner or to transfer the caring task to others; instead, he called on the pastoral practitioner to exemplify the best in ministry and urged him to educate laypersons for their mutual tasks. Moreover, Brister wrote for the church and the pastoral person with an awareness of and concern for the total task.

Change is a recurring reality to which Brister's work pointed. In the writings of Southwestern's premier pastoral theologian, change is both the framework and the occasion for pastoral care. For Brister, three types of change were especially significant: sociological, professional, and spiritual. Brister carefully chronicled change, analyzed its impact, and proposed constructive attitudes and actions in light of it. Although Brister's focus on change did not set forth a model for social change, his understanding of personal change offered helpful insights for understanding and managing change.

A third theme in the writings of this pastoral theologian was that of the minister as hope bearer. According to Brister, "True to their own versions of 'the heavenly vision,' authentic Christian ministers are *hope bearers*—advancing faith in a perplexed world."[11] Moreover, Brister acknowledged, "I have introduced the metaphor *hope bearer* to depict numerous aspects of pastoral work."[12]

Brister's thought also reverberated with an emphasis on the worth of human personality. In part, Brister's focus on such worth grew out of his experience of "the fragility of life and the force of time." Further, Brister interpreted and anchored his understanding in the life and ministry of Jesus. The Lord "insisted that God's love is universal. It includes the sinners, poor, handicapped, captives, and oppressed persons everywhere. . . . We learn from him that service to persons must cross all human barriers of race, culture, politics, and social standing."[13]

Like his early theology teacher, Frank Stagg, the Southwestern professor of pastoral care understood polarities in human experience. Alongside his focus on the worth of personality, Brister highlighted the dark side of the human story. Brister used two images to communicate this truth: (1) human bondage and the need to be liberated; and (2) the loss of home with its attendant "search for home."

Two chapters of *Change Happens* dealt with the concept of home in detail and with sensitivity. One focused on "losing the place we call home" and the other on "the struggle to be home at last." In both instances, Brister's perspective resounded with the power of hope.

Care, which Brister defined and described carefully in *The Promise of Counseling*, is the central and centering quality of the Christian community. The word itself stood at the center of four titles in Brister's work. Significantly, although his signature treatise dealt with the total ministry of the church, Brister used "pastoral care" for the title, not "pastoral ministry." Such "Christian concern is a fundamental attitude or disposition motivated by the love of God and needs of persons."[14]

Brister viewed the church as a community of shared caring. Among traditional interpreters, pastoral care belonged to the clergy in the church or to the professional pastoral counselor outside the church. Not so for Brister. In the preface to *Pastoral Care in the*

Church, Brister addressed pastoral care "in the light of the Christian pastor's unique heritage and resources" and the "layman's shepherding tasks."[15] Brister firmly rejected the idea that "pastoral care . . . [is] *the pastor's* work."[16] Although Brister clearly acknowledged "the biblical principle of the priesthood of all believers," he also contended that "the appointment and work of a formal ministry is clear in the New Testament."[17] Thus, in his foundational work, Brister wrote both of the pastoral role of the Protestant pastor and the "pastoral" tasks of responsible laypersons. Although Brister dealt with a wide range of ministry-related issues, he seldom ventured far from this emphasis and wove this theme in varied combinations, patterns, and cadences into his multifaceted ministry.

For Brister, however, shared caring was more than pastor and laity working alongside each other, both doing caring tasks within and as extensions of the church's ministry. Caring was also a process of mutuality, with pastor and laity each caring for the other. To this end Brister wrote *Caring for the Caregiver*.

A concern for context is another recurring theme in Brister's thought. The theme appeared in Brister's writing in at least five emphases. He fixed attention on the immediate sociological context in which care takes place and modeled sensitivity to human development throughout the life cycle. Likewise, he called for serious consideration of an individual's family system and chronicled the impact of the tides and times of history on persons and church. Further, from his initial writing to his most mature work, Brister addressed "the primary moments of life" and "life's crises" as key components of Christian care. Although Brister might not have called himself a contextualist, his thought and approach were contextually sensitive. He wisely observed and weighed the many dimensions of context—for churches and individuals alike. In turn, he called for and modeled ministry practice crafted for the context.

Counting Apples in a Seed

A needlework sampler that hung in a kitchen in Pineville, Louisiana, declared, "Anyone can count the seeds in an apple; only God can count the apples in a seed." True enough, but with C. W. Brister one can see some of the fruit grown from the life that he planted in the seedbed known as Southwestern Seminary.

In Brister's literature of pastoral care, readers found insights and approaches for enabling the church's ministry as well as strengthening one's own service. In an age when many had jettisoned hope and many ministers seemed to have their fingers crossed, readers found a resounding message of hope, a word that encouraged and emboldened the practicing minister.

Brister wrote for the church and the pastoral person with an awareness of and concern for the total task. Clearly, Brister was no stranger to the life of the congregation or the work of the pastoral person and wrote with evident love for both. Hence, alongside his contributions of understanding and skills, Brister added a sense of joy in the calling and confidence concerning its value.

Other contributions can be identified both in broad strokes and in specific terms. Brister invested heavily in the field of pastoral care and contributed to its development as a department at Southwestern and to its impact as a force in American church life. The Founder's Day address, delivered by Brister on 8 March 2001, chronicled and interpreted "Fifty Years of Pastoral Education at Southwestern Seminary." Early in the address, Brister issued a disclaimer: "While I have been closely involved with this department's development, I am unwilling to claim too much."[18] In the address that followed, the pastoral theologian identified four emphases that comprise "Southwestern's unique contributions of ministry studies" and ten core values that guided the mission of the Department of Pastoral Ministry. To read those segments of the address and to know C. W. Brister is to recognize his influence within the seminary and beyond among diverse constituencies.

He put his best efforts into classroom and seminar assignments and thereby demonstrated a model of excellence and challenged the best from his students. He taught thousands of students and sent them to their waiting world with tools crafted for use with people hungry for compassion, care, and concern. In his seminars, Brister provided structure and direction to the learning process but infused that with an air of freedom that encouraged doctoral candidates to be themselves and to develop uniquely.

Brister wrote widely and invested in the ongoing lives of people—laypersons and ministers alike—and strengthened them both in their faith and in their calling. Furthermore, in a sense like Wesley, he saw the world as his parish and contributed richly to Christians around the world.

Brister's greatest contribution, however, may have been more personal. He has extended friendship to students and colleagues, cheered them on, and encouraged them. He has lived as a "man of care"—a life-style far too rare among people who give allegiance to the Man from Nazareth.

CONCLUSION

In one of his popular works, Brister reported, "When a friend heard the title of this book, he reported dubiously: 'You mean there are still some of *those* people [who care] around?'" Brister put his answer into writing across four decades of service—an unequivocal, firm, hope-filled "Yes!" As a minister himself, living between the biblical ideal and human shortcomings, Brister called the church and individuals, clergy and laity alike, to embody Christian care and to permeate life and ministry practice with care. More importantly, he himself was a man of care who practiced what he preached. With his life and his words, he interpreted one meaning of the corporate slogan, "When you care enough to send the very best."

BIBLIOGRAPHY

1. Primary

DISSERTATION

"The Ethical Thought of Harry Emerson Fosdick: A Critical Interpretation." Ph.D. diss., Southwestern Baptist Theological Seminary, 1957.

BOOKS

Becoming You. Nashville: Broadman, 1980.
(coauth.) *Beginning Your Ministry*. Nashville: Abingdon Press, 1981.
Caring for the Caregivers: How to Help Ministers and Missionaries. Nashville: Broadman, 1985.
Change Happens: Finding Your Way through Life's Transitions. Macon, Ga.: Peake Road, 1997.
Dealing with Doubt. Nashville: Broadman, 1970.
It's Tough Growing Up. Nashville: Broadman, 1971.
Life under Pressure: Dealing with Stress in Marriage. Nashville: Sunday School Board of the Southern Baptist Convention, 1976.
Pastoral Care in the Church. New York: Harper and Row, 1964. 2d ed.: New York: Harper and Row, 1977. 3d ed. rev.: San Francisco: Harper Collins, 1992.
    El Cuidado Pastoral en la Iglesia. Trans. Daniel Tinao, Juan Sowell and J. David Fite. El Paso: Casa Bautista de Publicaciones, 1974. [Spanish]
People Who Care. Nashville: Broadman, 1967.
The Promise of Counseling. San Francisco: Harper and Row, 1978.
Take Care. Nashville: Broadman, 1978.

CHAPTERS CONTRIBUTED TO BOOKS

"Pastoral Care in a New Age." In *Contemporary Christian Trends: Perspectives on the Present*, ed. William M. Pinson, Jr. and Clyde E. Fant, Jr., 40–53. Waco, Tex.: Word, 1972.

"Person-Centered Ministry." In *Toward Creative Urban Strategy*, ed. George A. Torney, 122–41. Waco, Tex.: Word, 1970.

"The Liberation of Life." In *Southwestern Sermons*, ed. H. C. Brown, Jr., 29–35. Nashville: Broadman, 1964.

"To Colleagues." In *An Approach to Christian Ethics: The Life, Contribution, and Thought of T. B. Maston*, ed. William M. Pinson, Jr., 52–55. Nashville: Broadman, 1979.

JOURNAL ARTICLES

"Australia through My Eyes: Observations of a North American Guest." *Southwestern Journal of Theology* 34 (Spring 1992): 44–49.

"Impressions from a China Journey." *Southwestern Journal of Theology* 40 (Summer 1998): 65–75.

"The Ministry Today: Crises and Challenges." *Southwestern Journal of Theology* 15 (Spring 1973): 15–29.

"The Making of a Southwesterner." *Southwestern Journal of Theology* 25 (Spring 1983): 118–27; 37 (Summer 1995): 4–8.

"The Ministry in an Age of Stress." *Southwestern Journal of Theology* 2 (October 1959): 63–71.

"The Ministry in 1 Corinthians." *Southwestern Journal of Theology* 26 (Fall 1993): 18–31.

"Witnessing: The Redemptive Community." *Southwestern Journal of Theology* 8 (Spring 1966): 49–60.

MISCELLANEOUS

"Biblical Images of Leadership: The Stewardship of Power." *Baptist World*, January–March 1997, 13–14.

Dictionary of Pastoral Care and Counseling. Gen. ed., Rodney J. Hunter. Nashville: Abingdon, 1990. S.v. "Friendship, Pastor-Parishioner" and "Trust in Pastoral Relationships."

Disciple's Study Bible: New International Version. Nashville: Holman, 1988. S.v. "Ministry of Service."

"The Future Outlook of Pastoral Care." *Caregiving*, April–May–June 1994, 1–4.

"This Is My Story." *The Family: The Faculty/Staff Newsletter of Southwestern Seminary*, October 1993, 1,4.

2. Secondary

Brister, Elaine H. *Once upon a River: A History of Pineville, Louisiana*. Baton Rouge: Claitor's Publishing Division, 1968.

Cheslik, Mark and Matt Sanders. "C. W. Brister Retires after 44 Years at Southwestern." *Southwestern News*, Fall 2001, 20.

Howell, Thomas. *The History of First Baptist Church, Pineville, Louisiana*. Pineville: First Baptist Church, 1986.

"Professor's Book Enters Third Edition." *Southwestern News*, May/June 1992, 7.

Stone, Howard W., ed. *Strategies for Brief Pastoral Counseling*. Minneapolis: Fortress Press, 2001. Pp. 177, 203, 207, 209, 213–15.

Thornton, Edward E. "The Man of the Month: C. W. Brister." *Pastoral Psychology* 22 (June 1971): 4, 66.

William Lawrence Hendricks

(1929–)
Theology

William David Kirkpatrick

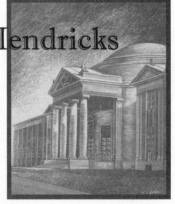

"Frail creatures of dust?" Yes, "frail creatures of dust!" Often greeted in this manner, the students of William L. Hendricks sat prepared to encounter one of the most stimulating lecturers on Seminary Hill. With his classes filled to capacity, he would enter the classroom with a presence that demanded respect and often intimidated. Each student came armed with at least two, if not three, pens or pencils. If one instrument failed to write, she or he would have just enough time to switch to the second. The structure of the lecture was always Roman one, subheading after sub-heading in pursuit of the next Roman numeral. The sequence was invariably as logical and as consistent as any symphony by Haydn and, on rare occasions, as surprising and as emotive as a Beethoven composition. Questions by the class were few and far between—no one dared to interrupt. If a question did manage to make it into "the rhythm" of the well-prepared words dancing across the room, it was quickly answered, accompanied by the gesticulation of an up-lifted arm and a turned down wrist, a well-rehearsed movement that allowed "the conductor" easily to return to the precise point in the outline before the less than sacral interruption. The tests? Well, if one wanted to make a good grade, every word of the lecture had to be taken down and committed to memory. The student's responsibility was to *replicate* every word, dot every I, and cross every T. In effect the student's memory was asked to represent the lecture verbatim with each sacred Roman numeral. Hence the challenge! While structure helped to manage the time, the professor would often offer a frequent reminder—"*tempus fugit*." If anyone did manage to make a perfect score, or better because of added bibliography, the good-natured response with mannerisms in full bloom was invariably: "Never again, creatures of frailness, never again!"

When and where the good Dr. Hendricks mastered the Turrettini method of teaching he has never divulged. Over the years, the lecture method and classroom performance were modified only slightly to accommodate writing requirements and advanced studies programs such as seminars and colloquies. The memory-demanding method, coupled with the mannerisms and personality of this master teacher, made it possible to run into "hendricksisms" long after the initial classroom experience. For the majority of Hendricks's theology students, the classroom provided an encounter with the precise language of theology, "spiced up" with a few well-worn Latin phrases, and an opportunity to expand the student's own theological imagination. Looking back over old notes and checking with Hendricks's students from other seminaries, one finds that the lecture material remained a constant combination of biblical references, pertinent material from the history of doctrine, and something called "theological reconstruction." "Frail creatures of dust" brings back fond memories.

BIOGRAPHY

Bill Hendricks was born in Butte, Montana, on 10 March 1929. Living in a certain amount of poverty, he moved to Wichita, Kansas, with his adoptive mother and almost immediately experienced the love and compassion of the Immanuel Baptist Church. Unable to participate in athletics, young Hendricks substituted reading, church activities, music appreciation, and a love of Latin for more rigorously Spartan activities. With interests in Latin and music, Hendricks was prepared for college and beyond—not a bad combination for a prospective young minister who at the age of seventeen had already envisioned a career as a missionary to Africa.

In 1947, armed with a few war bonds, a desire to excel, and not much else, this budding scholar set out for Oklahoma Baptist

University. Quickly realizing that potential had to be undergirded by hard work, the resourceful Hendricks financed academic interests with a less than stimulating job in a shoe store. In addition, he used his three years of high school Latin to earn more spending money by tutoring less-than-enthusiastic Latin students. With the help of friends and a little scholarship money he was able to make ends meet. Even though the African missionary vision never materialized, Hendricks's commitment to world missions never faded. His college education had further stimulated his love for the Bible and had done nothing to quell his interest in ministry.

After graduating from college and marrying on the same day, 4 June 1951, Hendricks found his way to Southwestern Seminary primarily because Lois Ann Lindsey Hendricks had secured a teaching position at the Buckner Children's Home in Dallas. E. D. Head was in the next to last year of his presidency when Hendricks enrolled in 1951. Hendricks took classes from W. Boyd Hunt, James Leo Garrett, Ray Summers, W. W. Barnes, Jack MacGorman, Curtis Vaughan, Ralph L. Smith, T. B. Maston, Robert A. Baker, and John P. Newport. In 1956, he completed the Th.D. degree in theology, writing a dissertation entitled "The Concept of Satan: A Biblical and Historical Approach and Its Relevance to the Christian Life Today." It was also in 1956 that John Lawrence Hendricks was born. Unable to be appointed as a missionary to Brazil because of health reasons, Hendricks accepted an appointment to the faculty of Southwestern in the fall of 1957. Always the student, Hendricks used his first sabbatical to begin a Ph.D. program in theology at the University of Chicago, completing the second dissertation in 1972. Its title, "Death in the Theology of Karl Barth," expressed an obvious interest in the vicissitudes of existential theology as well as the insights of the Swiss theologian. The existential subject of death notwithstanding, the dissertation provided the basis for a career-long interest in the variations of Reformed theology.

Enviously popular as a guest speaker in churches and Bible conferences, Hendricks had a teaching ministry that not only reached fruition in theological education but also stretched itself out across Baptist life and beyond. Having taught in three seminaries, Southwestern Baptist Theological Seminary, from 1957 to 1978, Golden Gate Seminary in Mill Valley, California, from 1978 to 1984, and Southern Baptist Theological Seminary in Louisville,

Kentucky, from 1984 to retirement in 1994, this resolute personality extended the wisdom and grace of learning to enthralled students for more than four decades.

While at Southern Seminary, Hendricks began to develop his interest in an "aesthetic theology." His intent was to "begin on the faith side of Lessing's ugly ditch." Building on his notion that Christology is central, he sought to develop aesthetic interests that focused the resurrection as the foundational "principle of light, effulgence, and luminosity."[1] After retirement in 1994 and until the spring semester of 2000, Hendricks served as lecturer in theology and director of Baptist studies at Brite Divinity School, Texas Christian University, Fort Worth, Texas. The journey that had begun in the romantic and fertile mind of a seventeen-year-old as a commitment to missions became more influential and perhaps even more exciting than the young visionary from Montana could ever have imagined.[2]

WRITINGS AND THEIR INTERPRETATION

The complete bibliography of William L. Hendricks ranges from books to plays and includes hymns, pamphlets, articles, book reviews, poems, chapel messages, and special papers. The bibliography, influenced by the New Testament, Baptist roots, and denominational life, reflects an interest in traditional theological subjects as well as nontraditional themes such as aging, children, hymnody, and the arts. Hendricks's theological interests have been wide-ranging and have consistently bordered on the creative. Although Hendricks has produced no multivolume systematic theology, the constructs of systematic theology have dominated everything that he has written.

His first book, *The Letters of John: Tapestries of Truth* (1970), is a theological commentary offering an interpretation of themes that are woven through the letters of John. These biblical texts are presented as a "law of love." Redeeming love is not only the dominant thread that is woven through the tapestries but also the only thing that is capable of combating the incipient Gnosticism found behind the texts. Brief excursuses throughout the book use the themes of incarnation, Trinity, salvation, and ethics to expose the intent of the letters. The concluding line of the book is its critical summary: "Among the threads one pattern is firmly etched: It is the *face* of

Christ—the true Word about whom all of John's words have been written" (142).

A Theology for Children (1980) was written for those who work with children of all ages. It is replete with suggestions on how to help the child to understand the doctrines of the church. It offers a constructive and somewhat creative approach to theology while claiming that theology is undergirded by both revelation and history (30–41). The focal point of revelation's "drama of redemption" is Jesus Christ. Scripture was always the primary source of revelation for Hendricks; however, this commitment carried the strong admonition to refuse to use the Bible to answer questions that it is not prepared to answer (52).

The structure of Hendricks's theology followed topically from revelation to eschatology. The occasion for writing was always to introduce the basic doctrines of systematic theology.[3] The classical doctrines of Trinity, Christology, and Spirit were confessionally addressed, while the doctrines of creation-providence, anthropology, and election-redemption were written carefully to avoid hermeneutical extremes.[4] The chapter on the Christian life encouraged the believer to be consistently Christ-centered and offered insights on faith, repentance, striving, prayer, Bible study, and ethics. The last chapter dealt with eschatology and the question of where it "all will end." The answer to the question, one of Hendricks's favorite phrases, is "in him with whom it all began—in God." In his own inimical and playful but purposeful way, Hendricks suggested that at the eschaton God will punctuate the end of the world not with a "dot," which is a bland period, or with a questioning crooked mark, but with an exclamatory "bat and ball" (269)!

The theme of redemption that underlies Hendricks's theology is typically Baptist. There are, however, theological interpretations that are difficult for children to understand. For example, an excursus on eschatology begins as follows: "How do you teach a child about pre-trib-rap-pre, post-trib-rap-pre and the seven dispensations thereunto?" The answer? "I hope to goodness you never do" (268).

The Doctrine of Man (1977) addresses the subject of Christian anthropology. An "Adam-Christ typology" dominates the book. After juxtaposing time and eternity as well as faith and history, Hendricks worked to demonstrate the relationship of creation to its Creator, suggesting that "at every level [humanity] needs community" (19–21). But because the "goodness of creation is clouded by the reality of sin," humanity must face the consequences of alienation from the Creator.[5] In a brief creative discourse on original sin entitled "Adam Didn't Make Me Do It," Adam was taken to be a type representing all humanity with death the natural consequence of humanity's sin. Playing off of 1 Cor. 15:21, Hendricks refused to say that sin is "transmitted automatically or physically from parent to child." Consequently, the Corinthian text should not be used to condemn all "because of what Adam did unless one is also willing to say that all are saved because of what Christ did. If sin is automatic, so is salvation" (30). Probing the question of why all have sinned, Hendricks concluded that theology does not have a definitive answer. Instead of using the celebrated causes of *human freedom* and *divine intention* to solve the conundrum, Hendricks opted for *mystery*. He refused to endorse "radical freedom" because it suggests that God is not in complete control. "Divine intention" or determinism is also unacceptable because it not only makes God responsible for sin but also makes "the fall the inevitable prelude to the cross." For Hendricks, only the gospel's promise reverses our estrangement (31).

The subject of humanity's distinctiveness and the options related to *image and likeness* are addressed under the title of "Existential Man." Refusing to link the constructs to the physical, he turned to the categories of reason, "potentiality, ability, and responsibility," as well as the emotive and volitional aspects of humanity (48). The tragedy of humanity is that it has "distorted the image of God" and has fallen from God's original intention. The "fall" is "the denial of responsibility" (50). "Partial depravity" is rejected, as is the notion that humanity is "affected only partly by sin." Because fallen man, however, is not affected *essentially* by sin, he still has the capacity to discover God. On the other hand, Hendricks acknowledged the truth of "total depravity" even though the theory contains "unfortunate" language. If used, it should not be taken to mean "people cannot do anything good in any area of life"; rather it should be taken to mean that humanity is prevented from finding God "unless God takes the initiative" (52). According to Hendricks, "there is some reflection of the image of God that still shines through every person and makes him/her valuable—even in a fallen state." Accordingly, the "mirror of God's goodness" is only "cracked," not shattered.[6] Jesus Christ is the only true image of God (53–54).

The goal of redeemed humanity is to "strive to be like God." Acceptance is the meaning of *justification*, while striving to be like God is *sanctification* (104). Providentially, God guides the world he has created "to the good he desires by the means he chooses" (109). In this fallen-existential stage, "man is not able not to sin and to die; that is, he must sin, and he must die" (116).

The final section, "Eschatological Man," uses Johannine language to propose "that God is making all things new and good in Jesus Christ" (121). In fact, the God-man "is sent to destroy the works of the devil" (121). God's overall purpose for humanity is nothing less than "to secure our intended goodness and the fulfillment of our life . . . in Jesus Christ" (121). Death defeated, life is to be lived in anticipation of its completion at the final resurrection (123). Heaven, therefore, is "the state and place in which God fulfills his purpose for his creation" (130). The book's concluding declaration is that "'man's chief end is to glorify God and to enjoy him forever'"[7] (139).

Hendricks wrote *A Theology for Aging* (1986) as a "lived through" theological expression "from practical experience" (6). He argued that 2 Cor. 5:19 is the basis for and the substance of any Christian theology. Instead of revelation, Hendricks begins this book with the doctrine of eschatology and a discussion of death, which is called both a curse and a blessing. In the face of death, the "aging Christian" should remember that death is followed by resurrection.[8] The Christian's eschatological hope comes from living by faith, anticipating the second coming of the resurrected Christ. Hendricks purposefully avoided pitting any one millennial view against another, preferring to pray the eschatological phrase of the Lord's Prayer in hopeful anticipation: "Thy kingdom come, thy will be done" (21–39).

The theology of *A Theology for Aging* is consistent with the theology expressed in *A Theology for Children*. While Hendricks's theology is focused by the revelatory event of the Christ, the defining reference for each doctrine, in both books, is that "God is in charge." For example, God alone provides the means of atonement in the work of Christ, making salvation God's gift. Hendricks's

strong theology also understands that God alone sets the boundaries of human freedom (43–70).

In his section on ecclesiology, Hendricks discussed the
"marks of the church." Instead of using the classical marks of universality, oneness, holiness, and apostolicity, he developed the
language of "chosenness, corporateness, celebrativeness, and
caringness" as marks that should be used to identify the church's
unique essence (74). As unconventional as these marks are, his
purpose was to say that the church was created for service; that it
is a family of relationships responsible for the world as well as the
Christian community; that baptism and the Lord's Supper are acts
that celebrate the joy of salvation; and that, because it was established by God and commissioned by the living Christ, the church
is to be a caring and compassionate community (97). In other
words, the marks are not only marks of identification but are also
marks of responsibility (73–104).[9]

In his chapter entitled "A Look in the Mirror," Hendricks took
the position that a "relic of the image [of God] is left 'after the fall'"
(114), leaving an opening for a possible natural theology. Because
humanity's mirror is distorted by sin, Jesus Christ is the only true
image of God (107–41). Only by Christ's death and resurrection is
"the way opened to the Father's house" (218). Because Hendricks
saw divine revelation as a cosmic drama in which creation and providence are indispensable movements, the redeeming Christ necessarily takes center stage. Significantly, providence presupposes
creation as the drama begins. God's providence, implicit in the full
and final revelation of the Christ, not only upholds all of creation
but also works to provide peace in the midst of tribulation and a
future hope for all who believe (151–67). What then is the role of
the Spirit? Functionally Trinitarian, Hendricks tends to emphasize
the work of the Holy Spirit in the life of the church. For example, the
gifts of the Spirit enable the church "to breathe, to be sustained, and
to become an agent of God's reconciliation" (177).

In writing about the various attributes of God—eternality,
faithfulness, mercy, grace, mystery, holiness, love, strength, and
justice, he used hymnody to breathe life into theology's often used
scholastic language. Hendricks obviously enjoyed music, claiming
that it is more profitable to *sing* about God than to use "formal and
technical" language (222). Hendricks used hymnody to express

the nature of God in order to develop the reader's theological imagination. The poetics of language has the ability to express both mystery and experience—something that logic by its very nature refuses to do (221–45).

Who Is Jesus Christ? (1985) was written to chronicle the "history of Jesus" presented in the four Gospels. Referencing the pre-existence, the birth of the Christ, his teachings, his death and resurrection, his intercession, and his second coming, the book is a testimonial to Hendricks's interest in biblical theology. In one way or another the theme of "promise and fulfillment" undergirds the book's Christology. The New Testament's investment in the prophetic word of the Old Testament is "fulfilled" in the one called Immanuel (21–31). The early years of the Christ, his baptism, the temptations, the parables, and the miracles are treated as eschatological signs. The death of Jesus is interpreted as the clarion call of "God's redemptive love" and the "ultimate answer [to] the predetermined plan of God" (56). "The strong Son of God has overcome Satan in all his forms" (61). Hendricks refused to endorse any specific theory of atonement, whether example, substitution, or ransom, and concluded that the death of Christ gives humanity a "sense of ultimate worth." The death of Christ alone enables God's acceptance of sinful humanity (64–67).

Christ's resurrection is an unquestioned historical event. In fact, for Hendricks, "fact and faith are forever joined in Jesus' resurrection" (82). The resurrected Christ commissioned the earliest witnesses of the church, and because of the resurrection the New Testament admonishes the Christian to live in anticipation of Christ's second coming. The second coming will complete the drama of redemption, and Christ will judge all of humanity. With this judgment "the Christ event is complete," making eschatology the concluding bracket of human history (116–20). Hendricks ended the book searching for ways to express the beauty of the incarnation. In an attempt to move beyond the classical, he believed that the poetic imagination, found in painting, music, and poetry, would provide additional means for judging the content of Scripture and eventually help to bring to light that which is normative for the Christian faith (123–59).

CONCLUSION

Hendricks's theology is a kaleidoscope of theological interests. It is filled with the tensions of methodology and experience. As a professor of biblical and systematic theology, with an abiding interest in the arts, he attempted to keep the methods of both disciplines juxtaposed, occasionally punctuating conclusions and points of interest with historical and aesthetic excursuses. Thoroughly integrated, the theological offerings are creatively presented and mirror the personality of the writer. Above all else, Hendricks worked to be consistently biblical in his presentations. Intended more for information and praxis than for academically critical reflection, the theology of this master teacher should be recognized for its foundational commitment to the needs of the church. Perhaps because Hendricks's theology is functionally about life, he does not offer an extended analysis of the church's Trinitarian history. Missing is an in-depth discussion of the triune nature of God, a theological interest that not only has in large measure defined the theology of the twentieth century but an interest that cuts across all that Hendricks has written.[10] The theological legacy of William L. Hendricks is rich and diverse, creative and missional by design. At the end of the day, the commending words of "well done" will surely describe his ministry and life.

BIBLIOGRAPHY

1. Primary

DISSERTATIONS
"The Concept of Death in the Theology of Karl Barth." Ph.D. diss., University of Chicago, 1972.
"The Concept of Satan: A Biblical and Historical Approach and Its Relevance to the Christian Life." Th.D. diss., Southwestern Baptist Theological Seminary, 1958.

BOOKS
(coauth.) *Deepening Discipleship*. Nashville: Convention Press, 1981; rev. ed. 1990.
The Doctrine of Man. Nashville: Convention Press, 1977.
The Letters of John: Tapestries of Faith. Nashville: Convention Press, 1970.
    Las Epistolas de Juan. Trans. Francisco Almanza. El Paso: Casa Bautista de Publicaciones, 1970. [Spanish]
(ed.) *Pascal, Fénelon: Devotion in the Age of Enlightenment*. Christian Classics. Nashville: Broadman, 1980.
(ed.) *Resource Unlimited*. Nashville: Stewardship Commission of the Southern Baptist Convention, 1972.
A Theology for Aging. Nashville: Broadman, 1986.

A Theology for Children. Nashville: Broadman, 1980.

> *Theologie für Kinder: wie man mit Kindern über Gott spricht*. Trans. Friedrich Haubner. Marburg: Francke, 1985. [German]

Who Is Jesus Christ? Layman's Library of Christian Doctrine, vol. 2. Nashville: Broadman, 1985.

> *¿Quién es Jesucristo?* Trans. José Luis Martinez. Biblioteca de Doctrina Cristiana. El Paso: Casa Bautista de Publicaciones, 1986. [Spanish]

CHAPTERS CONTRIBUTED TO BOOKS

"The Age of Accountability." In *Children and Conversion*, ed. Clifford Ingle, 84–97. Nashville; Broadman, 1970.

"A Baptist Perspective." In *Encounters with Eternity*, ed. Christopher Jay Johnson and Marsha G. McGee, 61–84. New York: Philosophical Library, 1986; 2d rev. ed.: *How Different Religions View Death and Afterlife*, ed. Christopher Jay Johnson and Marsha G. McGee, 31–46. Philadelphia: Charles Press, 1998.

"A Biblical History of Children." In *The Ministry of Childhood Education*, ed. Ray F. Evette, 8–12. Nashville: Convention Press, 1985.

"The Difference between Substance (Matter) and Form in Relationship to Biblical Inerrancy." In *The Proceedings of the Conference on Biblical Inerrancy, 1987*, 481–89. Nashville: Broadman, 1987.

"Full Salvation." In *Southwestern Sermons*, ed. H. C. Brown, Jr., 122–28. Nashville: Broadman, 1960.

"Glossolalia in the New Testament." In *Speaking in Tongues: Let's Talk about It*, ed. Watson E. Mills, 48–60. Waco, Tex.: Word, 1973.

"Imagination and Creativity as Integral to Hermeneutics." In *Science, Faith and Revelation: An Approach to Christian Philosophy*, ed. Bob E. Patterson, 261–82. Nashville: Broadman, 1979.

"Salvation." In *Rightly Dividing the Word of Truth: Testimonies of Faith from the Faculty of Southern Seminary*, 24–48. Louisville: Southern Baptist Theological Seminary, n.d.

"The State of Theology in the United States." In *Addresses and Papers: Baptist International Conference on Theological Education, Ridgecrest, North Carolina, USA, January 14–17, 1982*, 179–92. Washington, D.C.: Baptist World Alliance, 1982?

"The Theology of the New Testament." In *Broadman Bible Commentary*, ed. Clifton J. Allen, vol. 8, 32–47. Nashville: Broadman, 1969.

"Two Faces of Christ: What Makes Religious Art Good Art?" In *Art as Religious Studies*, ed. Doug Adams and Diane Apostolos-Cappadona, 149–59. New York: Crossroad, 1987.

JOURNAL ARTICLES

"All in All: Theological Themes in Colossians." *Southwestern Journal of Theology* 16 (Fall 1973): 23–35.

"Baptism: A Baptist Perspective." *Southwestern Journal of Theology* 31 (Spring 1989): 22–33.

"Baptists and Children: The Beginnings of Grace." *Southwestern Journal of Theology* 28 (Spring 1986): 49–53.

"Biblical Interpretation: The Pastor and the Contemporary Scene." *Southwestern Journal of Theology* n.s. 2 (April 1960): 17–26.

"A Century of Excellence." *Review and Expositor* 91 (Summer 1994): 409–17.

"Church Music as a Shaper of Baptist Theology." *Baptist History and Heritage* 21 (July 1986): 3–8.

"Communicating Baptist Doctrine in the Classroom." *Baptist History and Heritage* 13 (October 1978): 11–13.

"Divorce, Remarriage, and the New Testament Concept of Forgiveness." *Search* 2 (Fall 1971): 36–43.

"Giving the Devil His Due: A Visual Approach." *Review and Expositor* 89 (Fall 1992): 488–501.

"Learning from Beauty." *Southwestern Journal of Theology* 29 (Summer 1987): 19–27.

"Learning from Beauty." *Review and Expositor* 85 (Winter 1988): 101–20.

"The Nature of Grace: A Baptist Perspective." *Southwestern Journal of Theology* 28 (Spring 1986): 15–17.

"On Seeing the Christ." *Review and Expositor* 88 (Fall 1991): 419–23.

"Ordination: A Composite View and Practical Suggestions." *Southwestern Journal of Theology* 11 (Spring 1969): 87–96.

"Proclamation through the Arts." *Review and Expositor* 84 (Winter 1987): 75–85.

"Scripture: A Southern Baptist Perspective." *Review and Expositor* 79 (Spring 1982): 245–57.

"Southern Baptist Theology Today." *Theological Educator* 11 (Spring 1981): 22–28.

"Southern Baptists and the Arts." *Review and Expositor* 87 (Fall 1990): 553–62.

"Stewardship in the New Testament." *Southwestern Journal of Theology* 13 (Spring 1971): 25–33.

"A Theological Basis for Christian Social Ministries." *Review and Expositor* 85 (Spring 1988): 221–31.

"Theology and Children: Remarks on Relationships between Christian Theology and Childhood Development Psychology." *Southwestern Journal of Theology* 20 (Spring 1978): 60–72.

"Theology in the Eighties: A Prophecy." *Search* 10 (Winter 1980): 32–39.

"A Theology of Aging." *Search* 17 (Spring 1987): 9–12.

"The Theology of the Electronic Church." *Review and Expositor* 81 (Winter 1984): 59–75.

"Where Do We Worship?" *Baptist History and Heritage* 31 (July 1996): 26–37.

"The Work of Christ in the Hymns of the Church." *Theological Educator* 7 (Spring 1977): 72–80.

ENCYCLOPEDIA AND DICTIONARY ARTICLES

The Dictionary of Art. Ed. Jane Turner. London: Macmillan, 1996. Vol. 3. S.v. "Baptists and Congregationalists."

The Encyclopedia of Death. Ed. Robert and Beatrice Kastenbaum. Phoenix: Oryx Press, 1989. S.v. "Survival Beliefs and Practices: Baptist."

Holman Concise Bible Dictionary. Ed. Trent C. Butler. Nashville: Broadman and Holman, 1997. S.v. "Predestination," "Resurrection," "Resurrection of Jesus," and "Temptation of Jesus."

Holman Bible Dictionary. Ed. Trent C. Butler. Nashville: Holman, 1991. S.v. "Predestination," "Resurrection," "Resurrection of Jesus," and "Temptation of Jesus."

Holman Bible Handbook. Ed. David S. Dockery. Nashville: Holman, 1992. S.v. "Spiritual Gifts."

Mercer Dictionary of the Bible. Ed. Watson E. Mills. Macon, Ga.: Mercer University Press, 1990. S.v. "God."

A New Handbook of Christian Theology. Ed. Donald W. Musser and Joseph L. Price. Nashville: Abingdon, 1992. S.v. "Symbol."

MISCELLANEOUS

"Art's for Your Sake." *The [Baptist] Student*, March 1983, 32–35.

"Bringing Beauty to the Baptist Community." *The Church Musician*, July–August–September 1993, 30–32.

Building Bridges: How Jesus Helped People. Nashville: Sunday School Board of the Southern Baptist Convention, 1980.

"The Call." *The [Baptist] Student*, December 1974, 12–16; also *The Commission*, June 1977, 10–15; *The [Baptist] Student*, August 1977, 13–17.

"Describing the Indescribable." *The Baptist Student*, February 1965, 51–58.

Disciple's Study Bible: New International Version. Nashville: Holman, 1988. S.v. "Summary of the Doctrine of Jesus Christ."

"The God Who Is . . . Is Different . . . and Is Here!" *The Baptist Student*, March 1965, 50–58.

"God's Head and Hands." *The Baptist Student*, April 1965, 51–58.

The Harrowing of Hell: A Morality Play for Eleven Characters and a Chorus. Nashville: Broadman, 1977.

"If You Always See Yourself as Right, You're Wrong." *Church Administration*, January 1972, 10–12, 30.

"The Local Church." *Beliefs of Other Kinds: A Guide to Interfaith Witness in the United States* [*Missions USA*, September–October 1984], 56–57.

"The New Hymnal: Its Theological Dimension." *The Church Musician*, March 1975, 7–11.

"Paul's Use of 'Flesh.'" *Biblical Illustrator*, Winter 1983, 50–52.

"The Priority of God and the Fulness of God." *The Baptist Student*, May 1965, 50–58.

"Reconciliation: The Life of the Reconciled." *Outreach*, November 1976, 32–34.

"Reconciliation: The Questions of Election and Grace." *Outreach*, October 1976, 37–39.

"Reconciliation: What It's All about." *Outreach*, September 1976, 33–35.

"A Risen Savior—Unique among Religions?" *Biblical Illustrator*, Spring 1987, 16–19.

"The Role of the Christian." *The Commission*, July 1977, 15–18.

"Spiritual Gifts." *The [Baptist] Student*, December 1972, 8–14.

"Toward True Religion." *The Baptist Student*, December 1967, 21–25.

"The Tradition of Men." *Biblical Illustrator*, Spring 1984, 52–54.

2. Secondary

Baptist Reflections on Christianity and the Arts; Learning from Beauty: A Tribute to William L. Hendricks. Ed. David M. Rayburn, Daven M. Kari, and Darrell G. Gwaltney. Lewiston, N.Y.: Edwin Mellen Press, 1997.

Harry Leon McBeth

(1931–)
Church History

Karen O'Dell Bullock

BIOGRAPHY

Harry Leon McBeth was born 5 August 1931 and reared near small Panhandle towns of far west Texas. His parents were Elmo Clinton and Agnes Booker McBeth, cotton-farmers of deep faith who knew the value of hard work and strong family ties. During the Dust Bowl years they plowed fields, raised stock, and watched the skies for rain, farming near Rotan, Lamesa, and Plainview. Twelve children were born to them, of whom eight sons survived: the fourth, Harry Leon, was named after a Frenchman and family friend.

Leon attended school before and after the harvest each year. He preferred tractor work over chopping cotton but knew them equally well. Luxuries were scarce; even so, the *Baptist Standard* was a welcome guest bringing weekly denominational news.

Leon became convicted of his soul's lost condition the summer before his twelfth birthday when the "Apostle of the West," Willis J. Ray, preached in a brush arbor revival at the First Baptist Church of Rotan. Leon and his brother Jeff both trusted Christ as Savior and were baptized by Lawrence L. Trott. It was a genuine transforming experience for both brothers, who often spoke of spiritual matters as they worked side by side in the fields.

The McBeth family moved to Plainview the year Leon started high school and joined the College Heights Baptist Church. Here Leon met his lifelong love and soul mate, Ada Lucille Miller, in

263

whose vivacious wit, warm empathy and laughter he never ceased to find delight. They graduated from high school and married in June 1950 and entered Wayland Baptist College the same year. Leon pursued a B.A. degree in English, being the first person in his family to attend college, and Ada a B.S. in education.[1]

God confirmed McBeth's call to ministry as he prepared for the pastorate. In 1953, anticipating graduation, he preenrolled in Southern Baptist Theological Seminary. Meanwhile, W. Boyd Hunt,[2] professor at Southwestern, came to Plainview to preach a series of messages. That week changed the course of Leon's life. He knew that God was redirecting him to Southwestern. After graduation from college in 1954, Leon and Ada moved to Fort Worth. When they arrived on campus, John P. Newport was the first person to greet them.

During his seminary days, McBeth pastored several churches in western and central Texas, including the First Baptist Church of Rio Vista (1956–60).[3] Leon was one of a group of several young friends, all rural Texas Baptist pastors, including Ebbie C. Smith, Jimmy Draper, Russell H. Dilday, Jr., and Jesse Fletcher, who car-pooled together into Fort Worth to attend seminary.[4] These were busy years for the couple: Leon earned his B.D. in 1957; their first child, Ruth Ann, was born the same year he became a teaching fellow (1958); Mark was born in 1959; Leon was elected to the faculty in 1960; and he graduated with his Th.D. in 1961. Their third child, David, was born two years later. As a young man, Leon made a prayer covenant with God that he would follow "wherever and as far as God would be pleased to take him."[5] Yet Leon knew his own limitations and that doctoral work would be particularly difficult, given his growing responsibilities.

McBeth's most influential seminary professors were T. B. Maston, the renowned ethicist, and the church historian, Robert A. Baker, both of whose lectures captivated students. Baker took McBeth under his wing. As a doctoral student, Leon graded for Baker, taught classes, studied hard, and mastered his discipline, using as his rule the old adage: "First he wrought; then he taught." God clarified his ministry purpose, engraving on his heart the passion to prepare pastors for churches and scholars for schools. As a fellow in 1958, Leon taught classes that were diploma-level Baptist and church history sections, and, despite little compensation, he was soon teaching a full load. He joined the Department of Church History in 1960.

For more than four decades, since his first class at Southwestern, McBeth has continued to study: at the University of Texas at Arlington, Union Theological Seminary and Columbia University in New York, and two research residencies in Oxford, England. His influence grew with publications and readership, although his primary energies still target the steady stream of students who sit in his classrooms, absorbing a deep appreciation for their heritage from this gracious, humorous, sometimes reticent, and always powerful storyteller.

WRITINGS

All of McBeth's publications were written while serving on the faculty of Southwestern. From his earliest research on early English Baptist religious liberty sources in 1961 to the sesquicentennial history of Texas Baptists in 1998, some thirty-seven years later, his pen has been tireless. At this time, McBeth has authored ten books, has contributed chapters to five others, and has a new volume on the way. His list of published monographs, journal articles, and lectures on topics related to American Christianity and Baptist history number in the dozens. Although his corpus encompasses a broader sphere, his focus has centered on and advanced the study of Baptist heritage. The following discussion highlights by decade those writings which distinctively contribute to the field of historical scholarship.

McBeth's 1961 dissertation, "English Baptist Literature on Religious Liberty to 1689," set the tone for the rest of his career by analyzing how early English Baptist activity and literature "exercised an influence far out of proportion to the numbers and social status of the Baptists" in an era when "absolute liberty was considered an invitation to disaster in church and state."[6] He demonstrated that the Baptist corpus on religious liberty crossed boundaries of geography and denominations, helping to bring to Patriot politicians the concepts and language that helped to bring this principle into American constitutional law.[7]

Next, McBeth published two congregational histories: one in Fort Worth and the other in Dallas. *Victory through Prayer: A History of Rosen Heights Baptist Church, 1900–1966* (1966) traced the growth of this suburban congregation as it responded to its expanding church field. His *The First Baptist Church of Dallas: Centennial History, 1868–1968* (1968) narrated the story of one of the most influential congregations in the state from the Reconstruction period of Texas through the pastorate of George Washington Truett to the early years of Wallie Amos Criswell. Set firmly into state and local historical contexts, the record of each church demonstrated McBeth's conviction that local Baptist church histories are critical to the study of denominational identity and that the Baptist story is only secondarily adduced by its national structures.

Men Who Made Missions (1967) isolated personalities whose evangelistic fervor still echoes across the centuries. McBeth considered those regarded as radicals within their own circles: Gregory, Patrick, Boniface, Lull, Xavier, Carey, Brainerd, Livingstone, and Judson, a diverse sampling of missionary leaders.[8]

In the decade of the 1970s McBeth explored two salient topics. The first was a concise look at the shifting American religious landscape and emerging groups within it. Writing with his own teenagers in mind, McBeth described in *Strange New Religions* (1977) the beliefs of the Unification Church, Hare Krishnas, Scientologists, Zen Buddhists, Children of God, and occult groups to help his readers "understand better the confusing smorgasbord of new religions today."[9]

The second book, groundbreaking in its topic, was *Women in Baptist Life* (1979), which sketched the influence of Baptist women through almost four centuries. He introduced Baptist women on each side of the Atlantic, like Anne Dutton, the theologian-writer; Mrs. Attaway, the she-preacher of Coleman Street in London; Dorothy Hazzard of Bristol, whose valor earned her the epithet, "the he-goat before the flock"; and Americans Martha Meuse Clay and Hannah Lee, both of whom suffered for religious liberty. Dozens of other Baptist women were mentioned: lay and ordained ministers, denominational leaders, and missionaries around the globe. He rightly asserted that the stories of Baptist women should be included in expressions of denominational history so that all Baptists might celebrate their faith heritage more accurately.

The decade of the 1980s revealed McBeth's mature scholarship. Having taught in the classroom for more than twenty-five years and acquired a reputation for precise, readable historical work, he was asked by Broadman's Johnnie Godwin to write a comprehensive study of Baptist history. A textbook trilogy was planned: in addition to the Baptist volume, W. Morgan Patterson of Golden Gate Baptist Theological Seminary was invited to write its complementary source book; and E. Glenn Hinson of Southern Seminary, W. R. Estep of Southwestern, and Glenn T. Miller of

Southeastern Baptist Theological Seminary were to coauthor a third text to span church history from the early church through the Reformation to the modern era.[10]

McBeth's task was daunting. A conscious decision set aside pedantry and exhaustive footnotes in favor of producing a readable, general text. *Baptist Heritage: Four Centuries of Baptist Witness* (1987) was written for laypersons as well as for the classroom. Researched carefully from primary sources and written both chronologically and topically, each chapter was designed to stand alone, a goal crucial for the casual reader, college readings-courses, or seminary survey supplemental material. He set into their historical contexts the often complex and overlapping histories of Baptist groups in Europe and America. While the scope is vast, far more extensive than had been otherwise attempted in the twentieth century, the value of the work lies in both its broad sweep and its detailed treatments, allowing the author to discuss as easily the Seventh-Day, Primitive, or Landmark positions on worship, ordinances, and polity as the Arminian and Calvinistic Baptist views on atonement. The weakness of the book is its silence with regard to Asian, African, and Latin American Baptist history, the inclusion of which, one is confident, would require an additional volume.

His fourth decade of teaching and writing ministry brought to McBeth joy and heartache. Classroom teaching was fulfilling, but the unity of the Southern Baptist Convention (SBC) was eroding. In 1988 Lloyd Elder, then president of the SBC Sunday School Board (SSB) in Nashville, invited McBeth to write an interpretive history for the institution's upcoming centennial in 1991, to be published by Broadman. The Southwestern professor turned down the commission twice before finally accepting at the behest of Harold Smith of the SSB. Unsuspected tremors lay ahead as McBeth initiated the research phase.

Widening internal rifts between some SSB administrators and trustees became apparent even as McBeth began compiling the story and became more serious as the months advanced. Because of the production timetable and looming anniversary deadlines, McBeth found himself narrating highly charged episodes as they unfolded, history-in-the-making, without the obvious benefit of objectivity that reflection and the passage of time afford all parties to such events. Questions about portions of the manuscript surfaced in 1989, and differing philosophies about the book's original vision and some of its viewpoints clashed in the editing process, which, as time passed, involved an ever-expanding circle of readers. Some readers thought that portions of the narrative were imbalanced and that these could potentially threaten a legal case which was pending at the time. The manuscript was at the typesetters in August 1990 when the SSB aborted the project. Within months Elder retired early from his position as president, and Jimmy Draper came to head the institution. The volume was candid, drawing on confidential primary documents offered, without restriction, for McBeth's research. It fulfilled its original contract as interpretive history. Yet, in a climate fraught with denominational volatility, single voices sometimes find themselves silenced between louder, colliding forces. The book drew internecine crossfire which was unexpected, ill-timed, and most unfortunate. At present "Celebrating Heritage and Hope: The Centennial History of the Baptist Sunday School, 1891–1991," the story of one of the most influential entities in SBC life, has yet to roll from a press.

However painful this experience was to him personally, McBeth did not cease writing. In the same year that his Sunday School Board history was recalled, Broadman published a fifth McBeth book, his *A Sourcebook for Baptist Heritage* (1990), the well-received companion to his Baptist history text. Reemphasizing his commitment to the value of primary sources, this book still provides the best single-volume collection of documentary excerpts to support Baptist heritage studies.

McBeth continued to research and write, finishing by the end of the decade the celebrated anniversary volume, *Texas Baptists: A Sesquicentennial History* (1998), commissioned by the Baptist General Convention of Texas. Written under the severe duress of caring for his wife, Ada, who suffered an incapacitating stroke in 1997, McBeth wrote many chapters at night in the hospital chapel while waiting to sit with her. Standing in the line of distinguished Texas Baptist historians, like Z. N. Morrell, J. M. Carroll, J. M. Dawson, and Robert A. Baker, McBeth continued the compelling story of a specific people called Texas Baptists, even though this volume was also written amidst chaotic upheavals of national and state convention strife. McBeth is currently overseeing the compilation of a companion source volume to support the Texas narrative.

McBeth's five chapter contributions to books dealt categorically with Baptist identity or doctrine, all but the first of which were published in the discordant decade of the 1990s. His first chapter paid homage to his beloved professor in the festschrift titled, *The Lord's*

Free People in a Free Land: Essays in Baptist History in Honor of Robert Baker (1976), edited by William R. Estep. This volume is remarkable in that all but one of the essays were written by Th.D. graduates in church history, students of Baker, who were then serving in positions of denominational leadership.[11] McBeth furnished the essay, "Southern Baptist Higher Education," in which he traced the vestiges of anti-education among Southern Baptists and the progress made toward overturning the notion.

In *Southern Baptists and American Evangelicals: The Conversation Continues* (1993), edited by David S. Dockery, McBeth's Southern Baptist perspective was paired with that of Stanley Grenz, a North American Conference Baptist, to answer the question of whether Southern Baptists should properly be called "evangelicals." McBeth used George M. Marsden's discussions of the topic as a starting place to delineate new definitions for the old term "evangelical" and expressed aversion to their narrowing implications.[12]

His third chapter was a 1987 Herschel H. Hobbs Lectureship in Baptist Faith and Heritage at Oklahoma Baptist University. Published with other lectures in *The Fibers of Our Faith* (1995), edited by Dick Rader, "The Society Method of Baptist Work" drew the important distinction between *missionary tasks* and *missionary methods* in Baptist life, the latter of which Baptists implement with great diversity.

McBeth's fourth chapter, in *Biblical Hermeneutics: A Comprehensive Introduction to Interpreting Scripture* (1996), edited by Bruce Corley, Steve Lemke, and Grant Lovejoy, dealt with the earliest Baptists' high view of Scripture: its authority, interpretation, and application. He noted that these convictions about Scripture largely shaped the Baptist witness and that Baptists today "maintain the same confident faith in the Bible as God's true word to mankind" (p. 88). His fifth chapter, in *Defining Baptist Convictions: Guidelines for the Twenty-First Century* (1996), edited by Charles Deweese, examined the doctrines of soul competency and priesthood of all believers, both basic biblical truths and fundamental Baptist tenets.

McBeth's writings reveal the convictions on which his life and ministry anchor and provide the best glimpse of his distinctive contribution to the thought of many generations of students.

THOUGHT

Leon McBeth's spiritual pilgrimage developed the convictions which shape his ministry, drawn from the concentric circles of heritage that still impact his life: Missionary Baptist, Southern Baptist, Protestant, descendant of Puritans.[13] In turn, the biblical groundings of these circles inform his research, reporting, and interpreting of history.

Research of History

Akin to his conviction concerning the need for sound, biblical exegesis, Leon McBeth's foundational emphasis for historical study is the demand for a balanced reading of primary documents. That critical records are not always extant is an ever-present reality in historical studies; however, those having survived must be allowed to speak for themselves. As research unfolds, specific contexts of any given event reveal the forces at work upon the ideas, persons, and structures of that era. These factors must inform the process rather than support *a priori* assumptions. Thus historiography requires familiarity with diverse fields of study, all of which bring depth and breadth to the interpretation. McBeth's preparation before teaching and intense personal development throughout his career evince his conviction that there is no shortcut to good scholarship.

Reporting of History

McBeth is a consummate storyteller, able to detect the humorous or ironic element within the narrative and relate it without rancor. He values incisive biographies over generic summaries, for the simple reason that a single biography often captures the essence of an era, much like a snapshot freezes details of a single moment. From such studies one may derive nuances of meaning or information from that which is exposed, albeit unintentionally. McBeth planes the larger context and then carves in bas-relief human interest details against that backdrop. His accounts captivate readers, who find themselves longing to know more, to travel to his places, and to identify with his characters.

Interpreting of History

Crucial to the historian's task is precise interpretation, since the relaying of pure, non-interpretive history is humanly impossible. At the same time it requires a commitment to integrity and modesty. "[H]istory requires interpretation. I was not content merely to dump factual data upon the page but tried to arrange it in some order and offer my own interpretations as to its meaning and significance,"[14] McBeth wrote. For him, interpretive history is never complete.

INFLUENCE

Like ripples on a pond, Leon McBeth's influence ever widens, immeasurable by human means. Nevertheless, perhaps those who teach daily in his shadow and observe his contributions firsthand may be permitted to proffer a sampling of the ways in which his ministry has affected both his discipline and persons who have known him.

First, McBeth's consistent model of scholarship, by precept and by example, contributes to the field of historical research. His vigilant attention to primary sources induced generations of scholars to do the same. His multifaceted narratives of the faith and work of a specific people of God called Baptists reveal the diverse, challenging, and faithful service rendered in the name of Christ. They also paint cameos of the few individuals, representing the millions, who have embraced the name "Baptist" across the centuries. One finds in his pages nobility and human frailty combined, comprising the human response to a holy God, and this inspires renewed commitment. McBeth's influence in educating Baptists and persons of other religious traditions in Baptist principles is profound.[15]

Next, throughout McBeth's four decades of teaching ministry at Southwestern, thousands of master's and doctoral students left his classrooms to fill positions of leadership in churches, mission fields, and denominational organizations. Furthermore, doctoral students whom he supervised teach today in Baptist educational institutions in America and other nations, including most of the women historians employed in Baptist life.[16] Each person represents the lifetime investment of this quiet, jovial historian, whose probing questions and willingness to dialogue still motivate students toward research excellence and a desire to serve Christ's kingdom.

Finally, McBeth has modeled Christian integrity, faithfulness, and service. He preached and taught across the United States, Mexico, Canada, Ukraine, Brazil, England, Scotland, Wales, Germany, Switzerland, France, and Italy. The gospel message he still shares is applied practically in local Baptist church contexts, particularly bridging racial and gender divides.

His devotion to his beloved Ada, who died on 27 October 2001, was a poignant but vivid expression of his character. During her four-year illness, he would say of her, "She is as dear as life to me. I love her more now than I ever have,"[17] often spending ninety hours per week tending to her needs. This he accomplished in addition to his duties in the classroom and without a breath of complaint. Theirs was a love story which taught volumes about Christlikeness. Under the strain of unspeakable grief, compounded by cataclysmic denominational strife, McBeth's life reveals the refining touch of God's grace. Sustained by his life-verse, "I can do everything through him who gives me strength" (Phil. 4:13, NIV), his gracious, gentlemanly disposition remains steadfast.

Those who search for models of Christian dignity and courage in the midst of unrest may find many champions in the pages of Baptist heritage. Leon McBeth's journey, from a young chopper of cotton to the teacher of thousands, has fashioned of him a most rare example.

BIBLIOGRAPHY

DISSERTATION

"English Baptist Literature on Religious Liberty to 1689." Th.D. diss., Southwestern Baptist Theological Seminary, 1961.

BOOKS

The Baptist Heritage: Four Centuries of Baptist Witness. Nashville: Broadman, 1987.
English Baptist Literature on Religious Liberty to 1689. New York: Arno Press, 1980.
The First Baptist Church of Dallas: Centennial History, 1868–1968. Grand Rapids: Zondervan, 1968.
Men Who Made Missions. Nashville: Broadman, 1968.
    Hombres Claves en las Misiones. Trans. Manolita Ballaguer. El Paso: Casa Bautista de Publicaciones, 1980. [Spanish]
A Sourcebook for Baptist Heritage. Nashville: Broadman, 1990.
Strange New Religions. Nashville: Broadman, 1977.
Texas Baptists: A Sesquicentennial History. Dallas: Baptistway Press, 1998.
Victory through Prayer: A History of Rosen Heights Baptist Church, 1906–1966. Fort Worth: Rosen Heights Baptist Church, 1966.
Women in Baptist Life. Nashville: Broadman, 1979.

CHAPTERS CONTRIBUTED TO BOOKS

"Baptist or Evangelical: One Southern Baptist's Perspective." In *Southern Baptists and American Evangelicals: The Conversation Continues*, ed. David S. Dockery, 68–76. Nashville: Broadman and Holman, 1993.
"Early Baptist Hermeneutics." In *Biblical Hermeneutics: A Comprehensive Introduction to Interpreting Scripture*, ed. Bruce Corley, Steve Lemke, and Grant Lovejoy, 88–98. Nashville: Broadman and Holman, 1996.
"God Gives Soul Competency and Priesthood to All Believers." In *Defining Baptist Convictions: Guidelines for the Twenty-First Century*, ed. Charles W. Deweese, 62–70. Franklin, Tenn.: Providence House, 1996.
"The Society Method of Baptist Work." In *The Fibers of Our Faith*, ed. Dick Allen Rader, vol. 1, 74–85. Franklin, Tenn.: Providence House, 1995.

"Southern Baptist Higher Education." In *The Lord's Free People in a Free Land: Essays in Baptist History in Honor of Robert A. Baker,* ed. William R. Estep, Jr., 113–26. Fort Worth: School of Theology, Southwestern Baptist Theological Seminary, 1976.

JOURNAL ARTICLES

"Baptist Beginnings." *Baptist History and Heritage* 15 (October 1980): 36–41, 65. Also in *Baptist Heritage* (pamphlet) series.

"Baptist Fundamentalism: A Cultural Interpretation." *Baptist History and Heritage* 13 (July 1978): 12–19, 32.

"The Broken Unity of 1845: A Reassessment." *Baptist History and Heritage* 24 (July 1989): 24–31, 48.

"Challenges to Religious Liberty." *Southwestern Journal of Theology* 36 (Summer 1994): 45–51.

"The Changing Role of Women in Baptist History." *Southwestern Journal of Theology* 22 (Fall 1979): 84–96.

"Cooperation and Crisis as Shapers of Southern Baptist Identity." *Baptist History and Heritage* 30 (July 1995): 35–44.

"Expansion of the Southern Baptist Convention to 1951." *Baptist History and Heritage* 17 (July 1982): 32–43.

"Fundamentalism in the Southern Baptist Convention in Recent Years." *Review and Expositor* 79 (Winter 1982): 85–103.

"George W. Truett: Baptist Statesman." *Baptist History and Heritage* 32 (April 1997): 9–22.

"Has It Been Worth the Cost? Some Theological Reflections." *Faith and Mission* 5 (Fall 1987): 27–30.

"Images of the Black Church in America." *Baptist History and Heritage* 16 (July 1981): 19–28, 40.

"J. Frank Norris and Southwestern Seminary." *Southwestern Journal of Theology* 30 (Summer 1988): 14–19.

"John Franklin Norris: Texas Tornado." *Baptist History and Heritage* 32 (April 1997): 23–38.

"The Legacy of the Baptist Missionary Society." *Baptist History and Heritage* 27 (July 1992): 3–13.

"The New Shape of Religion in America." *Southwestern Journal of Theology* 38 (Summer 1996): 19–27.

"The Ordination of Women [in the Southern Baptist Convention]." *Review and Expositor* 78 (Fall 1981): 515–30.

"Origin of the Christian Life Commission." *Baptist History and Heritage* 1 (October 1966): 29–36.

"Patterns of SBC Presidential Authority." *Baptist History and Heritage* 31 (April 1996): 12–22.

"Perspectives on Women in Baptist Life." *Baptist History and Heritage* 22 (July 1987): 4–11.

"Preaching Values in Baptist History." *Southwestern Journal of Theology* n.s. 6 (April 1964): 111–22.

"The Role of Women in Southern Baptist History." *Baptist History and Heritage* 12 (January 1977): 3–25.

"Southern Baptists and Race since 1947." *Baptist History and Heritage* 7 (July 1972): 155–69.

"The Texas Tradition: A Study in Baptist Regionalism (Part I)." *Baptist History and Heritage* 26 (January 1991): 37–57.

"Two Ways to Be Baptist." *Baptist History and Heritage* 32 (April 1997): 7–8, 39–53.

MISCELLANEOUS

"America's Southern Baptists: Who They Are." *Christianity Today,* 4 November 1988, 17–21.

Encyclopedia of Southern Baptists. 4 vols. Nashville: Broadman, 1958–82. Vol. 3. S.v. "Baptists Today, Analysis of." Vol. 4. S.v. "Women Deacons" and "Women in Ministry, Baptist."

"A Glance at Baptist Home Missions." *The Watchman Examiner,* 15 and 29 May 1969, 299–301.

William Meredith Pinson, Jr.

(1934–)
Christian Ethics

22

Paul Griffin Jones, II

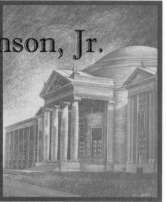

BIOGRAPHY

William (Bill) Meredith Pinson, Jr., was born in Fort Worth, Texas, on 3 August 1934, the only child of William M. and Ila Jones Pinson. His maternal heritage emphasized a strong Methodist background, and his paternal heritage was of the Baptist persuasion. His paternal great-grandfather, Josiah Fillmore Pinson, gave and sold the land for the original Buckner Orphans' Home and cooperated with R. C. Buckner, a lifelong friend from Kentucky, in the founding of the facility. Bill Pinson's family background would mold his commitment to civic and benevolent activities.

When he was ten years of age, he made a profession of faith and was baptized at the Baptist church in Lancaster, Texas, along with his mother, who came from the Methodist church. While in high school, his brilliant and probing mind prompted him to explore all the major world religions. He compared the different Christian denominations as he explored the validity of the Christian faith. The fact of the resurrection of Jesus led him to a renewed and deepened personal faith. Study and experience with churches of other denominations led him to conclude that the Baptist denomination was where he wanted to commit his life. He was the valedictorian of his Lancaster High School graduating class and subsequently entered North Texas State University (now University of North Texas).

Like his early life, his adult life and thought were shaped by a series of significant persons with whom he built meaningful relationships. The director of the Baptist Student Union, Doyle Baird, taught him about discipline, administration, and organization and in this context initiated a lifelong interest in Christian ethics. As president of the student body, Pinson worked with the president of the university to desegregate the institution and developed a lasting commitment to racial reconciliation. His interest in evangelism and preaching was encouraged by W. F. Howard, Texas state BSU director, who inspired him to preach youth-led revivals throughout Texas. While in college, Pinson also interacted with Foy Valentine, whose own social activism would create a permanent influence on him.

Upon graduation from college, Pinson married his high school/college sweetheart, Bobbie Judd, who provided validity to his understanding of the Christian home and family. In 1955 Pinson entered Southwestern Baptist Theological Seminary. In 1956, the Pinsons, along with Bill and Judith Moyers, enrolled in New College at the University of Edinburgh, Scotland. It was there that he met and was mentored by James S. Stewart, professor of New Testament and preaching. Stewart would become a dominant influence on Pinson's thought and writings. Stewart impressed upon Pinson the importance of heraldic preaching which focuses on the major aspects of the gospel, the kerygma, and not on less central issues. Stewart contended that there was no conflict between first-rate scholarship and evangelistic ministry and preaching.

When he returned to Southwestern Seminary, Pinson became a student of Thomas Buford Maston, who would have a profound influence on his thought and writings. Pinson's commitment to biblical rather than philosophical or theological ethics came from Maston, who would also instill in Pinson the understanding of a will-of-God ethic. Maston's training under H. Richard Niebuhr, along with his personal piety, demonstrated how outstanding scholarship could be linked with practical application and dedicated churchmanship. Pinson's dissertation on church-state relations shaped his devotion to the historic Baptist understanding of religious liberty and the separation of church and state. While completing his seminary degrees, Pinson served as an associate to Foy Valentine and later Jimmy Allen at the Texas Baptist Christian Life Commission.

After receiving his Doctor of Theology degree in 1963 and upon the retirement of Maston, Pinson was invited to join the faculty of Southwestern Seminary. Here he would continue to interact with several professors who helped shape his life and thought—William L. Hendricks, John P. Newport, Milton Ferguson, and James Leo Garrett. In 1969 Pinson on a sabbatical leave engaged in postdoctoral studies at Columbia University, studying how churches were meeting social and ethical needs in Atlanta, New York, and San Francisco. This was a life-changing time for Pinson, whose study of the dynamics of social change helped him to understand the difference between incremental and revolutionary change and reaffirmed his appreciation for the social and ethical emphasis of Baptists.

Prior to his sabbatical, Pinson began to interact with friend and colleague, Clyde E. Fant, Jr., on the role of preaching on ethical issues. This gave birth to the thirteen-volume *Twenty Centuries of Great Preaching*, jointly authored and edited by Pinson and Fant. Vester T. Hughes, Jr. greatly contributed to the project. The research for this set refocused Pinson's life on the role of preaching as he came to understand how "great" preachers had often preached on ethical themes.

Thus, when the seven-thousand-member First Baptist Church of Wichita Falls, Texas, invited him to become its pastor in 1975, Pinson was more open to respond than he might have been previously. He resigned from his position as professor of Christian ethics and chair of the Department of Christian Ethics to pastor the church and to apply what he had been teaching. The days at Wichita Falls affirmed the mentoring of Stewart, Maston, and others as Pinson witnessed that preaching, evangelism, and social action do indeed work together.

A sense of mission that had accompanied Pinson since BSU days, which had been heightened by the influence of Maston, led Pinson to resign the church to become president of Golden Gate Baptist Theological Seminary in Mill Valley, California. The multicultural, secular society of the Bay Area provided an additional dimension to his life and thought. It was here that his appreciation for other racial and ethnic groups was intensified. This period in his life heralded an end to the influence of provincialism that had begun its demise in his thoughts while in Europe and the East Coast cities.

Awareness that mission fields were dependent on "old line" Baptist conventions led Pinson in 1982 to become executive director of the Baptist General Convention of Texas. He came with the belief that the strength of Texas Baptists was a major factor in the strength of Southern Baptist missions. Until his retirement in February 2000, Pinson applied what he believed that God had taught him through those who had helped to shape his life and the places where he had served. His wife and soul mate, Bobbie, their children, Meredith and Allison, their spouses, and his grandchildren continue to add focus to his belief in a strong Christian home where missions begins. All the influences have converged to create a life that emphasizes the centrality of the Bible, the basics of Baptist beliefs, the importance of local congregations, the vital relationship of evangelism and ethics, the need to confront moral problems and social injustice through institutions as well as individuals, and the necessity to involve persons of all ethnic, racial, gender, and national groups in Baptist life.

WRITINGS

The review of each of the twenty-two published books by Bill Pinson would fill far more than space allows. For the purpose of this work, the books will be grouped by general purpose and addressed chronologically within each grouping. Many of his books were directed toward youth and young adults and form one group. *Out of Darkness* (1962) presented a dramatic history of the sources of religious liberty and was addressed to adolescents and their leaders. Likewise, *Ambassadors and Christian Citizenship* (1963) was addressed to participants in the Royal Ambassador program and focused on preparing such young men to be productive and effective citizens. In 1969 he produced *No Greater Challenge*, a guidebook for teenagers, which focused on this period of adolescent development as the most significant time in molding and shaping mature Christian adults.

In the following decade, many of his writings continued to focus on youth and young adults. In 1971 he helped T. B. Maston to revise his *Right or Wrong?* It was a guide for teenagers and their leaders for living by Christian standards and focused on the Christian life, Christian ethics, and conduct of life. He joined with professional football player Bill Glass in 1972 to produce *Don't Blame the Game*. It was a Christian examination of the value and need for appropriate sports activities while at the same time exposing the bankruptcy of "super star" motivation. The foreword to this book was written by professional football player

Roger Staubach. In 1974, *The Five Worlds of Youth* addressed the multiple problems and potential for youth during adolescence.

Another group of Pinson's books addressed major social issues and how the church can and should address them. He wrote *How to Deal with Controversial Issues* in 1966 in an attempt to spur Christian leadership to take responsible positions on the many contemporary issues that were challenging the church and society. He followed this with *Resource Guide to Current Social Issues* (1968), which provided a topical guide to addressing ethical issues. It provided organizational, philosophical, and bibliographical understanding on social problems for the church. In 1972 he teamed with Clyde Fant to coedit *Contemporary Christian Trends*, which examined twentieth-century trends in the church theologically, socially, and ethically.

In 1975 Pinson produced *Applying the Gospel*, which provided suggestions for Christian social action in the local church. Social problems were examined in light of Baptist polity and theology. *The Word Topical Bible on Issues and Answers* (1981) continued Pinson's interest in preparing the local church to address moral and social issues. The compendium addressed most issues that would conceivably confront contemporary Christianity. His most recent volume, written with Lloyd Elder in 2001, addressed *Decision Making for Life and Leadership* and continued his concern that the church community make appropriate, biblically based decisions on contemporary issues.

Another group of his books addressed the local church and its ministry and extensively focused on the role and privilege of proclamation. When Pinson and Fant joined together to produce *Twenty Centuries of Great Preaching* (1971; 2d ed., 1995), the role of preaching could never again be the same. These thirteen volumes challenged the assumption that kerygmatic or heraldic preaching did not have a strong social and ethical component by examining the sermons of the leading preachers of Christian history. In 1973 Pinson would produce *The Local Church in Ministry* to affirm the appropriate role of the pulpit and the people in ministry.

When in 1976 he joined with Nolan Howington and Alton McEachern to produce *Growing Disciples through Preaching*, Pinson challenged the church to use the act of biblical proclamation to disciple and nurture the community of faith. Preaching is the vitality of the church that enables and empowers the people to be the purposely called-out ones. In 1984 he wrote *Ready to Min-*

ister as a challenge to the church to assume its rightful place in the struggle for the souls and lives of the broken, bruised, and battered. His most recent work on the church, *Who in the World Are Baptists, Anyway?* (2000), affirms the historic Baptist principles that are central to the witness, ministry, and social action of the people called Baptists.

The remaining group of Pinson's books addressed the family and its need to be incarnational and intentional. *Families with a Purpose* (1978) challenged the church and its people to model purposeful living in relationships to each other and in their lives with those outside the faith community. This gave rise to an invitation from the Sunday School Board of the Southern Baptist Convention to prepare a major statement on the family with separate attention being given to each age group. This resulted in the publication of *The Biblical View of the Family* in 1981 and the youth version, *Youth Affirm: The Biblical View of the Family*, also published in 1981. These volumes affirmed the biblical basis for family relationships and the purposes for which God created the family structure.

This analysis and review reflect only the books written or edited by Bill Pinson. He has produced more than eighty video and audio productions and numerous articles in religious publications. An analysis of these must be left for a future time and a more focused volume.

INTERPRETATION OF THOUGHT

An integrated interpretation of the thought of Pinson must begin with his emphasis on the centrality of the Bible in the Christian life. His personal spiritual pilgrimage, the influence of James Stewart and T. B. Maston, and his writings all focus on the role of the Scriptures in the life of the people of faith. The introductory course in ethics became "Biblical Ethics" as he focused on "applied Christianity" in the life of the church. Many of his early writings held the title "The Bible Speaks on. . . ."

Pinson's understanding of biblical ethics in the decision-making process led him to embrace many of the concepts inherent in Maston's "will-of-God" ethic. An authentic biblical ethic would focus on seeking the will of God in every circumstance and decision. This practical hermeneutic established an ethical system that denied antinomianism as generally expressed in situationalism or contextualism as well as rejecting legalism and its accompanying literalism. Decisions should always be made in light of the biblical revelation of God's will for His creation.

Pinson's emphasis on the centrality of the Bible guided his early examination of other denominations and world religions. His conclusions affirmed historic Baptist beliefs as had been verified in the life of Baptist people for more than three and a half centuries. He affirmed the doctrines of soul competency and religious liberty and the corollary, the separation of church and state. These are reflected in his doctoral dissertation, "Contemporary Southern Baptist Involvement with the State." His writings and teaching give evidence that the historic Baptist tenets can be practically applied through the life and ministry of a local congregation.

The importance of the congregation is a major emphasis of Pinson. The local church is the place where the biblical message is proclaimed, the biblical material is studied, the biblical fellowship is realized, and the biblical ethic is affirmed in personal piety and applied in social relationships. For Pinson, the Christian ethic is not a concept to be debated but a means for the living out of God's plan by his people, the church, in the context of family, vocation, leisure, politics, and the other social interactions. The church's affirmation of applied Christianity through ethical living is the concomitant of its evangelistic message. For Pinson, the congregation is the appropriate focus of evangelism and ethics.

For Pinson there is no dichotomy between ethics and evangelism. He contends, with James Stewart, that evangelistic preaching is sound biblical preaching that focuses on the major aspects of the gospel. The biblical proclamation of the local church must be presented in a manner that draws unbelievers to the Lord and challenges believers to ethical living. With Maston he could contend that the preaching of the cross is the presentation of the integral concept of the Christian life. Evangelism and ethics form a vital relationship that energize the Christian life and authenticate the Christian experience. It is in biblical proclamation that the tension is created between the "oughtness" of the biblical expectation and the "isness," or reality, of the human experience. His call from academia to the pastorate is a major evidence of his belief that evangelism and ethics are best demonstrated through the proclamation and practice of the congregation.

Pinson realized that there is a biblical mandate to confront moral problems and social injustice through the institutions of society as well as through regenerated individuals. His understanding of biblical man in an immoral society was predicated on his understanding of the human condition as revealed in the biblical narratives. The institutions of society can be a means by which social justice can be brought to divergent segments of society. Social change should be a logical outcome of the Christian witness. The institutions of society work best when the change through them is incremental. As a social model, revolutionary change often destroys the institutions from which it springs. Congregations can encourage the institutions of society to bring about social change incrementally for large numbers of people and thus serve as a means to achieving social justice.

Pinson believed that the Baptist heritage demanded that the proclamation and the social action of the church be inclusive of all persons regardless of race, ethnicity, gender, or nationality. This intentionality should propel the church into the Christian world mission with a sense of urgency and freedom that arises from this inclusiveness. The gospel in its social context is a gospel that knows no boundaries, recognizes no limitations, accepts no preferences, and demands that all people receive just and equal care from the institutions of society. The central message of the Bible is that of One who heals the sick, lifts up the neglected, affirms the rejected, restores the wanderer, sets free the captives, and proclaims the acceptable year of the Lord.

The ethical thought of William Pinson is both congruent and coherent. Predicated on the centrality of the Bible, it espouses a view of humans as transformable, of a church that is intentional, of institutions that are viable, of failure from which there is recovery, and of evangelism and ethics that affirm that faith without works is a bankruptcy of the biblical message and model. When integrated into a consistent whole, the thought of Pinson demands a style of proclamation and practice that is reflective of the early church model and yet instructive to the contemporary church.

The ethical thought of Pinson is biblical rather than theological or philosophical. He predicates his thought on the Bible, which he finds to be the all-sufficient guide to matters of faith and practice. The congregation is the vessel through which the biblical message is filtered and furthered. In its proclamation and by its actions, the church affirms the living Lord, who called us all into a redemptive relationship and propels us all out to transform a fractured, faithless, and failing world.

INFLUENCE AND TENABILITY OF THOUGHT
The significance of William Pinson's thoughts can be noted in the impact which he continues to have in local churches, mission enterprises, and academia, and on Christian laity as well as his continued presence in the public forum. Through his students and his writings, Pinson continues to be a significant presence in the life, ministry, and social commitments of Southern Baptist churches as well as churches of other denominations. His writings on personal decision-making and on dealing with controversial issues have a unique place in the life of youth and youth leaders. His works on discipling through biblical preaching and the local church in ministry provide a corrective to contemporary complacent churchmanship. His analysis of contemporary trends serves as a means for evaluating changing values in church and society.

Pinson's impact on missions is seen in the number of former students who serve as a part of the Christian world mission. His thoughts on race, gender, and nationality have challenged the prejudicial biases that controlled much of twentieth-century missions. His emphasis on the will of God has provided the biblical and theological basis for an understanding of God's calling and gifting of his people. His emphasis on lay involvement in the life of the church has set the foundation for lay missionary work among Southern Baptists.

Bill Pinson's tenability in academia is established by the continued use of his writing as textbooks and research material. His study of twenty centuries of preaching is a standard in both preaching and ethics classes. In order to make the thirteen-volume set more available to students and faculty alike, more than a quarter of a century after it was first published the publisher recently reprinted the entire set in paperback. As an academician Pinson continues to teach as distinguished university professor at Dallas Baptist University and distinguished visiting professor at Baylor University.

The enduring and continued influence of the thought of Bill Pinson is evidence that his principal presuppositions and biblical models speak to the need of successive generations. The replication of many of his ideas in the thoughts and writings of others is another evidence that Pinson will continue to influence congregations, academia, and missions as well as to challenge Christian laypersons to model the faith in the public forum.

BIBLIOGRAPHY

DISSERTATION

"Contemporary Southern Baptist Involvement with the State." Th.D. diss., Southwestern Baptist Theological Seminary, 1963.

BOOKS

Ambassadors and Christian Citizenship. Memphis: Brotherhood Commission, Southern Baptist Convention, 1963.

Applying the Gospel: Suggestions for Christian Social Action in a Local Church. Nashville: Broadman, 1975.

(ed.) *An Approach to Christian Ethics: The Life, Contribution, and Thought of T. B. Maston*. Nashville: Broadman, 1979.

The Biblical View of the Family. Nashville: Convention Press, 1981.

(coauth.) *Building Sermons to Strengthen Families*. Nashville: Broadman , 1983.

(coed.) *Contemporary Christian Trends: Perspectives on the Present*. Waco, Tex.: Word, 1972.

(coauth.) *Decision-Making: For Life and Leadership*. Skilltrack, vol. 10. Nashville: Moench Center for Church Leadership, Belmont University, 2001.

(coauth.) *Don't Blame the Game: An Answer to Super Star Swingers and a Look at What's Right with Sports*. Waco, Tex.: Word, 1972.

Families with Purpose. Nashville: Broadman, 1978.

(coauth.) *The Five Worlds of Youth*. Nashville: Convention Press, 1975.

(coauth.) *Growing Disciples through Preaching*. Nashville: Broadman, 1976.

How to Deal with Controversial Issues. Nashville: Broadman, 1966.

The Local Church in Ministry. Nashville: Broadman, 1973.

No Greater Challenge. Nashville: Convention Press, 1969.

Out of the Darkness: A Pageant on Religious Liberty. Memphis: Brotherhood Commission, Southern Baptist Convention, 1962.

Ready to Minister. Nashville: Broadman, 1984.

Resource Guide to Current Social Issues. Waco, Tex.: Word, 1968.

(co-auth.) *Right or Wrong? A Guide for Teeners and Their Leaders for Living by Christian Standards*. Nashville: Broadman, 1971.

Bueno o Malo? Trans. Rubén Zorzoli and Alicia de Zorzoli. El Paso: Casa Bautista de Publicaciones, 1975. [Spanish]

(coed.) *20 Centuries of Great Preaching: An Encyclopedia of Preaching*. 13 vols. Waco, Tex.: Word, 1971; rpt. under title: *A Treasury of Great Preaching: An Encyclopedia of Preaching*. Dallas: Word, 1995.

Who in the World Are Baptists, Anyway? Beliefs Important to Baptists. Dallas: BaptistWay, 2000.

The Word Topical Bible of Issues and Answers. Waco, Tex.: Word, 1981.

Youth Affirm: The Biblical View of the Family. Nashville: Convention Press, 1981.

CHAPTERS CONTRIBUTED TO BOOKS

"Applying Christian Principles to the Problems of Society." In *The 70's: Opportunities for Your Church*, ed. James H. Daniel and Elaine Dickson, 88–111. Nashville: Convention Press, 1969.

"Christians Coping with Extremism." In *Extremism Left and Right*, ed. Elmer S. West, Jr., 132–52. Grand Rapids: Eerdmans, 1972.

"A Historical View of Christians and Peace." In *Peace! Peace!*, ed. Foy D. Valentine, 48–63. Waco, Tex.: Word, 1967.

"Issues and Priorities." In *Toward Creative Urban Strategy*, ed. George A. Torney, 43–55. Waco, Tex.: Word, 1970.

"Moral Crisis, U.S.A." In *The Cutting Edge: Critical Questions for Contemporary Christians*, ed. H. C. Brown, Jr., vol. 2, 119–30. Waco, Tex.: Word, 1969.

"Nationalism and Christian Allegiance." In *Baptists and the American Experience*, ed. James E. Wood, Jr., 225–33. Valley Forge, Pa.: Judson, 1976.

"A People-Centered Approach to Ministry." In *The Practice of Ministry: A Sourcebook*, ed. Doran C. McCarty and George W. Knight, 48–56. Nashville: Seminary Extension of the Southern Baptist Seminaries, 1995.

"A Plan of Action." In *The Gambling Menace*, ed. Ross Coggins, 106–28. Nashville: Broadman, 1966.

"Population Problems." In *Is It Moral to Modify Man?*, ed. Claude A. Frazier, 49–64. Springfield, Ill.: Charles C. Thomas, 1973.

"Preaching on Race Relations from 1954 to the Late 1960's." In *The Cutting Edge: Critical Questions for Contemporary Christians*, ed. H. C. Brown, Jr., vol. 1, 112–29. Waco, Tex.: Word, 1969.

"The Pulpit and Race Relations, 1954–1966." In *Preaching in American History: Selected Issues in the American Pulpit, 1630–1967*, ed. DeWitte Holland, 375–90. Nashville: Abingdon Press, 1969.

"The Pulpit and Race Relations, 1954–1966." In *Sermons in American History: Selected Issues in the American Pulpit, 1630–1967*, ed. DeWitte Holland, 502–6. Nashville: Abingdon Press, 1971.

"Theme Interpretation: The Witnessing-Giving Life." In *Witnessing Giving Life*, 11–26. Nashville: Stewardship Commission, Southern Baptist Convention, 1988.

"The Total Dimension of Renewal." In *Resources for Renewal*, ed. George E. Worrell, 53–62. Nashville: Broadman, 1975.

"The Visionary Leader: Contemporary Approaches to Christian Leadership." In *Evangelism for a Changing World: Essays in Honor of Roy J. Fish*, ed. Timothy K. Beougher and Alvin L. Reid, 51–65. Wheaton, Ill.: Harold Shaw, 1995.

"Why All Christians Are Called into Politics." In *Politics: A Guidebook for Christians*, ed. James M. Dunn, 9–28. Dallas: Christian Life Commission, Baptist General Convention of Texas, 1970.

JOURNAL ARTICLES

"The Church Creative: An Overview." *Southwestern Journal of Theology* 17 (Spring 1975): 3–8.

"The Contemporary Moral Crisis: A Christian Perspective." *Southwestern Journal of Theology* n.s. 7 (April 1965): 31–44.

"Texas Baptist Contributions to Ethics: The Life and Influence of T. B. Maston." *Baptist History and Heritage* 33 (Autumn 1998): 7–20.

MISCELLANEOUS

Disciple's Study Bible: New International Version. Nashville: Holman, 1988. S.v. "James, Introduction to."

"In Defense of Separation of Church and State." *Baptist Standard*, 12 February 1969, 8–9.

"Movies and Morals." *Baptist Standard*, 19 July 1961, 10–11.

F. B. Huey, Jr.
(1925–)
Old Testament

23

John L. Harris

BIOGRAPHY

F. B. Huey, Jr. was born in Denton, Texas, on 12 January 1925. After graduating from Denton High School in 1940, he attended the University of Texas at Austin, graduating with a B.B.A. degree in 1945. At the age of twenty-four, he began seeking for "peace of mind" and in a Paul-like experience made a commitment to follow Christ. This conversion also included a call, but although God's direction was clear, Huey refused. After five years of disobedience to God, Huey dedicated himself to pursuing a theological education; this five-year state of resistance combined with his act of obedience formed the basis of his theological thought. Huey had married Nonna Lee Turner of Longview, Texas, in 1950, and their children are Mary Anne, Linda Kaye, and William David.

Huey enrolled at Southwestern Baptist Theological Seminary and earned a B.D. degree in 1958 (updated to M.Div. in 1973) and a Th.D. degree in 1962 (updated to Ph.D. in 1979). He served as pastor of two Baptist churches in Denton County. He served as a missionary in Rio de Janeiro from 1961 to 1966, under the direction of the Southern Baptist Convention's Foreign Mission Board, and from 1962 to 1965 he was a professor of Old Testament at the South Brazil Baptist Theological Seminary. While in Brazil, he also served as pastor of the Fundação Baptist Church, Rio de Janeiro, during 1964–65.

287

In 1965, he returned to Southwestern on furlough to teach as a guest professor. At the invitation of Ralph Lee Smith and the seminary administration, Huey left the mission field and began his teaching career at Southwestern. After ten years of productive ministry, Huey experienced a life crisis in 1975. Since the beginning of his academic career, he had been striving to be known as an intellectual, with the primary goal of being accepted by the community of scholars. His dissatisfaction with this focus caused him to reexamine his theological thought. During this period of self-turmoil, he began a period of "theological realignment" and made a determination to be obedient to his theological nature and advocate theological thought corresponding to his conservative convictions. Huey taught until retirement in 1990, having served also as associate dean for the Ph.D. degree in the School of Theology from 1984 to 1990. He continued teaching as an adjunct professor until 1995.

WRITINGS

Huey's interpretive method and thought are clearly seen in his published works. In his writings, he is ever conscious of the layperson, or the "nonprofessional." He is careful to use language that communicates, for he believes that there is too much biblical interpretation that reflects the effort of scholars to write for other scholars. One of his great concerns is that the information gained by the educated is all too rarely communicated to the great masses of Christians.

"Capital Punishment." Huey's first published effort came in 1964.[1] In an article addressing the issue of capital punishment, he detailed its history, reaching as far into the past as the ancient laws of Hammurabi. Within the dialogue with the text, Huey presented the reader with the option that functions as both the core of his theology and the motivation that drives him as both a scholar and a Christian: obedience to God and the stated word. His final assertion was that when one appeals to the Bible as a defense for capital punishment, that person has a misplaced emphasis and an untenable exegesis.

Exodus. In 1977, Huey published his first book in the *Bible Study Commentary* series. Although limited in space, this work presents solid, conservative exegesis of the book of Exodus. Of particular value is the thorough outline of the biblical book. Consistent with Huey's approach to Scripture, he examined the historical setting and explained several Hebrew terms and phrases. His concern for practical application is seen in the "lessons" and at the end of each chapter with the inclusion of activities and questions under the heading of "For Further Study." Although the book of Exodus lends itself to an obedience/disobedience theme, Huey clearly focused on its value. He presented the obedience of the Hebrew midwives, the disobedience of Moses' killing the Egyptian, Moses' disobedience to God's commission, Pharaoh's disobedience, Israel's obedience to the Passover instructions, Israel's obedience/disobedience along the way to Mount Sinai, Israel's acceptance of and obedience to covenant conditions, the disobedience of Israel relating to the golden calf, and the obedience of the people in constructing the tabernacle.

Yesterday's Prophets for Today's World. Published in 1980, this work exemplifies Huey's methodology, his theological focus on obedience, and practical and ministerial concerns. This work was written for the layperson and is a good introductory study of the Hebrew prophets. It is both readable and practical. Of particular interest are his discussions on obedience and faithfulness.

Numbers. Huey's second book in the *Bible Study Commentary* series was published in 1981. Similar to his previous study on Exodus, this book is a solid, conservative exegetical interpretation of the book of Numbers. The commentary begins with an introduction, including a thorough outline of the biblical book. It does not take long for him to state his central theological concern: "Perhaps the most important lessons of the book are that God acts for the ultimate good of His people, demands obedience at all times, and is able to accomplish His purposes in spite of human sins."[2]

Jeremiah. Huey's third and final contribution to the *Bible Study Commentary* series is a commentary on the book of Jeremiah, published in 1981. In this work, as with the previous ones in this series, the grammatical-historical approach with a focus upon practical application is evident. Also detectable is his emphasis on obedience. In the introduction Huey stated, "God required only that Jeremiah obey Him by proclaiming His messages. An obedient servant of the Lord is not held accountable for the lack of response from those who hear him."[3]

Ezekiel-Daniel. This work, published in 1983, is Huey's only contribution to the *Layman's Bible Book Commentary* series and is written for the layperson. Each book in this series has as its basic purpose to show how the text was understood within the Hebrew community and how the truths of the text can be applied today. Huey accomplishes this by synthesizing linguistic study, historical context, archaeological data, and theological insight. It does not take the reader long to be made aware of Huey's theological trademark theme of obedience. In the introduction, Huey says of Ezekiel, "He was a man of rigid self-discipline and obedience to God's orders."[4]

"Esther." This section in *The Expositor's Bible Commentary*, appearing in 1988, is Huey's first major published contribution that had the goal of being a reference work providing pastors and other Bible students with a comprehensive and scholarly tool for the exposition of Scripture. The commentary contains an impressive exegesis of the Hebrew text, including textual notes and begins with a thorough introduction of ten parts: background, authorship, date, purpose, literary form, text, place in the canon, special problems, theological values, bibliography, and outline. Although the bibliography and outline are excellent, the real value of this introduction lies with the discussion of "the moral and ethical practices" provoked by the book of Esther. Within this presentation the reader is confronted with a departure from the conventional interpretation of the book. The characters are judged over and against the theme of obedience and are found deficient; not a single one exhibits noble qualities.[5] Concerning Esther, she was willing to hide her identity in order to become queen and did not appear to be reluctant to marry a Gentile; she showed no mercy when Haman pled for his life and even demanded that his sons be hanged; not content with deliverance of her people, she and Mordecai, with the king's permission, wrote a decree authorizing their people to slaughter and plunder their enemies.

Huey also raised some interesting questions: Should "God's silence . . . be interpreted as evidence that the people were working out their own affairs without consulting him [i.e., *disobedience*]?"; "Is it possible that Mordecai's pride [i.e., *disobedience*] is the key for understanding the events of [the book of] Esther?"; "Should Esther have refused to marry a pagan Gentile [i.e., *be obedient*]?"; "If she had, could not God have found another way to deliver his people?" Huey proposed that the book's "real message may prove to be that God's people are prone to use the same means as ungodly people for achieving their goals rather than taking a bold step of faith [i.e., *obedience*] that God will work out his purposes without human initiative . . . least of all resorting to immoral acts in a crisis situation."[6] The consideration of such questions and the answers that Huey gave provide the reader with an insightful, new understanding of the book of Esther.

Obedience: The Biblical Key to Happiness. Although not the typical academic publication, this book, published in 1990, more than any other of Huey's writings, reveals his heart, mind, soul, and thought. In a real sense, the book is an autobiography, presenting truths learned during his journey through life, and the message is clear: obedience to God is the key to happiness. In one instance, Huey allowed the reader entrance into his private life by telling that his awareness of the centrality of obedience for the Christian life came about unexpectedly as he was reading the autobiography of Helen Keller. This moment in time motivated him to begin a serious study of the biblical teachings on obedience, and as a result, he became firmly convinced that obedience is a neglected biblical emphasis in practice, though the principle is almost always affirmed. The results of this personal Bible study became the basis of the book.[7]

As the pages are read, one gets the sense that this is not simply a scholarly endeavor. In an echo of his life, Huey wrote:

> Obedience is the best evidence of trust in God. We make excuses for not living a consistent Christian life, for not answering God's call, for not going to the mission field, or for not giving up something that seems important to us. However, the real root of our problem is that we do not really have confidence that God's ways and plans for us are better than ours.[8]

In yet another section, Huey stated:

> I resisted for almost six years what I knew was God's certain call for me to enter the ministry. During that time I found all kinds of convincing reasons why I should not be a preacher, but I never was at peace with myself during those years, and they were largely unproductive years. Only when I finally said: "Lord, I am willing to do whatever You want me to do with my life" did that elusive peace and inner tranquility become a reality. Obedience truly is the gateway to happiness![9]

The book closes with words that could easily be viewed as a summary of Huey's theology and thought: *"Principle: Obedience to God is the key to finding happiness. Happy are those who obey God, for they are the ones who one day will hear, 'Well done, good and faithful servant.'"*[10]

Jeremiah-Lamentations. Huey's final written contribution is found in *The New American Commentary* series and was published in 1993. This series focuses on the intrinsic theological and exegetical concerns of each biblical book and engages the range of issues raised in contemporary biblical scholarship, having as its purpose to be a theological commentary rather than simply a text-critical, expositional, or devotional one. Huey's work is easily readable and serves as a bridge between the scholar and the layperson. It is built on the foundation of the grammatical-historical method of interpretation, thorough research, commendable exegesis, and applicable exposition. As with most of Huey's writings, the reader is confronted with the theme of obedience. Commenting on Jeremiah the prophet, Huey stated, "His is the test of obedience. God only required that Jeremiah obey him by proclaiming his message. Jeremiah was not responsible for a favorable response or lack of response. One who is an obedient servant of the Lord today is not held accountable for lack of response from those who hear his message."[11]

THOUGHT AND INFLUENCE

Rooted in a grammatical-historical methodology (i.e., seeking to determine the truth of the text grammatically, by applying rules of grammar and syntax, and historically, by determining the *Sitz im Leben*), Huey's theology includes *biblicism*, the theology of the text; *mission*, the equipping, encouraging, and challenging of Christians and the communication of the gospel to non-Christians; and *community*, linking the present people of faith with their Christian heritage. The content of Huey's thought may be summarized as a sustained commentary on the following proposition: Christian faith, happiness, and the abundant life are grounded on and sustained through obedience to God.

Pastoral work has always been important to Huey personally, and it has clearly impacted his theological thought.[12] The vast majority of Huey's writings reflect a concern for the faith of the

Christian community rather than an individual endeavor whose primary context and audience are academic. He is concerned with the communication of lay theology understood within a practical and ethical framework, with obedience serving as the center. The task is to assist the faith community to discover its theological identity, with the result that there are responsible and moral actions that contribute to the world's good. Huey's works are an attempt to draw Christians who are not professional theologians into the task of thinking deeply into Christian faith for the sake of living that faith more effectively.

Huey's thought and method of interpretation have directly influenced countless lives, particularly students whose theological heritage is Southwestern. Whether writing, lecturing to a class, overseeing a seminar, or preaching in a church, he displayed a brilliant intellect, unparalleled linguistic skills, and diligent work habits. He was constantly encouraging and challenging students to formulate and express their individual interpretations, never insisting on the adoption of his own opinions above all others. He was quick to praise and offered correction gently. For all his academic accomplishments, F. B. Huey, Jr., will most likely be remembered by those who know him best for his humility and unfettered obedience.

BIBLIOGRAPHY

DISSERTATION

"The Hebrew Concept of Life after Death in the Old Testament." Th.D. diss., Southwestern Baptist Theological Seminary, 1962.

BOOKS

Exodus. Bible Study Commentary. Grand Rapids: Zondervan, 1977.
    Chu Ai Ji Ji: Yan Jing Dao Du. Trans Yi-yi Hu. Hong Kong: Tien Dao Publishing House, Ltd., 1983. [Chinese]
Helps for Beginning Hebrew Students. Fort Worth: Alphagraphics, 1981; rev. ed., 1988; rev. ed.: Fort Worth: Scripta Publishing, Inc., 1990.
Jeremiah. Bible Study Commentary. Grand Rapids: Zondervan, 1981.
    Ye Li Mi Shu: Yan Jing Dao Du. Trans. Yi-yi Hu. Hong Kong: Tien Dao Publishing House, Ltd., 1982. [Chinese]
Jeremiah-Lamentations. New American Commentary, vol. 16. Nashville: Broadman, 1993.
Layman's Bible Book Commentary: Ezekiel-Daniel, vol. 12. Nashville: Broadman, 1983.
Numbers. Bible Study Commentary. Grand Rapids: Zondervan, 1981.
    Min Shu Ji: Yan Jing Dao Du. Trans. Yi-yi Hu. Hong Kong: Tien Dao Publishing House, Ltd., 1982. [Chinese]
Obedience: The Key to Biblical Happiness. Nashville: Broadman, 1990.

(coauth.) *A Student's Dictionary for Biblical and Theological Studies: A Handbook of Special and Technical Terms*. Grand Rapids: Zondervan, 1983.

Yesterday's Prophets for Today's World. Nashville: Broadman, 1980.

    Chen Xian Qi Ho Hua Xian Zhi. Trans. Yin-zun Lin. Taipei: Campus Evangelistic Fellowship, 1991. [Chinese]

CHAPTERS CONTRIBUTED TO BOOKS

(coauth.) "Are the 'Sons of God' in Genesis 6 Angels? Yes." In *The Genesis Debate: Persistent Questions about Creation and the Flood*, ed. Ronald Youngblood, 184–209. Nashville: Thomas Nelson, 1986; rpt. Grand Rapids: Baker, 1990.

"Capital Punishment." In *Crises in Morality*, ed. C. W. Scudder, 74–90. Nashville: Broadman, 1964.

"Esther." In *The Expositor's Bible Commentary*, vol. 4, ed. Frank E. Gaebelein, 773–839. Grand Rapids: Zondervan, 1988.

"Ruth." In *The Expositor's Bible Commentary*, vol. 3, ed. Frank E. Gaebelein, 507–49. Grand Rapids: Zondervan, 1992.

JOURNAL ARTICLES

"The Ethical Treatment of Amos: Its Content and Relevance." *Southwestern Journal of Theology* 9 (Fall 1966): 57-67.

"An Exposition of Malachi." *Southwestern Journal of Theology* 30 (Fall 1987): 12–21.

"Great Themes in Isaiah 40–66." *Southwestern Journal of Theology* 11 (Fall 1968): 45–57.

"Irony as the Key to Understanding the Book of Esther." *Southwestern Journal of Theology* 32 (Summer 1990): 36-39.

"A Poesia Hebraica no Velho Testamento." *Revista Teológica* 14 (July 1964): 3–13.

BIBLE TRANSLATIONS

(cotrans.) *Holy Bible: International Children's Version*. Fort Worth: Sweet Publishing, 1986. An adult version of this Bible was published as *The Everyday Bible*.

(cotrans.) *New American Standard Bible*. Anaheim, Calif.: Foundation Press Publications, 1971.

(contrib. to) *NIV Cross Reference Bible*. Grand Rapids: Zondervan, 1984.

(cotrans.) *New International Version of the Bible*. Grand Rapids: Zondervan, 1978.

ENCYCLOPEDIA, DICTIONARY, AND RELATED ARTICLES

Baker Encyclopedia of the Bible. Ed. Walter A. Elwell. 2 vols. Grand Rapids: Baker, 1988. Vol. 1. S.v. "Ammon, Ammonites," "Color," "Curse, Cursed," "Genealogy," "Hazor," and "Hezekiah." Vol. 2. S.v. "Korah," "Moses," and "Seal."

Disciple's Study Bible: New International Version. Nashville: Holman Bible Publishers, 1988. S.v. "Zephaniah: An Introduction."

Holman Bible Dictionary. Ed. Trent C. Butler. Nashville: Holman Bible Publishers, 1991. S.v. "Ezekiel."

Holman Bible Handbook. Ed. David S. Dockery. Nashville: Holman Bible Publishers, 1992. S.v. "Creation and Flood Stories," "Old Testament Numbers," and "Patriarchs."

Illustrated Guide to the Bible. Ed. David F. Payne. London: Marshall Pickering, 1986. S.v. "Jeremiah-Lamentations."

Mercer Dictionary of the Bible. Ed. Watson E. Mills. Macon, Ga.: Mercer University Press, 1990. S.v. "Human Being" and "Book of Zechariah."

NIV Bible Commentary. Ed. Kenneth L. Barker and John Kohlenberger, III. Grand Rapids: Zondervan, 1994. S.v. "Esther" and "Ruth."

F. B. Huey, Jr.

The Zondervan Pictorial Encyclopedia of the Bible. Ed. Merrill C. Tenney. 5 vols. Grand Rapids: Zondervan, 1975. Vol. 1. S.v. "Aphek" and "Bashan." Vol. 2. S.v. "Elder in the Old Testament," "Gebal," "Gilead," and "Great Sea." Vol. 3. S.v. "Idolatry" and "Kidron." Vol. 4. S.v. "Meals," "Oil," and "Ointment." Vol. 5. S.v. "Scroll," "Seal," "Table," "Threshold," "Throne," "Tomb," "Weaving," and "Weights and Measures."

PERIODICAL ARTICLES

"Being an Idealist in a Realist's World." *Christianity Today*, 31 January 1969, 6–7.
"The Folly of Ignorance." *Baptist Standard*, 17 September 1958, 4–5.
"God's Rebel [Roger Williams]." *Baptist Standard*, 16 March 1957, 4–5.
"Murder by Proxy." *Baptist Standard*, 20 April 1960, 18–19.
"Obedience: A Neglected Doctrine." *Christianity Today*, 19 January 1968, 6–7.

Justice Conrad Anderson
(1929–)
Missions/Church History

Robert I. Garrett, Jr.

J ustice Anderson has left an indelible mark on Southwestern
Seminary and on a generation of students who serve as Baptist missionaries all around the world. Many students and
colleagues remember him most fondly for his lanky form
sauntering down the hallways, face aglow with a wide and boyish
grin, greeting one and all with warm concern. For twenty-four
years (1974–98) his was the face of missions at Southwestern.[1]
Year after year of incoming students at their orientation believed
Anderson as they heard him proclaim enthusiastically: "the heartbeat of Southwestern Seminary is missions and evangelism, evangelism and missions."

Other missions professors could perhaps lay claim to a place
in a book on the legacy of Southwesterners.[2] There was a notable
young professor named Baker James Cauthen, who left the classroom in 1939 for China and a career as missionary statesman, but
that story is chronicled elsewhere.[3] One of the most colorful figures to grace Southwestern's faculty was certainly R. Cal Guy,
who singlehandedly convinced skeptical Southern Baptists that
they really needed to listen to those Church Growth people such
as Donald McGavran.[4] Perhaps the most unsung hero in Southwestern's Department of Missions would be Ebbie C. Smith, a
contemporary of Anderson, teaching from 1975 to 1999, whose
carefully crafted courses drilled decades of students on the latest

297

methods and strategies available to improve missionary practice.[5] Still, among these Justice C. Anderson stands tall as a figure who has helped Southwestern to define and live out its purpose, both in his contribution in the classroom and in the skillful administration of multiple projects and creative programs through the World Missions Center. Yet it is as an author in both Spanish and English languages and as both missiologist and Baptist historian that Anderson's thought and contribution will likely be most widely and enduringly received.

BIOGRAPHY

Justice Conrad Anderson was born in Bay City, Texas, on 13 February 1929 to Conrad Roy Anderson and Eunice Mae Justice, the older of two brothers. He quickly showed extraordinary abilities at Baylor University, where he was president of his sophomore class. In the youth revivals that swept across the campus and nation, he met many friends who remained colleagues for life. He was attracted to hone literary skills in an M.A. in English degree by the famous Browning scholar, A. Joseph Armstong.[6] While at Baylor he met his future bride, the beautiful Mary Ann Elmore of Orange, Texas. Their home is known as an international haven of hospitality. They have four children: Sandra Jean, Timothy Justice, Bradley Pryse, and Suzanne Renée.

Justice Anderson graduated from Southwestern Seminary in 1955 with the B.D. degree. His Th.D. degree was completed in 1965, but his studies were intercalated with pastorates in Texas and the beginning of his missionary career in Argentina.[7] Multitalented and multifaceted, Anderson has rarely done only one thing at a time. Upon his missionary appointment in 1957, Anderson served as professor at the Seminario Internacional Teológico Bautista in Buenos Aires, teaching church history and homiletics. Anderson was known among Baptists throughout Argentina as an outstanding preacher, passionate missionary, statesman in Baptist meetings, and counselor and friend to all.[8]

During his twenty-four years on the faculty at Southwestern, Anderson was a frequent speaker for missionary conferences, orientation for new missionaries, and Baptist churches all over the country concerned to ignite missionary zeal. He conducted lecture series at Baptist colleges and spoke at camps and assemblies. Not surprisingly,

Anderson was a favorite lecturer at Baptist seminaries around the world.[9] Yet of very great significance has been his fifteen-year (1981–96) tenure as the director of the World Missions Center.

WRITINGS

Anderson began to make significant contributions with his doctoral dissertation. In it he surveyed comprehensively the history of church-state relations in Argentina, noted the fascinating story of the Baptist contribution, and treated the challenge faced at the time of writing in 1965.[10] In fact, he carefully chronicled the extraordinary exploits of Baptist pioneer, Pablo Besson,[11] in championing the cause of religious liberty. He discussed the difficulty with which Santiago Canclini[12] had led Baptists to resist the religious intolerance promoted by the Peronistas.[13] This research established Anderson among Baptist historians as an expert on the history of Baptists in Latin America. Later, Anderson's broad missionary interests would expand that knowledge of Baptists globally.[14]

As a writer, Anderson has made his largest contributions in the Spanish language. His most significant work is *Historia de los Bautistas*[15] in three volumes, written under his Spanish *apodo* of Justo Anderson. Herein the influence of his missionary career is obvious. Also, Anderson's other writings bear the imprint of his missionary concerns. He wrote *La Iglesia Bautista: Ensayos Eclesiológicos*,[16] which gives simple explanations of how a local Baptist church should function. Believing that "ecclesiology determines missiology," Anderson showed a continuing interest in the nature of the church.[17] *Manual de Homilética para Laicos*[18] gave simple homiletical instructions to lay preachers. Clearly Anderson wanted to resist clerical tendencies among Latin American pastors and to legitimate the work of laymen in giving church leadership.

Anderson began his *Historia* by reviewing the "ecclesiastical etymology" of the name "Baptist" and the theories of Baptist origins in the light of historiography. Anderson took seriously his role in defining denominational identity for Latin Americans. The lengthy second section of volume 1 sets out Baptist distinctives helpfully under seven principles.[19] These are so significant that they are briefly restated here.[20] (1) The Christological principle provides a starting place in the lordship of Christ.[21] (2) The biblical principle reaffirms the authority of the New Testament as the only rule for faith and practice.[22] (3) The ecclesiastical principle affirms the importance of a regenerate church membership.[23] (4) The sociological principle espouses the practice of a democratic order.[24] (5) The spiritual principle heralds Baptists as incurably committed to religious liberty.[25] (6) The political principle treats the Baptist call for separation of church and state.[26] (7) The evangelistic principle recognizes the heartbeat of Baptists in personal evangelism and world missions.[27] The elaboration of Baptist principles in Anderson's *Historia* has provided a sense of denominational identity to a generation of Latin Americans who proudly compare their own convictions with Anderson's seven Baptist distinctives as carefully as budding Calvinists compare their reflections with the five points of TULIP.

As a historian, Anderson has a perspective highly influenced by the magisterial work of Kenneth Scott Latourette in his *A History of the Expansion of Christianity*.[28] Therefore Anderson deliberately set out to trace the expansion of Baptists around the world. Volume 1 of his *Historia de los Bautistas* dedicates a third section (115–91) to "The Place of Baptists in Church History." Here his conviction becomes clear that Baptist history cannot be an intramural exercise in today's world. Baptists must see themselves playing out their destiny on a global stage and in relation to other Christians.[29]

In the same way volume 2 shows clear influence of this global perspective in its structure. After a treatment of "immediate precursors" to Baptists (part 1, 15–87), Anderson considered in turn "Baptists in Great Britain" (part 2, 89–130), "Baptists in the USA" (part 3, 131–245), "Baptists in Continental Europe" (part 3, 247–361), and finally "Baptists in Canada, Australia and New Zealand" (part 5, 363–85). Volume 3 treated the global expansion of the Baptist people beyond the Anglo-Saxon world. Anderson considered the history and situation country by country across Latin America, Central America, the Caribbean islands, Africa, Asia, and Oceania.[30]

His magnum opus in three volumes, *Historia de los Bautistas*, has yet to be translated into English.[31] On a recent trip to the Baptist seminary in Havana, Cuba, this author found students memorizing pages from Anderson's *Historia*. They expressed more than a little consternation on learning that students at Southwestern could not study Baptist history from so venerable a scholar.

CONTRIBUTIONS

Confidence in God's Hand on Baptists

As an historian, Justice Anderson points out repeatedly that the successes and triumphs of Baptists are in no way the result of their deep commitment, their broad perspective, their high vision, their inherent abilities, or their "innate magnanimity." God has continually chosen to use Baptists in spite of themselves. Anderson opines: "Cooperation in missions is not something that we creatively developed in moments of spiritual illumination; to the contrary, it has gradually been discovered over a long period of time as we struggled against our pragmatic provincialism and our doctrinal fundamentalism."[32]

On first encounter this historical axiom may seem almost trite. In Anderson's writings, however, this principle appears again and again, representing a bedrock conviction, not a cliché. It certainly describes reality among Baptists better than other explanations. There must be a divine providence that aids and assists the people called Baptists, who find themselves used by God in spite of their best efforts to the contrary.

A Global View of Baptist History

A reading of Anderson's *Historia de los Bautistas* readily shows that he perceives Baptists on the stage of world history. The denomination has interconnections with all other facets of human life, so that Baptist history is correctly viewed as a concentric circle, nestled within other circles such as the "history of Christianity," "religious history," and "world history."

Anderson repeatedly invites Baptists to leave behind "their fierce individualism and provincial ecclesiology."[33] Like Winston Crawley, Anderson sees Baptists as coming of age after World War II.[34] The narrow sectarian views of earlier times must necessarily be discarded for a broader vision. Anderson lays out a global vision required for missiological thinking. Traditionally, in the Missionary Movement the "First World" of USA and NATO allies has been the *protagonist*, whereas the atheistic ideologies of the Soviet Union and Warsaw Pact countries ("Second World") put them in the role of *antagonist*. The "Third World" of nonaligned and often underdeveloped countries has been the *recipient* for missions. Now, the presence of strong

Christian movements in a "Fourth World," China, with one-fourth of the world's population, is demonstrating that the earlier work of missionaries had not been in vain. A "Zero" world was also coming into focus: that of "'unreached people groups'" whose ethnicity and language separate them entirely from gospel witness. Curiously, since the fall of Communism, the antagonist has turned into a very fertile mission field, while the traditional bastions of Christendom are rapidly becoming a spiritual desert.[35]

Missionary Impulse as the "Tie That Binds" Baptists Together

For Anderson, "the foreign missions challenge has constrained Southern Baptists to be a world-class denomination . . . Without doubt, the missions mandate has saved the convention from losing itself to racial prejudice, political provincialism, doctrinal pettiness, intellectual obscurantism, and economic stinginess."[36] Both as Baptist historian and missiologist Anderson sees as crucial the fact that Southern Baptists "have the largest singly-organized missionary enterprise in the history of Christianity."[37]

Anderson noted on the 150th anniversary of the Southern Baptist Convention that its motive for being and the concerns for its formation in 1845 had basically to do with the practicalities of implementing a missions program.[38] Indeed, "the missionary motif has been our 'northstar'" and "the missionary impulse has been our integrating center which became the occasion of our corporate life—the only cement which could hold us together in the midst of our amazing diversity and our occasional controversies."[39] In 1976 the challenge presented by Bold Mission Thrust inspired "evaluation and reform to many areas of SBC life." "Centered around an overarching goal to share the gospel with the whole world, the total convention program was revamped and redirected."[40]

Southwestern Seminary and the Missionary Impulse

The importance of the missionary impulse has been doubly true for Southwestern Seminary. Anderson summed up the driving principles of his own career at Southwestern when in his 1997 Founder's Day address[41] he expounded the founding principle of Southwestern. "Southwestern's 'dominant theme,' its 'integrating idea,' its 'energizing force' is 'the missions motif.'"[42]

He chronicled the perspective of Southwestern's founders, for whom "theological study sprang from missions praxis."[43] B. H. Carroll[44] and L. R. Scarborough founded Southwestern from a strong populist perspective. For them "the founding of SWBTS was the fulfillment of a divine mission—an errand in the wilderness. SWBTS would be a theological agency, teaching and practicing missions in a great mission field; a place where frontier preachers and missionaries, as well as promising scholars, would be prepared for evangelistic mission . . . while on mission!"[45] Their new kind of theological education has been "upheld in various ways by subsequent presidents."[46] Since both Carroll and Scarborough were "autodidacts,"[47] "theirs was a theology of the road, not of the balcony[48]—a theology of mission."

Anderson's thesis is reinforced by the fact that the last three presiding officers of the FMB (IMB) have been Southwesterners.[49] To this should be added the more impressive fact that a consistent average of slightly more than 50 percent of all Southern Baptist foreign missionaries appointed during the last three decades have studied at Southwestern.[50]

Acceptance of Missiology as a Legitimate Academic Discipline

Upon coming to the Southwestern faculty, Anderson identified with national efforts to advance missiology as a legitimate academic discipline within theological education.[51] Anderson noted that "the formal study of missions in theological education" has "not always been welcome in Protestant theological circles."[52] At Southwestern Seminary a glance at the missions course offerings in the catalog will suffice to show the extent to which his commitment to missiology is woven into the fabric of the present approach to the discipline. Anderson, with Ebbie Smith's help, also created the first M.A. degree offered at Southwestern, the M.A. in Missiology, to assist mid-career missionaries in advancing their academic training with the newest strategic tools for the practice of their profession.

The commitment to missiology as discipline will be most clearly seen in his role as co-editor of and contributor to the textbook *Missiology: An Introduction to the Foundations, History and Strategies of World Missions*.[53] The introductory chapter which he contributed defines missiology, describes its contours and relations to other academic disciplines, and outlines its task.[54]

The World Missions Center

Justice Anderson understood the significance of "networking" and "mobilization" before these terms became popular in missionary circles. He returned to Southwestern from Argentina determined to make Fort Worth a significant hub for Baptist life and the missionary enterprise. Recognizing that the structures and offices inherited from academic life were not within themselves capable of serving Southwestern Seminary's role as a protagonist for the missionary enterprise, Anderson worked with the seminary administration to establish the World Missions Center. This coordinating center has had an incalculable effect on the seminary and beyond in the life of the denomination. In the most recent reaccreditation study, Southwestern received commendation for its global outlook, almost all of the programs mentioned being the product of Anderson's years of creative labor through the World Missions Center.

The Priority of the Grassroots

As Baptist historian and missiologist Anderson saw that the secret power of Christianity always lay in the rank-and-file, ordinary believers who dedicated themselves to be soldiers of the cross. His writings in Baptist history repeatedly show the dangers of the centralizing tendency, of ecclesiastical authority committed to uniformity. He consistently saw that the cutting edge of Christianity was in the lives of simple saints who by their practice of missions and evangelism advanced Christ's kingdom. Everything should be done to support and foster that spirit; for Anderson, nothing should be done to quench it.

With this commitment to the grassroots, Anderson wrote his *Manual de Homilética para Laicos*[55] not for pastors but for laymen. He fostered one of the first groups of bivocational pastors. In his later years as a missionary in Argentina, he was widely known for promoting Theological Education by Extension, which proposed to take the education to church workers in the field rather than requiring students to come to a residential seminary to study.[56]

Protagonist of a Cooperative Spirit

In a generation of Baptists characterized by acrimony, Anderson was unswervingly committed to bridge-building and positive statements. All the writings and demeanor of Justice Anderson show him to have a solicitous and cheerful attitude towards others, even those who might take positions conflicting with his own. Ever the peacemaker, Anderson would always seek to build a consensus on a solid foundation in order to proceed ahead. Although in his later career he was disheartened by the directions of his beloved seminary and mission board, he chose to work positively within the framework of denominational realities. As such, his commitment to somehow "get along" with any and all, though not compromising his most strongly held convictions, should stand as a model for future generations of Christians, especially Baptists.

BIBLIOGRAPHY

THESIS AND DISSERTATION

"Church-State Problems among Baptists in Argentina in the Light of the Historic Baptist Perspective."
Th.D. diss., Southwestern Baptist Theological Seminary, 1965.
"Proverb Lore in Alexander Barclay's *Ship of Fools*." M.A. thesis, Baylor University, 1951.

BOOKS

(ed.) *El Crecimiento de las Iglesias Bautistas Argentinas*. Buenos Aires: Seminario Internacional
Teológico Bautista, 1969.
Historia de los Bautistas, Tomo 1: Sus Bases y Principios. El Paso: Casa Bautista de Publicaciones,
1978.
Historia de los Bautistas, Tomo 2: Sus Comienzos y Desarrollo en Europa y Norteamérica. El Paso:
Casa Bautista de Publicaciones, 1990.
Historia de los Bautistas, Tomo 3: Sus Comienzos y Desarrollo en Asia, Africa, y América Latina. El
Paso: Casa Bautista de Publicaciones, 1990.
La Iglesia Bautista: Ensayos Eclesiológicos. Buenos Aires: Junta Bautista de Publicaciones, 1974; El
Paso: Casa Bautista de Publicaciones, 1987.
Manual de Homilética para Laicos. Buenos Aires: Junta Bautista de Publicaciones, 1973; El Paso: Casa
Bautista de Publicaciones, 1987.
(coed.) *Missiology: An Introduction to the Foundations, History, and Strategies of World Missions*.
Nashville: Broadman and Holman, 1998.

BOOK AND CHAPTER TRANSLATED

(trans.) Juan C. Varetto, "Heroes and Martyrs of the Missionary Enterprise." In *Classics of Christian Missions*, ed. Francis M. DuBose, 403–9. Nashville: Broadman, 1979.
(coed. and cotrans.) *Manual de Eclesiología*. El Paso: Casa Bautista de Publicaciones, 1987. (Translation of H. E. Dana and L. M. Sipes, *A Manual of Ecclesiology*. 2d rev. ed. Kansas City, Kan.: Central Seminary Press, 1944.) [Spanish]

CHAPTERS CONTRIBUTED TO BOOKS

"Episodic North American Influence on Certain Baptist Beginnings in Latin America." In *The Lord's Free
People in a Free Land: Essays in Baptist History in Honor of Robert Baker*, ed. William R. Estep,
171–94. Fort Worth: School of Theology, Southwestern Baptist Theological Seminary, 1976.
"The Nature of Churches." In *The Birth of Churches: A Biblical Basis for Church Planting*, ed.
Talmadge R. Amberson, 48–72. Nashville: Broadman, 1979.
"Relación histórica de los Bautistas con las Sectas y con los Movimientos." In *Sectas y Movimientos en
América Latina*, ed. Daniel Carro, 95–105. Buenos Aires: Asociación Bautista Argentina de
Publicaciones, 1992.

JOURNAL ARTICLES

"Changing Patterns of World Mission Work." *Baptist History and Heritage* 27 (July 1992): 14–24.
"The Church and Liberation Theology." *Southwestern Journal of Theology* 19 (Spring 1977): 17–36.
"Foreign Missions as Shaper and Reflector of Southern Baptist Life." *Baptist History and Heritage* 29
(October 1994): 14–25.
"The Missions Motif: Southwestern's Integrating Principle." *Southwestern Journal of Theology* 41
(Spring 1999): 70–85.
"Old Baptist Principles Reset." *Southwestern Journal of Theology* 31 (Spring 1989): 5–12.

"Pablo Besson: The Argentine Roger Williams." *Quarterly Review* 33 (October–November–December 1972): 21–30.

"Santiago Canclini: The Argentine Isaac Backus." *Quarterly Review* 33 (April–May–June 1973), 56–68.

"The Southern Baptist Involvement in Spanish-Speaking South America." *Baptist History and Heritage* 3 (July 1968): 115–23.

"Southern Baptist Missions: *Quo Vadis?*" *Southwestern Journal of Theology* 40 (Summer 1998): 28–48.

"William Carey: A Bicentennial Tribute." *Southwestern Journal of Theology* 35 (Fall 1992): 40–44.

DICTIONARY AND ENCYCLOPEDIA ARTICLES

Comentario Bíblico Mundo Hispano. El Paso: Editorial Mundo Hispano, 1993. Vol. 22. S.v. "El Ministerio en el Nuevo Testamento."

Evangelical Dictionary of World Missions. Ed. A. Scott Moreau. Grand Rapids: Baker, 2000. S.v. "Southern Baptist Convention—International Mission Board," "Theological Education by Extension," and "World Missionary Conference (Edinburgh, 1910)."

Encyclopedia of Southern Baptists. 4 vols. Nashville: Broadman, 1958–82. Vol. 4. S. v. "Conferences, Student Missions."

CURRICULUM RESEARCH

Contextualizing the Gospel. Ministry Multiplication. Richmond, Va.: International Centre for Excellence in Leadership, International Mission Board of the Southern Baptist Convention, 2000.

Crossing Cultures: Living Incarnationally, Thinking Missiologically. Ministry Multiplication. Richmond, Va.: International Centre for Excellence in Leadership, International Mission Board of the Southern Baptist Convention, 1999.

What Kind of Church? Building a Biblical Ecclesiology for Culturally Relevant Church Planting. Ministry Multiplication. International Centre for Excellence in Leadership, International Mission Board of the Southern Baptist Convention, 1999.

MISCELLANEOUS

"Is Missions Optional?" *Baptist Program*, October 1987, 7–8.

"What about the Heathen?" *Baptist Standard*, 7 December 1994, 8–9.

William Jensen Reynolds

(1920–)
Hymnology/Church Music

David W. Music

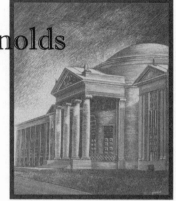

BIOGRAPHY

William J. Reynolds was born on 2 April 1920 in Atlantic, Iowa. Educated at Oklahoma Baptist University, Southwest Missouri State College (B.A., 1942), Southwestern Baptist Theological Seminary (M.S.M., 1945), North Texas State College (now the University of North Texas, M.M., 1946), and George Peabody College for Teachers (Ed.D., 1961), beginning in 1946 he served as full-time minister of music at the First Baptist Church of Ardmore and the First Baptist Church of Oklahoma City, Oklahoma. In 1947, Reynolds married Mary Lou Robertson, who was also on the staff of First Church, Oklahoma City, and they became the parents of two sons, Tim and Kirk.

In 1955 Reynolds joined the Church Music Department of the Baptist Sunday School Board, Nashville, Tennessee, where he served as an editor of musical and literary materials. He was named director of the Church Music Department in 1971, with responsibilities for overseeing both the editorial and consulting sections of the department and representing it both within the Sunday School Board and to its outside constituency.

Reynolds began his teaching career at Southwestern Seminary in 1980 as a guest professor. He was elected to the full-time faculty in the following year and, in 1994, was named Distinguished Professor of Church Music. Reynolds retired from the full-time faculty in

1998 but continued to teach on a part-time basis for several semesters following his official retirement.

In addition to his ongoing responsibilities as a church musician, denominational leader, and educator, Reynolds has been active in many other venues and received numerous honors and awards. He served as music director for meetings of the Baptist World Alliance (1960, 1975, 1980, 1985), Southern Baptist Convention (1958, 1972–86), and Baptist Youth World Congress (1958, 1963, 1968). He was elected to a two-year term as president of the Hymn Society of America (now the Hymn Society in the United States and Canada) in 1978–80 and was named a fellow of the Hymn Society in 1992. He also filled a term on the editorial advisory board of the society's journal, *The Hymn* (1998–2001). Reynolds received the W. Hines Sims Achievement Award from the Southern Baptist Church Music Conference (1971), the Music Alumni Award from the University of North Texas (1972), a Distinguished Alumnus Award from Southwestern Seminary (1975), the Distinguished Service Award from the School of Church Music at Southwestern Seminary (1991), the Distinguished Leadership Award from the Baptist Sunday School Board (1998), and an ASCAP Foundation Lifetime Achievement Award (1999). He has also been a leader in Sacred Harp singing circles, founding the annual Southwestern Seminary Sacred Harp Sing, and is highly respected as a leader of congregational singing.

WRITINGS

The writings of William J. Reynolds are both extensive and varied. Although it is his books and scholarly articles in hymnology that will be the primary focus of this study, it must be remembered that he was also a prolific composer and arranger of church music in various media and that he published numerous articles for popular consumption in magazines, journals, and newspapers.

Reynolds's first book was *A Survey of Christian Hymnody*. In the late 1950s, a fellow doctoral student who was working on his dissertation at Peabody College undertook a survey of colleges offering an academic major or degree program in church music. After visiting these schools, the student and his major professor, Irving Wolfe, became aware of the lack of an adequate textbook for courses in hymnology. Reynolds, with the approval of Wolfe—who was also his major professor—chose the writing of such a textbook for his doctoral dissertation. This was published in 1963 by Holt, Rinehart and Winston as *A Survey of Christian Hymnody*.

The year following, Reynolds's second book was issued, *Hymns of Our Faith: A Handbook for the Baptist Hymnal* (1964). Hymnal companions typically provide information on each text, tune, author, and composer represented in a particular hymnal; *Hymns of Our Faith* served this function for the 1956 *Baptist Hymnal*. Reynolds was in a unique position to do this work because of his educational background, his position in the Church Music Department of the Baptist Sunday School Board, and his service on the committee that had prepared *Baptist Hymnal*.

A publication of a different sort was *Christ and the Carols* (1967). This volume was designed for the lay reader rather than the hymnological student, pastor, or professional church musician as his previous books had been. *Christ and the Carols* was written in an engaging style that was suitable for reading at a single sitting.

During the decade of the 1970s Reynolds issued three book-length works, the first of which was a collection of *The Songs of B. B. McKinney* (1974) with an introduction by the compiler. For some time, Reynolds had been working with McKinney's widow on collecting and cataloging the music of Southern Baptists' most beloved gospel hymn writer. This collection of McKinney hymns was one result of that effort.

The other two books of the 1970s were directly related to the publication of the *Baptist Hymnal (1975 Edition)*, for which Reynolds served as general editor and chair of the hymnal committee. In the year of the hymnal's publication, Reynolds put out a small volume titled *Congregational Singing* (1975), which gave suggestions for making hymn singing more effective and vibrant. While many of the suggestions would work well with any body of song, the book was keyed to the *Baptist Hymnal* (1975). In the following year (1976), Reynolds's *Companion to Baptist Hymnal* was published, performing for the 1975 *Baptist Hymnal* what his earlier *Hymns of Our Faith* had done for the 1956 book.

By 1980, Reynolds was widely recognized as the foremost Southern Baptist leader of and writer on hymnody. In that year, however, he demonstrated his interest in other areas of music ministry by compiling *Building an Effective Music Ministry* (1980) with the assistance of Baptist Sunday School Board Church Music

Department staff. This sought to give guidance in administration and resources for the church music program as a whole. *Christian Hymnody: A Study Guide* (1983) was written at the request of the Seminary Extension Department to serve as a textbook for seminary extension classes. Reynolds's continuing interest in the work of B. B. McKinney found expression in a 1986 article on "The Contributions of B. B. McKinney to Southern Baptist Church Music."

In the fall of 1979, Reynolds began writing a weekly column titled "History of Hymns" for secular newspapers. (At the time of this writing the column still appears in the weekly *United Methodist Reporter* and monthly *Hoosier United Methodist Reporter*). In 1990, he collected many of these into a book, *Songs of Glory: Stories of 300 Great Hymns and Gospel Songs*. Two years later he was involved in another project aimed at the lay reader, Phillip Keveren's *The New Illustrated Family Hymn Book* (1992), for which he wrote the introduction and background to the hymns. He was also a major contributor to the companion for the 1991 *Baptist Hymnal, Handbook to the Baptist Hymnal* (1992), writing an introductory essay on "Baptist Hymnody in America," as well as numerous contributions on individual texts, tunes, authors, and composers.

The mid-1990s found Reynolds concentrating on the local scene. At the request of James McKinney, dean of the School of Church Music, Reynolds wrote a history of the School of Church Music at Southwestern Seminary, *The Cross & the Lyre* (1994). Upon the retirement of Dean McKinney, Reynolds served as editor for and contributor to a festschrift in his honor, *A Doxology for James McKinney* (1996). Slightly further afield, but still close to home, was Reynolds's *Heritage of Praise: The Story of the Church Music Department of the Baptist General Convention of Oklahoma* (1996). This was written at the invitation of Bill Green, director of the department, in celebration of the fiftieth anniversary of the department's founding.

Another subject of interest to Reynolds during the 1980s and 1990s was the life and work of his uncle, I. E. Reynolds, the first director of the Department of Gospel Music (subsequently the School of Church Music) at Southwestern Seminary. Reynolds published four articles on his uncle in *Baptist History and Heritage, The Quarterly Review*, and *Southwestern Journal of Theol-*

ogy. Throughout his career, he has also contributed articles on a variety of other hymnological topics to such journals as *The Hymn*, *The Church Musician*, *Southwestern Journal of Theology*, and *Christian History*.

INTERPRETATION

Reynolds's contributions to hymnological scholarship include a number of notable "firsts." His initial book, *A Survey of Christian Hymnody*, was the first book written specifically for use as a text in college and seminary courses in hymnology. *Hymns of Our Faith* was also a pioneering effort, for this was the first companion for a Southern Baptist hymnal. When *Companion to Baptist Hymnal* was published, this made Reynolds the first—and as of this writing the only—person to have written complete companions for two hymnals. With his work on the *Handbook to the Baptist Hymnal*, he has contributed to every hymnal companion published by Southern Baptists.

Aside from their status as pioneering works, *Reynolds's Survey of Christian Hymnody* and hymnal companions demonstrated innovative approaches to the study of hymns. Earlier books on hymnody—including such classics as Louis F. Benson's *The English Hymn* (1915), Henry W. Foote's *Three Centuries of American Hymnody* (1940), and Albert E. Bailey's *The Gospel in Hymns* (1950)—had tended to emphasize the texts of hymns, largely ignoring the music to which they were sung. Erik Routley's study of *The Music of Christian Hymnody* (1957) had gone to the other extreme, focusing primarily on tunes. When Reynolds wrote *A Survey of Christian Hymnody*, however, he treated texts and tunes as equal partners, a situation that more nearly reflects the use and significance of congregational song.

Another important feature of *A Survey of Christian Hymnody* was the section of 139 illustrative hymns in the back of the volume. This provided the student or other reader with immediate access to hymns mentioned in the body of the book and served as an effective guide to significant hymnic literature.

Reynolds's editorship of the 1975 *Baptist Hymnal* and his hymnal companions showed the same sort of insightful thinking and organization. An innovative feature of Reynolds's editorial work on the 1975 *Baptist Hymnal* was his placement of the author, composer, and tune names at the bottom of the page rather than the top, as was the case with almost all previous standard American hymnals. The result was a page that was much cleaner and easier for the congregational singer to read. The pattern established by Reynolds has been followed by a majority of subsequent hymnals of all denominations.

In earlier hymnal companions, the discussion of hymns was generally arranged according to the order in which they appeared in the corresponding hymnal; biographical notices on the authors and composers were often subsumed into the articles on the hymns themselves. While this organization might be adequate for persons who would use the handbook only in conjunction with its companion hymnal, it meant a multiplication of indexes and difficulty of use for anyone else. In his companions, Reynolds arranged the hymn discussions alphabetically by the first line of the hymn and placed the biographies in a separate section. This made referencing the contents easier and reduced the number of indexes to one (index of tunes; the *Companion to Baptist Hymnal* also included an index to the introductory essays in the volume).

Another interesting feature of Reynolds's companions is the use he made of personal contacts with hymn writers, their families, or descendants to acquire information that was not available anywhere else. His companion articles often cited letters written in response to his queries for information. Thus, the books contain much primary source material, in addition to their reliance upon previous scholarship. The companions are also notable for the information which they present on gospel songs and their authors and composers, a class of songs that had been largely ignored by earlier writers on hymnody.

One of Reynolds's most significant contributions to scholarship was his work in the history of Baptist church music, particularly that of Southern Baptists. Among his important works on this subject are the historical essays of the three hymnal companions; his publication of *The Songs of B. B. McKinney*, *The Cross & the Lyre*, *Heritage of Praise*, and *A Doxology for James McKinney*; and the articles he wrote on B. B. McKinney and I. E. Reynolds. The historical essay in *Hymns of Our Faith* and a chapter in William L. Hooper's *Church Music in Transition* (1963) were among the first published discussions of the hymnody of Southern Baptists.

314

Reynolds's work demonstrated that Southern Baptist hymnody was of intrinsic interest and that there were many facets of the subject that could profitably be explored.

Since congregational song is designed primarily for performance by laypersons, hymns should not need a considerable amount of explanation to make them meaningful. Knowing something, however, about the background of hymns can often increase the singer's understanding and appreciation of them. Although Reynolds's hymnal companions were designed in part for laypersons, his principal contributions in this area were his books *Christ and the Carols* and *Songs of Glory*. Many collections of "hymn stories" that are designed for nonspecialists repeat unfounded legends and half-digested truths. But Reynolds's books were based on thorough research and understanding of the subject, avoiding the pitfalls that are often found in such works. Nevertheless, these books were engagingly written and were quite suitable for use by their intended audience.

William J. Reynolds achieved renown not only as a hymnological scholar but also as a leader of congregational song. As demonstrated in conventions, hymn festivals, conferences at Ridgecrest and Glorieta Baptist conference centers, and other venues, he took a creative approach to hymn leadership that made congregational song more meaningful. Reynolds sought to share many of his insights into hymn performance through his book *Congregational Singing*. In this volume he discussed many facets of hymnody that are largely neglected in other books—items such as hymn tempos, keys, accompaniments, and so on. Reynolds took a commonsense, yet innovative approach to these subjects, which made his suggestions of considerable value to other hymn leaders.

While the focus of this article is on Reynolds's prose writings, brief mention must be made of his hymn tunes. The *Baptist Hymnal* (1975) included ten pieces credited to William J. Reynolds (not including arrangements of tunes by others), most of which had been previously published in other venues. These tunes demonstrate their composer's interest in a broad range of hymnody. For example, his work in shape-note folk hymnody is reflected in the use of the pentatonic scale in MORA PROCTOR, while the syncopations of "Washburn" show indebtedness to pop-music idioms.

EVALUATION AND INFLUENCE

William J. Reynolds's writings on hymnody have had a significant influence on the scholarly study of this subject. *A Survey of Christian Hymnody* has been used by several generations of students at Southwestern Seminary and many other institutions of higher learning, and, now in its fourth edition, remains in wide use in colleges and seminaries. The fourth edition was prepared by others but continues to follow the format, organization, and conclusions of the first edition and even retains much of the original wording. The primary changes in recent editions have been to take advantage of more recent research in hymnology and to cover new developments in hymn writing.

Reynolds's companions for the 1956 and 1975 Baptist hymnals are now out of print, since the hymnals they were written to accompany have been superseded. The companions, however, served as significant resources for the writers who compiled the *Handbook to the Baptist Hymnal* (to which Reynolds also contributed). Hymnologists, students, and church musicians continue to rely upon the *Handbook*—and thus much of the information from the earlier volumes—for accurate data on the songs they sing. Reynolds's companions have also been drawn upon frequently by authors of handbooks for other denominational and nondenominational hymnals.

While *Christ and the Carols* and *Songs of Glory* are both out of print, they remain models of their kind. *Congregational Singing*, like the *Companion to Baptist Hymnal*, also went out of print with the 1975 *Baptist Hymnal*, but the suggestions it presents are as valid now as when the book was first published. Reynolds's writings on B. B. McKinney and I. E. Reynolds and his studies of music at Southwestern Seminary and in the state of Oklahoma continue to be significant resources for understanding Baptist church music.

Baptists continue to sing Reynolds's original tune "Sullivan" (SHARE HIS LOVE) and his arrangements of WONDROUS LOVE, ASSAM, BREAK BREAD, PEACE LIKE A RIVER, COBBS, and CLONMEL, all of which appear in the 1991 *Baptist Hymnal*. Furthermore, several of Reynolds's tunes have enriched the hymnals of other denominations.

The scholarly and practical writings of William J. Reynolds have had a significant impact on the study and practice of church music.

His works have been influential far beyond the ranks of his own denomination, but they have been especially significant among Baptists. In many respects, it can be said that William J. Reynolds provided the foundation on which all subsequent studies of Baptist hymnody and church music will be based.

BIBLIOGRAPHY

1. Primary

THESIS AND DISSERTATION

"*Le devin du village*: A Product of the *Guerre des Bouffons*." M.M. thesis, North Texas State Teachers College, 1946.

"Sources for College Teaching of Christian Hymnody." Ed.D. diss., George Peabody College for Teachers, 1961.

BOOKS

Baptist Hymnal (1975 Edition). William J. Reynolds, gen. ed. Nashville: Convention Press, 1975.

Building an Effective Music Ministry. Nashville: Convention Press, 1980.

Christ and the Carols. Nashville: Broadman, 1967.

Christian Hymnody: A Study Guide. Nashville: Seminary Extension Department, Southern Baptist Convention, 1983.

Companion to Baptist Hymnal. Nashville: Broadman, 1976.

Congregational Singing. Nashville: Convention Press, 1975.

The Cross & the Lyre: The Story of the School of Church Music, Southwestern Baptist Theological Seminary, Fort Worth, Texas. Fort Worth: Faculty, School of Church Music, Southwestern Baptist Theological Seminary, 1994.

(ed.) *A Doxology for James McKinney*. Fort Worth: School of Church Music, Southwestern Baptist Theological Seminary, 1996.

Heritage of Praise: The Story of the Church Music Department of the Baptist General Convention of Oklahoma. Oklahoma City: Church Music Department, Baptist General Convention of Oklahoma, 1996.

Hymns of Our Faith: A Handbook for the Baptist Hymnal. Nashville: Broadman, 1964; rev. ed., 1967.

Keveren, Phillip. *The New Illustrated Family Hymn Book*. With introd. and bkgd. for the hymns by William J. Reynolds. Milwaukee: Hal Leonard Publishing Corporation, 1992.

The Songs of B. B. McKinney. Comp. William J. Reynolds, ed. Alta C. Faircloth. Nashville: Broadman, 1974.

Songs of Glory: Stories of 300 Great Hymns and Gospel Songs. Grand Rapids: Zondervan, 1990; rpt. ed., Grand Rapids: Baker, 1995.

A Survey of Christian Hymnody. New York: Holt, Rinehart and Winston, 1963. 2nd ed. as *A Joyful Sound: Christian Hymnody*, rev. Milburn Price, 1978. 3rd ed. as *A Survey of Christian Hymnody* by William J. Reynolds and Milburn Price. Carol Stream, Ill.: Hope Publishing Company, 1987. 4th ed. as *A Survey of Christian Hymnody* by William J. Reynolds and Milburn Price, rev. and enl. David W. Music and Milburn Price. Carol Stream, Ill.: Hope Publishing Company, 1999.

ARTICLES IN REFERENCE WORKS

Encyclopedia of Southern Baptists. 4 vols. Nashville: Broadman, 1958–82. Vol. 1. S. v. "Eugene Monroe Bartlett, Sr.," "Charles Butler," and "Hymn Writers, Baptist." Vol. 2. S.v. "John Gordon McCurry," "William Walker," and "Benjamin Franklin White." Vol. 3. S.v. "Hymn Writers, Baptist," "Hymnals, Baptist," "Music, Baptist," and "Sacred Harp." Vol. 4. S.v. "Hymn Writers, Baptist, "Hymnals, Baptist," "Minister of Music," "PraiSing," and "Sacred Harp."

Handbook to the Baptist Hymnal. Ed. Jere V. Adams. Nashville: Convention Press, 1992. S. v. "Baptist Hymnody in America" (30–54) and 168 brief articles (a few cowritten) on individual hymns, tunes, hymn writers, and composers.

SELECTED ARTICLES IN PERIODICALS

"Baptists, Music, and World War II." *Baptist History and Heritage* 36 (Summer/Fall 2001): 77–91.

"The Contributions of B. B. McKinney to Southern Baptist Church Music." *Baptist History and Heritage* 21 (July 1986): 41–49.

"Evidence of Isaiah in the Hymnal." *Southwestern Journal of Theology* 34 (Fall 1991): 36–52.

"The Graded Choir Movement among Southern Baptists." *Baptist History and Heritage* 19 (January 1984): 55–62.

"Henry Ward Beecher's Significant Hymnal." *The Hymn* 52 (April 2001): 17–24.

"The Hymnal 1940 and Its Era." *The Hymn* 41 (October 1990): 34–39.

"I. E. Reynolds, Church Music Crusader." *The Quarterly Review* 42 (January 1982): 72–77.

"I. E. Reynolds: Shaper of Church Music." *The Quarterly Review* 50 (January 1990): 66–71.

"I. E. Reynolds: Southern Baptist Church Music Crusader." *Southwestern Journal of Theology* 25 (Spring 1983): 76–88.

"Imagery in Christian Song." *Southwestern Journal of Theology* 37 (Summer 1995): 25–30.

"Isham Emmanuel Reynolds: Church Musician." *Baptist History and Heritage* 27 (April 1992): 31–41.

"John Rippon, Pioneer Hymnist." *The Church Musician* 15 (February 1964): 12–14.

"More about Southern Baptist Church Music." *The Church Musician* 15 (August 1964): 8–11.

"Our Heritage of Baptist Hymnody in America." *Baptist History and Heritage* 11 (October 1976): 204–17.

"The Practice of Congregational Singing." *The Church Musician* 26 (February 1975): 4–10, 16.

"Southern Baptist Music, 1900–1920." *The Church Musician* 15 (July 1964): 14–16.

"Three Hymnals That Shaped Today's Worship." *Christian History* 31 (1991): 36–37.

2. Secondary

Music, David W. "An Interview with William J. Reynolds." *The Hymn* 44 (October 1993): 15–19.

Music, David W., ed. *We'll Shout and Sing Hosanna: Essays on Church Music in Honor of William J. Reynolds*. Fort Worth: School of Church Music, Southwestern Baptist Theological Seminary, 1998. Includes "William J. Reynolds" by J. Stanley Moore (1–7) and "William J. Reynolds: A Bibliography" by David W. Music (267–83).

Afterword

William B. Tolar

W illiam Shakespeare declared there was a "tide in the affairs of men, which, taken at the flood, leads on to fortune" but if missed, people are "bound in shallows and in miseries."[1] Historians have long debated whether great people produce great times or great times produce great people.

Were the times simply great or the "tide" accidentally at its "flood" in the early twentieth century when that coterie of gifted scholars and passionate preachers started Southwestern Baptist Theological Seminary? Or was the school supernaturally founded, though the vision given to B.H. Carroll, and divinely superintended? To read about the lives and the writings of the twenty-five Southwestern professors in these pages leads one to the conclusion that God's special providence was active in both their lives and in the affairs of the seminary.

This writer has known personally all but four of the twenty-five scholars included in this book: Carroll, Scarborough, Conner, and Dana. The other twenty-one were or are my teachers and/or colleagues. Having minored in Greek in college under a world-class teacher who had been a Rhodes Scholar and therefore having experienced what excellent teaching and authentic scholarship were, I was profoundly impressed as a seminary student by the incredible gifts and talents, the intellectual acumen, and the profoundly deep spiritual commitment of these professors and colleagues. But these twenty-five do not exhaust the list. They are, in fact, representative of a much larger number of gifted, intelligent, selfless, Spirit-led rather than power-driven scholars, both men and women, who have served the cause of Christian higher education at Southwestern Seminary. They represent the best in Baptist theological education.

Tens of thousands of pastors, missionaries, teachers, evangelists, chaplains, ministers of education, ministers of music, youth directors, and other types of ministers have had their professional and personal lives forever enriched, enlightened, and trained by the scholars treated in this book and by others not included because of space limitations. These twenty-five were selected because of the special influence of their writings. Many other professors at Southwestern have written numerous articles for dictionaries, religious encyclopedias, study Bibles, scholarly journals, denominational papers, Sunday school lessons, and the like, and have created many cassette tapes and videos, but the professors discussed in this volume have been extraordinary in their production of scholarly books.

One of the amazing things about these scholars is that they were or are not simply ivory-tower academics who have spent all their time researching and writing for publication. They, while researching and writing, were simultaneously busy classroom teachers with heavy student loads who taught effectively and who, for the most part, were highly effective practitioners in local churches and in the denomination. They were not only excellent theorists but also exceptionally skilled "doers" of their churchly duties. They could apply in excellent practice what they so eloquently taught.

The scholars in *The Legacy of Southwestern* were or are not only gifted in thinking, writing, and doing but also in being. They have incarnated the spirit of Christ in loving, but demanding, discipleship. They have sought to educate and not simply to indoctrinate students with their own personal ideas. They have inspired their students to think intelligently, to study the Bible diligently, to love Christ supremely, and to serve others unselfishly.

If the current students and faculty follow in the spirit and practice of the scholars in this book, then the future is bright. B. H. Carroll's vision will continue to be fulfilled. God surely will be glorified. Then, hopefully, we too, like these twenty-five, will hear Christ say, "Well done, good and faithful servants!"

NOTES

Preface

1   Scarborough, *A Modern School of the Prophets* (Nashville: Broadman, 1939).

2   Baker, *Tell the Generations Following: A History of Southwestern Baptist Theological Seminary, 1908–1983* (Nashville: Broadman, 1983).

3   James Leo Garrett, Jr., "The Legacy of Southwestern: Writings That Have Helped to Shape a Theological Tradition," Founder's Day Address, 7 March 2002. Archives, Roberts Library, Southwestern Baptist Theological Seminary.

Chapter 1: Benajah Harvey Carroll

1   He was the seventh of thirteen children. His parents had migrated from North Carolina. His father, Benajah, was of Irish descent and a bivocational Baptist minister-farmer. His mother, Mary Eliza Mallad, was of French Huguenot stock. They reared twenty-four children: twelve of their own who survived, and twelve whom they adopted.

2   B. H. Carroll, "My Infidelity and What Became of It," in *Sermons and Life Sketch of B. H. Carroll, D.D.*, ed. J. B. Cranfill (Philadelphia: American Baptist Publication Society, 1893), 13–17. Carroll said that he was not an atheist. He believed in God but doubted the fundamental claims of Christianity: the divine inspiration of the Bible, Christ's deity, miracles, and the vicarious atonement.

3   They had nine children: B. H. Jr., Jimmie, Guy Sears, Charles, Kate, Louise, Hassie, Ellen, and Hallie. Jeff D. Ray, *B. H. Carroll* (Nashville: Sunday School Board of the Southern Baptist Convention, 1927), 46.

4   As leader of the McLennan County (1885–86) and statewide (1887) prohibition efforts, he was a formidable opponent in debates against U. S. Senators Roger Q. Mills and Richard Coke and Governor L. S. Ross. In 1894, he led Waco ministers in opposing the Sunday opening of the new Cotton Palace, even against resistance from his own members and his mentor R. C. Burleson. One of his own members, Governor Pat Neff, said that Carroll's influence for civic reform was profound and extensive.

5   This was a special committee of the Baptist General Association of Texas (BGAT), which led the consolidation from 1883 to 1886. At the same time he was president of the Waco Association Mission Board (1874–88; 1889–92) and vice-president of the BGAT (1871–85). He helped to start Buckner Orphan's Home (1877) and was an associate editor of R. C. Buckner's newspaper, *The Texas Baptist*.

6   This was in an address to the convention in Richmond, Virginia, in 1888.

7   This was in Fort Worth in 1890.

8   This was in the Chattanooga, Tennessee, meeting in 1906.

9   Pressured by his Texas constituency to do something about Whitsitt, Carroll at first showed restraint and recommended that the trustees conduct a private investigation. After they glossed this over at the Wilmington convention (1897), he insisted that the issue be discussed publicly. His position of high visibility made him the natural leader of the faction that eventually forced Whitsitt's resignation (1898).

10 He led the first campaign in 1871 as the chair of the BGAT Committee for Schools and Education. In the second campaign (1891–93) he was assisted by George W. Truett.

11 He eventually developed this material into a full theological course and integrated it into the university curriculum.

12 He was appointed professor of exegesis and theology in the newly created Bible Department.

13 Ellen died in 1897, Carroll resigned the pastorate in late 1898, and he started at the commission in January 1899.

14 Married in 1899, they had one son, Harrison.

15 The first faculty consisted of Carroll, A. H. Newman, L. W. Doolan, C. B. Williams, and Calvin Goodspeed.

16 L. R. Scarborough, pastor of First Baptist Church, Abilene, taught evangelism; Jeff D. Ray, pastor of Seventh and James Baptist Church, Waco, was elected professor of homiletics; and J. J. Reeve filled the Hebrew chair vacated by Doolan.

17 He was buried in Oakwood Cemetery, Waco.

18 Quoted by W. W. Barnes, *The Southern Baptist Convention, 1845–1953* (Nashville: Broadman, 1954), 209.

19 Baylor granted him the B.A. in absentia without his sitting examinations. He held honorary degrees from Baylor (M.A.), the University of Tennessee (D.D.) and Keatchie College in Louisiana (LL.D.).

20 *Communion, from a Bible Standpoint* (1876); *Baptism: Its Law, Its Administrator, Its Subjects, Its Form, Its Design* (1893); and *Four Good Works for 1895,* n.d. [1895].

21 *Personal Liberty* (1887); *Centennial Address on Home Missions* (1892); *Papal Fields* (1893); and *The Nature and Person of Our Lord* (1908).

22 *An Office Magnified* (1898); *Christian Education* (1900); and *Distinctive Baptist Principles* (1903).

23 *The Agnostic* (1884) and *My Infidelity and What Became of It,* n.d. [1892].

24 *Baylor University, at Waco, Texas: An Historical Sketch,* n.d. [c. 1890].

25 *The Bible Doctrine of Repentance: Lectures Delivered before the Bible School of Baylor University* (1897); *Course in the English Bible,* n.d. [c. 1900]; *Opening of the Course in the English Bible* (1902); and *Ecclesia—The Church: Bible Class Lecture,* n.d. [c. 1904].

26 *A Sermon on the Modern Social Dance* (1877); *Prohibition, A Sermon Delivered. . . in Waco* (1886); *The Statewide Prohibition Question,* n.d. [c. 1887].

27 Carroll's earliest published lectures and examination outlines survive in the *Texas Baptist Standard* editions of 18 January, 1 February, and 1 March 1894; and 17 June 1897. For his lectures in the "'Course in the English Bible," see the following editions of the *Standard* in 1902: 6, 20, and 27 February; 6 and 13 March; 3, 17, and 24 April; 1, 15, 22, and 29 May; 12 and 26 June; 10, 17, and 24 July; and 2 and 9 October. These continued in 1903: 22 January, 26 March, 1 October, and 8 October. One lecture was published 18 February 1904.

28 Most important among these are his "Opening Address before the Theological Department of Baylor University," *Texas Baptist Standard,* 14 September 1905, 1 ff., which outlined his vision of a separate seminary; and four articles in the *Standard* (12 and 26 March, and

2 and 16 April 1908) presenting the charter of the seminary, the need for a new location and endowment funds, and Carroll's philosophy of ministerial education. Most of his published articles about the founding of the seminary (1901–14) are in the manuscript, "Our Seminary, or The Southwestern Baptist Theological Seminary, Fort Worth, Texas," comp. J. W. Crowder (1938), located in Archives, Roberts Library, Southwestern Baptist Theological Seminary.

29   Carroll, "Cold Water," *Waco Daily Examiner*, 13 August 1885; "Whiskey Traffic," *Galveston Daily News*, 20 August 1885; and "The Cotton Palace and Sunday," *Texas Baptist Standard*, 6 December 1894.

30   *Texas Baptist Herald*, 10 May 1871, 2; and a series of articles from 24 April to 16 October, 1872.

31   Carroll, "Bro. Carroll Reviews Bro. Martin," *Texas Baptist Herald*, 13 February, 1889, 4; and "From Bro. Carroll," *Texas Baptist Herald*, 6 March 1889, 4, and 20 March 1889, 1. See also "Report Adopted by Waco Church," *Texas Baptist Herald*, 29 January 1890, 6.

32   See Carroll's articles in the *Baptist Standard*: "The Dallas County Episode," 13 September 1894, 1; "Cooperation," 12 March 1896, 6; "'The Responsibilities, Obligations, and Joys of Pastors in the Spread of the Gospel,' A Sermon by Pastor B. H. Carroll Preached at White Hall Church before the Board of Waco Association, Saturday, March 28, 1896," 21 May 1896, 6; "The Supreme Question at Houston," and "Statement of Dr. B. H. Carroll," 8 October 1896, 1, 5; "Dr. J. M. Robertson's Article on 'The Powers of Conventions,' A Review by B. H. Carroll," 31 December 1896, 1–3; "The Burleson Matter Once More," 23 September 1897, 1–2; and "Concerning Grayson County Association," 30 September 1897, 1–2. See also Joseph E. Early, Jr., "The Hayden Controversy: A Detailed Examination of the First Major Internal Altercation of the Baptist General Convention of Texas" (Ph.D. diss., Southwestern Baptist Theological Seminary, 2002.)

33   See Carroll's articles in the *Baptist Standard*: "Dr. Carroll Has a Word about the Whitsitt Controversy," 7 May, 1896, 13; "The Whitsitt Case at Wilmington," 20 May 1897, 1–2; "Back to the Realm of Discussion," 27 May 1897, 12; "The Real Issue of the Whitsitt Case," 5 August 1897, 5; and "A Word in Passing on the Seminary Issue," 9 September 1897, 1. See also Rosalie Beck, "The Whitsitt Controversy: A Denomination in Crisis" (Ph.D. diss., Baylor University, 1985), and Charles Bugg, "The Whitsitt Controversy: A Study in Denominational Conflict" (Ph.D. diss., Southern Baptist Theological Seminary, 1972).

34   See Cranfill's foreword to *The Day of the Lord* and *The Faith That Saves*. This was Carroll's response to J. D. Shaw, a deposed Methodist minister in Waco who had lapsed and had founded the Waco Religious and Benevolent Association for "infidelity." Cranfill distributed two thousand free copies of the sermon in pamphlet form throughout Waco.

35   During Cranfill's ownership of the *Standard*, he published 229 of Carroll's sermons. In the foreword of *The Providence of God*, Cranfill exaggerated by claiming that he had published more than six hundred of them in his paper. J. W. Crowder said that, altogether, 248 of Carroll's sermons were printed by various publishers and that all of these were contained in the eighteen volumes which he and Cranfill edited. In fact, that series contains only 245 sermons: two entries in *Sermons* (1893) were duplicated in *Jesus the Christ* (1937), and one of the entries in *Christ and His Church* (1940) is not a sermon by Carroll but the 1939 Founder's Day address by his son, Charles. See also J. W. Crowder, "B. H. Carroll's Literary Contribution," in *Dr. B. H. Carroll, The Colossus of Baptist History*, ed. J.

W. Crowder (Fort Worth: pvt. ptg., 1946), 176; and *Christian Education and Some Social Problems*, foreword.

36   J. B. Cranfill, *From Memory: Reminiscences, Recitals, and Gleanings from a Bustling and Busy Life* (Nashville: Broadman, 1937), 112.

37   Cranfill, *Dr. J. B. Cranfill's Chronicle: A Story of Life in Texas* (New York: Fleming H. Revell, 1916), 436.

38   Carroll had preached this at a ministers' institute in Nashville in February 1892.

39   See Cranfill's advertisement in the *Texas Baptist Standard*, 17 January 1895. *Sermons* was reprinted in 1908, 1957, and 1986. In 1936 it was translated into Spanish by Sara A. Hale.

40   Crowder, "B. H. Carroll's Literary Contribution," 169. Crowder succeeded Carroll as professor of English Bible.

41   This contains ten sermons.

42   This contains eleven sermons.

43   Five Old Testament and eight New Testament volumes were published by Fleming H. Revell and by the Sunday School Board under Revell's copyright. The order of publication was: Revelation; Genesis; Exodus-Leviticus; Numbers-Ruth; Daniel and the Interbiblical Period; The Four Gospels; The Pastoral Epistles; Acts; James; Thessalonians and Corinthians; The Hebrew Monarchy; Galatians, Romans, Philippians, and Philemon; and Colossians, Ephesians, and Hebrews. See L.R. Scarborough, "Book Review," *Southwestern Journal of Theology* o.s. 1 (April 1917): 71–73. The Spanish edition, translated by Sara A. Hale, was printed by Casa Bautista de Publicaciones (1932–47). Broadman obtained the copyright and published the second edition (thirteen volumes) in 1942 and the third edition (seventeen volumes) in 1947. Baker Book House published a new edition (six volumes) in 1976.

44   B. H. Carroll's Will in Roberts Library Archives (BX6495.C37 W54). Although Crowder had compiled material since 1906, no title pages acknowledged his contribution until *The Day of the Lord* (1936).

45   These thirteen sermons, first published in 1928, were reprinted by Broadman in *River of Pearls* (1936), which also included nine sermons from Robert Greene Lee, *Beds of Pearls*.

46   Published in 1930, this was derived mostly from Carroll's lectures at Baylor University and Southwestern Seminary.

47   Published in 1935, *Studies in Romans* was a study course adapted by the Sunday School Board from Carroll's lectures on the English Bible. This was reprinted in 1936 as a combined study course with E. Y. Mullins's work on Ephesians and Colossians.

48   Published in 1936, this contains twelve sermons. The original manuscript of this work, compiled by J. W. Crowder and located in the Archives of Roberts Library, was entitled "The Second Advent of Christ and Final Destinies," which included one sermon that was not published: "Funeral Sermon of Rev. M. V. Smith."

49   *Studies in Genesis* (1937) and *The Ten Commandments* (1938) were Sunday School training courses derived from Carroll's lectures on the English Bible.

50   The first of these manuscripts to be published was *The Day of the Lord*. As director of Southwestern's Extension Department, Crowder had a correspondence student, E.

Holbrook Waterman, who volunteered to pay for the typing of the manuscripts, and President L. R. Scarborough provided administrative support.

51 Cranfill, forewords to *The Holy Spirit, Saved to Serve, The Faith That Saves,* and *Jesus the Christ.* Florence, president of Republic National Bank of Dallas, underwrote four volumes; Mahon financed one volume.

52 Published in 1937, this contained fifteen sermons. Two sermons were reprinted from *Sermons* (1893): "My Infidelity and What Became of It" and "A Sermon to Preachers." Two sermons in the original manuscript were not published: "Jesus the Compassionate Christ" and "Christ Our Mediator." Cranfill distributed twenty-seven hundred free copies of this to all Southern Baptist ministerial students and to divinity students at Southern Methodist University.

53 Published in 1939, this contains sixteen sermons.

54 Published in 1939, this contains ten sermons.

55 Published in 1939, this contains fourteen sermons. The original manuscript, entitled "Life and Its Obligations," does not contain one of the published sermons: "Paul the Greatest Man in History." The published volume does not contain one sermon in the original manuscript: "Man's Forgiveness of Man."

56 Published in 1939, this contained thirteen sermons. The original manuscript was entitled "Faith and the Faith."

57 Published in 1940, this contained fourteen sermons. The original manuscript was entitled "God and His Church." Cranfill also included "An Appreciation," the 1939 Founder's Day address by Carroll's son Charles.

58 Published in 1940, this contains thirteen sermons.

59 Published in 1941, this contains fifteen sermons. The original manuscript was entitled "Stewardship and Missions."

60 Published in 1941, this contains fourteen sermons. The original manuscript was entitled "Good Works." Cranfill added Broadus's "A Catechism of Bible Teaching."

61 Published in 1941, this contains fourteen sermons. The original manuscript, entitled "The Law and the Gospel," contains one sermon not in the published volume: "Liberty for Man, Woman, and Child." This work contains two sermons not in the original manuscript: "The War between the Flesh and the Spirit" and "The Evils of Religious Compromise."

62 This edition added four volumes of previously unpublished material: Poetical Books, Divided Kingdom, Prophets of the Assyrian Period, and Prophets of the Chaldean Period.

63 Published in 1942, this contains eleven sermons. The original manuscript was entitled "Prayer and the Christian Warfare."

64 Published in 1947, this contains fourteen sermons.

65 Published in 1948, this contains eight sermons.

66 Published in 1952, this contains nineteen addresses and articles.

67 W. T. Conner, "A Sketch of the History and Ideals of the Seminary," *The Southwestern Evangel,* December 1925, 6.

68 Compiled by J. W. Crowder, these are found in Roberts Library Archives: "Addresses, Articles, and Reports of B. H. Carroll, " "Baptist Church Polity and Articles of Faith," "Biblical

Addresses," "Controversies," "The Davilla Debate," "Defending the Faith and Practice of Baptists," "Questions and Answers," and "Memorials, Meetings and Miscellanies."

69   Cranfill, "Editor's Foreword," in Carroll, *Inspiration of the Bible*, 8.

70   Strong, *Systematic Theology* (Philadelphia: Judson, 1907), 423–25.

71   This explains why his commentary on Revelation was the first volume of *An Interpretation* to be published.

72   J. B. Gambrell, "The Home-going of B. H. Carroll," in *Dr. B. H. Carroll: The Colossus of Baptist History*, 103.

73   Cranfill, "The Passing of B. H. Carroll," in *Colossus*, 112–13.

74   Carroll's successor at First Baptist Church, J. M. Dawson, said, "For eleven years I have found his deep, abiding footprints everywhere about here. He hovers like a great benign, inspiring spirit over us all." Quoted by Jeff D. Ray, *B. H. Carroll*, 77. Cranfill, "Preface," in Carroll, *Sermons*, said that many of the sermons in this volume were of great "historical interest" and had "permanently molded public opinion." For other sermons that influenced public opinion, see *Christian Education and Some Social Problems* and *Patriotism and Prohibition*.

75   Cranfill, "The Passing of B. H. Carroll," in *Colossus*, 105.

76   Truett, "B. H. Carroll, The Titanic Champion of the Truth," in *Colossus*, 90; Scarborough, "A Further Introduction," in Carroll, *Inspiration of the Bible*, 11–12.

77   During 1893–98, two hundred of Carroll's sermons appeared in the *Standard*. For the circulation and influence of the *Standard* under J. B. Cranfill, see Presnall H. Wood, "History of the Texas *Baptist Standard*, 1888–1959," (Th.D. diss., Southwestern Baptist Theological Seminary, 1964), 75–78.

78   Quoted by Cranfill, "Editor's Introduction," in Carroll, *The Day of the Lord*, 11.

79   Scarborough, "B. H. Carroll, A Kingdom-Builder," in *Colossus*, 127.

80   John R. Sampey to B. H. Carroll, 24 August 1896, Carroll Collection, File 208-1, Archives, Roberts Library, Southwestern Baptist Theological Seminary.

81   Most of this was published intermittently between 1902 and 1908.

82   George W. McDaniel, "B. H. Carroll, the Colossal Christian," in *Colossus,* 161.

83   P. E. Burroughs, "Benajah Harvey Carroll," in *Ten Men from Baylor*, ed. J. M. Price (Kansas City, Kan.: Central Seminary Press, 1945), 77. Four of his students became presidents of the SBC: George W. McDaniel, Truett, Scarborough, and Pat M. Neff. Samuel Palmer Brooks became president of Baylor University. Neff became governor of Texas and president of Baylor. Burroughs himself became educational secretary of the Sunday School Board.

84   Truett, "B. H. Carroll, the Titanic Champion of the Truth," 98–99.

Chapter 2: Lee Rutland Scarborough

1   *Lee Rutland Scarborough: A Life of Service* (Nashville: Broadman, 1942), 80–86, esp. 84.

2   *Abilene Reporter News*, n.d. Scarborough Collection, File 9, Archives, Roberts Library, Southwestern Baptist Theological Seminary.

3   Scarborough, *A Blaze of Evangelism across the Equator* (Nashville: Broadman, 1937), 67.

4   H. E. Dana, "Lee Rutland Scarborough," in *Ten Men from Baylor*, ed. J. M. Price (Kansas City, Kan.: Central Seminary Press, 1945), 157.

5   *The Southern Baptist Convention and Its People, 1607-1972* (Nashville: Broadman, 1974), 401-4.

6   Scarborough was buried in Greenwood Cemetery, Fort Worth.

7   Dana, *Lee Rutland Scarborough*, 87.

8   Scarborough, *How Jesus Won Men* (Nashville: Sunday School Board of the Southern Baptist Convention, 1926), v.

9   Scarborough, *Christ's Militant Kingdom: A Study in the Trail Triumphant* (Nashville: Sunday School Board of the Southern Baptist Convention, 1924).

10 Scarborough, *A Search for Souls: A Study in the Finest of Fine Arts—Winning the Lost to Christ* (Nashville: Sunday School Board of the Southern Baptist Convention, 1925), 8.

11 Scarborough, *Gospel Messages* (Nashville: Sunday School Board of the Southern Baptist Convention, 1922).

12 Scarborough, *Prepare to Meet God* (New York: George H. Doran, 1922).

13 Scarborough, *The Tears of Jesus* (New York: George H. Doran, 1922).

14 Scarborough, *Products of Pentecost* (New York: Fleming H. Revell, 1934).

15 Scarborough, *After the Resurrection, What?* (Grand Rapids: Zondervan, 1942).

16 Scarborough, *Holy Places and Precious Promises* (New York: George H. Doran, 1924).

17 Scarborough, *Recruits for World Conquests* (New York: Fleming H. Revell, 1914).

18 Scarborough, *Marvels of Divine Leadership*, or *The Story of the Southern Baptist 75 Million Campaign* (Nashville: Sunday School Board of the Southern Baptist Convention, 1920).

19 Ibid., 63.

20 Scarborough, *Ten Spiritual Ships* (Nashville: Sunday School Board of the Southern Baptist Convention, 1927).

21 Scarborough, *My Conception of the Gospel Ministry* (Nashville: Sunday School Board of the Southern Baptist Convention, 1935).

22 Scarborough, *A Modern School of the Prophets* (Nashville: Broadman, 1939).

23 Scarborough, *How Jesus Won Men* (Nashville: Sunday School Board of the Southern Baptist Convention, 1926), 33.

24 Ibid.

25 Scarborough, "Militant Evangelism." *Baptist Standard*, 1 July 1915, 1.

26 (New York: Macmillan, 1907).

27 Scarborough, *Christ's Militant Kingdom: A Study of the Trail Triumphant* (Nashville: Sunday School Board of the Southern Baptist Convention, 1925), 126.

28 Scarborough, *Recruits for World Conquests* (New York: Fleming H. Revell, 1914), 60.

29 Scarborough, *A Search for Souls*, 91.

30 Scarborough, "The Mastery of the Main Thing," unpublished manuscript, Scarborough Collection, File 424, Archives, Roberts Library, Southwestern Baptist Theological Seminary.

31   Scarborough, "The Methods of Harvesting Results of Revival Meeting," unpublished manuscript, Scarborough Collection, File 427, Archives, Roberts Library, Southwestern Baptist Theological Seminary.

32   Dana, "Lee Rutland Scarborough," 156.

33   A. D. Foreman, Jr., "The Evangelistic Thrust of L. R. Scarborough," *Southwestern Journal of Theology* n.s. 7 (October 1964): 55.

Chapter 3: Walter Thomas Conner

1   Conner, "Trip to Arkansas, January 1948," unpublished manuscript now deposited in the library of Southeastern Baptist Theological Seminary, Wake Forest, N.C., 1. Copy in Roberts Library, Southwestern Baptist Theological Seminary.

2   *Who's Who in America* (Chicago: A. N. Marquis Co., 1950), 26:547; Stewart A. Newman, *W. T. Conner: Theologian of the Southwest* (Nashville: Broadman, 1964), 19–20; Conner, "Autobiographical Sketch," in *Southwestern Men and Messages*, ed. J. M. Price (Kansas City, Kan.: Central Seminary Press, 1948), 41.

3   Conner, "Autobiographical Sketch," 41.

4   Conner, "Trip to Arkansas," 6; Newman, *W. T. Conner*, 19–20.

5   Conner, "My Religious Experiences," unpublished manuscript now deposited in the library of Southeastern Baptist Theological Seminary, Wake Forest, N.C., 1–4. Copy in Roberts Library, Southwestern Baptist Theological Seminary.

6   Conner, "Autobiographical Sketch," 41; Scarborough, *A Modern School of the Prophets* (Nashville: Broadman, 1939), 190; Newman, *W. T. Conner*, 29, based on the minutes of Harmony Baptist Church, Caps, Tex.

7   Conner, "Autobiographical Sketch," 41–42; Scarborough, *A Modern School of the Prophets*, 190.

8   Conner, "My Religious Experiences," 14–15; Conner, "Autobiographical Sketch," 42–43.

9   Hugh R. Peterson, registrar, Southern Baptist Theological Seminary, to James Leo Garrett, Jr., 18 September 1953.

10   For the documentation, see James Leo Garrett, Jr., "The Theology of Walter Thomas Conner" (Th.D. diss., Southwestern Baptist Theological Seminary, 1954), 12–13.

11   "Connerisms," *The Southwestern News* 10 (November 1952): 6.

12   Robert A. Baker, *Tell the Generations Following: A History of Southwestern Baptist Theological Seminary, 1908–1983* (Nashville: Broadman, 1983), 245–59, 263–66.

13   Mary Irene, John Davis, Arnette, Blanche Ray, Neppie Lee, and Sarah Frances.

14   Newman, *W. T. Conner*, 143. For additional biographical data, see Garrett, "The Theology of Walter Thomas Conner," 2–16.

15   Very similar was Conner's later article, "Eddyism versus Christianity."

16   It was dedicated to Conner's three teachers in theology: Calvin Goodspeed, A. H. Strong, and E. Y. Mullins.

17   Conner, like the first Southern Baptist writing theologian, John Leadley Dagg, did not in 1924 consider the doctrine of the church to be a necessary topic in systematic theology.

18   James Leo Garrett, Jr., "Walter Thomas Conner," in *Theologians of the Baptist Tradition*, ed. Timothy George and David S. Dockery (Nashville: Broadman and Holman, 2001), 202–15.

19   Much of the following is taken from the author's "Walter Thomas Conner," 211–12.

20   Homes Rolston, Review of Conner, "The Gospel of Redemption," *Interpretation* 1 (October 1947):527–28.

21   Conner at the end of his career affirmed "the infallibility of the fundamental teachings of the Bible" but questioned a strict inerrancy view. W. T. Conner to E. B. Atwood, 21 February 1948 and 13 April 1948. "W. T. Conner Collection," Archives, Roberts Library, Southwestern Baptist Theological Seminary.

22   James Leo Garrett, Jr., "W. T. Conner: Contemporary Theologian," *Southwestern Journal of Theology* 25 (Spring 1983): 59–60.

Chapter 4: William Wright Barnes

1   Robert A. Baker, "William Wright Barnes," *Baptist History and Heritage* 5 (July 1970): 144.

2   Barnes, "The Theological Curriculum of Tomorrow in the Light of the Past," *Review and Expositor* 44 (April 1947): 149.

3   Baker, "William Wright Barnes," 146.

4   (Seminary Hill, Tex.: pvt. ptg., 1934; rpt.: Paris, Ark.: Baptist Standard Bearer, Inc., 1997).

5   (Nashville: Broadman, 1954).

6   "Progress of Baptist Principles from Constantine to Luther and the Anabaptists," *Review and Expositor* 23 (January 1926): 44–62; "Progress of Baptist Principles from Jesus and Paul to Constantine," ibid. (July 1926): 303–18.

7   *The Chronicle* 1 (July 1938): 110–14.

8   Ibid., 112.

9   *Review and Expositor* 39 (January 1942): 3–8.

10   "The New Hampshire Confession of Faith: Its Origin and Uses." *Review and Expositor* 39 (January 1942): 3–8.

11   *Review and Expositor* 41 (January 1944): 3–17.

12   *Review and Expositor* 44 (April 1947): 135–57.

13   Ibid., 152.

14   Ibid., 154.

15   *Southwestern Journal of Theology* n.s. 2 (April 1960): 49–54.

16   P. 304.

17   Ibid., 306–7.

18   (Louisville: Charles T. Dearing).

19   This view was not really new. It was held by all the earliest English Baptists but was displaced by G. H. Orchard in 1838 and was picked up and popularized throughout the South by J. R. Graves, the father of the controversial Landmark movement.

20   "Progress of Baptist Principles from Jesus and Paul to Constantine," 303–18, and "Progress of Baptist Principles from Constantine to Luther and the Anabaptists," 44–62.

Chapter 5: John Milburn Price

1   It is probable that Price derived this axiom from the first stanza of Howard A. Walter's 1907 hymn, "I Would Be True."

2   L. R. Scarborough to J. M. Price, 12 March 1915, Price Collection, File 2554, Archives, Roberts Library, Southwestern Baptist Theological Seminary.

3   Price, *Jesus the Teacher* (Nashville: Sunday School Board of the Southern Baptist Convention, 1946), 4.

4   Ibid., 32, 33.

5   Ibid., 34, 35.

6   Ibid., 41, 42.

7   Joe Davis Heacock, "J. M. Price: Trailblazer in Religious Education" *Southwestern Journal of Theology* 17 (Fall 1974): 91. Heacock summarized Philip Henry Briggs, "The Religious Education Philosophy of J. M. Price," D.R.E. diss., Southwestern Baptist Theological Seminary, 1964.

8   William Lewis Howse, Jr., *Those Treasured Hours: The Adventure and Dividends of Sunday School Teaching* (Nashville: Broadman, 1960), 57.

9   Price, *Jesus the Teacher*, 1.

10   Ibid., 1–2.

11   Clyde Merrill Maguire, *J. M. Price: Portrait of a Pioneer* (Nashville: Broadman , 1960), 122.

12   Leon Marsh, "J. M. Price: Pioneer in Religious Education," *Southwestern Journal of Theology* 25 (Spring 1983): 61–62.

Chapter 6: Harvey Eugene Dana

1   Dana and Julius R. Mantey, *A Manual Grammar of the Greek New Testament* (New York: Macmillan Co., 1927).

2   Franklin M. Segler, "Harvey Eugene Dana: Lights and Shadows," *Southwestern Journal of Theology* 13 (Fall 1970): 72.

3   For treatments of the life and career of Dana, see J. Clark Hensley, *In the Heart of the Young* (Kansas City, Kan.: Central Seminary Press, 1952); Segler, "Lights and Shadows"; Wayne Ozment, "The Hermeneutics of Harvey Eugene Dana," Th.D. diss. New Orleans Baptist Theological Seminary, 1972, 8–29; Ray Earl Bennett, "The Contribution of H. E. Dana to the Southern Baptist Understanding of the Historical-Critical Method of New Testament Interpretation," Ph.D. diss. Baylor University, 1974, 1–54; James Leo Garrett, Jr., "The Bible at Southwestern Seminary during Its Formative Years: A Study of H. E. Dana and W. T. Conner," *Baptist History and Heritage* 21 (October 1986): 30.

4   Soon afterwards, Dana realized that his wife had emotional disturbances, an illness that continued for the entirety of the marriage and one that required hospitalization on various occasions. His commitment, devotion, and care for his wife were admired by those who knew him. See Segler, "Lights and Shadows," 69–70.

5   Scarborough served as the president of Southwestern for the entirety of Dana's career as student and professor. Scarborough wrote the preface to one of Dana's earliest publications, *The Authenticity of the Holy Scriptures*, and was himself the subject of a biography

written by Dana. See Dana, *Lee Rutland Scarborough: A Life of Service* (Nashville: Broadman, 1942). Rogers influenced Dana's methods of teaching the New Testament. Dana credited Williams with giving him his first insight into the critical interpretation of the New Testament. See Dana, *The Ephesian Tradition: An Oral Source of the Fourth Gospel* (Kansas City, Kan.: Kansas City Seminary Press, 1940), 5. The theology of W. T. Conner, professor of systematic theology, can be seen throughout Dana's writings. For a detailed assessment of these men and their influence, see Ozment, "Hermeneutics of Dana," 16–18, and Bennett, "Historical-Critical Method," 19–23.

6   Data noted in a later book Votaw's influence on his work. See *Searching the Scriptures: A Handbook of New Testament Hermeneutics* (New Orleans: Bible Institute Memorial Press, 1936), 7.

7   Bennett, "Historical-Critical Method," 33.

8   Segler, "Lights and Shadows," 71.

9   Ibid., 67.

10   Garrett, "Bible at Southwestern," 30.

11   Bennett, "Historical-Critical Method," 52–54.

12   Ibid., 80.

13   Concerning the book Scarborough wrote: "It strengthens one's faith in the Book of Books, and gives a hopeful view of the relation between religion and science. It is conservative. There is not a stain of radicalism or modernism in it. It is a sane presentation of the ortho-dox position on this great subject." Dana, *The Authenticity of the Holy Scriptures: A Brief Story of the Problems of Biblical Criticism* (Nashville: Sunday School Board of the South-ern Baptist Convention, 1923), vii.

14   Bennett, "Historical-Critical Method," 139.

15   Ibid., 53.

16   These works include *The Jewish Christian Message* (Fort Worth: Seminary Book Store, 1934); *The Heavenly Guest: An Expository Analysis of the Gospel of John* (Nashville: Broadman, 1943); *The Epistles and Apocalypse of John: A Brief Commentary* (Kansas City, Kan.: Central Seminary Press, 1937); *Jewish Christianity: An Expository Survey of Acts I to XII, James, I and II Peter, Jude, and Hebrews* (New Orleans: Bible Institute Memorial Press, 1937); *A Life of Christ* (Philadelphia: Judson, 1945); and *The Life and Literature of Paul* (Fort Worth: Taylor Co., 1937). At the end of his life, Dana was working on a one-thousand-page manuscript on Paul. It was never published and was lost for some time but now resides in the Archives of Roberts Library at Southwestern Seminary.

17   A small eleven-page pamphlet arguing for the first day of the week as the proper day of Christian worship.

18   A publication consisting of the Holland Foundation Lectures delivered at Southwestern Seminary in 1943.

19   Bennett, "Historical-Critical Method," 173.

20   Dana, "Ecclesia in the New Testament and Early Christian Literature," Th.D. diss., South-western Baptist Theological Seminary, 1920.

21   Dana and L. M. Sipes, *A Manual of Ecclesiology* (2d ed. rev.: Kansas City, Kan.: Central Seminary Press, 1944), 149.

22   Segler, "Lights and Shadows," 70.

23 See, for example, Dana, *Searching the Scriptures: A Handbook of New Testament Hermeneutics* (2d ed.: Kansas City, Kan.: Central Seminary Press, 1946), 137–39.

24 In the preface to his book on the Holy Spirit in Acts, Dana wrote, "The fixed and decisive line which in recent years has been drawn between spiritual and historical interpretation is too largely assumed and is inimical to the best results." Dana, *The Holy Spirit in Acts* (Kansas City, Kan.: Central Seminary Press, 1943), 8.

25 Dana, *Authenticity of the Holy Scriptures*, 15.

26 Dana and Sipes, *Manual of Ecclesiology*, 33–150.

27 In *The Ephesian Tradition*, Dana argued that three strata of tradition (Palestinian, Pauline, and Ephesian) could be detected in the Gospel of John.

28 Segler, "Lights and Shadows," 71.

29 Hensley, *Heart of the Young*, 61–68.

30 Dana, *A Neglected Predicate in New Testament Criticism* (Chicago: Blessing Book Stores, 1934), 5.

31 Dana contended that principles of exegesis must be consistent with the mind of the Spirit and a coherent message of redemption. On the other hand, the New Testament's human character necessitates considerations of authorial intent, literal meaning, historical conditions, meaning of words, and the literary quality of the passage under investigation. See *Searching the Scriptures: A Handbook of New Testament Hermeneutics*, 2d ed., 182–201.

32 Dana, *New Testament Criticism: A Brief Survey of the Nature and Necessity, History, Sources and Results of New Testament Criticism* (Fort Worth: World Co., 1924), 18; Dana, "Biblical Criticism and Inspiration," *Southwestern Evangel* 14 (February 1930): 139.

33 Dana, *New Testament Criticism*, 11.

34 Dana, *The Science of New Testament Interpretation* (Fort Worth: Southwestern Press, 1930), 5.

35 Dana, "The Bearing of Luke's Preface upon the Doctrine of Inspiration," *Southwestern Evangel* 11 (February 1927): 195.

36 Dana, *A Neglected Predicate*, 48.

37 Dana, *Jewish Christianity*, 15.

38 Dana, *Searching the Scriptures*, 136.

39 Ibid., 132–39.

40 Hensley, *Heart of the Young*, 137–44.

41 See, for example, the recent revision of an earlier work on New Testament interpretation: David Alan Black and David S. Dockery, eds., *Interpreting the New Testament: Essays on Methods and Issues* (Nashville: Broadman and Holman, 2001).

42 Bennett also noted that Dana's writing was greatly limited by the fact that many of his books were privately published and confined to limited circulation. Only *The Ephesian Tradition* was written with the wider scholarly world in view. For the most part, Dana's works were influential only within Southern Baptist ranks. See Bennett, "Historical-Critical Method," 174–76.

43 Bennett, "Historical-Critical Method," 176.

Chapter 7: Thomas Buford Maston

1   "Hall of Faith" (featuring T. B. Maston), hosted by Bill Weber (Dallas: Discovery Broadcasting Network, 1988), Videocassette, VHS 1200, Roberts Library, Southwestern Baptist Theological Seminary.

2   Vance C. Kirkpatrick, "The Ethical Thought of T. B. Maston" (Th.D. diss., Southwestern Baptist Theological Seminary, 1972), 16–19.

3   Ibid., 22.

4   Ibid., 23–24.

5   Keith C. Wills, "Through Writing," in *An Approach to Christian Ethics: The Life, Contribution, and Thought of T. B. Maston*, ed. William M. Pinson, Jr. (Nashville: Broadman, 1979), 82.

6   Kirkpatrick, "The Ethical Thought of T. B. Maston," 192–93.

7   James E. Giles, "Biblical Ethics," in *An Approach to Christian Ethics*, 99.

8   Maston, *Why Live the Christian Life?* (Nashville: Thomas Nelson, 1974), 161–66.

9   Not locatable in Maston's published works but in notes taken in his Th.D. seminar, "Current Issues of Christian Ethics," 1969.

10 Ibid., 174–86.

11 Julian C. Bridges, "Citizenship," in *An Approach to Christian Ethics*, 140.

12 Browning Ware, "War and Peace," in *An Approach to Christian Ethics*, 150.

13 Ralph A. Phelps, Jr., "Church and the World," in *An Approach to Christian Ethics*, 195.

14 Ibid., 196.

15 Maston, *God's Will and Your Life* (Nashville: Broadman, 1964), 9.

16 Maston, *Why Live the Christian Life?* 94–96.

17 John C. Howell, "Marriage and Family," in *An Approach to Christian Ethics*, 121–22.

18 Ibid., 123–26.

19 A. Jase Jones, "To Race Relations," in *An Approach to Christian Ethics*, 63.

20 Maston, *The Christian, the Church, and Contemporary Problems* (Waco, Tex.: Word, 1968), 47.

21 Ebbie C. Smith, "Economics and Daily Work," in *An Approach to Christian Ethics*, 158–59.

22 Maston, *Christianity and World Issues* (New York: Macmillan, 1957), 241, 240.

23 Ware, "War and Peace," 151.

24 Ibid., 152.

25 Jimmy R. Allen, "To His Denomination," in *An Approach to Christian Ethics*, 38.

26 Ibid., 41.

27 James M. Dunn, "Through Graduates," in *An Approach to Christian Ethics*, 92.

28 Foy D. Valentine, "To Christian Ethics," in *An Approach to Christian Ethics*, 51.

Chapter 8: Ray Summers

1   *Oral Memoirs of Ray Summers* (11 August 1980 – 29 August 1980), Interviewer Daniel B. McGee. Texas Baptist Oral History Project. (Waco, Tex.: Baylor University Institute for Oral History, 1984), 194. Subsequently referred to as *OMRS*.

2   This need was created by the resignation of H. E. Dana to become president of Central Baptist Theological Seminary in Kansas City, Kansas.

3   In going to Southern Baptist Seminary, Summers was responding to a critical need caused by the dismissal of eleven faculty members.

4   For a more complete presentation of his publications, see the secondary bibliography at the end of this chapter.

5   The amillennial approach to the Book of Revelation may be found also in H. E. Dana's *The Epistles and Apocalypse of John* (Kansas City, Kan.: Central Seminary Press, 1947). He was professor of New Testament at Southwestern Seminary from 1919 to 1938 and so was Summers's mentor, having significant influence upon him.

6   Summers, *Ephesians: Pattern for Christian Living*, v.

7   *OMRS*, 587.

8   Cassette tape (TC 6068), Audio-Visual Department of A. Webb Roberts Library, Southwestern Baptist Theological Seminary. The Archives Department has a transcription of this tape.

9   Ibid.

10   Ibid. At an earlier time H. E. Dana had written an article entitled "Why I Do Not Sign," explaining why he, a strong anti-evolutionist, did not sign the SBC McDaniel statement opposing evolution. He wrote: "I do not believe in compulsory signing of creedal statements because the New Testament teaches the general principle of voluntary, uncoerced, and absolutely free acceptance of the redeeming work and redemptive truth of Jesus Christ." (Article available in the H. E. Dana Collection in the Archives Department of A. Webb Roberts Library.)

11   Summers, *The Life Beyond*, 87.

12   *OMRS*, 576.

13   (50th anniv. ed.: Nashville: Holman Bible Publishers, 1986).

14   (New York: Macmillan Company, 1944).

Chapter 9: Robert Andrew Baker

1   Baker had two older step-sisters. "Robert A. Baker: Baptist Biography File," Samuel B. Hesler, "Robert Andrew Baker," Archives, Roberts Library, Southwestern Baptist Theological Seminary.

2   Baker had no memories of his father and little discussion with his mother about his father.

3   Robert A. Baker, *The Oral Memoirs of Robert Andrew Baker* (Dallas: Baptist General Convention of Texas, 1981), 2–5; Jesse Fletcher, "Robert Andrew Baker," in *The Lord's Free People in a Free Land: Essays in Baptist History in Honor of Robert A. Baker*, ed. William R. Estep (Fort Worth: School of Theology, Southwestern Baptist Theological Seminary, 1976), 1–2.

4   The church was but a few blocks from the Baker home.

5   Baker, *Oral Memoirs*, 3.

6   Baker felt responsible for the financial care of his mother and assisted his siblings in financing their college education.

7   Baker, *Oral Memoirs*, 6–8. W. H. Moran, chief of the United States Secret Service, wired the appointment to special agent with the simple instructions: "Have Baker take the oath of office." Normal prerequisites for appointment as a field agent included a law degree or one year of police work. Baker possessed neither qualification. Baker served as the inside man on several assignments, investigating counterfeiting rings, stolen government bonds, gambling, and forged checks. Baker was sent to Washington, D. C., and trained in counterfeiting techniques.

8   Baker enjoyed investigative work. He acknowledged, "my own investigative methods and research since I've come into teaching were influenced by the thoroughness of the investigative work that I did in the Secret Service." Baker, *Oral Memoirs*, 8.

9   T. L. Holcomb left First Baptist to lead the Sunday School Board (SBC) in Nashville; W. R. White formerly served as executive secretary of the Baptist General Convention of Texas and would later become president of Baylor University.

10   Baker, *Oral Memoirs*, 11–18; Fletcher, "Robert Andrew Baker," 2. Years later White, then president of Baylor, tried to persuade Baker to leave Southwestern Seminary to head Baylor's Department of Religion.

11   Baker, *Oral Memoirs*, 19–21. Baker accepted the Bell Mead position after declining a call to pastor a church near Belton because he had neither a wife nor a car and "the church wanted both of those."

12   Baker, *Oral Memoirs*, 21–24; Fletcher, "Robert Andrew Baker," 3. Baker considered his marriage to Fredona "the best day's work I've ever done." Mary Crutcher, "Summer Sketchbook," *Fort Worth Press*, 27 August 1964.

13   Baker, *Oral Memoirs*, 27–28; Fletcher, "Robert Andrew Baker," 3.

14   Baker, *Oral Memoirs*, 27–34. Further encouraged by new faculty member Stewart A. Newman, Baker began his Th.D. work by studying Greek and theology at the behest of Conner. Barnes, however, won the recruiting war as Baker switched to church history in his second year of studies.

15   Fletcher, "Robert Andrew Baker," 5.

16   "Faculty Addition," *Southwestern News* (May 1943): 2. Baker joined Southwestern's faculty as instructor in church history and New Testament.

17   W. W. Barnes began to teach only Baptist history in his final years at Southwestern. Baker covered the remainder of the church history courses. Baker, *Oral Memoirs*, 52. Upon completion of his Th.D. at Southwestern, Baker was promoted to assistant professor of church history. "Commencement," *Southwestern News* (May 1944): 2.

18   Stewart Newman was scheduled to spend his sabbatic leave at Yale, but a change in Newman's plans led to a request from the faculty for Baker to fill Newman's spot in New Haven. Baker had met Kenneth Scott Latourette when the eminent Baptist church historian from Yale had lectured at Southwestern in 1944. Latourette suggested that Baker consider further training in church history. Fletcher, "Robert Andrew Baker," 4.

19   Robert A. Baker, "The American Baptist Home Mission Society and the South, 1832–1894." (Ph.D. diss., Yale University).

20   Baker served as vice-chairman of the Historical Commission (SBC) from 1970 to 1973 and chairman from 1973 to 1976. He was the first recipient of the commission's distinguished

service award in 1981. Baker served as the first president of the reorganized Texas Baptist Historical Society in 1977.

21   Baker, *Oral Memoirs*, 153.

22   On one occasion while Baker was lecturing on the Apostles' Creed, as he was writing the text of the creed on the blackboard in Latin, a student muttered that he did not understand Latin. Hearing the comment, Baker calmly erased the board and began to write the creed in Greek; this was followed by the admonition that the student had better understand what was presently being written.

23   Robert A. Baker, *The Baptist March in History* (Nashville: Convention Press, 1958), preface.

24   Robert A. Baker, *Relations between Northern and Southern Baptists* (Fort Worth: pvt. ptg., 1948) is the published version of Baker's Yale dissertation.

25   No doubt Baker's pastorate at Highland Baptist Church, Dallas, cut into Baker's time research and writing. Baker resigned that pastorate in 1952. Topics covered by Baker during this decade included continued assessment of North/South Baptist relations, examination of the Rocky Mount Baptist Church legal battle, and local church autonomy. All exhibit Baker's trademark of detailed research.

26   Robert A. Baker, *A Summary of Christian History*, rev. John M. Landers (Nashville: Broadman and Holman). Baker's original text went through more than eight printings and was translated into Chinese and Spanish.

27   Baker, *The First Southern Baptists* (Nashville: Broadman, 1966). Baker recounts his adventures investigating the whereabouts of William Screven from 1682 to 1696, including a search for Screven's grave under a South Carolina home. Baker spent a sabbatic leave combing through records from South Carolina to Maine in an effort to thoroughly document William Screven's life. Baker, *Oral Memoirs*, 74–76. See also "Four Professors on Sabbatic Leave," *Southwestern News* (July 1962), 8.

28   Barnes, *The Southern Baptist Convention, 1845-1953* (Nashville: Broadman, 1954).

29   Baker, *Oral Memoirs*, 77. When it came to writing, Baker admitted, "The hardest part has always been the limitations on space imposed by publication specifications." Fletcher, "Robert Andrew Baker," 6.

30   In six vignettes Baker unfolded the stories four preachers (Adiel Sherwood, John G. Landrum, Lewis Lunsford, Zacharius N. Morrell), a layman (Joseph Cole Stalcup), and a devoted Christian mother (Ann Graves). Baker, "Lewis Lunsford," *Quarterly Review* 37 (October–November–December 1976): 18–22; "Adiel Sherwood," *Quarterly Review* 37 (January–February–March 1977): 17–22; "Ann Graves," *Quarterly Review* 37 (April–May–June 1977): 20–24; "Zacharius N. Morrell." *Quarterly Review* 38 (October–November–December 1977): 20–25; "John G. Landrum," *Quarterly Review* 38 (January–February–March 1978): 20–25; "Joseph Cole Stalcup," *Quarterly Review* 38 (April–May–June 1978): 18–23.

31   Mary Crutcher, "Summer Sketchbook," *Fort Worth Press*, 27 August 1964. Baker viewed causation as the key contribution of the historian: "We emphasize causation, digging in to find why something happened."

32   Ibid.

33 When asked to forecast the future, Baker replied, "[I] can't see much beyond the end of my nose, as a Baptist historian." Baker, *Oral Memoirs*, 201. Baker was much more comfortable applying history to the present: "I don't think you can understand Southern Baptist life or religious life unless first you go back and pull out the whole context: religious, economic, social, political, and so on." Baker, *Oral Memoirs*, 212.

34 One can find census reports, population growth/decline, church statistics, and financial records. The introductory paragraph to Baptist life in Louisiana is typical of the wealth of statistical data found in the text: "*Louisiana*. This state was admitted to the Union in 1812, the first state to be formed from the Louisiana Purchase of 1803. The population in the first census in which it was shown in 1810 was 75,556, of which 34,660 were slaves. By 1840, it had increased to 352,441, with 168,452 slaves. This represented an annual average population increase of 11.62%, and an average increase annually in slaves of 12.29%, slightly larger than the population gain. It is likely that there were fewer than 100 Baptists in Louisiana in 1814. By 1845 there were 5 associations, 50 ministers, 73 churches, and 3,311 members." Baker, *The Southern Baptist Convention and Its People, 1606–1972* (Nashville: Broadman, 1974), 141.

35 "Barnes-Baker Collection," Robert A. Baker Research Room, Scarborough Hall, Southwestern Baptist Theological Seminary. The collection is privately held by H. Leon McBeth.

36 Baker, *Tell the Generations Following* (Nashville: Broadman, 1983), 392, 302. Baker's treatment of the building of the current president's home at Southwestern and of the faculty tension during E. D. Head's administration serve as two prominent examples. Without divulging the rancor among students, faculty, and Southern Baptists over the plans and cost for the new residence for the Southwestern's president, Baker writes: "After much discussion by the trustees and others, the plans for the house were approved in the spring of 1971." In a similar vein Baker refused to identify faculty personalities that clashed with Southwestern president E. D. Head, writing:

> It is not surprising that this inevitable process of organizational modernization was greeted less than enthusiastically by some of the more mature members of the theological faculty. Just a few years earlier, they had been a part of the small Faculty Council who sat in a circle around the desk in President Scarborough's office and dialogued with him about almost every administrative and academic decision. Now, without any warning, one of their younger colleagues had been elected by the trustees to supervise their work, and they no longer had a part in any administrative decisions.

It was enough said; there was no need to expose private debates among the faculty.

37 Fletcher, "Robert Andrew Baker," 7.

38 "Our history department," explained Baker in a 1964 interview, "is making history relevant. . . making it useable . . . illustrative . . . informative . . ." Crutcher, "Summer Sketchbook," *Fort Worth Press*, 27 August 1964.

39 Fletcher, "Robert Andrew Baker," 6.

40 Among Baker's doctoral students were Southwestern historians William R. Estep and H. Leon McBeth: Jesse C. Fletcher, chancellor of Hardin-Simmons University; Roy J. Fish, Southwestern evangelism professor; Justice C. Anderson, missionary to Argentina and later professor of missions at Southwestern; Presnall H. Wood, editor of *The Baptist Standard*, and H. K. Neely, professor at Southwest Baptist University and Hardin-Simmons University.

41   H. Leon McBeth, *The Baptist Heritage: Four Centuries of Baptist Witness* (Nashville: Broadman, 1987); Jesse C. Fletcher, *The Southern Baptist Convention: A Sesquicentennial History* (Nashville: Broadman and Holman, 1994). H. Leon McBeth, *A Sourcebook for Baptist Heritage* (Nashville: Broadman, 1990), reflects Baker's emphasis upon access to and use of primary sources to understand better Baptist life.

42   Baker, "Divided We Stand," in *The Fibers of Our Faith*, ed. Dick Allen Rader, vol. 1 (Franklin, Tenn.: Providence House, 1995), 147, emphasized Baptist commitment to liberty of conscience:

> For. . .[Baptists] the words 'liberty of conscience' must be written large. The doctrine of priesthood of the believer means for them that all Christians have a right, nay the duty, not only to come to God without aid of priests or prelate but also to interpret for themselves the meaning of the Scriptures. A concomitant belief is that all Christians have a freedom to voice their distinctive views, whether about doctrine or church polity. There are no first lieutenants among Baptists; they are all generals.

43   Ibid., 146–58.

44   Fletcher, "Robert Andrew Baker," 7.

Chapter 10: John (Jack) William MacGorman

1   MacGorman, *The Gifts of the Spirit* (Nashville: Broadman, 1974), 26–27.

2   Ibid., 44–45; MacGorman, *Romans, 1 Corinthians*, Layman's Bible Book Commentary, vol. 20 (Nashville: Broadman, 1980), 23. See also MacGorman, "Glossolalic Error and Its Correction: 1 Corinthians 12–14," *Review and Expositor* 80 (Summer 1983): 396.

3   MacGorman, "Galatians," in *The Broadman Bible Commentary*, Vol. 11, *2 Corinthians—Philemon* (Nashville: Broadman, 1971), 119.

4   MacGorman, *Acts: The Gospel for All People*, Adult January Bible Study (Nashville: Convention Press, 1990), 7–8.

5   MacGorman graciously shared a copy of the correspondence with the writer.

6   *Romans, 1 Corinthians*, 80–81.

7   *The Gifts of the Spirit*, 75; see also *Romans, 1 Corinthians*, 140–41.

8   MacGorman, "Problem Passages in Galatians," *Southwestern Journal of Theology* 15 (Fall 1972): 49–51.

9   MacGorman, "Introducing the Book of James," *Southwestern Journal of Theology* 12 (Fall 1969): 17–19.

10   MacGorman, "The Law as Paidagōgos: A Study in Pauline Analogy." In *New Testament Studies: Essays in Honor of Ray Summers in His Sixty-fifth Year*, ed. Huber L. Drumwright, Jr., and Curtis Vaughan (Waco, Tex.: Markham Press Fund of Baylor University Press, 1975), 110–11.

11   Ibid., 111.

12   *Acts: The Gospel for All People*, 7–8.

Chapter 11: James Leo Garrett, Jr.

1   Garrett, *Living Stones: The Centennial History of Broadway Baptist Church, Fort Worth, Texas, 1882-1982*, 2 vols. (Fort Worth: Broadway Baptist Church, 1984, 1985).

2   Garrett, *Southwestern Journal of Theology* 37 (Summer 1995): 36–46. See also Garrett, "Who Are the Baptists?" *The Baylor Line*, June 1985, 11–15.

3   Garrett, "Major Emphases in Baptist Theology," 37.

4   Ibid., 44.

5   Garrett, "Epilogue," in Garrett, ed., *Baptist Relations with Other Christians* (Valley Forge, Pa.: Judson, 1974), 195. This was a volume of Baptist World Alliance study commission papers. Garrett's long-term responsibilities with the BWA began in 1965.

6   Garrett, "The Distinctive Identity of Southern Baptists *vis-à-vis* Other Baptists," *Baptist History and Heritage* 31 (October 1996): 6–16.

7   Ibid., 10.

8   Ibid., 12.

9   Garrett, "Preface," *Baptist Relations with Other Christians*, 11.

10   Garrett, "Preface," in Garrett, ed., *The Concept of the Believers' Church: Addresses from the 1967 Louisville Conference* (Scottdale, Pa.: Herald, 1970), 5.

11   Ibid. For more insights on Garrett's ecumenism, see William L. Pitts, "The Relation of Baptists to Other Churches," in *The People of God: Essays on the Believers' Church*, ed. Paul A. Basden and David S. Dockery (Nashville: Broadman, 1991), 235–50. This book was a festschrift for Garrett.

12   Garrett, "Seeking a Regenerate Church Membership," *Southwestern Journal of Theology* n.s. 3 (April 1961): 25.

13   Garrett, *Baptist Church Discipline* (Nashville: Broadman, 1962), 1.

14   Garrett, "The Biblical Doctrine of the Priesthood of the People of God," in *New Testament Studies: Essays in Honor of Ray Summers in His Sixty-Fifth Year*, ed. Huber L. Drumwright and Curtis Vaughan (Waco, Tex.: Markham Press Fund of Baylor University Press, 1975), 137, 147.

15   Ibid., 149.

16   Garrett, "The 'No . . . Establishment' Clause of the First Amendment: Retrospect and Prospect," *Journal of Church and State* 17 (Winter 1975): 13.

17   Garrett, "The 'Free Exercise' Clause of the First Amendment: Retrospect and Prospect," *Journal of Church and State* 17 (Autumn 1975): 397.

18   Garrett, "The Dialectic of Romans 13:1–7 and Revelation 13: Part One," *Journal of Church and State* 18 (Autumn 1976): 433–42; "Part Two," ibid., 19 (Winter 1977): 5–20, esp. 20.

19   Garrett, E. Glenn Hinson, and James E. Tull, *Are Southern Baptists "Evangelicals"?* (Macon, Ga.: Mercer University Press, 1983), vii.

20   Ibid., 62–63.

21   Ibid., 126 [italics his].

22   (Nashville: Broadman, 1965).

23   Ibid., 7.

24   Ibid., 9–27. The "Rebuttalists" answered the case for the Roman church, the "Exposurists" pointed out "alleged immoralities or moral abuses" in the Roman church, the "Successionists" countered Roman claims to Petrine primacy and apostolic succession by

positing a Landmark view of Baptist succession, and the church-state writers attacked church-state union and defended church-state separation.

25   Ibid., 28–34.

26   Ibid., 35–37.

27   For a closer look at Garrett's thought as found in *Systematic Theology*, see Paul A. Basden, "James Leo Garrett, Jr.," *Theologians of the Baptist Tradition*, ed. Timothy George and David S. Dockery (Nashville: Broadman and Holman, 2001), 308–14.

28   Garrett, *Systematic Theology: Biblical, Historical, and Evangelical*, 2 vols. (Grand Rapids: Eerdmans, 1990, 1995). The second edition, 2 vols. (North Richland Hills, Tex.: BIBAL Press, 2000, 2001) exceeds seventeen hundred pages.

29   Dwight A. Moody, "The Bible," in *Has Our Theology Changed? Southern Baptist Thought since 1845*, ed. Paul A. Basden (Nashville: Broadman and Holman, 1994), 10.

30   Garrett, *Systematic Theology*, 1st ed., 1:121.

31   Ibid., 1:142.

32   Ibid., 1:158.

33   Ibid., 1:167.

34   Ibid., 1:181–82. On Garrett's doctrine of the Bible, see Dwight A. Moody, "The Bible," 7-40.

35   Garrett, *Systematic Theology*, 1st ed., 1:261.

36   "Christians can seek to 'de-patriarchalize' the language and concept of God as Father and yet to preserve the abidingly valid dimensions of divine fatherhood." Garrett, *Systematic Theology*, 2d ed., 1:303.

37   Ibid., 2d ed., 1:661.

38   Ibid., 663.

39   Ibid., 1st ed., 2:214–15.

40   Ibid., 443–48, 453–54.

41   Ibid., chaps. 65, 67, 68, 72.

42   Ibid., chaps. 79–87.

Chapter 12: Ralph Lee Smith

1   Harry B. Hunt, Jr., "Ralph Lee Smith: A True Prophet," *Southwestern Journal of Theology* 32 (Summer 1990): 8.

2   "Preface," *Wycliffe Bible Encyclopedia*, 2 vols. (Chicago: Moody, 1975), 1:v.

3   David A. Hubbard, Glenn W. Barker, John D. W. Watts, and Ralph P. Martin, "Editorial Preface," in Ralph L. Smith, *Micah—Malachi*, Word Biblical Commentary, vol. 32 (Waco, Tex.: Word, 1984), x.

4   Smith, *Old Testament Theology: Its History, Method, and Message* (Nashville: Broadman and Holman, 1993), 13.

5   Smith, "Interpretation of Scriptures—Principles of Interpretation," *Encyclopedia of Southern Baptists*, 4 vols. (Nashville: Broadman, 1958–82), 1:690; *Micah–Malachi*, 1984, ix; *Job: A Study in Providence and Faith* (Nashville: Convention Press, 1971), 6; cf. *Old Testament Theology*, 76–77, 91–92.

6   Smith, *Old Testament Theology*, 14.

7   Smith, *Job*, 6; *Old Testament Theology*, 91–92. In "Pentateuch," *Holman Bible Dictionary*, ed. Trent C. Butler (Nashville: Holman, 1991), 1091, he attributed the same view to W. T. Conner, citing *Revelation and God* (Nashville: Broadman, 1943), 99.

8   Smith, *Micah–Malachi*, 1984, 9–10; Smith, *Old Testament Theology*, 91–92.

9   Smith, "Interpretation of Scriptures—Principles of Interpretation," 1:690; *Job*, 8, 12; *Israel's Period of Progress* (Nashville: Convention Press, 1970), vii-viii.

10   Smith, *Old Testament Theology*, 18–20.

11   Smith, *Israel's Period of Progress*, ix–xi, 5–95; "Covenant and Law in Exodus," *Southwestern Journal of Theology* 20 (Fall 1977): 34–35; "Exodus," *Holman Bible Dictionary*, 451–55.

12   Smith, *Israel's Period of Progress*, 27–30.

13   Smith, "Exodus," 451–55; Smith, *Israel's Period of Progress*, 18–19.

14   Smith, "Exodus," 454; Smith, *Israel's Period of Progress*, ix.

15   Smith, "Red Sea (Reed Sea)," *Holman Bible Dictionary*, 1170.

16   Smith, "Pentateuch," 1091.

17   Smith, *Israel's Period of Progress*, 151.

18   Smith, *Old Testament Theology*, 89–90.

19   Smith, "The Theological Implications of the Prophecy of Amos," *Southwestern Journal of Theology* 9 (Fall 1966): 56; Smith, "Amos," *Broadman Bible Commentary*, vol. 7, *Hosea-Malachi*, (Nashville: Broadman, 1972), 87.

20   Smith, *Micah–Malachi*, 1984, 8–11, 29, 37, 40–41.

21   Smith, *Micah–Malachi*, 1984, 219, 249.

22   Smith, *Israel's Period of Progress*, 164–65, 169–70; Smith, "Introduction to the Book of Job," *Southwestern Journal of Theology* 14 (Fall 1971): 12–13.

23   Smith, "Some Theological Concepts in the Book of Deuteronomy," *Southwestern Journal of Theology* 7 (October 1964): 17; Smith, "Introduction to the Book of Job," 13–14; Smith, *Old Testament Theology*, 72–74.

24   Smith, *Old Testament Theology*, 76.

25   Ibid., 77.

26   Smith, "Covenant and Law in Exodus," 34, 36–37; Smith, *Micah–Malachi*, 1984, 259; Smith, *Old Testament Theology*, 151–61.

27   Smith, *Old Testament Theology*, 242.

28   Smith, *Old Testament Theology*, 227, 331–33, 370–72.

Chapter 13: Henry Clifton Brown, Jr.

1   Brown, *Walking toward Your Fear* (Nashville: Broadman, 1972), 17–18.

2   Brown, *A Quest for Reformation in Preaching* (Waco, Tex: Word, 1968), 16.

3   Ibid., viii.

4   Ibid., p. 71.

5   Ibid., p. 71.

6   Ibid., 87.

7   Brown, Gordon Clinard, and Jesse Northcutt. *Steps to the Sermon* (Nashville: Broadman, 1963), vii-viii.

Chapter 14: William Curtis Vaughan

1   No biographical sketch of Vaughan has been published; this account depends upon Curtis Vaughan, "Personal Memoirs," an unpublished manuscript in possession of the author, at Southwestern Baptist Theological Seminary.

2   In 1992 the Roellen Baptist Church invited Vaughan back to celebrate his fiftieth year in the gospel ministry. The church presented him a plaque acknowledging his first sermon, and he preached there a second time. The second sermon was longer.

3   These distribution figures from three publishers do not include volumes translated into foreign languages (Chinese, Spanish, and Portuguese).

4   See the bibliographical entries for fourteen New Testament writings: Acts, Colossians and Philemon, Ephesians, Galatians, James, 1, 2, and 3 John, Romans, 1 Corinthians, 1 and 2 Peter, Jude.

5   Cf. *The Biblical Sunday School Commentary* (1968–70); *The Teacher's Bible Commentary* (1972); and *Master Design: Your Calling as a Christian* (1986).

6   See *The New Testament from 26 Translations* (Grand Rapids: Zondervan, 1967); *The Old Testament Books of Poetry from 26 Translations* (Grand Rapids: Zondervan, 1973); and *Twenty-Six Translations of the Bible* (Atlanta: Mathis, 1985); republished as *The Word: The Bible from 26 Translations* (Moss Point, Miss.: Mathis, 1991).

7   *Elementary Greek: A Summary of the Essentials* (Fort Worth: Southwestern Baptist Theological Seminary, 1980); and *New Testament Greek: Grammatical Notes* (Fort Worth: Southwestern Baptist Theological Seminary, 1996).

8   Vaughan, *James: A Study Guide* (Grand Rapids: Zondervan, 1969), 36.

9   Spurgeon, *Lectures to My Students* (new ed.: Grand Rapids: Zondervan, 1955), 305.

10   Vaughan, *Ephesians: A Study Guide Commentary* (Grand Rapids: Zondervan, 1977), 14-15.

11   For example, Vaughan, *1, 2 Peter, Jude: Bible Study Commentary* (Grand Rapids: Zondervan, 1988), 94–111, re "Preaching to the Spirits in Prison."

12   Vaughan, *James: A Study Guide*, 57.

13   Vaughan, *Ephesians: A Study Guide Commentary*, 21–22.

Chapter 15: Franklin Morgan Segler

1   *A Man in Christ: The Vital Elements of St. Paul's Religion* (New York, London: Harper and Bros., 1935).

Chapter 16: Huber Lelland Drumwright, Jr.

1   "A Mosaic of Jesus: John 2:12–4:54," in *New Testament Studies: Essays in Honor of Ray Summers in His Sixty-fifth Year*, ed. Huber L. Drumwright, Jr., and Curtis Vaughan (Waco, Tex.: Markham Press Fund of Baylor University Press, 1975), 55–67, esp. 59.

2   "The Appendix to the Fourth Gospel," in *The Teacher's Yoke: Studies in Memory of Henry Trantham*, ed. E. Jerry Vardaman and James Leo Garrett, Jr. (Waco, Tex.: Baylor University Press, 1964), 129–34.

3   "A Re-evaluation of the Significance of John's Gospel," *Southwestern Journal of Theology*, n.s. 8 (October 1965): 13–16.

4   Ibid., 16–20.

5   "Problem Passages in the Johannine Epistles: A Hermeneutical Approach," *Southwestern Journal of Theology* 13 (Fall 1970): 53–62, esp. 59.

6   Ibid., 62–64.

7   "Problem Passages in Luke: A Hermeneutical Approach," *Southwestern Journal of Theology* 10 (Fall 1967): 45–48, 55–58.

8   *Southwestern Journal of Theology* 17 (Fall 1974): 7–9.

9   Ibid., 9, citing Dana, *The Holy Spirit in Acts* (Kansas City, Kan.: Central Seminary Press, 1943), 44.

10   Ibid., 10.

11   Ibid., 10–14.

12   Ibid., 14–17.

13   "A Study of the Epistle to the Hebrews with Special Reference to the Hebraic Mind" (Th.D. diss., Southwestern Baptist Theological Seminary, 1957), esp. Introduction and chaps. 1–3.

14   "A Homiletic Study of the Sermon on the Mount: The Ethical Motif in Matthew 5–7," *Southwestern Journal of Theology* n.s. 5 (October 1962): 65–76, esp. 76.

15   (Nashville: Broadman, 1978), esp. 9.

16   *Saints Alive! The Humble Heroes of the New Testament* (Nashville: Broadman, 1972), esp. 11–12.

Chapter 17: John Paul Newport

1   In addition to student pastorates in Kentucky, Newport was pastor of Clinton Baptist Church, Clinton, Miss. (1944–46) and Immanuel Baptist Church, Tulsa, Okla. (1948–1949). Subsequently he served as interim pastor of more than fifty churches in five states and conducted more than two hundred revival meetings and Bible conferences.

2   Frank Louis Mauldin, Personal Interview with John P. Newport, September 1983.

3   Newport, "Biblical Philosophy and the Modern Mind," *Baptist Faculty Paper* 6 (Winter 1963): 1–2, 4.

4   Newport to Louis Mauldin (letter), 2 June 1983; John P. Newport to Louis Mauldin (letter), 20 August 1984; Frank Louis Mauldin, Personal Interview with John P. Newport, September 1983.

5   See Newport, "Preface," in Frank Louis Mauldin, *The Classic Baptist Heritage of Personal Truth* (Franklin, Tenn.: Providence House, 1999), ix-x; *Southwestern News*, Spring 2000, 25.

6   An extensive bibliography of Newport's writings from 1952 to 1987 may be found in *Southwestern Journal of Theology* 24 (Summer 1987): 7–9.

Chapter 18: William Roscoe Estep, Jr.

1   For more complete biographical information on Estep, see the bibliography of secondary literature at the end of this chapter. The most accessible article is by Paul L. Gritz in the *Southwestern Journal of Theology* (Summer 1994). This issue was dedicated as a "Festschrift for William R. Estep, Jr.: A Statement for Religious Liberty" and contained articles by his former students and colleagues. Estep edited the *Journal* from 1963 to 1967. He was buried in Valley View, Texas.

2   For complete bibliographical information on Estep's writings, see the bibliography of primary literature at the end of this chapter.

3   Estep issued in 1955 a typescript revision in book form of his Th.D. thesis, "Church Union and Southern Baptists."

4   Estep added to his original historical survey and evaluation of ecumenism and his discussion of contrary Baptist stances a survey of World Council of Churches meetings to 1961. He also included a review of Roman Catholicism's changed posture towards the Orthodox and Protestants arising from Vatican Council II. In addition he described alternative forms of interdenominational cooperation among Fundamentalists and Evangelicals. In "The Changing Ecumenical Scene: A Baptist Perspective" (1968) he provided a synopsis of the sections added to his dissertation by his book, *Baptists and Christian Unity*.

5   Estep also sketched the changes in the Roman Catholic posture towards other world religions and various secular, contemporary challenges.

6   For the BWA, Estep collaborated with Richard Pierard and James Leo Garrett, Jr., in producing "Baptists: A Global Community of Faith" (1999), a historical and geographical survey of the global expansion of the Baptist movement.

7   In the introduction and first chapter, Estep acknowledged his indebtedness to Harold Bender and other Mennonite scholars who had found the roots of normative or evangelical Anabaptism in the Swiss Reformation. Estep became the primary spokesman for this viewpoint among Baptist scholars in America. In "The Significance of the Reformation" (1967), Estep pinpointed the evangelical breakthrough of Luther, which he believed that the Anabaptists had implemented more consistently than others.

8   Estep expanded on his argument in "A Baptist Reappraisal of Sixteenth Century Anabaptism" (1958).

9   The chapter was an address on the heritage of the Anabaptist vision which Estep had delivered at the first Believers' Church Conference (1967). In it he noted Anabaptism's lineal descendants, the Hutterites, Amish and Mennonites, as well as its impact on Quakers, Pietists, Restorationists like Alexander Campbell, Holiness groups, and Pentecostals. Estep concluded with a list of seventeen characteristic features defining the believers' churches.

10   The paper, first presented to the Conference on Faith and History, focused on differing church-state viewpoints among Christians. Estep later presented a popularized version of his arguments in "Separation as Sedition: America's Debt to the Anabaptists" (1976).

11   Estep included writings by Conrad Grebel (translating letters to Vadian, the Reformer at St. Gall), Felix Manz, Michael Sattler, Hans Denck (translating his *Recantation*, 1527), Pilgram Marpeck, and Hans Schlaffer. Estep translated the relevant sections of the October, 1523, Zürich Disputation in which Zwingli and his students (the future Anabaptist leaders) disagreed publicly. Estep also translated an anonymous Anabaptist pamphlet on

the Christian and the state. He translated Hubmaier's "Eighteen Theses" for reform at Waldshut, "Supplication to the City Council of Schaffhausen" and "Concerning Heretics and Those Who Burn Them" (his two religious liberty tracts). He supplemented his own efforts with the text of the Twelve Articles of the Peasants endorsed by Hubmaier, translations by Henry C. Vedder of Hubmaier's "On the Sword" and his hymn "God's Word Stands Forever," and Leo T. Crismon's translation of Hubmaier's interrogation by John Faber. Two European Baptist scholars, Gunnar Westin and Torsten Bergsten, had edited *Balthasar Hubmaier Schriften*, Quellen zur Geschichte der Täufer, vol. 9 (Gutersloh: Gerd Mohn, 1962), which Estep used for his translation.

12   Documents by Erasmus, Luther, and Zwingli made up the volume along with items by Anabaptist leaders, Peter Rideman and Menno Simons, together with confessions by the Waterlander Mennonites, with whom early Baptists had contact.

13   The German title was *Balthasar Hubmaier: Seine Stellung zu Reformation und Täufertum* (Kassel: Oncken, 1961).

14   A preliminary survey by Estep of various evangelical leaders of the 1500s had appeared in a self-study workbook for students, *The Reformation and Protestantism* (1983). As early as 1983, he had noted in "Zwingli" and "Conflict over the Sacraments in the Reformation" that the Anabaptists carried on Zwingli's view of the Lord's Supper more than did the Reformed churches. Estep also observed that the Anabaptists such as Hubmaier stressed the gospel-proclaiming significance of the ordinances more than did other Reformers. In "Contrasting Views of the Lord's Supper in the Reformation of the Sixteenth Century" (1997), Estep provided in some detail the views of the Zurich Anabaptists and Hubmaier concerning the Lord's Supper, which he had presented at a Believers' Church Conference on this subject.

15   Estep rounded out the textbook by discussing the legacy of Calvin and others in elaborating the Reformed tradition, the Anglican middle way, the Roman Catholic reaction, the spread of the Reformation to various countries, and the devastation of the Wars of Religion.

16   Estep presented his paper at a 1986 meeting of the Baptist World Alliance Commission on Baptist Heritage. Estep had pointed to the written evidence for such a link in (John) "Smyth" (1983). In "Thomas Helwys: Bold Architect of Baptist Policy on Church-State Relations" (1985), he explained the modifications which Helwys made to the Mennonite stance on church-state separation.

17   Estep outlined Baptist views on worship, doctrine, and church ordinances and polity, as well as on church and state. In the last chapter of the book, Estep highlighted the early history of Baptists, especially in shaping America's constitutional guaranties on religious freedom, in pioneering modern missions, and in promoting interdenominational cooperation. He had presented these materials at Hong Kong Baptist Theological Seminary (1994–95).

18   He recounted the opposition of Roger Williams and John Clarke to church-state linkage in Massachusetts and their "livelie experiment" of religious liberty in Rhode Island. Estep emphasized how the spiritual awakening of the mid 1700s yielded Isaac Backus and other Separate (New Light) Baptists in New England who campaigned for religious liberty. He noted how Virginia's New Light Baptists influenced the revolutionary leaders, James Madison and Thomas Jefferson, in this regard. Furthermore, John Leland and the Virginia Baptists lobbied successfully for the end of a state-sponsored church and secured the religious

free exercise and no establishment guarantees of the First Amendment to the U S Constitution. Estep concluded by calling on Baptists and others to hold onto the principles of their forefathers.

The book project developed from a series of lectures to the Christian Legal Society which Estep prepared and distributed as a typescript notebook, *An Introduction to the Historical Development of Baptist Church-State Relations, 1612–1833* (1986). In 1987 he delivered these lectures again at Bethel College, North Newton, Kansas, and they were printed as a book, *Religious Liberty: Heritage and Responsibility* (1988). Estep summarized his argument in "The Struggle for Freedom in the Historical Context" (1989). After the book's publication in 1990, he edited "Portraits of Baptist Heritage" for *Discipleship Training* (1991), in which he wrote several articles about the witness for religious liberty among early Baptist leaders. He repeated the points of *Revolution within the Revolution* in a condensed form with "Church and State" (1991). With "Respect for Nonconformity Permeates the Baptist Conscience" (1996), Estep stated some personal implications of the Baptist advocacy of religious freedom. In "The English Baptist Legacy of Freedom and the American Experience" (1999), he added to his case a discussion of the negative stance of Presbyterians and the limited support given to religious liberty by Independent Congregationalists in England during the 1640s. He also expanded on his earlier treatment by showing the positive views of the Levellers and some General and Particular Baptist leaders whom he had not discussed in *Revolution within the Revolution*. Estep also indicated possible antecedents for the English arguments of the 1600s for liberty of conscience in writers of the 1500s such as Hubmaier.

19 Estep presented the same arguments in "Baptists and Authority: The Bible, Confessions, and Conscience in the Development of Baptist Identity" (1987) and "The Nature and Use of Biblical Authority in Baptist Confessions of Faith, 1610–1963" (1987).

20 The original title of the article was "Calvinizing Southern Baptists." The specific rebuttals which appeared in the *Founders Journal* were: Tom Ascol, "Do Doctrines Really Lead to Dunghill?" R. Albert Mohler, "The Reformation of Doctrine and the Renewal of the Church: A Response to Dr. William R. Estep"; and Roger Nicole, "An Open Letter to Dr. William R. Estep."

21 Estep wrote *And God Gave the Increase* (1972) for the First Baptist Church, Beaumont; *The Gaston Story* (1987) and *A New Chapter in the Gaston Story* (1993) for the Gaston Avenue (now Gaston Oaks) Baptist Church, Dallas; and *A Brief History of the Iglesia Templo Bautista Emanuel* (1996) for the Spanish-speaking congregation in Fort Worth (a former mission of Gambrell Street Baptist Church) with whom Estep regularly worshipped.

22 Estep had earlier addressed the relationship of Baptists and others to African Americans in "The Negro and American Christianity in Historical Perspective" (1969). Even earlier in "A Baptists Chapter of Texas History" (1957) Estep had sketched the contributions of Baptists to the creation of the Republic of Texas as a state committed to religious liberty. With "Religion in the Lone Star State" (1989) he expanded this account for the benefit of non-Texans. Estep saw the publication of several chapel addresses including "The Place Called Calvary" (1960), "The Making of a Prophet: An Introduction to Charles Hadden Spurgeon" (1984), and "Reflections on Eighty Years of Theological Education at Southwestern" (1988/1995).

23   From 1959 to 1960 Estep taught in Spanish at the International Baptist Theological Seminary, Cali, Columbia. He published his lectures on the witness of the church in the New Testament era as *La Fe de los Apostoles* (1961).

24   In "Course-Changing Events in the History of the Foreign Mission Board, SBC, 1845–1994" (1994) and "Southern Baptist Global Evangelism, 1950–1994: Strategies, Tensions, Achievements" (1995), Estep summarized his research and analyses.

25   *The Anabaptist Story*, 3d ed., xiii.

26   "On the Origins of English Baptists," 24.

27   See Estep's Founder's Day address, "A. H. Newman and Southwestern's First Faculty" (1978).

Chapter 19: C. W. Brister

1   Tim O'Brien (Boston: Houghton Mifflin, 1990).

2   Elaine H. Brister, *Once upon a River: A History of Pineville, Louisiana* (Baton Rouge: Claitor's Publishing Division, 1968) and Thomas Howell, *The History of the First Baptist Church, Pineville, Louisiana* (Pineville: First Baptist Church, 1986).

3   Brister, *Pastoral Care in the Church* (New York: Harper and Row, 1964), xi.

4   Brister, "The Liberation of Life," in *Southwestern Sermons*, ed. H. C. Brown, Jr. (Nashville: Broadman, 1960), 29–35.

5   Brister, James L. Cooper, and J. David Fite, *Beginning Your Ministry* (Nashville: Abingdon, 1981), 10.

6   Brister, *Caring for the Caregivers* (Nashville: Broadman, 1985), 13.

7   William M. Tillman, Jr. "Editorial Introduction," *Southwestern Journal of Theology* 37 (Summer 1995): 3.

8   Natalie Goldberg, *Writing Down the Bones* (Boston, London: Shambhala, 1986), 4.

9   Brister, *The Promise of Counseling* (New York: Harper and Row, 1978), 18.

10   Brister, *Pastoral Care in the Church* (3d ed. rev.: San Francisco: Harper Collins, 1992), 102.

11   Ibid., 8.

12   Ibid., 10.

13   Brister, *People Who Care* (Nashville: Broadman, 1967), 26–27.

14   Ibid., 47.

15   Brister, *Pastoral Care in the Church*, 1964 ed., xii.

16   Ibid., xxiii.

17   Ibid., 91.

18   Brister, "Fifty Years of Pastoral Education at Southwestern Seminary: Looking Back and living Forward," Founder's Day Address, Southwestern Baptist Theological Seminary, 8 March 2001 (Videocassette TC 19463, Roberts Library), 1.

Chapter 20: William Lawrence Hendricks

1   *Baptist Reflections on Christianity and the Arts: Learning from Beauty, A Tribute to William L. Hendricks*, ed. by David M. Rayburn, Daven M. Kari, and Darrell G. Gwaltney

(Lewiston, N.Y.: Edwin Mellen Press, 1997), 21; see also Hendricks, "Learning from Beauty," *Review and Expositor* 85 (Winter 1988): 101–20; "Proclamation through the Arts," *Review and Expositor* 84 (Winter 1987): 75–85; and, "Southern Baptists and the Arts," *Review and Expositor* 87 (Fall 1990): 553–62.

2   The biographical data were gathered from *Baptist Reflections on Christianity and the Arts: Learning from Beauty,* 2–22, from personal conversations with the subject, and from having known William L. Hendricks for more than thirty-five years.

3   The order was invariably revelation, the doctrine of God, creation-providence, humanity, Christology, the Holy Spirit, salvation, church, which included baptism, the Lord's Supper, and worship, the Christian life, and eschatology. One suspects that these subjects have been tweaked through the years but that the foundational sequence and the basic content never changed.

4   The doctrine of creation-providence includes a brief look at the problem of evil and suffering.

5   Hendricks's point is that alienation is bifocal; that is, sin impairs our relationship with God as well as with one another (28–29).

6   This conclusion suggests the rejected theory of "partial depravity" in another form (see 51–52).

7   Quoted from *Westminster Shorter Catechism* (Richmond: John Knox Press, 1964), 391.

8   An understanding made possible by the resurrection of Jesus Christ.

9   For a rather detailed outline of the marks of the church as they correspond to the classical ideals as well as the offices of Christ as prophet, priest, king, and shepherd, see *A Theology for Aging* (Nashville: Broadman, 1986), 104.

10   See Hendricks, *A Theology for Aging,* 246–48. Hendricks's method was to "work through theology as life" (243). For this reason and the fact that he sought to relate his theological understanding to other than academic types, he did not develop a more formal theological-historical construction of doctrine.

Chapter 21: Harry Leon McBeth

1   As a young man, McBeth pastored two "half-time" churches in the Panhandle: Becton Baptist Church in Lubbock County (1948–50); and Duncan Flat Baptist Church in Dickens County (1947–50), the latter on land that was once part of the old Matador Ranch.

2   Now distinguished professor emeritus of theology, Hunt taught at Southwestern Seminary from 1944 to 1946 and from 1953 to 1987 and as an adjunct professor in the years following retirement.

3   In 1955 McBeth served as pastor of Charlie Baptist Church, north of Wichita Falls, before moving to Rio Vista Baptist Church.

4   Among his other seminary friends were David King, later an FMB missionary in Lebanon; Finlay M. Graham, FMB missionary in the Near East; Glenn O. Hilburn, professor and chairman of the Department of Religion at Baylor University; Presnall Wood, pastor and editor of the *Baptist Standard*; Justice Anderson, FMB missionary in Argentina and professor at Southwestern; Roy J. Fish, professor at Southwestern; and Francis DuBose, professor in Golden Gate Baptist Theological Seminary.

5   Oral Interview with Leon McBeth, 11 September 2001.

6   McBeth (Th.D. diss., Southwestern Baptist Theological Seminary), 1.

7   In this decade McBeth also participated in a study authorized by the SBC Executive Committee and sponsored by the SBC Education Commission called the Baptist Education Study Task (BEST), which established him as a research scholar and resulted in two writings by McBeth. BEST used these findings to establish guidelines for SBC-related educational institutions for the remainder of the century. See McBeth, "The Loss of Baptist Colleges" (1964) and "The History of Southern Baptist Higher Education" (1966) in Roberts Library, Southwestern Baptist Theological Seminary. These papers were presented to the First National Conference of the Baptist Education Study Task, 13–16 June 1966, and the Second National Conference of the same group, 12–15 June 1967, both in Nashville, Tennessee.

8   The book was translated into Spanish by Manolita Ballaguer and published in 1980.

9   (Nashville: Broadman), 4. McBeth also expressed appreciation in the preface to his wife, Ada, "who is the most convincing argument I know against the Krishna doctrine of marriage."

10   The history trilogy was never completed according to the Broadman plan. All three of the latter volume's writers chose to publish independently of each other: Hinson, *The Church Triumphant: A History of Christianity up to 1300* (Macon, Ga.: Mercer University Press, 1995); Estep, *Renaissance and Reformation* (Grand Rapids: Eerdmans, 1986); Miller, *The Modern Church: From the Dawn of the Reformation to the Eve of the Third Millennium* (Nashville: Abingdon, 1997). McBeth was also left to write the companion source book, *A Sourcebook for Baptist Heritage* (1990).

11   The only exception is the essay of Keith C. Wills, who was at that time director of SWBTS libraries.

12   See Marsden, *Fundamentalism and American Culture: The Shaping of Twentieth Century Evangelicalism, 1870–1925* (New York: Oxford University Press, 1980), and Marsden, *Reforming Fundamentalism: Fuller Seminary and the New Evangelicalism* (Grand Rapids: Eerdmans, 1987).

13   McBeth, "Baptist or Evangelical: One Southern Baptist's Perspective," in *Southern Baptists and American Evangelicals: The Conversation Continues* (Nashville: Broadman), 69–71.

14   McBeth, *The Baptist Heritage: Four Centuries of Baptist Witness* (Nashville: Broadman, 1987), 5.

15   McBeth's participation in and leadership of the various historical entities with which he has been associated is substantial: chairman of the BGCT Bicentennial Committee (1975–76) and member of its Baptist Distinctives Committee; president of the Southern Baptist Historical Society (1977–78); chairman of the SBC Historical Commission (1980–83); member of the SBC Sesquicentennial Planning Committee (1994–95); chairman of the Texas Baptist Historical Committee; and a member of the board of trustees of Wayland Baptist University. He was also honored as distinguished alumnus of Wayland (1992) and Southwestern Seminary (2001) and served on various Baptist editorial boards. These entities preserve, inculcate, and implement Baptist tenets. McBeth's involvement over the years enhanced the work of all of these bodies.

16   Among McBeth's many master's and doctoral-level women students serving in theological education are Rosalie Beck, Baylor University; Vicki Crumpton, senior editor, Broadman

and Holman; Susan Day Pigott, Hardin-Simmons University; Carol Crawford Holcolmb, University of Mary-Hardin Baylor; and Dinorah Mendez, Mexican Baptist Theological Seminary.

17   Oral Interview with Leon McBeth, 11 September 2001.

Chapter 23: F. B. Huey, Jr.

1   Huey, "Capital Punishment" in C. W. Scudder, ed., *Crisis in Morality* (Nashville: Broadman, 1964), 74–90.

2   Huey, *Numbers*, Bible Study Commentary (Grand Rapids: Zondervan, 1981), 8.

3   Huey, *Jeremiah*, Bible Study Commentary (Grand Rapids: Zondervan, 1981), 8.

4   Huey, *Layman's Bible Book Commentary: Ezekiel-Daniel*, vol. 12 (Nashville: Broadman, 1983), 11.

5   In "Irony as the Key to Understanding the Book of Esther," *Southwestern Journal of Theology* 32 (Summer 1990): 39, Huey stated, "Is it not possible that Esther could also be interpreted, along with Nehemiah and Malachi, as another example of the post-exilic failure to become the exemplary, obedient people that God meant for them to be, instead of trying to 'whitewash' the acts of Mordecai and Esther by convoluted interpretations?"

6   Huey, "Esther" in *The Expositor's Bible Commentary*, vol. 4, ed. Frank E. Gaebelein (Grand Rapids: Zondervan, 1988), 787–88.

7   The first attempt to communicate his conclusions in writing can be seen in Huey, "Obedience: A Neglected Doctrine." *Christianity Today*, 19 January 1968, 6–7.

8   Huey, *Obedience: The Biblical Key to Happiness* (Nashville: Broadman, 1990), 49.

9   Ibid., 63.

10   Ibid., 124.

11   Huey, *Jeremiah-Lamentations*, New American Commentary, vol. 16 (Nashville: Broadman, 1993), 24.

12   Huey served as pastor of Rush Creek Baptist Church, Arlington, Texas, from 1989 to 1993.

Chapter 24: Justice Conrad Anderson

1   Anderson is often remembered as "Mr. Missions" by those who knew him during his years at Southwestern Seminary.

2   Although a complete history of the Department of Missions at Southwestern is outside the purview of the present study, many have served with distinction, including Charles T. Ball (1911–18), William Henry Knight (1919–23; 1929–31), William Richardson White (1923–1927), Earl R. Martin (1982–87), and Marion G. [Bud] Fray (1989–94).

3   Jesse C. Fletcher, *Baker James Cauthen: A Man for All Nations* (Nashville: Broadman, 1977). Cauthen served from 1935 to 1939. His successor, Frank K. Means, who taught from 1939 to 1947, also left the classroom, to serve as Latin American administrator for the Foreign Mission Board (SBC).

4   Guy had a long tenure from 1947 to 1982. Generations of missionaries were highly influenced by his dictums, such as: "The job of a missionary is to win people to Jesus, to give them a Bible, and to organize them into a church. As soon as that is done, the missionary must work himself out of a job."

5   A brief history of key Southwestern missions professors is chronicled by Anderson himself. "The Missions Motif: Southwestern's Integrating Principle," *Southwestern Journal of Theology* 41 (Spring 1999): 78–84. Yet another important professor was L. Jack Gray, who taught from 1956 to 1984 and whose quiet and passionate demeanor inspired many students to learn the importance of prayer in missions and in their ministries.

6   His thesis on *Ship of Fools* was supervised by Charles G. Smith. Anderson, "Proverb Lore in Alexander Barclay's *Ship of Fools*" (M.A. thesis, Baylor University, 1951).

7   In his dissertation, "Church-State Problems among Baptists in Argentina in the Light of the Historic Baptist Perspective" (Southwestern Baptist Theological Seminary, 1965), one can see the fusion of concerns with missiology and Baptist history that has characterized his entire career.

8   The present author served in Argentina from 1979 to 1994 and from multiple first-hand experiences can vouch that Justice Anderson left significant footprints in multiple churches, denominational structures, and other spheres of influence. Anderson served for one year as interim president of the seminary in Buenos Aires (1968–69). Upon his resignation to join the faculty at Southwestern in 1974, he was serving with distinction as president of the body of almost one hundred missionaries in Argentina.

9   The *ATLA Database* contains fifty-four entries for Justice C. Anderson and another three for Justo Anderson. The Roberts Library at Southwestern shows sixty-four entries. Of these, thirty-two are recordings of his chapel addresses. Since Anderson prepared carefully for these and spoke to the critical issues of his day, they contain priceless insights. Another seventeen entries reflect lectures given in conferences, workshops and seminars—many of which he created himself through the World Missions Center—treating a wide variety of topics that indicates many of his concerns. One could wish that the pearls of wisdom contained in these might be collected and made available to readers in English, but by far his most significant written works are in Spanish.

10   Anderson, "Church-State Problems among Baptists in Argentina in the Light of the Historic Baptist Perspective." One sees in this early work both the carefully crafted outlines which clarify broad issues and the extensive research and citation that characterize Anderson's writings.

11   Besson's significance is further described in "Pablo Besson: The Argentine Roger Williams," *Quarterly Review* 33 (October–November–December 1972): 21–30.

12   Canclini is treated in "Santiago Canclini: The Argentine Isaac Backus," *Quarterly Review* 33 (April– May–June 1973): 56–68.

13   Anderson may have the singular honor of having his dissertation made into movies. In 1968 Broadman Films produced "Giants in the Land," treating the struggle of Baptists in Argentina for religious liberty, and also "For Many Tomorrows" on the work of the Seminario Internacional Teológico Bautista in preparing ministers and church leaders.

14   See, for example, his survey of early efforts to plant Baptist churches in Latin America: Anderson, "Episodic North American Influence on Certain Baptist Beginnings in Latin America," in *The Lord's Free People in a Free Land: Essays in Baptist History in Honor of Robert A. Baker*, ed. William R. Estep (Fort Worth: School of Theology, Southwestern Baptist Theological Seminary, 1976), 171–94.

15   3 vols. (El Paso: Casa Bautista de Publicaciones, 1978, 1990).

16   (Buenos Aires: Junta Bautista de Publicaciones, 1974). His interest in Baptist ecclesiology was closely wedded to his concern for church growth; see also the symposium of studies he edited: *El Crecimiento de las Iglesias Bautistas Argentinas* (Buenos Aires: Seminario Internacional Teológico Bautista, 1969).

17   Anderson, "The Nature of Churches" in *The Birth of Churches: A Biblical Basis for Church Planting*, ed. Talmadge R. Amberson (Nashville: Broadman, 1979), 48–72. Here both the universal church and local churches are seen as expressions of the concept of the kingdom of God.

18   (Buenos Aires: Junta Bautista de Publicaciones, 1973). His missiological concern for empowering the laity and bivocational ministry is found in his affirming that not only the "pastor-preacher" but also the "lay-preacher" needs guidance for the task.

19   Anderson's elaboration of these principles appears in English in his article, "Old Baptist Principles Reset," *Southwestern Journal of Theology* 33 (Spring 1989): 5–12.

20   A clear distinction can be drawn between the history of the Baptist denomination and the history of Baptist principles. The principles existed long before they provided the basis for a denomination. These distinctive Baptist principles do not include all Baptist doctrine. Many basic beliefs, such as salvation by faith, are shared with other denominations, but these provide a nucleus for distinctive convictions. With other radical Reformers the first Baptists were not conformists; they saw an institutional church allied with the "world" that had lost its way. The New Testament was the permanent and definitive rule by which they critiqued and revised the church. The highest authority was never any institution, but Baptists decried dogmatism, sacramentalism, priestly authority, and legalism so as to embrace and promote personal involvement, high moral standards, lay leadership, and dynamism.

21   The first and defining Baptist principle is the lordship of Christ, graphically portrayed at the center of all the other principles which serve as its corollaries. John Smyth echoes the New Testament confession, "Jesus is Lord," when he declares in 1610: "Christ alone is King, Judge of the church and of conscience." Although some Baptists would place the Scriptures or a spiritual principle as their first article of faith, it is just to begin with the Person of our redemption. The sovereign and absolute lordship of Christ in his churches is the source of all Baptist life. Christ's lordship responds to the most profound needs of all people and inflames the highest ideals of his followers. Peace, justice and understanding can only emerge where Christ reigns.

22   Throughout history, church politics has always been determined on three bases—tradition, Scripture, and convenience. Baptist churches consider the Bible, especially the New Testament, as the only source of authority. This principle is intimately connected to the first: the authority of the New Testament derives from the authority of the Lord of the New Testament. The Bible is not a fetish; one does not believe in Christ because of the Bible; rather one believes in the Bible because one believes in Christ. From the text of the New Testament all theology and ecclesiology are derived. The New Testament is the objective revelation that provides a guide and standard for the subjective experiences of individuals and churches. The New Testament is the definitive "tradition" for all Baptists. Baptists believe that they are apostolic because they follow the New Testament—which is the product of apostolic tradition. It is the high privilege and solemn responsibility of every Baptist to read and to interpret for oneself the Scriptures under the direction of its Author, the Holy Spirit. Thus, Baptists are aptly described as considering the Bible the only source for

theological certainty, when by custom they suspect the interpretations of scholars and prefer to take down "their" Bible and "see what it says."

23   The peculiar doctrine of the church is the most distinctive characteristic of Baptists. The Christian church may be defined as the fellowship of all believers in Christ, a spiritual community whose concrete expression in the world is a local congregation, whose purpose is the extension of the kingdom of God. Baptists emphasize local "churches" which are true expressions of a universal and spiritual "Church," which is God's people. Each church achieves its identity by serving as a small agency of Christ's kingdom. The autonomy of the local congregation protects the primitive purity of the New Testament doctrine of the church as universal and spiritual. Before admitting new members, the church will require evidence of personal and genuine conversion, and baptism. Baptism should be biblically correct (by immersion), psychologically true (by believers who identify with Christ), intellectually free (voluntary step of obedience), and symbolically rich (portraying a mystical union of the believer with the death and resurrection of Jesus). As baptism is the symbol of a new birth of an individual believer and thus celebrated only once, so the Lord's Supper is a symbol of continuing growth and the sanctification of life that is often repeated. Both ordinances proclaim the death of Christ in graphic terms.

24   Universally accepted among Baptists, but sometimes misunderstood in practice, is that a local congregation of Baptists is theoretically a pure democracy. The concept of social equality and the absence of elitism and classes derive directly from the lordship of Christ equally over all. Also the principle comes from the "priesthood of the believer," which means that a believer is regenerated by grace once for all through faith, that he has free access to God through Jesus Christ as the only high priest, and that he assumes the priestly responsibility of ministry to others. This is a New Testament teaching, although Martin Luther rediscovered and emphasized it in the sixteenth century. Baptists fight for democracy in both ecclesiastical and political spheres in order to submit themselves to the absolute monarchy found in the lordship of Christ, or in other words, the kingdom of God. This New Testament principle has suffered long under ecclesiastical authority, including deliberations of councils and edicts of popes, so that the local church must have autonomy. Baptists emphasize the separation of church and state, toleration between ecclesiastical bodies, voluntarism, and freedom of conscience. Baptists educate all church members to exercise their democratic responsibilities. Domingo Sarmiento often said: "If the people is sovereign, then the sovereign must be educated."

25   The greatest contribution of Baptists to Protestantism has been their obsession with religious liberty, as enunciated by the Anabaptists and given prominence in the earliest confessions of English Baptists. The incorporation of religious liberty into a political system is the great achievement of Baptists in North America. All persons are personally responsible to God, for each has been made "in his image" and bequeathed an inalienable right to be free. Religious tolerance, no matter how benevolent, is not religious liberty. Liberty cannot be conceded by governments, but must be respected as a gift of God to every human being—without governmental coercion or clerical interference. Such liberty includes freedom of worship, freedom of conscience, and freedom to propagate. The biblical basis and historical development of these concepts is part of the Baptist identity.

26   This cardinal principle is a conviction of Baptists from their beginnings, not simply an idiosyncratic expression of North American politics. But the triumph of the principle, now

incorporated in the Constitution of the United States, is a Baptist trophy. The principle does not depend upon this constitution but derives from the Scriptures. The Bible recognizes the legitimacy of government: law and order are part of God's design for human welfare. Thus the state can be the "instrument" for this divine purpose and should be respected, obeyed, supported and prayed for by Christians—so long as it acts uprightly and within its prescribed limits. When Christ taught that we should "Render unto Caesar," he ratified this view of the state, but when he required that we should "Render unto God," he asked for supreme loyalty. This biblical basis is foundational, since others have argued for separation of church and state for other reasons. The Baptist cry for liberty is supported often by atheists, socialists, and humanitarians on the basis of purely humanistic motives. In Latin America, where revolutions were widely inspired by the Encyclopedists and the values of the French Revolution, the cry of liberty has not proved to be so successful. The Baptist cause has ever been to free men for religion, not from it.

27   Missions is the heartbeat of Baptists. Baptists are "evangelicals" because they share with others a serious commitment to fulfill the Great Commission of Christ (Matt. 28:18–20). The numerical growth of the denomination and the growing geographic extension of Baptists around the world bear witness to this principle. Jesus Christ was sent to the world to redeem it. To evangelize is to participate in his ministry to the world, living in the power of the Holy Spirit who makes this work possible. Baptist identity is inextricably intertwined with the decision of William Carey that Christians have the obligation to use all means possible for the conversion of the lost. Luther Rice and Adoniram Judson helped Baptists in North America to form a Missionary Convention, called "Triennial" because it met every three years. So the missionary impulse was the motive for the organization of Baptists in the USA. Evangelism is the leaven in the Baptist lump of dough. Because of this evangelistic and missionary zeal, Baptists may be found today throughout the world.

28   Latourette, *The History of the Expansion of Christianity*. 7 vols. (New York: Harper and Brothers, 1937–45).

29   In a manner unique to Anderson, Baptists are viewed in relation to "the New Testament churches" (up to AD 100), to the early catholic church (100–400), to "schismatic groups" (AD 150–800), to the Roman Catholic Church (AD 440–present), to "medieval dissenters" (AD 800–1517), to Protestant churches (AD 1517–present), to the free churches (AD 1525–present), and to the ecumenical movement (AD 1910–present).

30   Anderson deduces from his studies that "the Baptist tradition is an integral and important part of the Christian faith in the contemporary world. . . . The Baptist denomination is becoming free of its identification with the West, and with North America and Europe; it is becoming universal. " *Historia de los Bautistas*, 3: 11–12.

31   Anderson's treatment of the international growth of Baptists is in many respects more profound and detailed than subsequent publications in English, such as Albert W. Wardin, ed., *Baptists around the World: A Comprehensive Handbook* (Nashville: Broadman and Holman, 1995).

32   Anderson, "Foreign Missions as Shaper and Reflector of Southern Baptist Life," *Baptist History and Heritage* 29 (October 1994): 14.

33   Anderson, "Changing Patterns of World Mission Work," *Baptist History and Heritage* 27 (July 1992): 14.

34 Crawley, *Global Mission: A Story to Tell; An Interpretation of Southern Baptist Foreign Missions.* (Nashville: Broadman, 1985), esp. 20–26.

35 Ibid., 14–17.

36 Anderson, "Foreign Missions as Shaper and Reflector of Southern Baptist Life," 14.

37 Anderson, "Changing Patterns of Mission Work," 16–17.

38 Anderson, "Foreign Missions as Shaper and Reflector of Southern Baptist Life," 14, quoted the 1902 statement by B. H. Carroll, Jr., *The Genesis of American Anti-Missionism* (Louisville: Baptist Book Concern), 7–8: "I believe the foreign mission movement has furnished the centripetal force which holds our denomination together and which counteracts the centrifugal force of church sovereignty and independence; which if it operated without the check of fraternal sympathy, comity and co-operation, would cause us to fly off at a tangent into chaos."

39 Anderson, "Foreign Missions as Shaper and Reflector of Southern Baptist Life," 15.

40 Ibid., 23.

41 For the full text of this message, see Anderson, "The Missions Motif: Southwestern's Integrating Principle," *Southwestern Journal of Theology* 41 (Spring 1999): 70–86.

42 Ibid., 70.

43 Ibid., 71.

44 Carroll, addressing the SBC in 1888, demonstrated his own identity with missions:

> Brethren, when God converted me from infidelity, he made me a missionary. My heart is in it. May that heart stop its beating when it fails to love any man from any shore who is a child of God . . . . Texas is your gateway to Mexico and the Pacific slope. Texas before the days of the Republic was an integral part of that Coahuila in whose capital [W. D.] Powell now preaches. . . . By this principle let Texas as a field of missionary operations be tried. . . . Tongues of missionary fire rest on their heads.

Quoted by Alan J. Lefever, *Fighting the Good Fight: The Life and Work of Benajah Harvey Carroll* (Austin: Eakin, 1994), 150,147.

45 Anderson, "The Missions Motif," 71–72, holds that this zealous fervor for evangelism and missions was far more important than the clearly documented relation that both Carroll and Scarborough had with W. O. Carver's innovations along these lines at Southern Seminary.

46 Ibid, 73.

47 Curiously for founders of a great theological institution, "both had keen minds and super intellects, but neither finished a theological degree." Ibid.

48 See John A. Mackay, *A Preface to Christian Theology* (London: Nisbet, 1942), chap. 2.

49 Baker James Cauthen, R. Keith Parks, and Jerry Rankin.

50 As documented year after year in reports from Personnel Department, International Mission Board.

51 He personally showed a strong commitment to the discipline by his active participation in the American Society of Missiology.

52 Anderson, "The Missions Motif," 70.

53 John Mark Terry, Ebbie C. Smith, and Justice C. Anderson, eds. (Nashville: Broadman and Holman, 1998).

54 Anderson, "An Overview of Missiology," in ibid., 1–17. Anderson also wrote historical chapters on "Medieval and Renaissance Missions (500–1792)" (183–98) and "The Great Century and Beyond (1792–1910)" (199–218).

55 (Buenos Aires: Junta Bautista de Publicaciones, 1973; El Paso: Casa Bautista de Publicaciones, 1987).

56 See Anderson, "Theological Education by Extension," in *Evangelical Dictionary of World Missions*, ed. A. Scott Moreau (Grand Rapids: Baker, 2000), 944.

Afterword

1 *Julius Caesar*, act 4, scene 3, line 217.